AutoCAD® in 3 Dimensions

Third Edition

Using Release 14

Stephen J. Ethier
Christine A. Ethier
CADInnovations

Prentice Hall
Upper Saddle River, New Jersey   *Columbus, Ohio*

Library of Congress Cataloging-in-Publication Data
Ethier, Stephen J.
    AutoCAD in 3 dimensions / Stephen J. Ethier,
Christine A. Ethier.—3rd ed.
  p. cm.
    Includes index.
    ISBN 0-13-796301-7
    1. Computer graphics. 2. AutoCAD for Windows. 3. Three-dimensional
display systems.   I. Ethier, Christine A. II. Title.
  T385.E783 1998
  620′.0042′02855369—dc21   97-46787
                                         CIP

Cover art: Stephen J. Ethier
Editor: Stephen Helba
Production Coordination: Lisa Garboski, bookworks
Design Coordinator: Karrie M. Converse
Text Designer: STELLARViSIONs
Cover Designer: Raymond Hummons
Production Manager: Deidra M. Schwartz
Marketing Manager: Frank Mortimer, Jr.

This book was set in Dutch 801 and Swiss 721 by STELLARViSIONs and was printed and bound by Courier/Kendallville, Inc. The cover was printed by Phoenix Color Corp.

AutoCAD® is a registered trademark of Autodesk, Inc. All rights reserved. Screen representations used by permission.

Printed in the United States of America

10 9 8 7 6 5 4 3 2 1

ISBN: 0-13-796301-7

Prentice-Hall International (UK) Limited, *London*
Prentice-Hall of Australia Pty. Limited, *Sydney*
Prentice-Hall of Canada, Inc., *Toronto*
Prentice-Hall Hispanoamericana, S. A., *Mexico*
Prentice-Hall of India Private Limited, *New Delhi*
Prentice-Hall of Japan, Inc., *Tokyo*
Simon & Schuster Asia Pte. Ltd., *Singapore*
Editora Prentice-Hall do Brasil, Ltda., *Rio de Janeiro*

This text is dedicated
first,
to each other,
        a tenacious bond between the best of friends
and
a wonderful 3-dimensional marriage.

Next,
to our strongest supports,
Dorothy and Vic Evans,
for
unfailing help,
intelligent guidance,
and unconditional love.

And, finally,
in memory of my father,
George Ethier,
who was always for me.
        Stephen and Christine Ethier

Warning and Disclaimer

This book is designed to provide tutorial information about the AutoCAD computer program. Every effort has been made to make this book complete and as accurate as possible. But no warranty or fitness is implied.

The information is provided on an "as-is" basis. The author and Prentice Hall Publishing, Inc., shall have neither liability nor responsibility to any person or entity with respect to any loss or damage in connection with or arising from the information contained in this book.

Preface

My own interest in CAD began many years ago, when the phrase "technological revolution" was not yet a household phrase. It was my feeling then that computerized drawing would drastically change the field of drafting and design, but even I couldn't have guessed the far-reaching implications of the changes. Today, drafting students—although still being introduced to work on the boards—are universally exposed to the computer early in the game and are being hired into the job market based on their familiarity with and skill in this area. And, as always, in this skill-intensive age, the more information we have, the better we are able to compete.

AutoCAD in 3 Dimensions was written to provide the information students need to compete in a competitive job market. The text covers AutoCAD Release 14 and is a hands-on, lab- and exercise-intensive look at all the important concepts needed to draw in true 3D. It is my hope that even the beginner, who has had only an introduction to CAD, will be able to pick up this text, follow the activities and the labs, and turn to the book for answers to possible questions—leaving the instructor relatively question free!

Features

To aid student understanding of AutoCAD, the text includes the following pedagogical features:

- More than 600 illustrations of 3D drawings help students visualize the concepts.
- Part 7, Application Projects, includes six chapters (18–23) that act as independent labs with step-by-step guidelines. These labs cover architectural (residential and commercial), mechanical, structural, and civil projects.
- Part 4, Solid Modeling, gives the most thorough look at AutoCAD's Advanced Modeling Extension currently available.
- Most chapters have a series of labs that move the student from simple to complex projects (all chapters except those in Section 7 where the chapters themselves are labs).
- Chapters end with questions that test student understanding of chapter concepts.

- Chapters also end with assignments that allow students to explore the chapter concepts interactively.
- The text is accompanied by an *Instructor's Manual* that includes answers to chapter questions; suggestions for additional assignments and discussion topics; and chapter tests with a mix of multiple choice, true/false, matching, and short-answer questions.

Organization

The text is organized into eight parts covering all aspects of 3-dimensional AutoCAD:

Understanding 3D
Preparing for Construction of 3D Models
Construction of 3D Surface Models
Solid Modeling
Enhancing the Use of 3D
Presentation
Application Projects
Application Programs

There is no question that 3-dimensional modeling is here to stay. In what direction it will eventually take the reader and the author is anyone's guess, but there is no question that it will be an exciting trip.

Acknowledgments

I would like to thank the following people for their assistance with the text: Stephen Helba, whose constant guidance and considerable expertise have been invaluable; Patty Kelly, for lending us her technical know-how and her encouraging words; Linda Thompson, for her vigilance and tenaciousness in every manuscript check she performs; all of my colleagues at New Brunswick Community College (Moncton, NB), both current and retired, especially John Wadman and Bert Rioux for their special support and contributions; David Fenety, a past student of mine, for his graphic contributions to the text; Vic Evans for his classy contribution to the introductory section of the text; David Devereaux-Weber, Craig Burgess, and Charles Michal for their individual work in 3 dimensions; Lisa Senauke at Autodesk, who manages to keep me posted on all that's new with AutoCAD.

I would also like to thank the following reviewers for their comments and advice: Donna P. English, Gaston College; Clair S. Hill, Northern Arizona University; Richard C. Mason, II, Pennsylvania College of Technology; and Tami L. Schultz, Northern Arizona University.

I would like to extend a special thank you to Lisa Garboski for her careful and thorough accuracy check of the manuscript.

COORDINATES
Out of your time
the ancient quest
for Holy Grail
beyond your time
to ride astride
a comet's tail
but here and now
to seek and find
new dimensions in the mind
D. V. Evans

Brief Contents

Contents

14   3D Parametric Design   241

PART 6   Presentation   261

15   Display of 3D Models for Presentation   262

16   Plotting   285

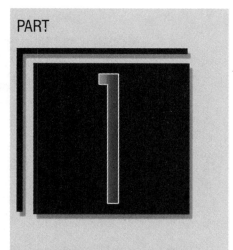

Understanding 3D

In this first part, basic 3D terminology is defined and explained to help you thoroughly understand each central concept and the many terms associated with each concept. In addition, a number of disciplines in which 3D CAD is used are discussed, and we explore how each of these disciplines would utilize the central concepts presented. It is in this discussion that the *why* of 3D CAD is disclosed: its benefits when dealing with nontechnical people, such as clients; its greater tangibility; its ability to impress; and its cost-saving benefits in design and prototype creation.

CHAPTER 1

Theory Behind 3D Modeling

Overview

It is essential for 3D users to understand the concepts of extrusion, wireframe, surface models, and solid models. This chapter defines these terms and others in simple language and demonstrates them with both illustrations and diagrams.

Concepts Explored

- The purpose and benefits of 3D computer modeling
- The different model building and displaying options
- A basic vocabulary of 3D terminology.

1.1 Introduction

The more tangibly a concept can be presented, the more quickly and easily it can be understood. Take the example of a pyramid: It is a difficult shape to describe, but once you have seen it in concrete form, it is easily pictured in your mind's eye. Humans learn first by knowing an object physically. Being able to touch or hold an object is the best way to understand its operation or purpose. After learning through physical interaction, humans can progress to learning through pictorial means and finally to understanding something symbolically—without contact with the actual object or even its pictorial representation.

Before three-dimensional creation on computers was possible, a model maker physically constructed a prototype of a design, either full size or to a smaller scale if, for instance, a house or bridge was being built. This allowed the designers and clients to see something tangible, something three dimensional; to interpret the ramifications of the design; and, in some cases, to actually apply operating conditions to the models and observe the results. This was a good method, and it continues to be. However, problems arise when the design needs to be altered. A new model has to be physically constructed, which is expensive and time consuming.

This is where 3D steps in. It is the ideal solution for model makers, designers, and clients alike because it allows them to construct a model whose form can be altered at will such that the results can be immediately observed. And, because computer-generated images are three dimensional in nature, the user has the added bonus of a tool that has elements of a concrete object—its three dimensionality—combined with the ease of creation of a pictorial image.

The art of three-dimensional construction on computers is referred to as *geometric modeling*. To save confusion, we will refer to it as *modeling* throughout this book.

A model generated on a computer consists of numeric data that describes the geometry of the object. The object geometry can include edges, surfaces, contours, or other features. Once this model database is built (created), the computer program "knows" the model has three dimensions. This allows the manipulation and display of the model in a variety of ways—some of which are not possible or not easily done with an actual physical model.

1.2 Benefits

Models provide us with a wide range of benefits. Most are described under "what-if" situations, or questions such as "what if this were changed—what would be the results?" Initially, models were created so that mechanical parts could be tested under what-if situations. This continues to be a major reason for the creation of models. Using finite element analysis (FEA), stresses can be applied to the computer model and the results graphically displayed. FEA makes use of a grid of meshes and analyzes the amount of deflection at each intersection or node point to determine allowable stresses.

With the advent of smaller, faster, and less expensive computers and powerful computer programs like AutoCAD that run on these computers, the applications of models that can be generated on computer have increased by leaps and bounds. Chapter 2 details actual applications of AutoCAD 3D models. For now, consider the following examples.

Because computer models can be altered easily, a multitude of design options can be presented to a client before any construction or manufacturing takes place. In the mechanical discipline, volume and mass calculations can be done automatically when the model is altered. FEA can be applied to the model. Robotic work cells can be designed on the computer and animated to show the results of the end effector (robot's hand) paths as the robot goes through its programmed movement. In the architectural discipline, once a structure is created, the effects of sun passage can be depicted and walkthroughs can be simulated, all while the client observes. These things are not easily done with a physical miniature model. In the area of marketing, a multitude of textures or surface finishes can be applied to a model until the desired results are obtained. The benefits are virtually endless and are limited only by the imagination of the designer. And the greatest benefit is that, once the model is created, it can be used over and over again with an endless adaptability to new modifications. If the old adage is true and a picture is worth a thousand words, an animated three-dimensional model must be worth millions!

1.3 Modeling Versus Drafting and AutoCAD

Exploring the possibilities of modeling is exciting. And making the transition from drafting (2D) to modeling (3D) does not have to be a difficult experience. First, to make the transition virtually painless, it is essential to understand a variety of terms, which will appear in the exercises and labs that reinforce the concepts explored in the following chapters.

The mental skills required to work in 3D are different from those needed for drawing in 2D. In drafting, the user translates the three-dimensional attributes of an object into flat two-dimensional views—top (plan), front (elevation), and side (elevation). Refer to Figure 1.1.

In modeling, all three dimensions are taken into consideration. This sounds complicated, but actually it allows the design to be formulated faster because the user can see the entire model at any time, instead of having to work on one view at a time.

In drafting, the creator works within two dimensions—the X and Y axes, as illustrated in Figure 1.2. In modeling, a third axis is added—the Z axis, as illustrated in Figure 1.3.

Both 2D and 3D creation rely on an origin point. In 2D, that origin point is described as 0,0. In 3D it's 0,0,0. When working with AutoCAD, the third dimension has always been available, but the program automatically assigned the Z coordinate the value of 0 while working in 2D. Every entity stored the Z portion of its geometry at the 0 point. By accessing the Z value, you allow for the creation of true three-dimensional models. Coordinate entry in 3D is the same as in 2D. Coordinates can be entered with absolute values based on the origin 0,0,0 or using relative or polar coordinates. The only difference is the addition of the third coordinate point—Z.

Figure 1.1
Transforming a 3D object into a 2D drawing

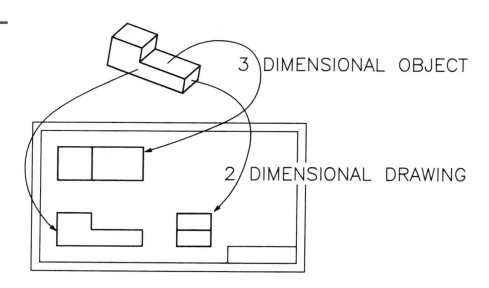

Figure 1.2
Two-dimensional axes

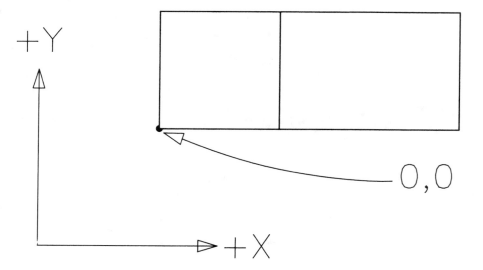

Figure 1.3
Three-dimensional axes

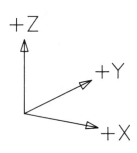
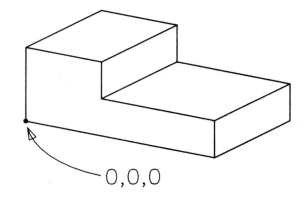

1.4 Model Building Options

In 2D drafting, the drafter used flat geometry, putting straight lines and curves into complex finished drawings. In 3D, these same simple geometric forms are used, but the third *Z* axis expands upon them. The techniques learned in 2D are not forgotten; instead they are utilized in a different fashion.

Basically, the development of 3D modeling using microcomputers has followed the path from 2-1/2D line extrusions, through 3D line wireframes, to surface generations, and finally to solids. This development went hand in hand with the increasing power of the microcomputer. As the building options developed, the model database's complexity increased, putting heavier demands on the computer's processing. Although the software developers already had the techniques used to create solids on larger computers, they had to wait until the hardware (computer) caught up with the software (Auto-CAD). Now, happily for users, microcomputers can make use of the most complex model creation options available—solids. There are still developments to come, but the advances to date have been revolutionary.

In our learning process, we'll follow the same path as the building options—from simple to complex. What follows is an introduction to the different building options; this will prepare us for the detailed work to come. It is up to the user to decide which of these building options would best achieve the desired effect. Luckily, they can be used in combination.

Extrusion: 2-1/2D

The first method of building a model is through the use of extrusion. Extrusion is the process of taking an outline of a shape and pushing or drawing it along an axis. In CAD, this process, which is the simplest yet one of the most useful, is the same.

As Figure 1.4 shows, an outline of a shape is drawn. Then, through a series of commands, the shape is drawn along the *Z* axis, forming a three-dimensional shape (see Figure 1.5). Basically, the first outline is copied along the *Z*

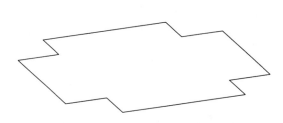

Figure 1.4
Shape-defining profile

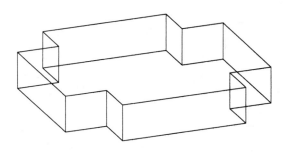

Figure 1.5
The extruded profile

axis at a set distance, and then connecting lines are automatically extended from the start and end point of each line. This connects the first outline to the corresponding points on the second, copied, outline.

The reason extrusion is the most useful process is that most graphically displayed objects are made up of an extrusion of some sort. Walls, wooden pencils, structural members, pipes, and filing cabinets are all forms of extrusions. If not the total form, then some parts of all everyday objects have extrusions. The label of 2-1/2D indicates the fact that, although not truly three dimensional, the resulting image is amazingly close to the real thing.

Wireframe: 3D Lines

Extrusion has one basic limitation—all the extruded lines going from one outline to the next are parallel to each other. This is fine for residential walls, but what about modeling the Great Pyramid at Cheops? To draw true three-dimensional shapes, the ability to draw lines on an oblique plane must be available. A true three-dimensional line must have the possibility of a start point at one set of X, Y, Z coordinates and a stop point at a different set of X, Y, Z coordinates. Refer to Figure 1.6.

The two X, two Y, and two Z coordinates must be differentiated. If a CAD program cannot do this, then it cannot create in true 3D. Drawing 3D lines to represent an object is referred to as creating a wireframe of the model. Each edge is represented by a wire. Looking at it is like looking at a skeleton of the object. You can see right through it.

Surface Generation

Now that the wireframe of the model has been created, wouldn't it be great to be able to see how it would look with some "clothes" on? This is where surface generation comes in. Wireframe is very useful during the initial complex construction of a model, but the need to see the model in a more tangible form remains. The frame must be covered with sheets of material, referred to as *surfaces*, as shown in Figure 1.7. These surfaces will display the model in an easier-to-comprehend form—the hiding of edges behind one another. This is very important in the presentation stage.

Methods of Surface Generation

There are four main methods of generating surfaces: extrusion, area definition, sweep profile, and contour mesh. Each of the methods covers a defined boundary with a surface using semiautomatic techniques.

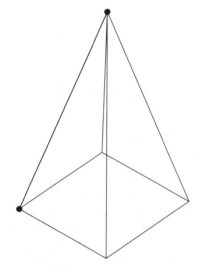

Figure 1.6
True 3D geometry

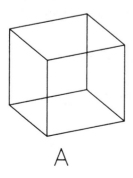 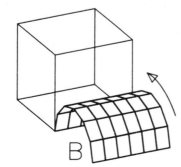 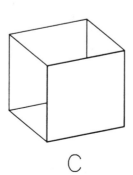

Figure 1.7
Applying a surface

Figure 1.8
Extruding a line

Surface extrusion is similar to the extrusion technique mentioned earlier, but instead of using individual connecting lines from several key vertices on one outline to the next, every possible point along the edge of one outline is used to form the corresponding edge of the second outline, thus completing two tasks—forming the surface and forming the second profile edge. Refer to Figure 1.8. Initially, a two-dimensional entity (line) is created, and then the entity (line) is extruded to form a surface.

In area definition, the user identifies an area to be covered with a surface by indicating the nodes (the vertices of perimeter edges) that define the area, as shown in Figure 1.9. The area can be as simple as the triangle shown in the figure or as complex as the user desires. The only limitation is that the surface be planar; that is, it must have a "two-dimensional" quality. In area definition, then, the surface generated must be flat. It is possible to form nonplanar surfaces with area definition; however, the results displayed may differ from what the user expected. Often, the surface will be twisted, as if you had taken a playing card and twisted it between your left and right hands.

Sweep profile is a higher order of surface generation. It generates a multitude of surfaces based on an initially created two-dimensional profile. First, a profile is created, as in Figure 1.10A. Then, using that profile, surfaces are formed around a central axis, creating a cylindrical shape with an unlimited profile, as in Figure 1.10B. The modeled surfaces can be created through a continuous 360 degrees around the axis and any part thereof. Any semicylindrical shape can be created—wine glasses, soda bottles, light bulbs, cockpit cowls. Each surface created is planar, but because of the number of surfaces created, the contour appears to be curved. The larger the number of surfaces, the smoother the model appears. This result is similar to the drawings produced on the popular children's two-dimensional drawing toy, the Etch A Sketch. As you probably remember from your childhood sketching, the greater the number of linear bits used to draw a circle, the smoother that shape appeared.

Figure 1.9
Defining a surface area

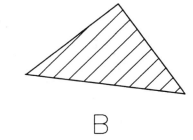

Figure 1.10
Sweeping a profile

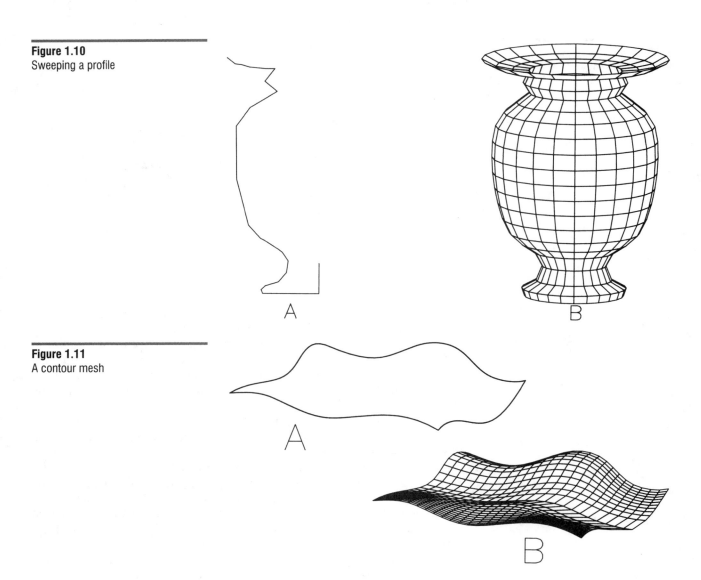

Figure 1.11
A contour mesh

Contour mesh is similar to sweep profile in that it also generates multiple surfaces. First, contour mesh generates several profiles; then, it creates surfaces to form a contoured shape, as shown in Figure 1.11. This can be quite calculation intensive, because the intersection nodes that will allow the blending of two or more curves to each other have to be calculated. However, the results can be quite amazing. This type of creation is used for items where irregular surfaces are the norm, such as automobiles, airplanes, and terrain modeling.

Solid Modeling

Up to this point, our discussion has focused on how wireframes are covered with flat surfaces to illustrate a model. This type of model is excellent for most applications that require only the exterior shell. Solid modeling is the culmination of the model building options. As the name implies, the user works with three-dimensional solids that have mass and density. As might be imagined, this is the most math/calculation-intensive building option, but it is the most accurate for model creation.

The process of manipulation is very simple: The user may take varied solid forms and add them together to form a complex object, as in Figure 1.12, or the user may subtract solid forms from each other to form the final object, as in Figure 1.13. In contrast to the user's simple manipulations, the CAD program is going through a lot of necessary calculations to generate the form. The

Figure 1.12
Adding two solids

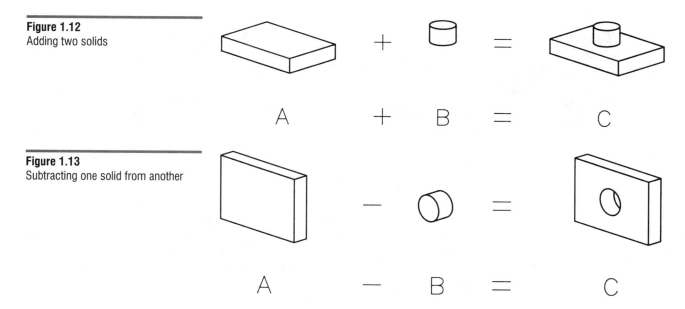

Figure 1.13
Subtracting one solid from another

resultant model, though accurate, can be time consuming and can create enormous CAD databases.

1.5 Model Display Options

Just as there are a variety of building options, there are also a variety of ways in which the model can be presented on the screen to the viewer. The displaying and the building of the model are linked. Some methods of model building will allow only certain methods of display. The three methods of model display representation are wireframe, edge removal, and rendering.

Wireframe is the most common way of displaying models in 3D CAD packages. Basically, it displays the model with all the edges visible to the viewer, regardless of where they are placed on the model, as shown in Figure 1.14. Think of the model as being made out of glass, so that all edges can be seen. This method is necessary for construction purposes; when constructing, it is important to be able to see where each line is going and how its path can affect other lines.

Edge removal (or, as it is commonly called, the hidden line removal option) displays the model to the viewer with foreground surfaces obstructing background surfaces. Those edges that would be obstructed by a surface between the edge and the view are not displayed. The lines or edges are not really removed, they just are not displayed. Refer to Figure 1.15. This is the same cylinder as the one shown in Figure 1.14, only in Figure 1.15 all that is

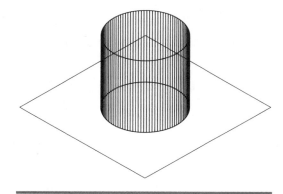

Figure 1.14
Wireframe display

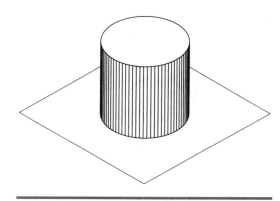

Figure 1.15
Hidden lines removed display

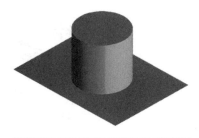

Figure 1.16
A rendered display

visible are the unobstructed edges. It is also possible to redefine temporarily the hidden edges in edge removal so that, instead of not showing up at all, they are displayed in a different fashion, such as in a different color. The edge removal option requires surfaces or solids to function.

Rendering is the technique of applying surface shades. The created surfaces are colored to accent the model, as shown in Figure 1.16. This shading can be of different types: (1) The surface can be plainly colored, based on the created surface color, or (2) the surface can be tone shaded, which is the process of giving tones to the surface color, based on different light sources, resulting in a range of light to dark tones. You can also create shadows as cast by the light sources hitting the model. Finally, rendering may assign surface textures or finishes as well. The surface can be very rough or smooth, or it may be a material such as wood, glass, or steel. The rendering option, like edge removal, requires surfaces or solids to function.

Again, it is up to the user to identify which method of display best suits the purpose of the project. But time must be considered when choosing a model display option: The more sophisticated the display, the more time required to generate it. Edge removal takes only a couple of key strokes, whereas rendering can require the integration of a separate application program to achieve the desired results.

1.6 Model Viewing

Whereas model display defines how the model is illustrated, model viewing tells how the model is depicted according to the position of the viewer. The model will behave in a certain fashion based on the viewer position, regardless of whether it will be shown in wireframe, with edges removed, or rendered. The viewing position will determine how large or small the model appears or whether it will be shown axonometrically or perspectively.

When the model is viewed with axonometric viewing, the edges that represent the model are parallel along the *X, Y, Z* axes, as shown in Figure 1.17. In axonometric viewing, the model can be turned and viewed from any direction, and the node points that define the edges are projected orthographically (straight) toward the viewer. This is extremely useful for construction purposes.

Perspective viewing makes use of converging lines, as opposed to parallel lines, to represent the model. See Figure 1.18. This viewing represents more closely how the human eye sees the model, and it is a useful way to present the model to clients. In perspective viewing, the lines or objects that are going away from the viewer appear smaller as the distance increases, and finally they converge into a vanishing point.

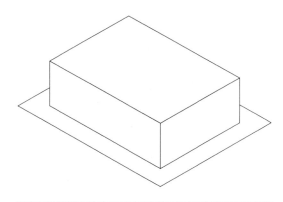

Figure 1.17
An axonometric view

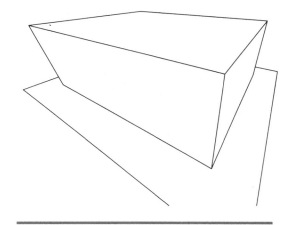

Figure 1.18
A perspective view

In both axonometric and perspective viewing, the model can be turned to any viewing position and can be reduced or enlarged. At any point, the user can apply the type of display desired—wireframe, hidden line removed, or rendered.

1.7 Working Planes

Almost all 3D creation is based on flat planes, referred to as *working planes*. Working planes form the reference point on which the building options are established. The final form is not necessarily flat, but its original creation point is built on a flat working plane. Refer to Figures 1.19 through 1.22. In Figure 1.19, a cube has already been created. To construct a cylinder on the top of the cube, a working plane is defined, as shown in Figure 1.20. Then the cylinder is added based on that working plane. Similarly, in Figure 1.21, a working plane

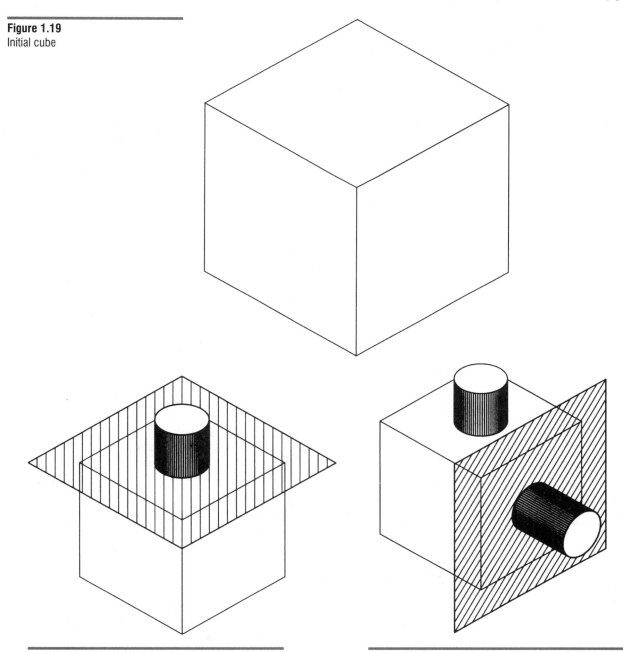

Figure 1.19
Initial cube

Figure 1.20
Creating a top working plane

Figure 1.21
Creating a side working plane

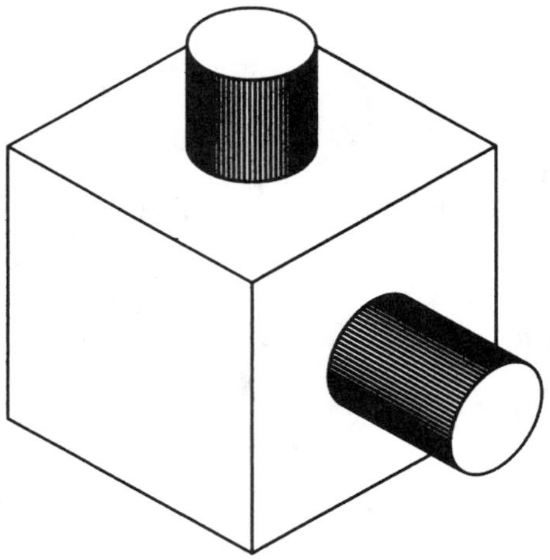

Figure 1.22
The final model

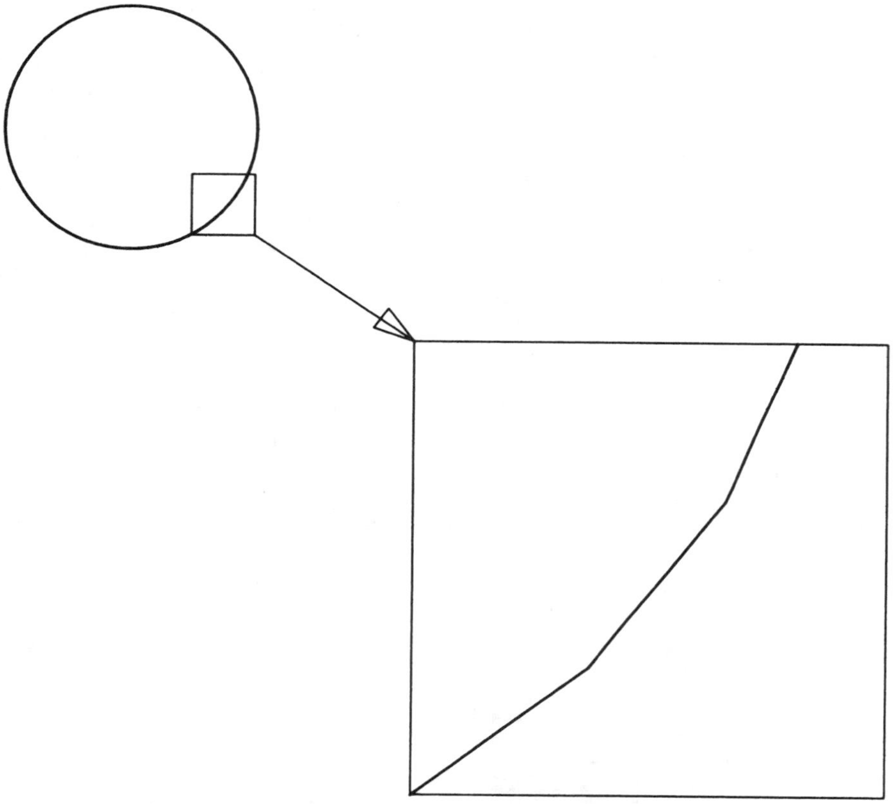

Figure 1.23
A close-up of a circle

is defined on the side of the cube and, from that plane, the second cylinder is added. Finally, as shown in Figure 1.22, the model is displayed.

Note that, even though most curved geometry appears smooth, it is based on flat surfaces in its creation, as shown in Figure 1.23.

1.8 The Text and Lab Framework

Before we get into the thick of things, there are a few facts about the text and the labs we must note. These pointers should help you avoid unnecessary confusion when you're performing the labs. Where possible, the labs have been written in a standard format, with the major objectives and the primary commands to be used outlined for you. The labs reinforce the theories and concepts explained in the chapter through hands-on interaction.

AutoCAD Version

This text is written primarily for use with AutoCAD Release 14. This does not mean that users of earlier versions are excluded. Users of Release 10, 11, 12, or 13 will find that the majority of the text applies to them as well. If you are *not* using Release 14, simply watch out for those specific areas where Release 14 has enhanced commands or rearranged menus.

3D Viewpoint Boxes

Throughout the text, you will find boxes entitled "3D Viewpoint." These boxes emphasize some of the important do's and don'ts of 3D modeling. The following illustrates the concept.

3D Viewpoint

File Naming

When completing the labs, adopt a file naming convention that contains your initials. The length of the file name leaves space for at least two initials at the end, as in the case of the file name PLANSE, for "PLAN Stephen Ethier." It is a good idea to practice this initialing throughout the text, because it automatically distinguishes your work from others for the instructor's or your benefit. Remember that the file name, including initials, cannot exceed eight characters.

File Referencing

As the book progresses, you will create models that build on each other. The initial labs may seem simple, but they will be used as stepping stones to more complicated model-creation techniques. When a model created in a lab or assignment is going to be used in later chapters, we will explicitly mention it so that you will know of the requirement. We will also mention when a previously constructed model will be required in a lab or assignment. This way, if you did not create the model the first time, you may go back, construct the model, and then use it for the required assignment.

Model Creation and the Use of Color

Virtually all the information required to construct a model is outlined in the labs. However, the mention of color for entities has been left out, mainly because this text is in black and white. Do not ignore the use of color if the computer you are using is capable of displaying color. Models are customarily broken down into sections. You should use these sections to assign different colors; this will prove exceedingly useful when viewing the model during the construction stage. At a later time in the book, you will be creating composite models that involve, among other things, an orientation cube, wireframe techniques, 3D faces, and surface meshes. Making each of these elements a separate color is an excellent way to enhance visual distinction in the models. If you want to see one particular aspect of the model, you can turn all the other parts off, leaving only, say, the blue orientation cube or the red surface meshes.

Also, when all parts are being viewed, you can distinguish each part of the model by its color on the viewing screen. Being able to distinguish the separate parts is essential during the construction phase of the more complex three-dimensional models.

Model Space and Paper Space

Within AutoCAD, there are two working environments: model space and paper space. Practically all design and creation take place in model space, and all three-dimensional work must take place in model space. Paper space is useful for preparing the model for presentation. The user creates and locates the necessary views and annotates these views in paper space. Usually, title blocks and borders are inserted in paper space. All entities created in paper space are flat, two-dimensional entities. Even the floating viewports created in paper space are flat. However, the displayed view inside the viewport can be, and often is, three dimensional. Entities created in the two working environments are kept separate, allowing each to be modified independently.

The two environments are managed and kept separate with the TILE-MODE system variable. When it is set to 1 (on), you are working solely in model space and the creation of tiled viewports using the VPORTS command is possible. The use of tiled viewports is the reason for the TILEMODE system variable. Prior to Release 11 of AutoCAD, this was the only method of creation and is still the default when you enter AutoCAD. When TILEMODE is set to 0 (off) you can create floating viewports in the paper space environment using the MVIEW command and work inside the viewports in model space using the MSPACE (MS) command. The paper space floating viewports can be created in any rectangular shape and can overlap, allowing more control over the layout. While TILEMODE is set to 0, you can switch to a paper space layout using the PSPACE (PS) command and enter model space in a floating viewport by using the MSPACE (MS) command. The methods of using paper space are explained in more detail in Chapter 16.

Tilemodes and Labs

As stated earlier, the creation of three-dimensional models must occur in model space, but it is up to you whether you choose to work in model space with TILEMODE set to 1 or 0. With TILEMODE set to 1, the working environment feels as it used to feel and, if you are just starting in 3D, this can be comforting. But with TILEMODE set to 0, you have more control over the creation of viewports and may find this more beneficial. Basically, it is up to you to decide which method to employ. The labs do not specify which method to use unless they involve specifically practicing paper space capabilities.

Plotting

The chapter on plotting is placed later in the book so that you may have produced some complex 3D work by that time. However, feel free to review the chapter earlier if you wish to see some of your early 3D work on paper.

Commands and Menus

Command entry in AutoCAD can be accomplished in several ways, including using the command line through the keyboard, the sidebar (screen) menu, a pull-down menu, the cursor menu, a tablet menu, and a button menu.

This text concentrates on the access of commands through on-screen visual methods, acknowledging the fact that many individuals have access to a mouse rather than a digitizer for input. In addition, because of the versatility of on-screen icons, more people may make use of these icons rather than the tablet method of input.

The commands to manipulate AutoCAD practically never change from release to release, although they are usually enhanced or added to. However, the order of pull-down menus and sidebar (or screen) menus does change from release to release, demonstrating AutoCAD's attempts to make the menus more user-friendly. This can cause some confusion with users progressing to new releases. In any case, the method of accessing commands through the pull-down menus is given in the theoretical portion of the chapter concerned with that menu, and the use of direct commands at the command prompt is added in the labs. This should make your entry into 3D easier, regardless of which version of AutoCAD you are using.

1.9 What's Ahead

Now you have some grounding and you are ready to move on. Your basic understanding of the various 3D terms will enable you to master 3D construction. Before we embark on the ways in which AutoCAD can be used to accomplish the amazing feats described in the previous pages, we will explore how others have applied AutoCAD's 3D capabilities. The next chapter is devoted to actual user applications and should give you some insight in the uses of 3D. Then, Chapter 3 begins your introduction to AutoCAD's 3D commands.

Questions

1. Identify three benefits of 3D computer modeling.

2. Which discipline was the first major user of 3D, and what did it use 3D for?

3. Explain what-if situations.

4. Identify the three axes that are used in 3D modeling, and explain how they are used.

5. What are the four 3D building options? How do they build on each other?

6. Surface generation can be accomplished by four different methods. Explain each.

7. What are the pros and cons of solid modeling?

8. What is the difference between displaying and viewing a 3D model?

9. Explain edge removal.

10. What is the difference between axonometric and perspective viewing?

11. What is the function of working planes?

CHAPTER 2

Applications

Overview

This chapter explores the ways in which a variety of drafting and design disciplines use 3D models as well as the reasons why uses differ between disciplines. This very visual chapter includes examples from industry, business, and the arts to illustrate how these disciplines use 3D modeling techniques.

Concepts Explored

- Which 3D models are used in which disciplines
- How approaches differ when used on different model types.

2.1 Introduction

As outlined in Chapter 1, the benefits of 3D modeling are numerous. 3D modeling can be applied in practically any discipline, from designing a better mousetrap to creating a digitized model to aid in the restoration of the Sphinx.

Although a variety of techniques and procedures may be used to create 3D models, each discipline relies mainly on specific techniques, depending on the design. Architects rely heavily on extrusion techniques for building walls, and they tend to use perspective views in the display of the final structure. Civil engineers use irregular 3D meshes to achieve results in terrain modeling. Mechanical manufacturers make use of solids to create accurate models of machined or welded parts and use axonometric views to detail the model. Structural designers rely on the use of 3D parametric symbols for the construction of structural members.

In the following pages, a myriad of disciplines and applications are discussed, and these examples show some of the possible hows of construction. As these discussions progress, we'll use a number of terms with which you probably are not yet acquainted. Although we cite a chapter and sometimes a section reference for each term, don't feel an obligation to follow up each reference at this point. These terms are included for two reasons: First, they give you a brief taste of things to come and a better understanding of how each of these constructions is achieved through specific AutoCAD commands. Second, after completing later chapters and learning the terms by using the commands within your own constructions, you can come back to Chapter 2 with a greater understanding of the terms.

2.2 Model Illustrations

Building Complex

When constructing a model of a building complex, such as the one shown in Figure 2.1, a model maker could use a variety of 3D techniques. Extruded lines (Chapter 5) would be used for flat, rectangular surfaces such as the vertical building walls and retaining wall tops, whereas irregularly shaped flat surfaces created with 3D faces (Section 7.3) would be used to cover the variable surfaces, such as roof tops and sloped retaining walls. In the case of surfaces that radiate from a central point, such as the main entrance way, the polygon mesh generating RULESURF (Section 8.3) command would automate the process. To construct items such as the rectangular box-shaped skylights, simply specifying the shape and size desired would automatically create a 3D object (Section 8.2) to suit.

Park and Streetcar Station

The drawing shown in Figure 2.2, which was prepared by Pietz and Michal Architects in Keene, New Hampshire, and created by modeler Charles Michal, displays a complex park setting generated with a variety of extruded lines and circles (Chapter 5). Because the trunks of the trees are tapered and truncated, a truncated cone would be used (Section 8.2). The leaf structure of the trees could be made from the linking of flat irregular surface constructed from 3D faces (Section 7.3). When the design requires a series of parallel surfaces such as the walkways, the TABSURF (Section 8.3) command can create them automatically. After this drawing was produced, it was rendered (Chapter 17) in

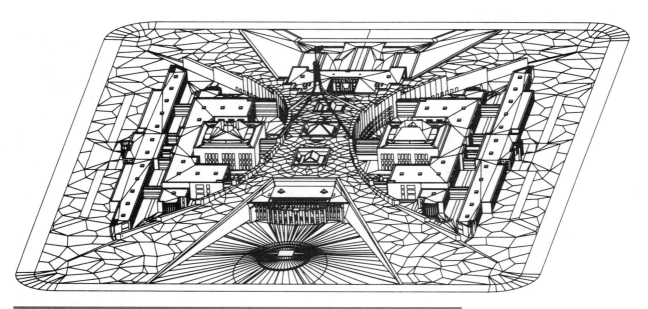

Figure 2.1
Model of a building complex (hidden lines removed)
Source: Courtesy of Autodesk

Figure 2.2
Model of a park setting with streetcar station (hidden lines removed)
Source: Courtesy of Pietz and Michal Architects

ink and pencil to enhance its artistic appearance for 3D animated walk-throughs on video tape.

Steel Arch Bridge

With bridges such as the one modeled in Figure 2.3, symmetry is the key. The bridge shown here is a very impressive structure, but it can be broken down into unique pieces to make the task of 3D construction easier. Because of the many related members, parametric symbols (standard designs that can be applied to differing sets of parameters; Chapter 14) can be employed to make the job of construction proceed more quickly. Parametric symbols could also be used for the light standards, and the roadway could be created by drawing its profile and then extruding it to form its length (Section 14.2).

Office Layout

The office layout model in Figure 2.4, generated by Charles Michal of Pietz and Michal Architects, uses many extruded lines and forms in the construction of the office furniture and cabinets (Chapter 5). The rounded reception desk, which is the focal point of the drawing, uses an extruded arc in a most effective way.

Turboprop Airplane

For the creation of the airplane shown in Figure 2.5, a wireframe skeleton would be constructed initially. Once this was done, the skeleton would control the automatic application of surface skins, relying heavily on Coons surface patches created by the EDGESURF command (Section 8.3), to construct such items as the wings and tail pieces. The fuselage (body) could be constructed out of either Coons surface patches or a series of ruled surfaces using the RULESURF command.

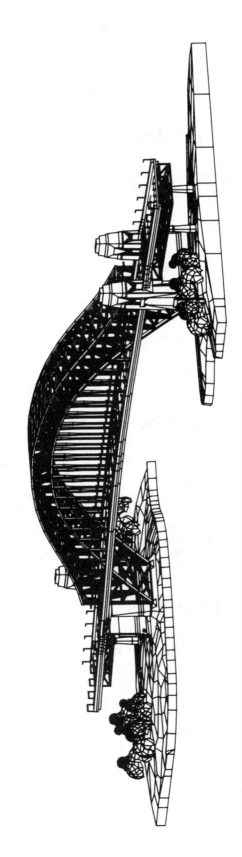

Figure 2.3
Steel arch bridge model (hidden lines removed)
Source: Courtesy of Autodesk

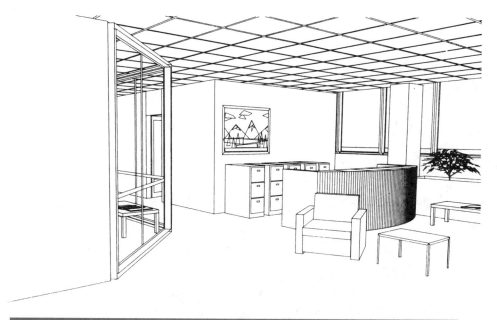

Figure 2.4
Model of an office layout (hidden lines removed)
Source: Courtesy of Pietz and Michal Architects

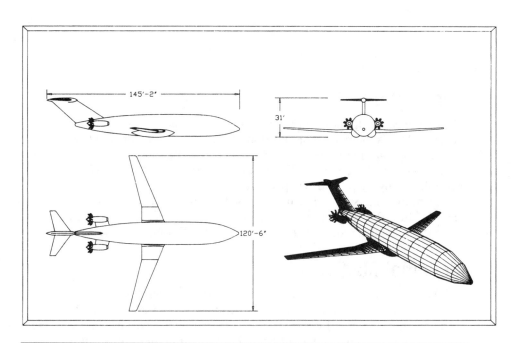

Figure 2.5
Turboprop airplane model (hidden lines removed)
Source: Courtesy of Autodesk

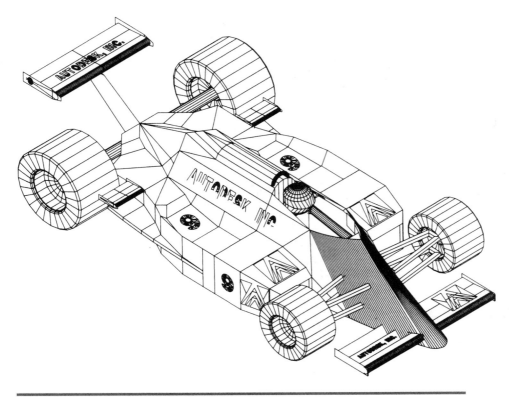

Figure 2.6
Racing car model (hidden lines removed)
Source: Courtesy of Autodesk

Racing Car

The racing car body shown in Figure 2.6 is composed of many flat but irregular surfaces. This is the perfect application of the 3DFACE command (Section 7.3). Because tires are naturally round but tend to have a unique tread profile, they require the use of the REVSURF command (Section 8.3), with its ability to take a profile of any shape and revolve it about an axis to create a series of surfaces that form the final shape. The nose of the body uses radial surfaces formed with the RULESURF command. The tips of the spoilers are rounded but parallel along their lengths, requiring use of the TABSURF command (Section 8.3).

Memorial Stadium

The complex model of the new south stands and memorial colonnade for Memorial Stadium at the University of Illinois was created by modeler Craig Burgess from a design by architect John Severns at Severns, Reid & Associates, Inc. This model, shown in Figure 2.7, has a minimum of detail because of the building's size and complicated appearance. The stands, vomitories, and colonnades are drawn in true 3D, thereby lending themselves to the production of video walk-throughs. The stadium was a project of the University of Illinois, Urbana–Champaign. The campus architect was Roland Kehe and the project manager was George Hendricks.

Crane Hook

The model of a crane hook presented in Figure 2.8 uses a variety of surface techniques, most of which require wireframe construction to create cross-sec-

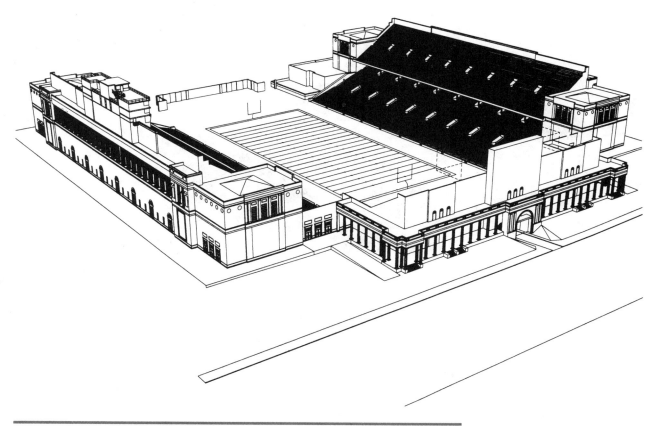

Figure 2.7
Model of Memorial Stadium at University of Illinois (hidden lines removed)
Source: Courtesy of Severns, Reid & Associates, Inc.

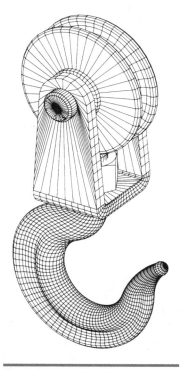

Figure 2.8
Crane hook (hidden lines removed)
Source: Courtesy of Autodesk

tional profiles. Then surface techniques would be applied, similar to the creation of the airplane model in Figure 2.5; the pulley wheel would use surfaces of revolution created by the REVSURF command (Section 8.3), the hook would require a combination of Coons surface patches and surface revolutions (EDGESURF and REVSURF commands), and the nut could be constructed from an extruded polygon.

Hilly Terrain

The three-dimensional construction of the model shown in Figure 2.9 would rely totally on the use of topologically rectangular meshes created with the 3DMESH command (Section 8.3). The user or an outside program supplies all the coordinates, including elevations of all the vertices, and AutoCAD automatically links the various surfaces to generate the topographic map. Then, 3D polylines could be used to add rivers and roads.

Boardroom

A model such as the one shown in Figure 2.10 would use 3D faces (Section 7.3) for most of the construction because of the irregular flat surfaces, such as the table top and the chair backs. The pedestal supports for the table could be made of extruded polylines (Section 5.3) as could the chair columns and legs.

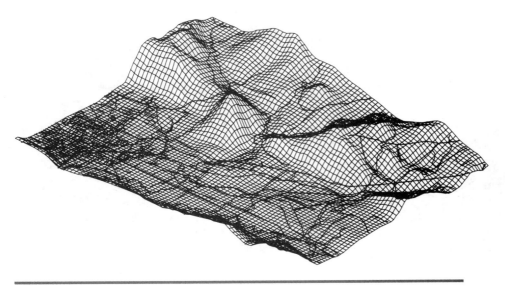

Figure 2.9
Hilly terrain topographical model (wireframe)
Source: Courtesy of Autodesk

Figure 2.10
Boardroom table and chairs model (hidden lines removed)
Source: Courtesy of Autodesk

Antenna Tower

The model of an antenna tower depicted in Figure 2.11 is interesting in that it illustrates one of the practical purposes of 3D modeling. This 80-foot tower designed for cable television was produced by modeler David Devereaux-Weber of American Communications Consultants, Inc. The model uses a 3D approach to ensure that none of the structural members of the antennas is in the same place at the same time—something that drawing in 2D could not guarantee. With the aid of this drawing created from the 3D model, the tower erector will know at what height and azimuth to install the antennas.

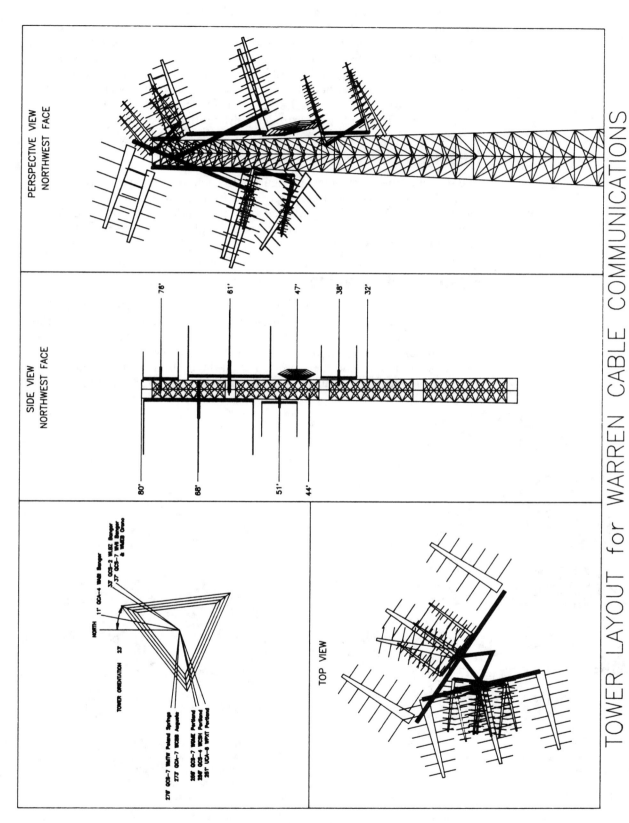

Figure 2.11

Antenna tower model (wireframe)

Source: Courtesy of American Communications Consultants, Inc.

Diver's Helmet

The helmet shown in Figure 2.12 is composed of many curved surfaces allowing semiautomatic means to be employed in its creation. The head piece and the spherical knobs on the front of the shoulder yoke would be constructed with revolved surfaces using the REVSURF command (Section 8.3). The rim of the shoulder yoke would use the RULESURF command because it requires radial surfaces. The base of the shoulder yoke would be created through parallel tabulated surfaces with the use of the TABSURF command and the front of the faceplate base would be made from extruded polylines that have width (Section 5.3).

Heart

The model of the heart shown in Figure 2.13 could be initially created in wireframe. Wires (lines) would be constructed from point to point and then 3D faces (Section 7.3) would be placed over the model to allow hidden edge removal and surface shading. Terrain modeling, illustrated in Figure 2.9, could also use the 3DMESH command (Section 8.3).

Residential Dwelling

Figure 2.14 presents an attractive model of a house with attached garage. Initially constructed from extruded lines to define the preliminary model, the extrusions were replaced with 3D faces (Section 7.3) once the overall shape had been defined. 3D symbols (Chapter 13) of windows and doors were created as separate files and then inserted at all the desired locations. Finally, to accent the model, 2D hatching was applied for siding, brick, and roofing tiles.

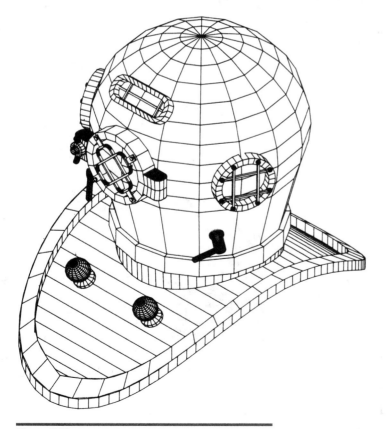

Figure 2.12
Deep sea diver's helmet model (hidden lines removed)
Source: Courtesy of Autodesk

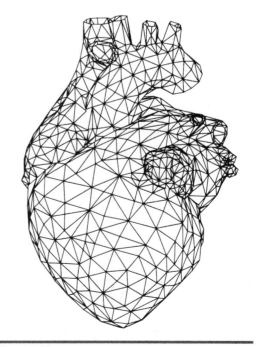

Figure 2.13
Heart model (hidden lines removed)
Source: Courtesy of Autodesk

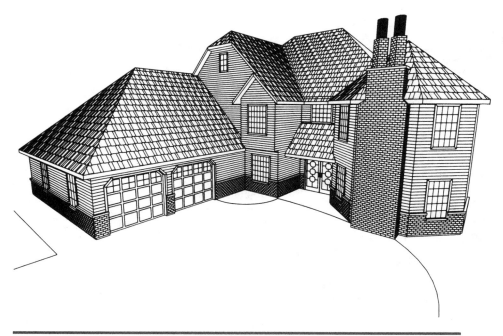

Figure 2.14
Residential dwelling model (hidden lines removed)

Miniature Pneumatic Cylinder

The miniature pneumatic cylinder body modeled in Figure 2.15 was constructed initially using solid modeling (Chapters 9 through 12). Solid three-dimensional entities such as cylinders and boxes were added to and subtracted from each other to create the final shape. Using the finished solid model, mass calculations can be performed to find its weight, its center of gravity, and much more. Because it is a solid model, its three-dimensional data could be sent to a stereolithography apparatus (SLA) and a physical, tangible part could be created. As a finishing touch to the illustration, this model was rendered (Chapter 17) inside of AutoCAD.

Figure 2.15
Solid model of a miniature pneumatic
cylinder body (rendered)

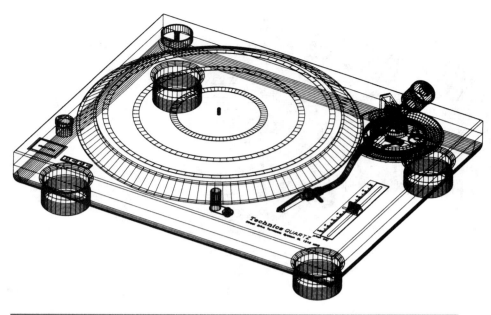

Figure 2.16
Record turntable model (wireframe)
Source: Courtesy of Autodesk

Record Turntable

Refer to the turntable model in Figure 2.16. Here, where circular symmetry is prominent, surfaces of revolution would be created using the REVSURF (Section 8.3) command. Such items as the support legs and the platter bed would be constructed in this way. The slider control could be constructed out of a tabulated surface using the TABSURF command. To construct the needle arm, a Coons surface patch must be used, created through the EDGESURF command. The base could be formed with extruded lines (Section 5.3) and the top covered with a 3D face (Section 7.3).

Kitchen

The illustration in Figure 2.17 shows a rendered kitchen model created with 3D symbols (Chapter 13). The symbols of the refrigerator, sink, cabinetry, and other similar components were created in their own files and then assembled to create the final kitchen model. These components use extruded lines capped with 3D faces. Specifically, the countertop was created with 3D faces (Section 7.3) with an opening left for the sink. The mug and coffeepot are made of revolved surfaces using the REVSURF command (Section 8.3). Once the model was finished, it was rendered using advanced rendering (Chapter 17). Advanced rendering is an add-on application program from Autodesk that enhances the rendering ability of AutoCAD. With advanced rendering, surface materials can make objects appear transparent or shadows can be automatically calculated and shown. Look closely at the screen of the laptop computer on the countertop; it is displaying the rendered model of the kitchen. Release 14 rendering allows the modeler to apply previously created images to 3D geometry.

2.3 Summary

Now that you have seen what can be done with three-dimensional modeling, its time to learn how to do it. Throughout the following chapters, you will learn

Figure 2.17
Rendered kitchen model

and apply three-dimensional modeling techniques in a steadily advancing process until you are able to create models as complex or even more complex that those shown in this chapter. In Part 2, you will prepare yourself by learning how to move around in 3D space and how to create working planes. Then you will dig into the actual construction techniques outlined in Part 3. In Part 4 you will learn about solid modeling, building on the techniques presented in preceding chapters, but using another area of 3D modeling—the formation of models from true solids.

When you have mastered the various methods of creation, you will then learn how to produce the models more efficiently and how to present them to others in Parts 5 and 6. At this point, you'll be ready to tackle any type of 3D construction and can move on to any of the applications presented in Part 7.

Part 8 contains an introduction to three programs, Autodesk Designer, 3D Studio (R4), and 3D Studio MAX, that can be integrated within AutoCAD or used separately to enhance your models.

Questions

1. What is the 3D modeling technique upon which architects rely so heavily? Why?

2. What technique do civil engineers most commonly use? Why?

3. What techniques described in Chapter 2 might be used when creating the model of a working farm? Explain where you would use these techniques.

4. From what you have learned of 3D modeling techniques in Chapter 2, list some 3D modeling procedures that would be helpful for the construction of a train.

5. Upon which technique do mechanical engineers rely heavily? Why?

6. Sketch a model of your own that would require at least three of the techniques already explored. Label the drawing locations where these techniques could be applied.

7. Look ahead at Figure 4.1 in Chapter 4. What 3D techniques might have been used to create these models?

2

Preparing for Construction of 3D Models

Before you actually create a 3D model, it is essential that you become familiar with the commands that allow movement through the 3D space created on the screen. This part includes step-by-step explanations and a number of suggested exercises to familiarize you with this three-dimensional movement. Chapters 3 and 4 introduce some simple labs that are designed to involve you quickly and prepare you for the more complex creation of geometric constructs that begin in the next part.

CHAPTER **3**

Display of 3D Models for Construction

Overview

The techniques you'll learn in this chapter will serve as the foundation of the skills you'll need for 3D model construction in later chapters. In simple terms, this chapter could be entitled, "how to walk around and look." The chapter will instruct you in how to create a simple cubic model so that you'll be able to thoroughly explore a variety of processes for moving around the on-screen model, for viewing the model in a number of ways, and for altering the display of the model to enhance the visual imagery. In addition, this chapter will give you your first lesson in saving a 3D model.

Concepts Explored

- The difference between axonometric and perspective displays
- The importance of axonometric display in the construction phase of modeling
- The manipulation of viewpoints
- The various methods of changing the viewpoint
- Controlling the orientation of view
- The need for multiple viewports
- The creation techniques used in configuring viewports
- How to apply hidden line removal to enhance the viewing of the model.

3.1 Introduction

To facilitate the construction of 3D models, proper procedures for viewing need to be adopted. First, the operator needs to choose the manner in which the model will be viewed. As mentioned in Chapter 1, there are two main ways of viewing a model—axonometrically and perspectively. Although perspective views display a very realistic image of how the viewer would see the actual model, it is often hard to distinguish whether the geometry has been designed correctly. (For instance, are corners square or at right angles?) For example, look at the perspective view of Figure 3.1. With axonometric views, on the other hand, it is much more apparent whether corners are square or edges are parallel to each other. See Figure 3.2 for a sample. Because of this difference, axonometric viewing is the primary method of viewing the model during the construction phase.

Figure 3.1
A perspective view

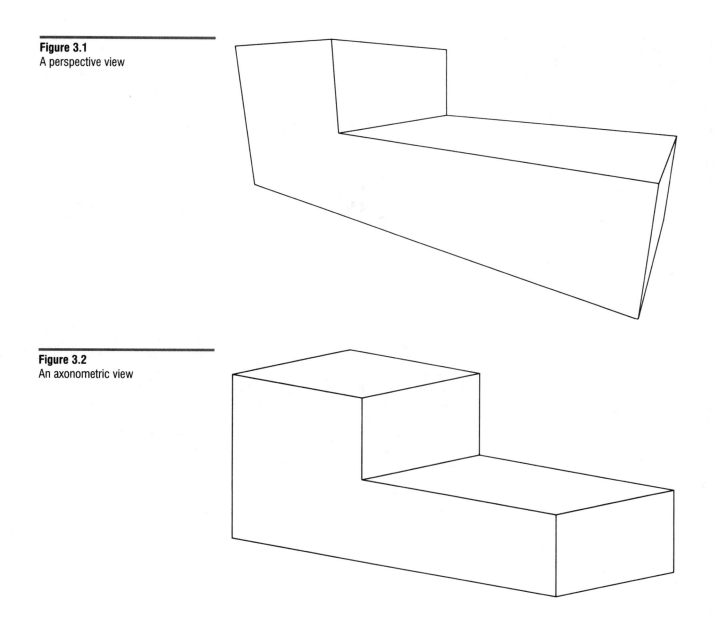

Figure 3.2
An axonometric view

Let's consider some techniques of on-screen model display. Axonometric viewing makes use of orthographic techniques to view an object. With axonometric viewing, the object is turned on any axis and the view is projected straight toward or perpendicular to the viewer. Then it is outlined on a viewing or picture plane, thereby generating the image that shows three sides of the object. This method of on-screen display is accomplished in AutoCAD by means of the VPOINT command, which stands for viewpoint.

A second technique of on-screen model display utilizes multiple views of the model at one time. This technique allows the construction to move along at a faster pace because the designer can see the effects of construction on different locations on the model at the same time. Referring to Figure 3.3A, you can see the three-dimensional aspect of the addition of the cylinder to the angle bracket. At the same time, looking at Figure 3.3B, you can see that the cylinder is off-center of the horizontal plate. And, finally, observing Figure 3.3C, you can see that the cylinder is not actually touching the horizontal plate. By maintaining several different views of a model on the screen at one time, design deficiencies can be caught early in the design, saving time and preventing errors from accumulating. This method of on-screen display is accomplished in Auto-CAD by using the VPORTS command, which stands for multiple viewports.

Figure 3.3
The need for multiple viewpoints of the
same model

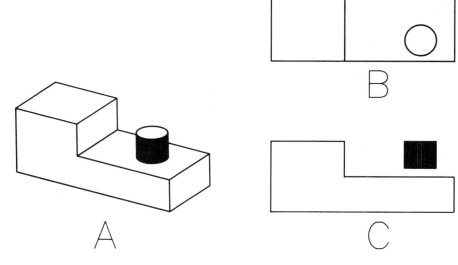

A third technique involves displaying the model with normally viewed
obstructed edges in wireframe hidden from the viewer, thereby presenting an
enhanced view. This enhanced view can clarify the construction of the model,
especially when lines appear to be overlapping each other but are actually in
front of or behind each other, separated by a distance. Refer to Figure 3.4,
where a model appears in wireframe display, and to Figure 3.5, where the
same model is shown with edges hidden from the viewer. It is useful to check
the model construction periodically by viewing the model in this mode. This
method of on-screen display is accomplished in AutoCAD by using the HIDE
command, which stands for hidden line removal.

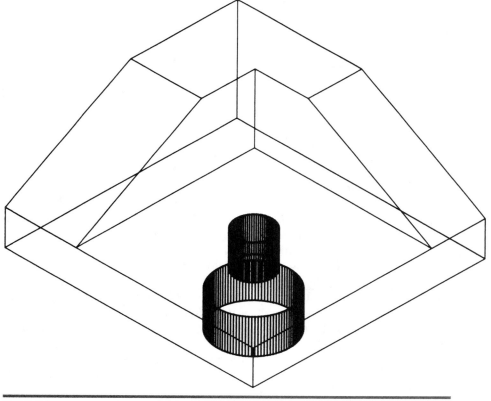

Figure 3.4
Wireframe view

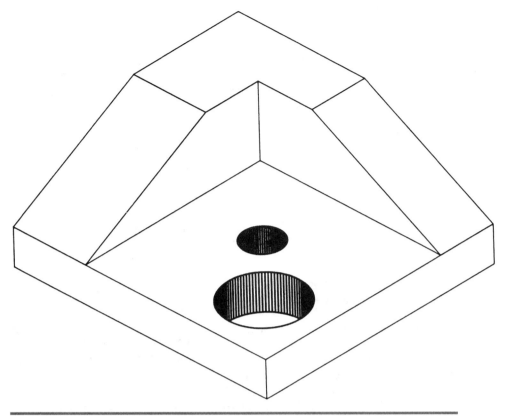

Figure 3.5
Hidden line removed view

3.2 Viewpoint Manipulation

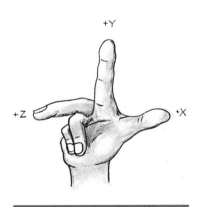

Figure 3.6
The right-hand rule

The first step in the proper viewing of a model is to identify two crucial components: (1) the center of interest (the piece of the image at which the viewer is looking) and (2) the viewer's position in relation to the model. The center of interest is set with the AutoCAD system variable TARGET. This variable is set to the default location of 0,0,0. In most cases, to generate the axonometric views, all you need do is enter the position of the viewer. The VPOINT command has four methods of entering this location: (1) entering the three-dimensional X, Y, Z coordinates, (2) rotating the model through angles, (3) rotating the model by the use of a compass, and (4) using preset locations.

To help with the visualization of the model in three-dimensional space, AutoCAD uses the right-hand rule to define all coordinate systems. This rule is illustrated in Figure 3.6. To try it yourself, hold your right hand in front of the screen, with the back of the hand parallel to the screen, and make a fist. Now extend the thumb out, toward the right; this points in the positive X direction. Extend the index (or first) finger upward; this points in the positive Y direction. And, finally, extend the middle finger toward yourself; this points in the positive Z direction.

3D Viewpoint

The VPOINT Command

The VPOINT command does not function in paper space. This is because paper space is designed for flat, two-dimensional layouts, whereas the VPOINT command is designed for 3D viewing.

Figure 3.7
3D axes

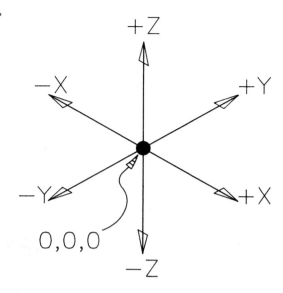

VPOINT Coordinate Input

Entering coordinates to set the location of the view is an accurate way to get the required view of the model. When the VPOINT command is first selected, two things happen. First, the UCS icon switches to WCS orientation. This is to tell the user that the entering of coordinates is based on the World Coordinate System, which is outlined in Chapter 4. In simple terms, the WCS is the main X, Y, Z coordinate system that keeps track of all the coordinate entries. Its 0,0,0 point is the reference point of all geometric creation.

Second, the user is prompted for the X, Y, Z viewpoint location. At this time, the user enters the X, Y, Z coordinates, which may be positive or negative and may have any numerical value. Refer to Figure 3.7. The positive and negative values of the coordinates control whether the viewer is viewing from above or below the model, behind or in front of it, or to the right or left side of it. See Figure 3.8. Positive means the viewer is moving along an axis in the positive direction, away from the model. Negative means the viewer is moving along

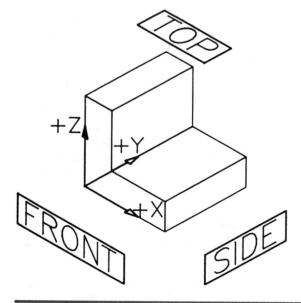

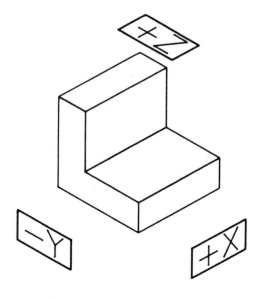

Figure 3.8
Relation of views to axes

Figure 3.9
Viewpoints and their coordinates

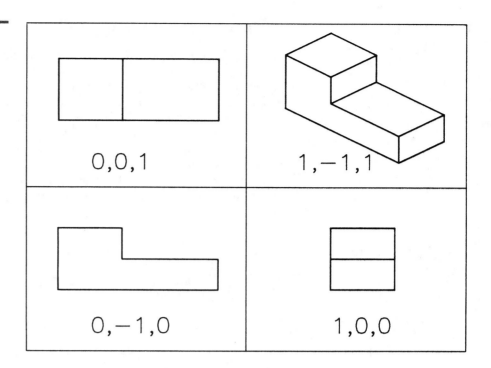

the axis in a negative direction, away from the model. Zero input means that there is no movement along that axis.

Entering a number, whether positive or negative, in only one axis generates a standard orthographic view (that is, top, front, or side view). Entering a number in all three axes generates a pictorial axonometric view, as shown in Figure 3.9.

Because the view generated in all cases is based on parallel projection, the numerical value of the input has no effect on the size of the object. VPOINT always generates a zoom extents view. The user then makes use of the regular zoom functions to manipulate the size or placement of the view. The numerical value does have an effect on rotation of the model. Refer to Figure 3.10. When all three axis values are set to the same quantity, whether positive or negative, an isometric view is generated. *Isometric* means all three axis angles are equal. If only two of the three axis values are the same numerical value, then a dimetric view is generated. *Dimetric* means two axis angles are different. If all three axis values are different, then a trimetric view is generated. *Trimetric* means all three axis angles are different.

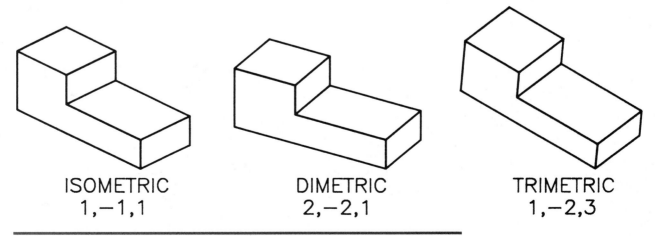

Figure 3.10
The three types of axonometric views

37

VPOINT Rotation Input

Rotation input is the method of entering angular values to rotate planes away from the 0,0,0 location, as illustrated in Figure 3.11. To access this procedure, select the VPOINT command and then enter R for rotate at the option prompt. The user is first asked for the rotation angle (A) from the X axis along the X–Y plane (see Figure 3.12). This is almost the same as a 2D rotation command. The second angle input required (B) is the rotation from the X–Y plane in the Z direction (see Figure 3.13). This is similar to tilting the viewer position away from the model up or down in the Z axis. Once both angles are input, the resulting view is displayed (see Figure 3.14). By entering different values, isometric, dimetric, and trimetric views can be created.

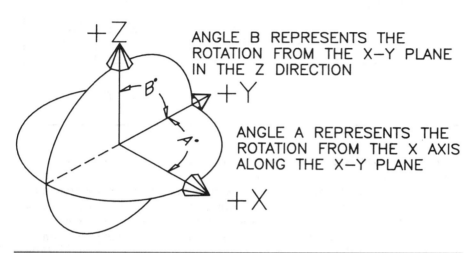

Figure 3.11
Spherical coordinates used in rotation

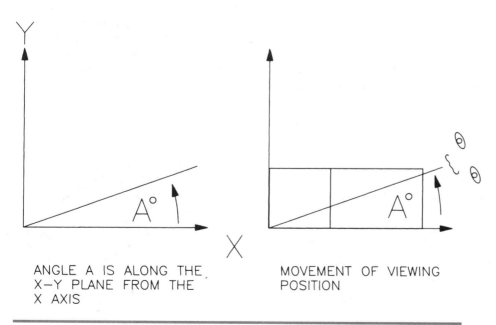

Figure 3.12
Rotation in the Z axis

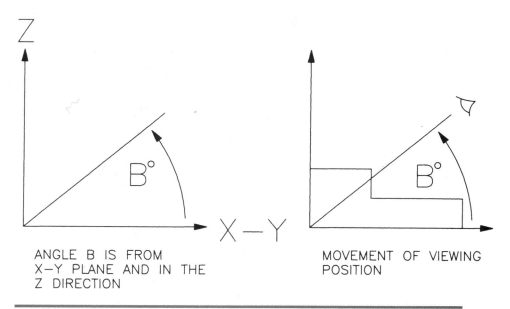

ANGLE B IS FROM
X–Y PLANE AND IN THE
Z DIRECTION

MOVEMENT OF VIEWING
POSITION

Figure 3.13
Rotation in the *X–Y* plane

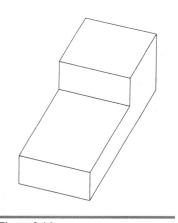

Figure 3.14
The final viewpoint

VPOINT Compass Input

The compass method of input is the most visual and quickest way of displaying an axonometric view of a model using the VPOINT command. To access the compass command, select the VPOINT command and then simply press the enter key. At this point, the screen switches from the graphics screen to the compass input screen, which is shown in Figure 3.15.

Contained in the compass input screen are two movement feedback icons. The first is the compass, which is displayed in the upper right-hand corner of the screen. By moving the cursor, represented by a small cross, around the compass icon, a desired orientation is achieved. As the cross is moved about the compass, the second feedback icon reflects that movement. The second icon is a tripod representation of the three (*X, Y, Z*) axes. It will turn, twist, and flip based on the placement of the cursor on the compass. The compass is a two-dimensional representation of the World Coordinate System.

Look at Figure 3.16. The center of the compass represents the north pole, or the positive *Z* axis. The outer ring of the compass represents the south pole,

Figure 3.15
The compass input screen

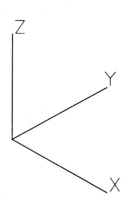

Figure 3.16
The compass defined

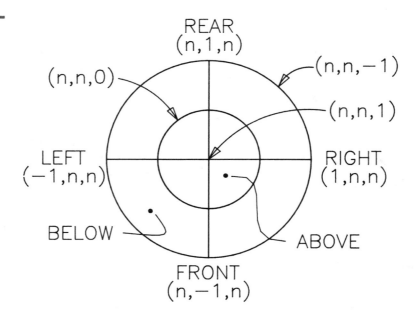

Figure 3.17
The compass point and the resulting view above

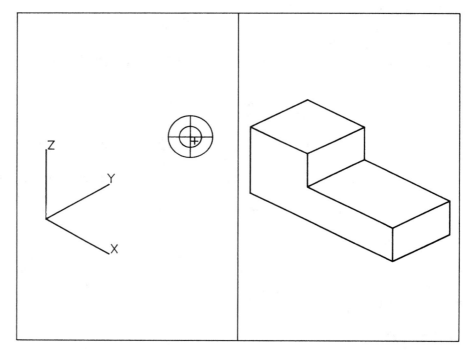

or the negative Z axis. The inner ring represents the equator, or the 0 point on the Z axis. By moving the cursor around in a circular fashion, you can achieve a front, side, or rear view combination, either above or below the model. Figures 3.17 and 3.18 illustrate these views.

VPOINT Preset Input

As part of the Advanced User Interface (AUI), AutoCAD provides a pop-up dialog box containing preset viewpoints. Using Release 13, this box is accessible from the View pull-down menu under the View/3D Viewpoint/Select heading. Here, the user is presented with two feedback icons. The one on the left controls the angles from the X axis along the X–Y plane, which affects movement around the model. The one on the right controls the angles from the X–Y plane, which affects the viewer's elevation. The preset settings are a combination of

Figure 3.18
The compass point and the resulting view below

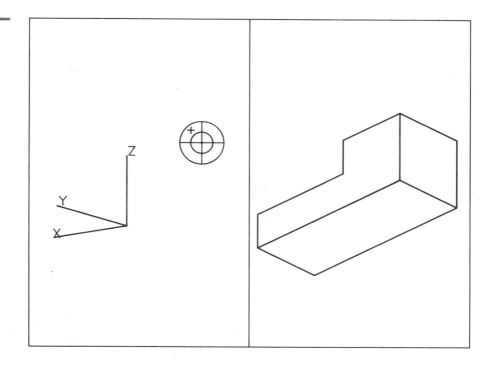

VPOINT rotation input and VPOINT compass input, allowing for the precision of the rotation input while retaining the graphical feedback of the compass input. Exact values can be entered in the two boxes provided below the icons.

Figure 3.19 illustrates the access to the preset input viewpoints through pull-down menus.

The VPOINT Command

Listed here are the various options that are available under the VPOINT command or from dialog boxes:

Figure 3.19
Pull-down menu access to VPOINT

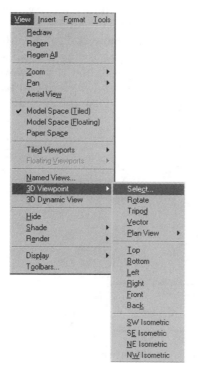

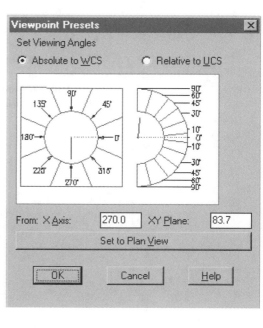

OPTIONS	DESCRIPTION
VPOINT X, Y, Z	Places the viewpoint based on coordinates.
VPOINT R	Places the viewpoint based on rotation of the model using specific angles.
VPOINT <Enter>	Calls up the compass screen, allowing placement of the viewpoint based on the rotation of the model using a compass and tripod.
PRESET	Provides preset viewpoints by means of dialog boxes.

3.3   The PLAN Command

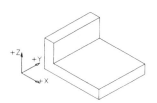

To provide a quick way of displaying a plan or top view of the model, Auto-CAD has included a command called PLAN. The PLAN command has two functions. The first is to display the plan view of the WCS, and the second is to display the plan view of the current User Coordinate System (UCS), which is explained in detail in Chapter 4. Using the WCS option of the PLAN command has the same effect as entering 0,0,1 for VPOINT coordinates.

Figure 3.20
Model oriented to the X, Y, Z axes

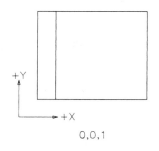

0,0,1

Figure 3.21
Standard top view

> ### 3D Viewpoint
>
> **The PLAN Command**
> *The PLAN command is a fast way of displaying the current UCS parallel with the screen. Simply type PLAN on the command line and press two enters.*

Orientation Control

When entering coordinates to place the viewpoint for the standard orthographic views shown in Section 3.3, the final orientation of the model on the screen is always the same. However, it is not necessarily the orientation that would best suit construction or viewing. Take, for instance, the model shown in Figure 3.20. To display a top or plan view, the coordinates 0,0,1 are entered; the resulting view is shown in Figure 3.21.

It is possible to have more control over the orientation by entering almost nondiscernible values for an axis input instead of entering a zero. Refer to Figure 3.22. The values entered to display this view were –0.0000001,0,1. A very small value for the X axis was given, which caused the model to be displayed with the –X direction pointing down. Figures 3.23 and 3.24 illustrate other orientations.

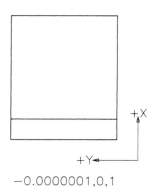

−0.0000001,0,1

Figure 3.22
Top view turned 90 degrees

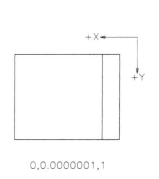

0,0.0000001,1

Figure 3.23
Top view turned 180 degrees

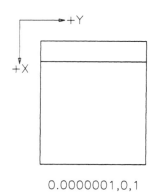

0.0000001,0,1

Figure 3.24
Top view turned 270 degrees

Any viewpoint displayed on the screen can be saved by using the common VIEW SAVE command. Then, at any time, that viewpoint can be restored using VIEW RESTORE and giving the previously saved name.

3.4 Multiple Viewports

As you probably know from your 2D drafting with AutoCAD, multiple tiled viewports are available using the VPORTS command. These viewports are useful in displaying different two-dimensional locations of a drawing. But multiple viewports are even more important to three-dimensional modeling. Not only do viewports display different locations on a drawing, but they are capable of displaying totally different viewpoints. This allows the user to observe construction of the model from different vantage points, as illustrated in Figure 3.25.

The discussion in this chapter is concerned with viewports where TILE-MODE is set to 1. Viewports using a tilemode set to 0 behave differently as discussed in Chapter 16.

Viewport Control

Once viewports are displayed, you need only set the various viewpoints in each viewport. This can be achieved in a variety of ways, depending on the user. But one constant is that you need to activate the viewports first. This is accomplished simply by moving the cursor into the particular viewport. If a cursor is displayed, then the viewport is already activated. If an arrow is displayed, the viewport has not been activated yet, and you'll need to use the pick button to change the arrow to a cursor. Once activated, you can use the VPOINT, PLAN, or VIEW RESTORE command to set the viewpoint. If a similar scale is desired in each viewport, then the ZOOM scale command can be used. To set the scale to 1, enter the following command in each activated viewport:

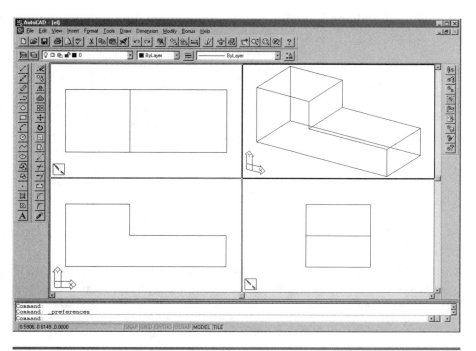

Figure 3.25
Multiple viewports (four)

3D Viewpoint

Viewports

Remember that when you save the viewport configuration, it is saved inside the current drawing only. You cannot pass viewport configurations to other drawing files through insertion. If you begin a new drawing, and the prototype drawing contains viewports, those viewports will be passed to the new drawing.

```
Command: ZOOM
All/Center/Dynamic/Extents/Previous/Scale(X/Xp)/Win-
dow/<Realtime>: 1X
```

With this feature, any common scale can be displayed in any viewport when TILEMODE = 1. With TILEMODE = 0, 1XP would be used to set the scale in a viewport. Refer to Chapter 16.

Like views, viewport configurations can be saved and recalled in the model. This is accomplished by using the VPORTS SAVE and VPORTS RESTORE commands. The layout of the viewport is saved, as are the current viewpoints. If you have a combination of viewpoints that are associated with each other, you can group them into a viewport configuration for easy redisplay. To redisplay the combination of viewpoints, you simply recall that particular viewport.

Note also that it is possible to display layers independently in different viewports. But this technique is used when tilemode is set to 0 and is explained in detail in Chapter 16.

The VPORTS Command

Listed here are the various options that are available under the VPORTS command:

OPTION	DESCRIPTION
Save	Saves the viewport configuration and the associated viewpoints.
Restore	Recalls a previously saved viewport configuration.
Delete	Removes a named viewport configuration.
Join	Merges two viewports that are next to each other.
Single	Displays only a single viewport.
?	Lists the names of saved viewport configurations.
2	Divides the current viewport into two viewports.
3	Divides the current viewport into three viewports.
4	Divides a single viewport display into four viewports.

Note that there can be as many viewports on the screen as desired. The only limitation is size. AutoCAD will notify you when a viewport is too small to be created.

3.5 Hidden Line Removal

The HIDE command displays an enhanced view by removing edges that would be obstructed by other features. This command will work only if surfaces or solids are present. If the model is composed solely of wireframe, evoking the HIDE command will have no effect. Using this command periodically during construction of the model helps you to check the behavior of edges. With the HIDE command, you can tell whether objects are actually intersecting the model or running behind it. Let's look at a wireframe display. Refer to Figure

3.26. Note that parts A and B appear to be identical. Now look at Figure 3.27, which is the same model, but with hidden lines removed. You now can easily see that the two boxes intersect each other in part A and that one box is in front of the other in part B. It is also helpful to use the HIDE command when you cannot tell whether viewing is from above or below the model.

When using hidden line removal on complicated models, generating the final view can take a significant amount of time. The easiest way to speed up the process is to break the model into different layers. This is a good practice in any drawing. But in the case of a complicated model, using different layers allows you to freeze those layers that are not important to the HIDE command. AutoCAD's HIDE command ignores any entities that are on a frozen layer. However, the HIDE command will still factor in entities that are on a turned-off layer. (Turning off layers can create some interesting effects; for instance, you can blank out a portion of the model in order to accent text.)

Figure 3.26
Two seemingly identical wireframe models

Figure 3.27
Using HIDE to distinguish differences

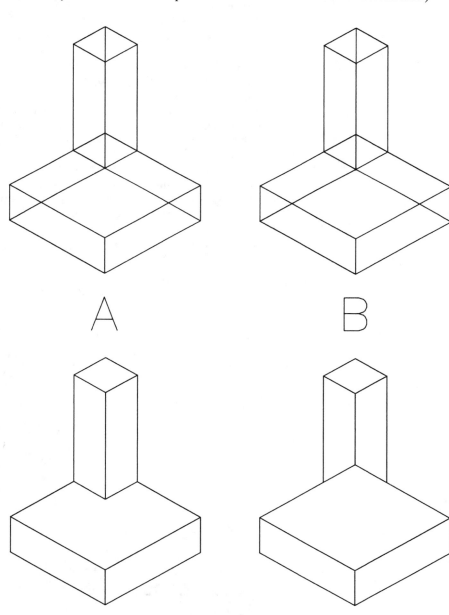

3.6 AutoCAD and Shading

Two levels of rendering can be performed directly within the AutoCAD program. The first level makes use of the SHADE utility. Though limited compared to separate rendering programs, the SHADE utility is nonetheless extremely useful in giving a more expressive view of a 3D model, as Figure 3.28 shows. This utility shades or colors in each surface with a choice of options. The surface may be shaded with its property color, generating a model whose surfaces appear as a solid color, or the surface may be shaded with the background color and outlined with its property color, generating a hidden line removed type of image. The image can also be shaded using a combination of techniques, producing outlined shaded surfaces. If the computer used can display 256 colors on the screen, then AutoCAD can display a limited tonal image, giving a light to dark representation of the model. The use of tones creates an effect similar to that of having light shone onto the model. It is even possible to adjust this effect so it appears that the amount of light shone on the model varies, thereby making the generation of the displayed model even more versatile.

AutoCAD's SHADE Utility

To generate a shaded model with AutoCAD, use the SHADE command, which is invoked in a manner similar to the invocation of the HIDE command. Auto-

Figure 3.28
A shaded model from AutoCAD

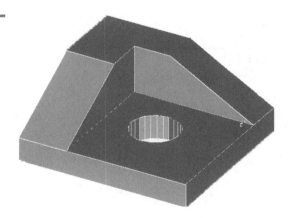

CAD then goes through the calculation process to generate the image. To make adjustments to the outcome of the SHADE command, you can modify some variables. Those variables associated with the SHADE command are listed next.

AutoCAD SHADE Variables

The following is a list of variables that have an effect on the final shaded model within AutoCAD.

SYSTEM VARIABLE	VALUE	DESCRIPTION
SHADEDGE		Controls the final result of the shaded image.
	0	Shades surfaces with entity color and no edge definition; requires 256 colors.
	1	Shades surfaces with entity color and defines the visible edges with the background color; requires 256 colors.
	2	Shades surfaces with background color and defines the visible edges with entity color; similar to hidden line removal; works with any display.
	3	Colors surface with solid entity color and defines the visible edges in the background color; works with any display. (AutoCAD recommends a value of 2 with monochrome displays.)
SHADEDIF		Controls tonal shading if 256 colors are present. (SHADEDIF represents the percentage of light reflected off of a surface—diffuse reflection—as opposed to the amount of light around the surface—ambient. The value can be from 0 to 100. The higher the value, the greater the percentage of diffuse reflection and the greater the contrast between reflecting surfaces.)

3.7 View Toolbar

The View toolbar can be used to recall previously named views or display preset viewpoints. The toolbar is displayed by checking the Viewpoint box from the Toolbars dialog box. The Toolbars dialog box is displayed by selecting Toolbars from the View pull-down menu. If you move the cursor onto a tool without picking it, a tooltip may appear. Tooltips are words that describe the function of the tool. Tooltips can be turned on by checking the Show Tooltips box in the Toolbars dialog box.

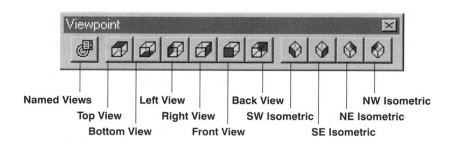

Viewpoint Coordinates

Lab 3.A will familiarize you with the VPOINT command, focusing your attention on the coordinate input method of setting the viewpoint.

You will be able to:

- Create a simple three-dimensional model.
- Add text to the model.
- Display isometric and orthographic views.
- Use the HIDE command for clarity.

VPOINT (Coordinates)
HIDE

1. Start a new drawing called OCUBE (Orientation CUBE) with the following settings:

```
Units  =  decimal
Limits  =  0,0 to 2,2
Grid  =  0.125
Snap Incr  =  0.125
Current Layer  =  OCUBE
```

Creating the 3D Cube

2. Select the ELEV command, and enter 0 for the elevation and 1 for the thickness.

```
Command: ELEV
New current elevation <0>:0
New current thickness <0>:1
```

This will give a 3D thickness of 1 to any entities that are drawn from this point on.

3. Turn off the fill for coloring solids:

```
Command: FILL
ON/OFF<On>:OFF
```

Filled-in solids are not very useful in 3D modeling. They are much more effective when only the outline shows.

4. Using the SOLID command, draw a solid that is 1″ wide and 1″ long, as shown in Figure 3.29. P1 represents the start point of the solid, and P2, P3, and P4 represent the other points.

Creating the X and Y Projections

5. Select the ELEV command, and enter 0 for the elevation and 0.5 for the thickness.

```
Command: ELEV
New current elevation <0>: 0
New current thickness <0>: .5
```

This will give a 3D thickness of 0.5 to any entities that are drawn from this point on.

6. Now use the SOLID command to add the two features, as shown in Figure 3.30. These will be used as positive directional pointers for the X and Y

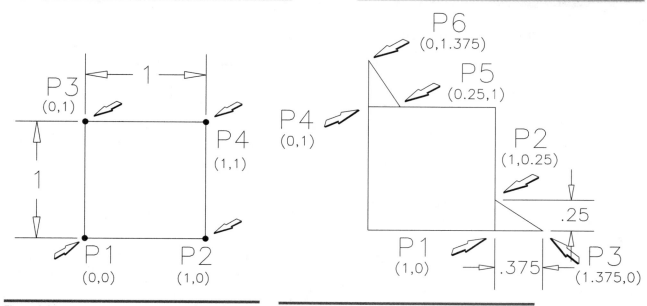

Figure 3.29
Cube dimensions

Figure 3.30
Addition of solid projections

axes. Create the top (*Y*) solid in red and the right (*X*) in green to help with the visualization.

At this point, a three-dimensional model has been created. Save it under the name OCUBE (Orientation CUBE).

Adding Text to the Cube

7. Select the ELEV command, and enter 1 for the elevation and 0 for the thickness.

```
Command: ELEV
New current elevation <O>: 1
New current thickness <O>: 0
```

This will place any entities added at an elevation of 1, which will place the text on top of the cube.

8. Using the TEXT command, enter text and place it as shown in Figure 3.31. The text should have an approximate height of 0.125.

Adding Text to the Projections

9. Select the ELEV command, and enter 0.5 for the elevation and 0 for the thickness.

```
Command: ELEV
New current elevation <O>: .5
New current thickness <O>: 0
```

This will place any entities added at an elevation of 0.5, which will place the text on top of the solid features.

10. Using the TEXT command, enter text and place it as shown in Figure 3.32. The text should have an approximate height of 0.125. Return elevation to 0.

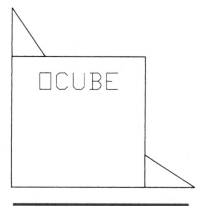

Figure 3.31
Addition of text to the top of the cube

Figure 3.32
Addition of text to cube and projections

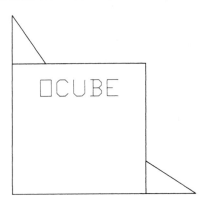

Again, save the model as OCUBE. It is useful to save periodically. Should anything happen to the workfile, you want to avoid the very difficult task of duplicating models.

Viewing the Model Isometrically

11. Select the VPOINT command and enter isometric coordinates.

```
Command: VPOINT
Rotate/<Viewpoint><current>: 1,1,1
```

The display will show a rear-right view above the model, as shown in Figure 3.33.

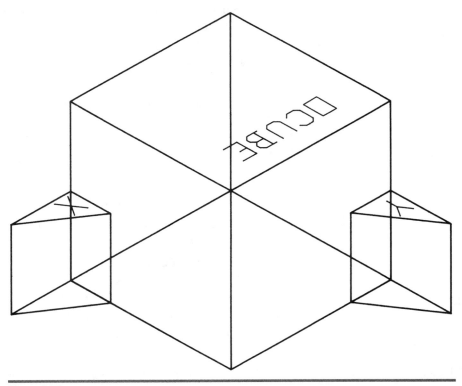

Figure 3.33
Rear-right view from above

Displaying a Hidden Line Removed Model

12. Select the HIDE command.

    Command: **HIDE**

    The results should be similar to those shown in Figure 3.34. Note that the HIDE command has no effect on the text.

    Experiment at this point: Generate different viewpoints and use the HIDE command. Observe the display of text.

    Note that to be able to hide text, the text must have some thickness. Even a value as small as 0.001 will produce these results. You may want to experiment. Save your model.

Generating Orthographic Views and Saving the Viewpoints

13. Using the VPOINT coordinates, display the front orthographic view.

    Command: **VPOINT**
    Rotate/<Viewpoint><current>: **0,−1,0**

    The display will show the front orthographic view.

14. Using the VIEW SAVE command, save the orthographic viewpoint as FRONT.

    Command: **VIEW**
    ?/Delete/Restore/Save/Window: **SAVE**
    View name to save: **FRONT**

    Not only does this save the current view, but it also saves the viewpoint.

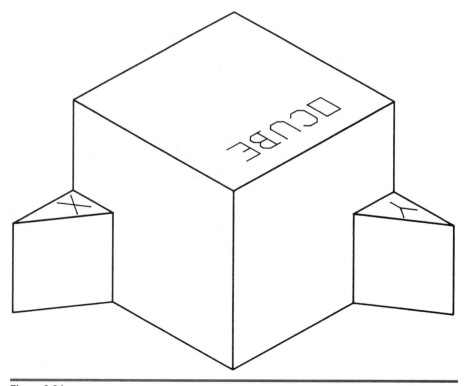

Figure 3.34
Hidden line removed display

15. Repeat steps 13 and 14 for the other five viewpoints: top, right side, left side, rear, and bottom.

Save the model at this point as OCUBE.

Recalling a Previous Viewpoint

16. Using the VIEW RESTORE command, recall the FRONT view.

```
Command: VIEW
?/Delete/Restore/Save/Window: RESTORE
View name to restore: FRONT
```

The front viewpoint should now be displayed on the screen. Experiment saving and recalling different viewpoints.

Lab 3.B

Viewpoint Rotation/Compass/Preset

Purpose

Lab 3.B will familiarize you with the VPOINT command, focusing your attention on the rotation, compass, and preset input methods of setting the viewpoint.

Objective

You will be able to rotate the model, displaying any angular viewpoint.

Primary Commands

```
VPOINT (Rotation, Compass, Preset)
PLAN
HIDE
```

Procedure

1. Open the OCUBE drawing created in Lab 3.A.

2. Display the top view, using the PLAN command.

```
Command: PLAN
<current UCS>/Ucs/World: W
```

Moving the Viewpoint Through Rotation

3. Using the VPOINT ROTATE command, display an isometric view.

```
Command: VPOINT
Rotate/<Viewpoint><current>:R
Enter angle in XY plane from X axis <current>: —45
Enter angle from XY plane <current>: 45
```

The display should look similar to that shown in Figure 3.35.
Use the HIDE command to display the model.

Moving the Viewpoint Through Compass

4. Using the VPOINT compass command, rotate the object to display the lower left rear.

```
Command: VPOINT
Rotate/<Viewpoint><current>: press the <Enter> key
```

The display should switch to show the compass input screen. Place the cursor as shown in Figure 3.36.

Figure 3.35
Viewpoint through rotation

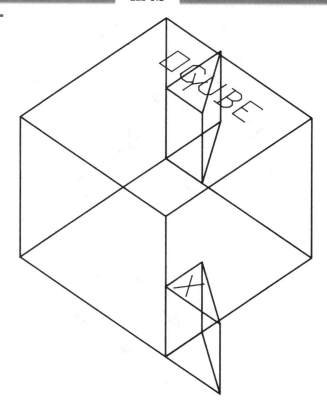

Figure 3.36
Compass input screen

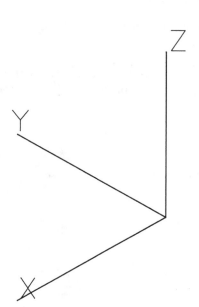

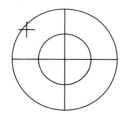

Once the cursor has been digitized in the compass area, the display should look similar to Figure 3.37.

Now use the HIDE command to see the effect. Experiment at this point: Use the compass and HIDE command to move around the model.

Figure 3.37
Viewpoint through the compass input
screen

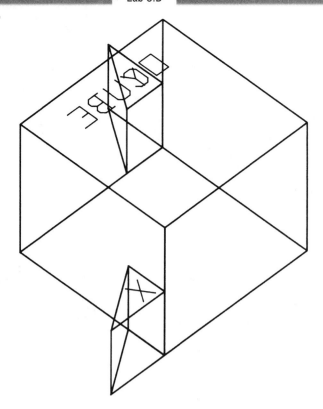

Using the Preset Viewpoints

5. Select the pull-down menu View/3D Viewpoint/Select to select a preset
view of the front of the model. The dialog box should appear as shown in
Figure 3.38.

Enter 270 for the angle from the *X* axis and 0 degrees for the
angle from the *X–Y* plane. The display should look similar to Figure 3.39.

Figure 3.38
Viewpoint Presets dialog box

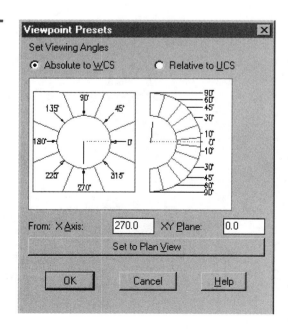

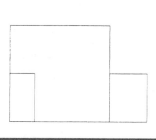

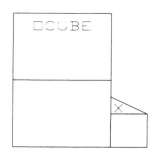

Figure 3.39
Viewpoint through dialog box

Figure 3.40
Hidden line removed display

6. Now tilt the model using a preset view of the front (270 degrees) and an angle other than 0. Enter an angle of 45 degrees from the *X–Y* plane.

Use the HIDE command. The display should look similar to Figure 3.40.

Lab 3.C

Multiple Viewports

Purpose

Lab 3.C will familiarize you with multiple viewports used in conjunction with 3D modeling when TILEMODE is set to 1.

Objectives

You will be able to:

- Configure multiple viewports.
- Display multiple viewpoints.
- Save multiple viewport configurations.

Primary Commands

VPORTS
VPOINT
HIDE

Procedure

1. Open the OCUBE model created in Lab 3.A and make certain TILE-MODE is set to 1.

2. Display the bottom viewpoint.

Displaying a Multiple Viewport Display

3. Using the VPORTS command, pick the four equal viewport configurations.

   Command: **VPORTS**
   Save/Restore/Delete/Join/Single/?/2/<3>/4: **4**

Displaying Multiple Viewpoints

4. Activate the top left viewport.

5. Display the top viewpoint in the now active viewport. Use the Coordinate option to accomplish this.

   Command: **VPOINT**
   Rotate/<Viewpoint><current>: **0,0,1**

55

Figure 3.41
Viewpoint Presets dialog box

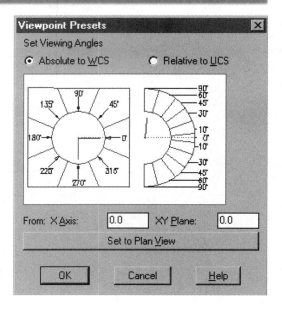

6. Activate the bottom left viewport and display the front view using the VIEW RESTORE command.

```
Command: VIEW
?/Delete/Restore/Save/Window: RESTORE
View name to restore: FRONT
```

7. Activate the bottom right viewport and display the right-side viewpoint using the Viewpoint Presets dialog box. Refer to Figure 3.41.

8. Activate the top-right viewport and display an axonometric viewpoint using the Compass option. The display should look similar to Figure 3.42.

Figure 3.42
Four viewports: top, front, right, and isometric

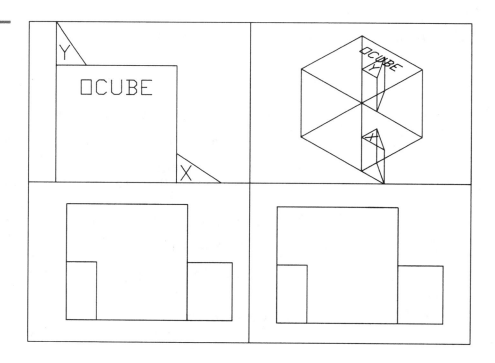

Figure 3.43
Adding a cylinder

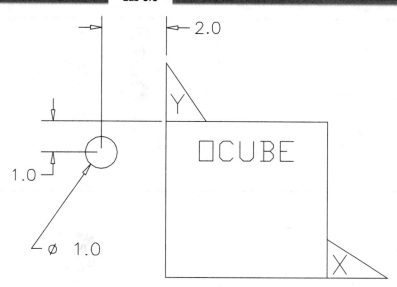

9. Activate each viewport and use the HIDE command on each.

Drawing Between Viewports

10. Activate the top view viewport. Set the elevation to 0 and the thickness to 0.75.

11. Draw a circle as shown in Figure 3.43.

12. Set the elevation to 0 and the thickness to 0.

13. Draw the start of a line from the top of the circle (in the top viewport) in the center (use the filter .XY and give a Z value of 0.75).

14. Activate the isometric view.

15. Finish the line by using the object snap midpoint and snap to the midpoint of the lower front line of the cube, as shown in Figures 3.44 and 3.45.

16. Observe the results in all four viewports.

17. Save the viewport configuration with the name ORTHO1.

Figure 3.44
Start and finish locations of line

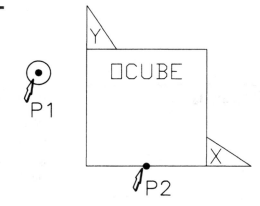

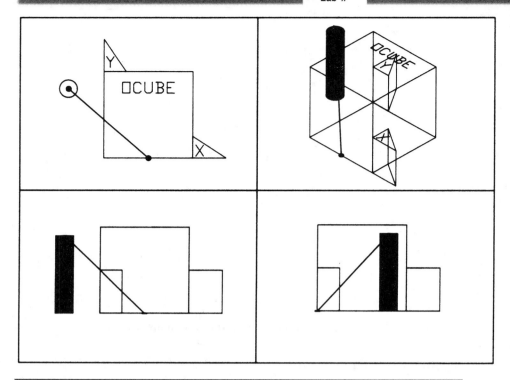

Figure 3.45
Line shown in all viewports

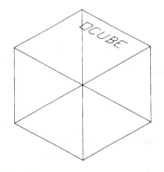

Figure 3.46
Final saved model with deletions made

18. Display a single viewport configuration.

19. Save the model as OCUBE2.

20. Delete the cylinder and the *X* and *Y* solid projections. The model should look like Figure 3.46. Save the model as OCUBE.

Questions

1. What is the advantage of displaying an axonometric view of a model?

2. What two crucial components must be considered in generating a proper view?

3. Is the VPOINT command used to generate an axonometric or a perspective view?

4. Does VPOINT use UCS or WCS for reference?

5. Explain the four ways of setting a viewpoint.

6. What do the terms *isometric, dimetric,* and *trimetric* mean?

7. Draw a diagram to indicate the compass position that would display a left-front view looking underneath a model.

8. What is the function of the PLAN command?

9. Explain the procedure for controlling the orientation of an orthographic view generated by VPOINT.

10. In what way are viewports independent and in what way are they linked?

11. Why is it useful to use the HIDE command during construction?

12. What is the effect of freezing a layer before accessing the HIDE command? How does this compare to the effect of turning a layer off?

13. How does using the VPOINT command affect the size of the displayed model?

14. Explain the procedure for maintaining multiple viewpoints. How can they all be displayed on the screen at one time?

Assignments

Read the complete assignment before beginning.

Note: Assignment 1 must be completed because it will be used in the labs in Chapter 5.

1. Set up a prototype drawing that has the following preset:

    ■ A configuration of four equal viewports that contains the top, front, and right-side views plus the front-right-above isometric view. Save the configuration as ORTHO1 using the VPORTS command. Refer to Figure 3.47.

    ■ A configuration of four equal viewports that contains the bottom, rear, and left-side views plus the rear-left-below isometric view. Save the configuration as ORTHO2 using the VPORTS command. Refer to Figure 3.48.

    ■ A single viewport that contains the front-right-above isometric view. Save it as ISO1 using the VPORTS command. Refer to Figure 3.49.

Figure 3.47
Four-viewport configuration: ORTHO1

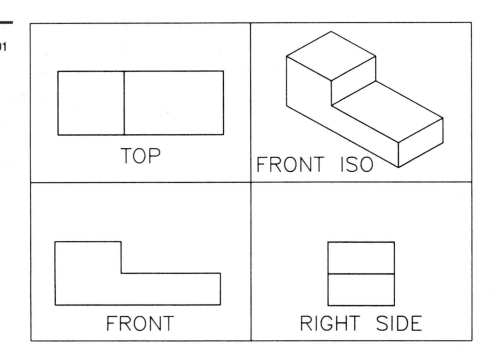

Figure 3.48
Four-viewport configuration: ORTHO2.

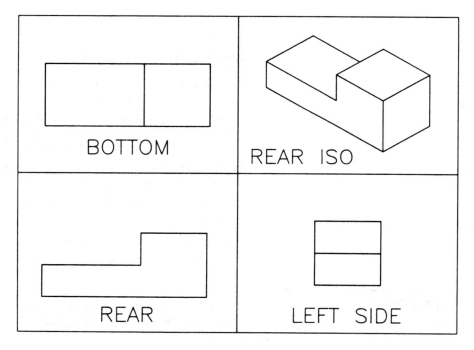

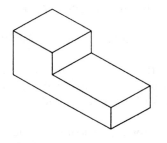

Figure 3.49
Single-viewport configuration: ISO1

Name all the various viewpoints as well as the viewports. Call the file 3DSET. This prototype drawing now can be utilized anytime you start a project in 3D.

Note: In Figures 3.47, 3.48, and 3.49, the angle bracket is used as an example, but any model can be used to test the configurations. However, the final file 3DSET should not contain any geometry.

2. Recall the OCUBE model created during the labs in this chapter. Using the VPOINT ROTATION option, display the following viewpoints in a four-viewport configuration: Viewport 1 is an isometric view, 2 is a dimetric view, 3 is a trimetric view, and 4 is a bottom view. Refer to Figure 3.50.

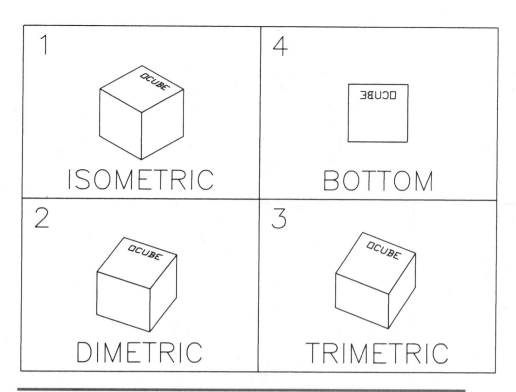

Figure 3.50
Different viewpoints using rotation

3. After recalling the OCUBE model created during the labs, display four identical views of the model using the four VPOINT options in a four-viewport configuration: Viewport 1 is displayed using the Coordinate option, 2 uses the Rotation option, 3 uses the Compass option, and 4 uses the Viewpoint Preset dialog box option. Refer to Figure 3.51.

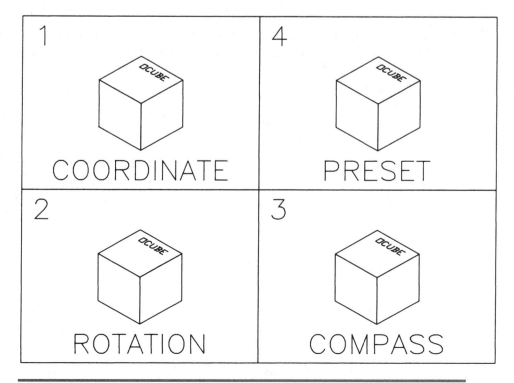

Figure 3.51
Different methods for displaying the same view

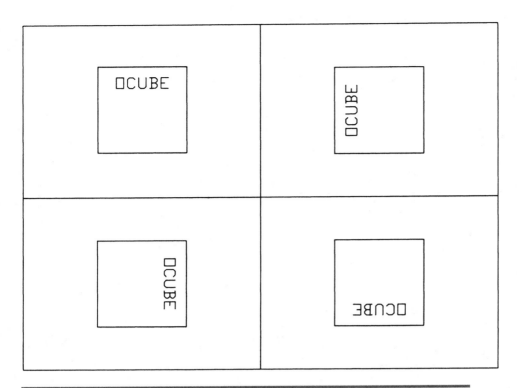

Figure 3.52
Different orientations of the same view

4. Again, recall the OCUBE model. Display the top/plan view. Use the LIST command to display the data about the text "OCUBE." Record the information. Once this is done, display a front-right-above isometric view. Use the LIST command a second time to display the data about the text "OCUBE." Compare the first data with the second data. Is there any difference? What conclusions do you reach?

5. With the OCUBE model recalled, use the Coordinate option of the VPOINT command to display the four different orientations of the top view. See Figure 3.52.

CHAPTER **4**

Working in 3D Space

Overview

In Chapter 4, you will learn how to break a model into working planes and define these planes for retrieval in order to simplify the construction and modification of the model itself. The techniques discussed here range from the easy-to-learn ones for beginners to the more exotic techniques (which can, in fact, be made simpler under specific circumstances). When you have mastered these procedures, you will be ready to construct your own 3D models.

Concepts Explored

- The purpose of the working plane
- How the World Coordinate System and the User Coordinate System are related
- The different forms of the UCS icon
- How to set elevated working planes
- How to manipulate the UCS icon
- How to create working planes.

4.1 Introduction

When creating three-dimensional models, almost all PC-based CAD systems construct their geometry out of flat surfaces (see Figure 4.1). To perform this construction, the systems need a flat plane base. These planes, which we call *working planes,* are the bases on which all 3D construction takes place. Even when the CAD user is only drawing a view in two dimensions, the constructing geometry still uses a working plane. Because the geometry being drawn is simply a flat outline of the object, the use of a working plane is not apparent. It is only when 3D construction takes place that the various working planes become evident.

The working plane can be thought of as a flat surface similar to a sheet of paper. As can be said of a sheet of paper, you can draw on the working plane no matter where it is placed or at what angle.

When working in three dimensions, the user must align the working plane to the surface where creation of the model is to take place. This align-

Figure 4.1
Models created with flat surfaces

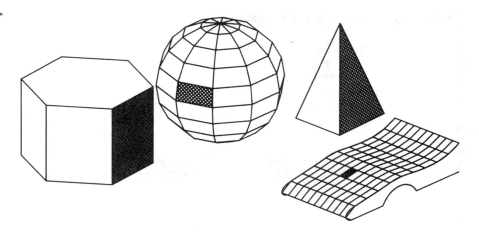

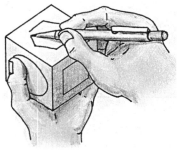

Figure 4.2
Manually drawing on a cube

ment (making parallel) is the key to all three-dimensional modeling. Figure 4.2 shows a hand holding a cube. If that were your hand holding the cube, and you wanted to draw on it with a pencil, all you would need to do is pick the side to draw on, get a pencil, and proceed to draw. The procedure is similar in AutoCAD. You must tell the program on which surface (side) the drawing or construction is going to take place. This is done using two systems of coordinates—the World Coordinate system (WCS) and the User Coordinate System (UCS).

4.2 World Coordinate System

The WCS is AutoCAD's master coordinate system. This system has X, Y, and Z coordinates with origin points of $0x$, $0y$, $0z$. However, the orientation of these axes cannot be changed or moved in any way. Using this system of coordinates, AutoCAD keeps track of all geometry, whether 2D or 3D. All dimensional information is related back to the WCS. This guarantees that the user cannot get "lost" in 3D space. The WCS can always be used as a frame of reference.

4.3 User Coordinate System

The UCS is the means by which AutoCAD allows the user to create and save the various working planes required to generate any complex 3D model (see Figure 4.3). Like the WCS, this system of coordinates has X, Y, and Z axes. The difference is that the UCS axes can be rotated, moved, or aligned to any location on the 3D model. Think of the UCS as telling the program which side of the cube you want to draw on and which point is going to be used as the origin point $0x$, $0y$, $0z$.

3D Viewpoint

Working Planes
You can create and save as many UCS working planes as you desire, but only one can be active at any one time. UCS working planes are saved with the UCS command, and are retained in the drawing.

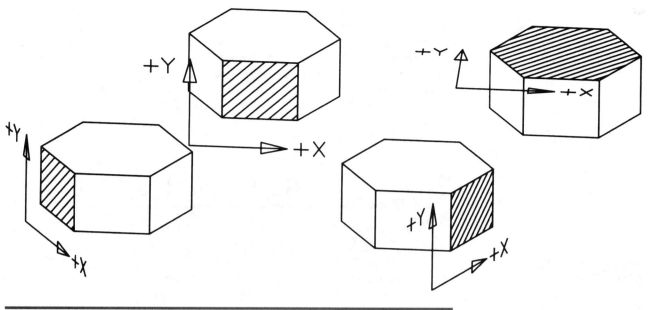

Figure 4.3
3D object illustrating working planes

When a user draws in 2D, the UCS automatically aligns to the WCS, thereby matching the coordinates of the two systems. This working plane is customarily referred to as the *top* or *plan* view.

The UCS Command

In 3D, the working plane can be created in a number of ways, all requiring the alignment of the UCS to a set of WCS coordinates. Thankfully, doing the alignment with AutoCAD is easy because most of its commands use existing geometry.

The following lists alignments and the UCS commands that achieve them:

UCS COMMAND	DESCRIPTION OF ALIGNMENT
UCS World	Aligns the UCS to the WCS.
UCS 3Point	Defines the UCS by entering three points to define a plane; these points are the origin, positive *X*-axis direction, and the positive *Y*-axis direction.
UCS Origin	Moves only the origin point; the alignment stays the same.
UCS ZAXIS	Defines the new direction of the positive *Z* axis.
UCS OBject	Aligns the UCS to an existing object.
UCS View	Aligns the UCS to the plane of the current view.
UCS X or Y or Z	Rotates the UCS about a selected axis.
UCS Save	Saves the current UCS under a name.
UCS Restore	Restores a saved UCS by name.
UCS Previous	Returns UCS alignment to the last UCS.
UCS Delete	Removes a named UCS.
UCS ?	Displays a list of named UCSs.

The UCS options can be accessed by typing the commands at the prompt, using the sidebar menu, or using the pull-down menus. The method of accessing the UCS commands from the pull-down menus is shown in Figure 4.4.

Note that the UCS automatic dialog selection sets the new UCS based on the current UCS. For instance, if the current UCS was set to the top of the model and the FRONT UCS automatic dialog selection was made, the UCS would switch to the front of the model. If the same selection was made again, the UCS would switch to the bottom of the model. Think of the TOP option as the current UCS and the rest as based on it.

3D Viewpoint

UCS and 3Point Option

It is easier to establish the UCS using the 3Point method if you are looking at an axonometric view because you can see the corners to which you will snap when setting the three points. Use the VPOINT command to display such a view.

The UCS Icon

The UCS icon is used to help the user keep track of the *X*, *Y*, and *Z* axes of the current UCS. The UCS icon is a directional beacon, telling you in what direction the axes of your UCS are pointing. The icon's display can be turned off or on, and it normally appears in the lower left corner of the screen's graphics display (refer to the next section and Lab 4.A). Remember, because any number of UCS working planes can be created, it is essential to know which one is currently active. The UCS icon aids in identifying which working plane is active by letting the user know where the UCS origin point 0,0,0 is located and in which directions the *X*, *Y*, and *Z* axes are pointing. Look at Figure 4.5. The icon is formed in the shape of an "L," with arrowheads on the ends of the *X* and *Y* axes pointing in the positive direction of the axes. In addition, each arrowhead is labeled with the appropriate axis letter.

Now look at Figure 4.6. Notice the "W" below the *Y*-axis letter. The "W" on the icon indicates that the UCS is aligned to the WCS. That is, the

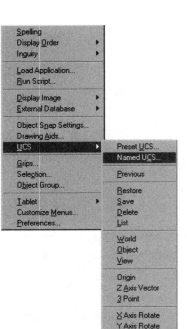

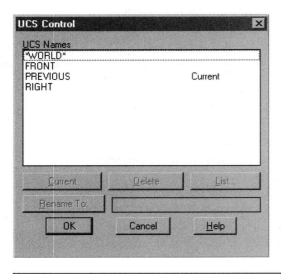

Figure 4.4
Accessing the UCS pull-down menus

Figure 4.5
UCS icon

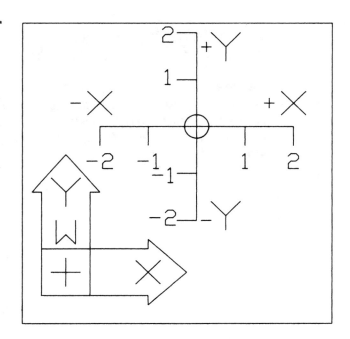

Figure 4.6
UCS aligned to the WCS

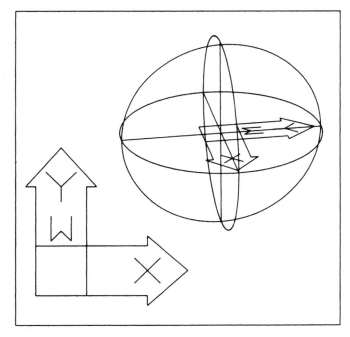

coordinates used when constructing with the UCS match those of the master WCS coordinates.

In the illustration of the UCS icon in Figure 4.7, there is a "+" sign displayed in the center of the junction of the X and Y axes. This tells the user that the icon has been set to display itself on the origin of the X, Y, Z axes of the UCS. The plus sign coincides with the origin point 0,0,0.

By observing the direction of the icon arrowheads, you can easily tell which way the X and Y axes are pointing. To identify the Z axis for you, AutoCAD forms a box at the base of the icon, as shown in Figure 4.8. Notice that the box is formed by the extension of the two lines indicated by arrows in the figure. When those lines are displayed, it means that the Z axis is going in a positive direction toward the viewer. To help identify the directions in which the axes are pointing, refer to the right-hand rule explained in Section 3.2.

3D Viewpoint

UCS Icon

The UCS icon will only appear on the origin point (0,0,0) if it is set to do so and if there is room on the screen to display the entire icon. If some of the icon would be cut off by an edge of the display screen, the icon jumps to the lower left corner of the screen. The current UCS does not move, however, only the icon.

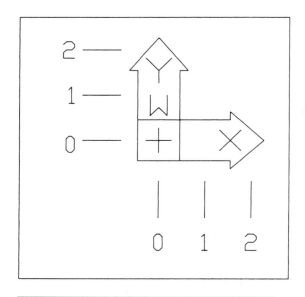

Figure 4.7
UCS icon on the origin

Figure 4.8
Z axis pointing toward the viewer

When the lines on the *X* and *Y* axes do not form a box, it means that the *Z* axis is going in a positive direction away from the viewer, as shown in Figure 4.9. The object is usually viewed from the bottom in this situation.

It is possible to rotate the displayed view so that the UCS icon is displayed completely flat. When this happens, the icon is replaced by a broken pencil symbol, as illustrated in Figure 4.10. The broken pencil is a warning that using the pointing device to locate coordinates will be virtually useless or, worse, disastrous. When this symbol appears, the cursor can move in only one axis, and thus it is impossible to be certain which coordinate is going to be used for the other immobile axis.

The UCSICON Command

The commands used to manipulate the UCS icon are as follows:

UCS ICON COMMAND	DESCRIPTION
UCSICON ON	Displays the icon.
UCSICON OFF	Turns the icon off.
UCSICON All	Displays the icon in all the viewports.
UCSICON No origin	Shows the icon is not on the origin.
UCSICON OR	Displays the icon at the origin of the UCS.

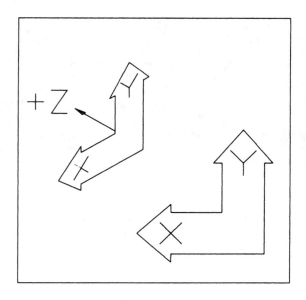

Figure 4.9
Z axis pointing away from the viewer

Figure 4.10
Warning! The working plane is not visible to the viewer

4.4   Elevated Working Planes

It is possible to draw above or below the current working plane by using the ELEVATION command. When you need to insert geometry above or below an already set working plane, the ELEVATION command allows you to do so. Consider, for example, one design situation: An AutoCAD user is laying out a kitchen plan. If the user sets the working plane to floor level of the kitchen plan, then to insert cabinetry at the desired distance above the floor the user must use the ELEVATION command.

When using the ELEVATION command, entering positive distances causes the working plane to be temporarily elevated in the positive Z direction. Entering negative distances causes the working plane to be lowered in the negative Z direction. Figure 4.11 illustrates these effects. If the ELEVA-

Figure 4.11
Elevated working planes—positive and negative

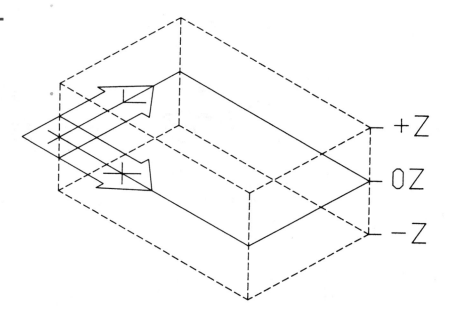

3D Viewpoint

The ELEVATION Command

Always remember to return the elevation setting back to 0 when completed. If forgotten, when you try to draw on a UCS working plane, you will instead draw above or below the plane by the previously set elevation distance. This can give annoying results.

TION command is activated from the command line, it has an effect on the extrusion thickness of the geometry. This is explained in the next chapter. At this point, it is enough to note that the extrusion thickness starts from the elevation point.

The ELEVATION Command

The ELEVATION command is activated by typing ELEV at the command prompt.

```
Command: ELEV
New current elevation <current>: Enter positive or
negative distances
New current thickness <current>: Enter the desired
positive or negative extrusion thickness
```

4.5 UCS Toolbar

The UCS toolbar can be used to access all the options of the UCS command. The toolbar is displayed by checking the UCS box from the Toolbars dialog box. The Toolbars dialog box is displayed by selecting Toolbars from the View pull-down menu. If you move the cursor onto a tool without picking it, a tooltip may appear. Tooltips are words that describe the function of the tool. Tooltips can be turned on by checking the Show Tooltips box in the Toolbars dialog box.

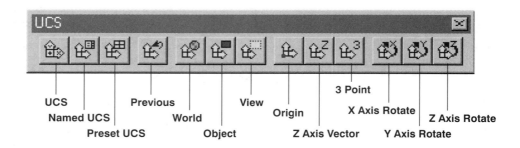

The UCS Icon

Lab 4.A will familiarize you with the UCS icon and its functions.

You will be able to:

- Activate and deactivate the UCS icon.
- Align the UCS icon to the origin of the UCS.

UCSICON

Activating the UCS Icon

1. Open the orientation cube drawing that was created in the labs in Chapter 3. The filename is OCUBE.

2. Set the display to show the plan view of the OCUBE.

```
Command: PLAN
<current UCS>/Ucs/World: W
```

This displays the plan view of the World Coordinate System.
Use ZOOM 0.5X to reduce the displayed view.

3. Activate the UCS icon.

```
Command: UCSICON
ON/OFF/All/Noorigin/ORigin <current ON/OFF state>: ON
```

This turns on the UCS icon, displaying it in the lower left corner of the graphics screen. At this point, the display should look similar to Figure 4.12.

Figure 4.12
The activated UCS icon

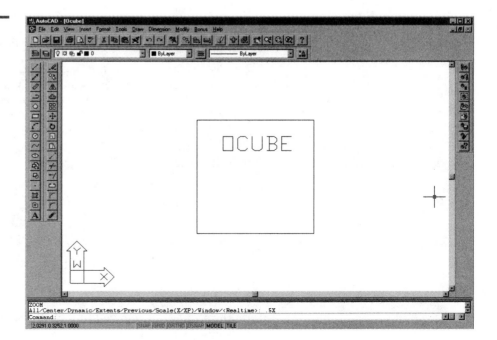

Figure 4.13
Turning the UCS icon off

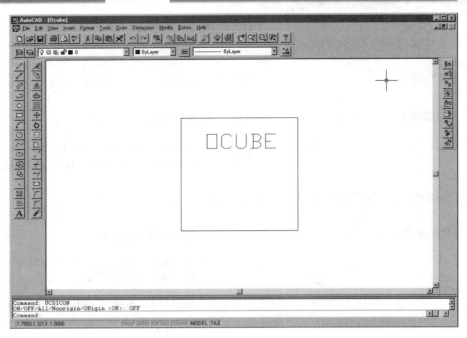

Deactivating the UCS Icon

4. Select the UCSICON command.

   Command: **USCICON**
   ON/OFF/All/Noorigin/ORigin <current ON/OFF state>: **OFF**

   This turns off the display of the UCS icon. At this point, the display should look similar to Figure 4.13.

   Turn the icon back on now.

Aligning the UCS Icon to the UCS Origin

5. Select the UCSICON command.

   Command: **UCSICON**
   ON/OFF/All/Noorigin/ORigin <current ON/OFF status>: **OR**

   This displays the icon at the 0,0,0 location of the current UCS. At this point, the display should look similar to Figure 4.14.
   If the UCS is changed, then the icon moves with it. Remember, the icon will only display at the 0,0,0 location if there is enough room for the entire icon to be displayed. If some of the icon would be cut off, the icon is displayed in the lower left corner of the screen, regardless of the 0,0,0 point. Refer to Figure 4.15.

6. Use the ZOOM Window and PAN commands to manipulate the view of the orientation OCUBE so that the icon either displays at the 0,0,0 point or is forced to be displayed in the lower left corner.

7. Use the Noorigin option of the UCSICON so that the icon does not align itself with the origin of the UCS.

8. Use the ZOOM command to move about the screen and observe the UCS icon.

9. Use the VPOINT command to look at the cube from below using a negative value for the Z axis as in 1,1,–1. Notice what happens to the UCS icon. Refer back to Figure 4.9 if you are unsure.

Figure 4.14
Displaying the UCS icon on the origin

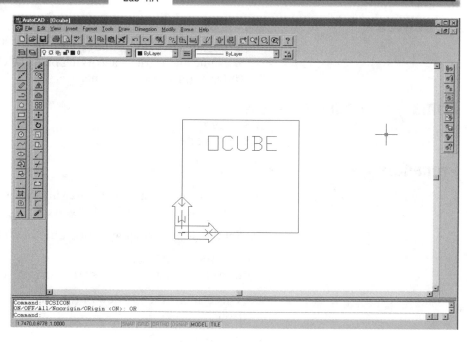

Figure 4.15
The UCS icon forced off the origin

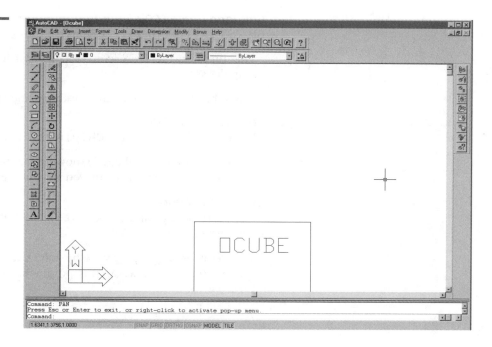

Lab 4.B

Creating Working Planes Using the 3-Point Method

Purpose

Lab 4.B will show you how to create a working plane using the 3-point method. This method of aligning the UCS to create a working plane is the most useful, the simplest, and hence the most commonly used. The 3-point method normally uses existing geometry, but it can align to the UCS using coordinates alone. This lab demonstrates the method using existing geometry.

Objectives

You will be able to:

- Create a working plane (UCS).
- Name and retrieve a working plane (UCS).
- Draw on a working plane.

Primary Commands

```
UCS 3Point
UCS Save
UCS Restore
```

Procedure

Activating the UCS Icon

1. Open the orientation cube drawing that was created in the labs in Chapter 3. The filename is OCUBE.

2. Set the display to show an isometric view of the cube.

   ```
   Command: VPOINT
   Rotate/<View point><current>: 1,-1,1
   ```

   This displays the iso-view of the orientation cube looking from above right front.

3. Activate the UCS icon.

   ```
   Command: UCSICON
   ON/OFF/All/Noorigin/ORigin<current ON/OFF state>: ON
   ```

   This turns on the UCS icon, displaying it in the lower left corner of the graphics screen.

4. Align the icon to the current working plane (UCS).

   ```
   Command: UCSICON
   ON/OFF/All/Noorigin/ORigin<ON>: OR
   ```

   If the icon is not aligned (showing the plus sign), use the ZOOM command to scale down the displayed view of the orientation cube.

   ```
   Command: ZOOM
   All/Center/Dynamic/Extents/Previous/Scale(X/Xp)/Win-
   dow/<Realtime>: .5X
   ```

   This reduces the display view by half. Experiment with this command to achieve the best view. At this point, the display should look similar to Figure 4.16.

Creating a New Working Plane

5. Align the working plane to the front side of the orientation cube. Refer to Figure 4.17: The front side is the side facing toward the left.

   ```
   Command: UCS
   Origin/ZAxis/3point/OBject/View/X/Y/Z/Prev/Restore/
   Save/Del/?/<World>: 3
   Origin point<0,0,0>: refer to text below
   ```

   At this point, the command is asking you where the new origin point would be located. Refer to Figure 4.17. Pick point P1. Remember to use the object snap endpoint to lock the cursor at the correct location. The use of object snaps is extremely important when performing operations in 3D.

   ```
   Point on positive portion of the X axis <default>:
   refer to text below
   ```

Figure 4.16
The activated UCS icon

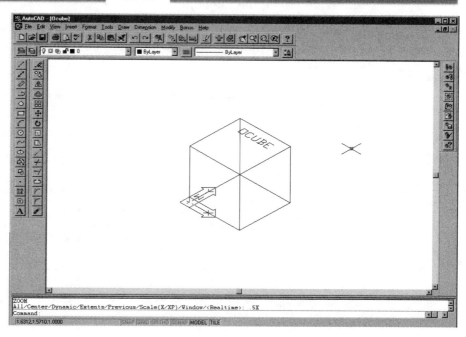

Here, the program needs to know which direction the positive *X* axis will be pointing. An imaginary line is calculated from the new origin to the point picked for the positive direction of the *X* axis. Refer to Figure 4.17. Pick point P2. (Use object snap endpoint.)

```
Point on the positive-Y portion of the UCS XY plane
<default>: refer to text below
```

This is where the program needs a point to calculate where the working plane is going to be. It pivots the plane around the new *X* axis based on the point picked for the positive *Y*. Refer to Figure 4.17. Pick point P3. (Use object snap endpoint.)

Figure 4.17
Defining a new working plane

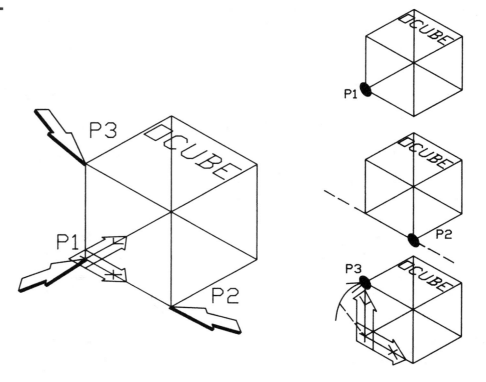

Notice that the UCS icon has moved to indicate the new working plane. This indicator can be invaluable when performing 3D modeling on complex models.

Giving the Current Working Plane a Name

6. Use the UCS command to give a name to the current working plane. This allows quick retrieval (aligning) of previous working planes whenever necessary.

```
Command: UCS
Origin/ZAxis/3point/OBject/View/X/Y/Z/Prev/Restore/
Save/Del/?<World>: Save
?/Name of UCS: FRONT
```

The name "FRONT" is used to describe that working plane uniquely. If you enter a question mark instead of a name, the previously named working planes (UCS) will be listed.

Aligning the Screen to the Current Working Plane

7. To facilitate the creation of entities in the *X–Y* plane, it is often desirable to have the display screen parallel to the working plane. This is accomplished by using the PLAN command.

```
Command: PLAN
<current UCS>/Ucs/World: press the <Enter> key
```

When you press enter at this point, you instruct the screen to align itself to the current UCS or working plane, which should be similar to Figure 4.18.

Drawing on the Working Plane

8. Using either the TEXT or DTEXT command, add the word "FRONT" to the upper left of the Orientation cube, as shown in Figure 4.19.

9. Add geometry to the front face and observe the results with step 10.

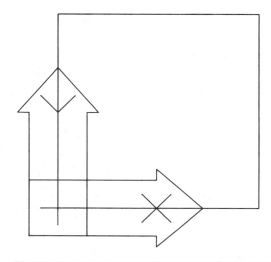

Figure 4.18
Displaying a plan view of the current working plane

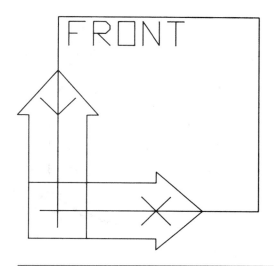

Figure 4.19
Adding text to the new working plane

Figure 4.20
Displaying an isometric view

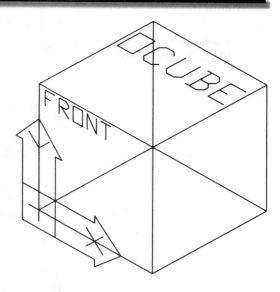

10. Use the VPOINT command to display the ISO (1,–1,1) view again. The view should be similar to Figure 4.20. Notice the location of the UCS icon, the polygon, and the text.

11. Using the 3Point option of the UCS command, repeat steps 5 to 10 for each of the remaining sides of the Orientation cube. The final rendering should look similar to Figure 4.21.

    At this point, the working plane should be on one of the five sides other than the front. If it is not, set it to one of the other sides.

Figure 4.21
Text to be added to the sides of the cube

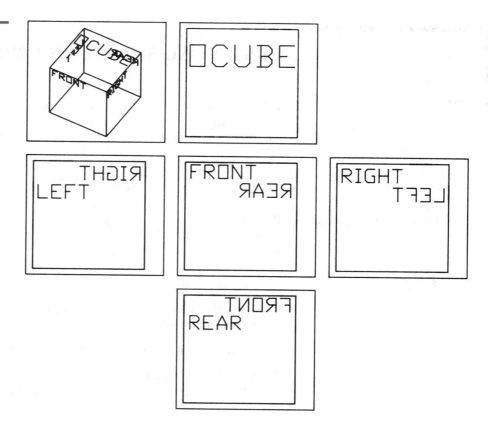

Restoring a Previously Saved Working Plane

12. Restore the working plane named FRONT.

```
Command: UCS
Origin/ZAxis/3point/OBject/View/X/Y/Z/Prev/Restore/
Save/Del/?<World>: R
?/Name of UCS to restore: FRONT
```

Notice how the UCS icon switched to the front working plane. It is important to save working planes so that you can align them quickly for construction. If you name planes as you create them, then you do not have to repeat several commands to realign a plane. Instead, you simply restore the previously named plane.

13. Display on the screen a list of the newly created working planes.

```
Command: UCS
Origin/ZAxis/3point/Entity/View/X/Y/Z/Prev/Restore/
Save/Del/?<World>: ?
```

14. Align the UCS with the WCS.

```
Command: UCS
Origin/ZAxis/3point/Entity/View/X/Y/Z/Prev/Restore/
Save/Del/?<World>: press the <Enter> key
```

Hitting the return or enter key aligns the UCS with the WCS. Notice the "W" on the icon.

15. Save the model as MOCUBE for Modified Orientation CUBE.

Lab 4.C

Creating Working Planes Using the Axes

Purpose

Lab 4.C will demonstrate how to create various working planes quickly by revolving the UCS about the *X*, *Y*, and *Z* axes. The lab is straightforward and easy to perform. However, this method of creating working planes is very useful to master early.

Objective

You will be able to rotate the UCS about the *X*, *Y*, and *Z* axes.

Primary Commands

```
UCS X
UCS Y
UCS Z
```

Procedure

Activating the UCS Icon

1. Open the orientation cube drawing that was modified in Lab 4.B. The file name is MOCUBE.

2. Set the display to show an isometric view of the cube.

```
Command: VPOINT
Rotate/<View point><current>: 1,-1,1
```

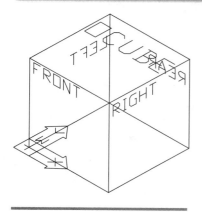

Figure 4.22
UCS icon displayed at lower left corner

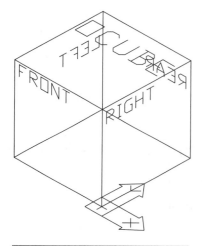

Figure 4.23
The new origin point

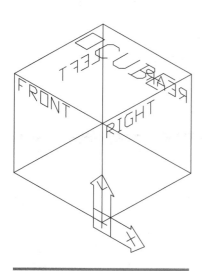

Figure 4.24
Rotating the UCS using the *X* axis as
the pivot

This displays the iso-view of the orientation cube looking from above right front.

3. Reduce the displayed view of the cube using the ZOOM command to see the UCS icon better when it is on.

```
Command: ZOOM
All/Center/Dynamic/Extents/Previous/Scale(X/Xp)/Win-
dow/<Realtime>: 0.8X
```

This reduces the displayed view to 80% of its current size.

4. Use the UCS command to ensure that the working plane is set to the World Coordinate System (WCS).

```
Command: UCS
Origin/ZAxis/3point/OBject/View/X/Y/Z/Prev/Restore/
Save/Del/ ?/<World>: press <Enter> to accept the
default of world
```

5. Activate the UCS icon if it is not displayed.

```
Command: UCSICON
ON/OFF/All/Noorigin/ORigin<ON>: ON
```

6. Align the icon to the current working plane (UCS).

```
Command: UCSICON
ON/OFF/All/Noorigin/ORigin<ON>: OR
```

The UCS icon should now be displayed on the origin of 0,0,0 at the lower left corner of the cube. Refer to Figure 4.22.

Moving the Origin Point

7. Using the Origin option of the UCS command, move the origin point to the lower right corner of the cube. The Origin option will allow you to move the origin point of the working plane but maintains the orientation of the *X–Y* plane.

```
Command: UCS
Origin/ZAxis/3point/OBject/View/X/Y/Z/Prev/Restore/
Save/Del/ ?/<World>: Origin
Origin point <0,0,0>: endpoint
of pick the lower right corner of the cube
```

Notice how the UCS icon moved to indicate the new origin point. Refer to Figure 4.23.

Rotating the UCS About the *X* Axis

8. Repeat the UCS command, except use the X option to rotate the UCS 90 degrees about the *X* axis.

```
Command: UCS
Origin/ZAxis/3point/OBject/View/X/Y/Z/Prev/Restore/
Save/Del/ ?/<World>: X
Rotation angle about X axis <0>: 90
```

Notice the UCS icon has now rotated to show the movement of the UCS working plane. Refer to Figure 4.24

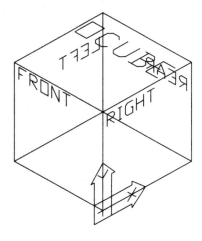

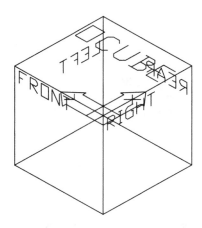

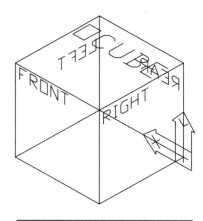

Figure 4.25
Rotating the UCS using the Y axis as the pivot

Figure 4.26
Moving the UCS to the top of the cube

Figure 4.27
Moving the UCS to the rear of the cube

Rotating the UCS About the *Y* Axis

9. Repeat the UCS command, except use the Y option to rotate the UCS 90 degrees about the *Y* axis.

```
Command: UCS
Origin/ZAxis/3point/OBject/View/X/Y/Z/Prev/Restore/
Save/Del/ ?/<World>: Y
Rotation angle about Y axis <O>: 90
```

The UCS working plane should now be aligned to the right side of the cube as shown in Figure 4.25.

Repositioning the UCS

10. Using the Origin option and any of the X, Y, or Z options of the UCS command, reposition the UCS so that it is in the same position as in Figure 4.26.

11. Using the Origin option and any of the X, Y, or Z options of the UCS command, reposition the UCS so that it is in the same position as in Figure 4.27.

12. Save the model as MOCUBE.

Questions

1. What is the WCS?

2. What is the UCS and how does it relate to the WCS?

3. Explain the UCS icon and how it can be used to indicate the 0,0,0 origin point.

4. Why are working planes important?

5. Why is it useful to name working planes (UCS)?

6. What does the "W" displayed on a UCS icon mean?

7. What is the function of the ELEVATION command?

8. How can using the PLAN command help in the construction of geometry?

9. What is the most commonly used method to create a working plane?

10. What function does the OBject option of the UCS command serve?

Assignments

1. Determine different applications of the ELEVATION command.

2. Open the OCUBE model. Display an isometric viewpoint. Align the UCS to the top of the cube. Use the LIST command to display the data about the text "OCUBE." Record the *X, Y, Z* coordinate information. Once this is done, align the UCS to the front of the cube. Use the LIST command a second time to display the data about the text "OCUBE." Compare the first data with the second data. Is there a difference? What conclusion can you draw?

3. Open the 3DSET drawing file that was created in Assignment 1 in Chapter 3, or set up a four-viewport configuration showing the top, front, right-side, and isometric viewpoints. Use the 3D Object Construction option and construct a wedge. Use the UCS 3Point option to enable you to draw a circle on the sloped surface. (*Hint:* It is easier to use the 3Point option by picking snap points on an isometric view.) Observe the results in all four viewports. Note the orientation of the UCS in all the viewports.

4. Use the 3D Object Construction option to construct a sphere. Using the UCS 3Point option, place your first name around the sphere (placing one letter per rectangle) by aligning the UCS to each rectangle that makes up the sphere. (*Hint:* Explode the sphere into individual 3D faces.)

5. Open the OCUBE model. Display a single viewport configuration. Set the UCSFOLLOW system variable to 1 (on). Change the UCS to various locations on the model. What happens to the display? To return to the normal display, set the UCSFOLLOW variable back to 0 (off).

Construction of 3D Surface Models

In this part, you will learn the commands required to create and modify a 3D model on the screen. Chapter by chapter, you'll progress from the simplest processes to the most complex models allowed within the confines of the software (and these are impressive models by anyone's standards). As in previous chapters, you'll follow a step-by-step approach and be provided with many illustrative training activities.

CHAPTER **5**

2-1/2D Extrusion

Overview

Even with very little experience in the method, any user will find 2-1/2D to be simple, fast, and visually effective. For this reason, it is a good stepping stone to 3D modeling.

Concepts Explored

- How extruded forms are commonplace
- How the extrusion process works and the way entities behave under extrusion
- How to manipulate extruded forms using the thickness property
- How to create models through extrusion.

5.1 Introduction

Most objects have their basis in extrusion techniques. Figure 5.1 shows some familiar items that can be created easily with extrusion methods: walls, tables,

Figure 5.1
Familiar items created through extrusion

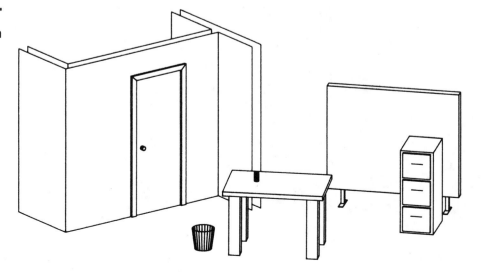

Figure 5.2
Mechanical objects created through extrusion

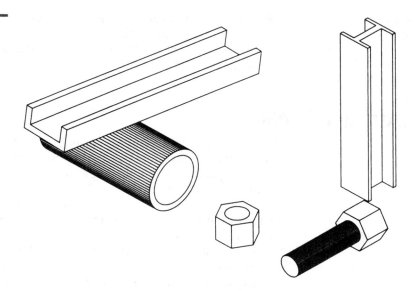

soda cans, file cabinets, wall dividers, wastebaskets, and many more. Figure 5.2 displays ordinary mechanical objects: a pipe, structural shapes, and a nut and bolt. What all of these shapes have in common is that, in each object, the outline or profile controls its final shape.

To be extruded, the profile does not have to be as simple as that of a file cabinet; it can be as complex as the outline of a floor plan or an I-beam. What is important to note is that the surfaces are parallel in the direction the profile is going to be extruded. The first step in the construction of any model should always be an analysis to determine which portion of the model can be constructed through extrusion. The method of extrusion is perhaps the easiest and fastest way to generate a model. You need make only three commands to turn a flat 2D floor plan into a three-dimensional model.

5.2 Extrusion and Thickness Concepts

Extrusion is the act of taking an entity—perhaps a line—and pushing its shape along an axis to form a 3D object—such as a sheet. AutoCAD assigns a property to each entity, thus allowing the operator to transform it from a two-dimensional shape into a three-dimensional shape. AutoCAD refers to this property as *thickness*. This property should be considered like any other property, such as color or linetype. The thickness of an object can be added, removed, or altered at any time, just like any other property of an entity. The thickness property operates only in the *Z* direction. The entity is drawn along an *X–Y* plane and is extruded along the *Z* axis.

Access to the thickness setting can be gained through the ELEVATION command. Here, the thickness can be entered as a positive or negative distance, and the distance will go either in the positive direction or negative direction along the *Z* axis. The elevation of the entity also can be added here. Elevation is not a property but a location in 3D space along the *Z* axis. The elevation can be different at the start of the entity than at its finish. The thickness, on the other hand, applies to the entire length of the entity because it is a property. Think of an entity with the color red. The color property covers the whole entity. You couldn't have a line half red and half green without breaking the entity into two separate pieces.

Note that AutoCAD's Thickness option not only extrudes the entity, forming a three-dimensional shape, but also creates a surface over the extruded area. Some other CAD packages extrude the shape but do not cover the area with a surface. A covered surface is a requirement for the display of a hidden line removed picture. So the thickness option actually performs two functions. This way, a user new to 3D can display an interesting 3D model using relatively few commands.

5.3   Extrusion Behavior

The act of extruding entities through the thickness property has different effects on different entity types. Also, the orientation of the entity can alter the extrusion process. The following figures illustrate the effects of the thickness property on different entities.

Figure 5.3 shows the line entity. If the UCS is aligned with the entity, the extrusion takes place in a normal fashion, as shown in part A of the figure. However, as part B shows, if the UCS is not aligned with the line, the extrusion takes place along the Z axis, regardless of the inclination of the line. This type of extrusion is useful when a certain effect is desired.

Figure 5.4A shows a circle extruded. A circle drawn with the thickness property has a surface over its top and bottom, forming an enclosed shape. The arc shown in Figure 5.4B does not have a surface on either its top or bottom. Two arcs can be used to create an open cylinder.

Figure 5.5A shows a polyline with no width (2D). In Figure 5.5B, width has been added to the polyline, and its possible graphic uses increase. Finally, in Figure 5.5C, a polyline with curves and width has been given thickness. When width is given to a polyline, the surface covering the area is defined by the width.

Figure 5.6A displays a polyline donut that behaves like a regular polyline. Figure 5.6B shows a polygon that does not have a surface covering its area, either at top or bottom.

Figure 5.7 shows an entity created with the SOLID command. This is a 2D command not to be confused with 3D solids. An irregular shape created by the SOLID command has a top and bottom surface when given a thickness.

Figure 5.3
Extruded lines

Figure 5.4
Extruded arcs

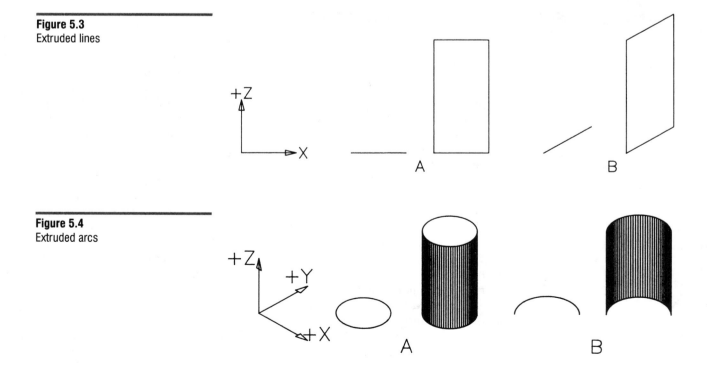

Figure 5.5
Extruded polylines

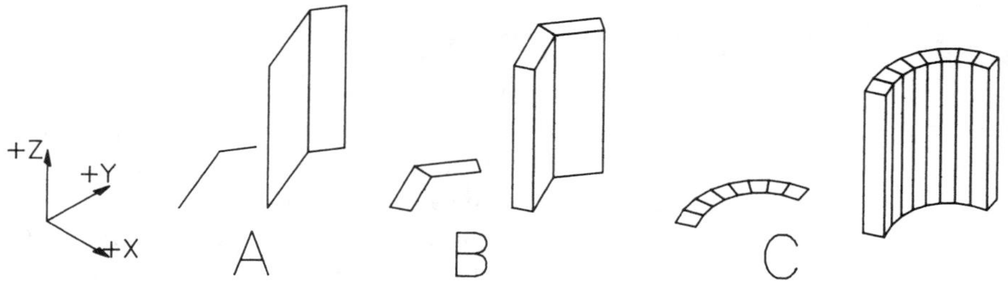

A   B   C

Figure 5.6
Extruded polylines: donut and polygon

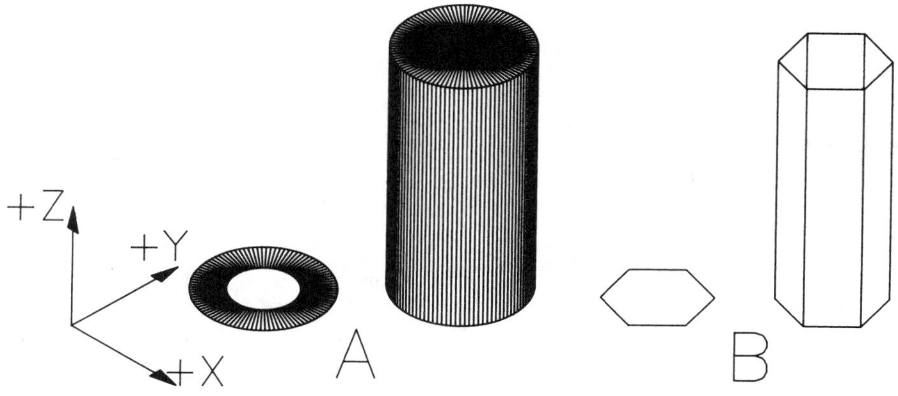

A   B

Figure 5.7
Extruded 2D solid (not a 3D solid)

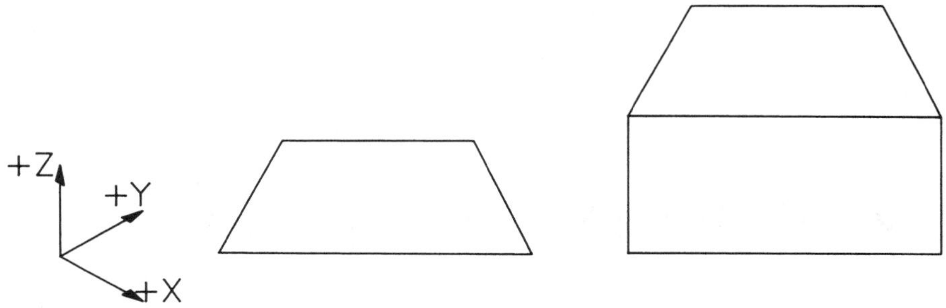

Figure 5.8
Pull-down menu/dialog box to access
entity creation

5.4   Thickness Property

Normally, the best practice is to set the thickness property before drawing an entity. As mentioned earlier, to access the Thickness option, the ELEV, or Thickness, command is used. This command sets the thickness and sets the elevation above or below the current working plane, as described in Section 4.4. The Thickness option also can be accessed through a pull-down menu and a dialog box, as shown in Figure 5.8.

3D Viewpoint

Thickness Property

Remember to return the thickness setting to 0 when you are finished. If left at some value and forgotten, it can result in some unpredicted results—namely, numerous entities with unwanted three-dimensional thickness.

5.5   Thickness Modification

The thickness of any entity can be altered through the CHPROP or the DDMODIFY command, both of which allow changes to any property of an entity. One property—such as color, layer, or thickness—common to several entities may be changed at once with these commands. In Figure 5.9A, several lines have uneven thickness. Using the CHPROP command, the thickness of all the lines can be changed to match, as shown in Figure 5.9B.

Figure 5.9
Using CHPROP to align thicknesses

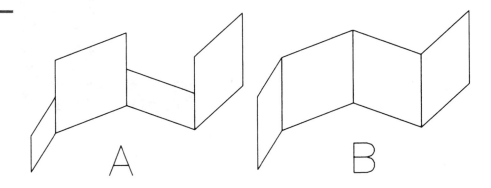

5.6   Thickness Effect on Object Snap

Because a form with thickness is bound by the originating entity, the snap locations on the extruded form reflect the original object snap points. Figure 5.10 shows common entities and the various snap points on their extruded forms: A is a line, B is a polyline, C is a circle, and D is a polygon. Remember that polylines that have a width are bound by the original "no-width" start and stop points (vertices). This means that there are no snap points around the perimeter of a polyline with a width.

Figure 5.10
Snap points on extruded entities

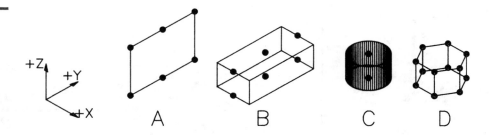

Lab 5.A

Purpose

Objectives

Primary Commands

Final Model

Procedure

Figure 5.11
Extruded bolt model

Bolt Extrusion

Lab 5.A will show you how extrusion methods are used to create the model of a bolt. This model will be used again in Assignment 1 in Chapter 7.

You will be able to:

- Set the Elevation and Thickness options.
- Display multiple viewpoints.
- Create a 3D model through extrusion.

```
ELEV—Elevation/Thickness
VPORTS
VPOINT
HIDE
```

Figure 5.11 shows the completed extruded bolt model.

1. Start a new drawing called BOLT. (*Note:* Use drawing file 3DSET from Assignment 1 of Chapter 3 for the prototype drawing. This will establish the initial settings and then proceed with the following lab-specific settings.)

```
Units  =  decimal
Limits  =  −1,−1 to 1,1
Grid  =  0.25
Snap Incr  =  0.125
Current Layer  =  0
Viewport Configuration  =  single/plan viewpoint
```

Creating the Bolt Head

2. Select the ELEV command and enter 0 for the elevation and 0.25 for the thickness. This will give thickness to the bolt head.

3. Using the POLYGON command, draw the bolt head as shown in Figure 5.12. The center of the polygon should have the coordinates 0,0.

4. Display an isometric view (1,−1,1) and use the HIDE command. The results should be similar to Figure 5.13. Note that there is no top to the polygon. This will be added in Chapter 7, after surfaces are explained.

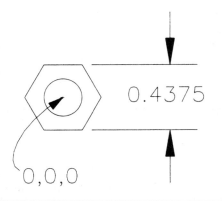

Figure 5.12
Top view of bolt head hexagon

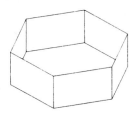

Figure 5.13
Isometric view of bolt head

90 Lab 5.A
Bolt Extrusion

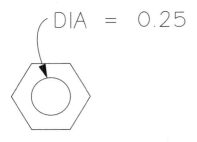

DIA = 0.25

Figure 5.14
Top view showing circle placement
and size

Displaying Multiple Viewports

5. Using the VPORTS command, restore the four-viewport configuration called ORTHO1.

Creating the Bolt Shaft

6. Select the ELEV command and enter 0 for the elevation and –1.5 for the thickness. This will give thickness to the bolt shaft along the negative *Z* axis.

7. Activate the top viewpoint viewport. Using the CIRCLE command, draw the shaft as shown in Figure 5.14. Do not use object snap. Object snap will override the elevation settings.

8. Experiment with the ZOOM CENTER command to display all three orthographic views at the same scale. (Try a factor of 2.)

9. Save the model as BOLT.

Lab 5.B

Purpose

Objectives

Primary Commands

Final Model

Procedure

Table Extrusion

Lab 5.B will show you how extrusion methods can be used to create a model of a table. This model will be used again in Assignment 1 in Chapter 13.

You will be able to:

- Set the Elevation and Thickness options.
- Display multiple viewpoints.
- Create a 3D model through extrusion.

```
ELEV–Elevation/Thickness
VPORTS
VPOINT
HIDE
```

Figure 5.15 shows the finished extruded table model.

1. Start a new drawing called TABLE with the following settings. (*Note:* Use drawing file 3DSET from Assignment 1 of Chapter 3 for the prototype drawing.)

```
Units  =  architectural
Limits  =  0,0 to 6',4'
Grid  =  6"
Snap Incr  =  1"
Current Layer  =  0
Viewport Configuration  =  single/plan viewpoint
Fill  =  OFF
```

Creating the Table Top

2. Select the ELEV command and enter 2'5" for the elevation and –1" for the thickness. This will place the table top at an elevation of 2'5" and give it a thickness of 1".

Figure 5.15
Extruded table model

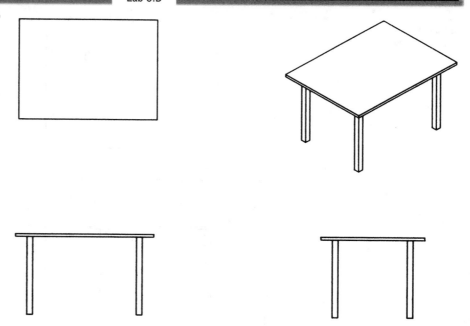

3. Using the PLINE (polyline) command, draw the table top as shown in Figure 5.16. (*Note:* The polyline should have a width of 3'.) The polyline was used because of its simplicity to create and its characteristic of allowing surfaces on its top, bottom, and sides.

Displaying Multiple Viewports

4. Using the VPORTS command, restore the four-viewport configuration called ORTHO1.

Creating the Table Legs

5. Select the ELEV command and enter 0 for the elevation and 2′4″ for the thickness. This will place the legs on the ground and give a thickness that will extrude to meet the top. Do not use object snap. Object snap will override the elevation settings.

6. Activate the top viewpoint viewport. Using the LINE command, draw the legs as shown in Figure 5.17.

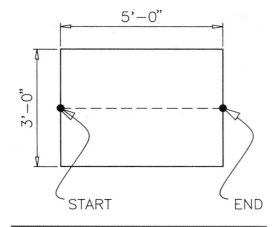

Figure 5.16
Top view showing polyline size

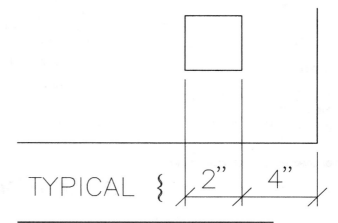

Figure 5.17
Top view showing leg size and placement

Figure 5.18
Viewports showing final model

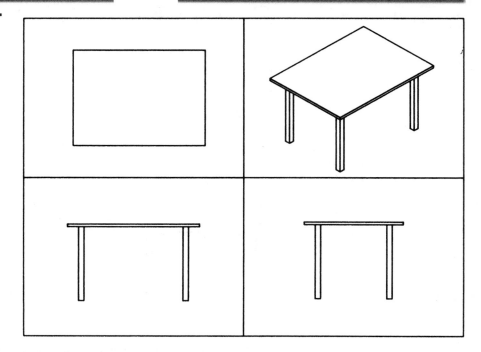

Displaying a Hidden Line Removed Model

7. Use the ZOOM CENTER command in each viewport to set a matching scale. Try a scale factor of 4′.

8. Activate each viewport and use the HIDE command. Refer to Figure 5.18. Note that the table top has a surface covering it.

Setting the Base Point

9. Because this model will be used later in Chapter 13, a new base point needs to be set. The base point is the cursor handle point when the block (the table) is inserted into another model. It is used to identify where the block will be placed. This base point should have an elevation of 0Z, and the X and Y location should be in the center of the table. Refer to Figure 5.19. To set the new base point:

   ■ Activate the top viewpoint viewport.
   ■ Select the BASE command.
   ■ Select the .XY filter (if desired, more can be learned about filters in Section 6.2).
   ■ Select the object snap midpoint option.
   ■ Select the top width of the polyline of the table top.
   ■ Enter 0 for the request of the Z coordinate.

   A new base point has now been set.

10. Save the model as TABLE.

11. Experiment with moving around the model using the VPOINT and HIDE commands.

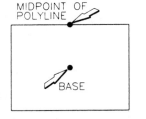

MIDPOINT OF
POLYLINE

BASE

Figure 5.19
Top view showing base point

Lab 5.C

Purpose

Chair Extrusion

Lab 5.C will show you how extrusion methods can be used to create a model of a chair. This model will be used again in Assignment 1 in Chapter 13.

Objectives

You will be able to:

- Set the Elevation and Thickness options.
- Display multiple viewpoints.
- Create a 3D model through extrusion.

Primary Commands

```
ELEV—Elevation/Thickness
VPORTS
VPOINT
HIDE
```

Final Model

Figure 5.20 shows the final extruded chair model.

Procedure

1. Start a new drawing called CHAIR with the following settings. (*Note:* Use drawing file 3DSET from Assignment 1 of Chapter 3 for the prototype drawing.)

```
Units  =  architectural
Limits  =  −1",−1" to 2',2'
Grid  =  2"
Snap Incr  =  0.5"
Current Layer  =  0
Viewport Configuration  =  single/plan viewpoint
Fill  =  OFF
```

Creating the Chair Seat

2. Select the ELEV command and enter 1′6″ for the elevation and −1″ for the thickness. This will place the chair seat at an elevation of 1′6″ and give it a thickness of 1″.

Figure 5.20
Extruded chair model

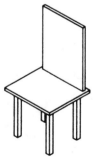
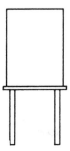
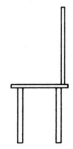

3. Using the PLINE command, draw the chair seat as shown in Figure 5.21. (*Note:* Set the width of the polyline to 1′5″.) As in Lab 5.A, the polyline was used because of its simplicity to create and its allowance of surfaces on its top, bottom, and sides.

Displaying Multiple Viewports

4. Using the VPORTS command, restore the four-viewport configuration called ORTHO1.

Creating the Chair Legs

5. Select the ELEV command and enter 0 for the elevation and 1′6″ for the thickness. This will place the legs on the ground and give a thickness that will extrude to meet the seat. Do not use object snap. Object snap will override the elevation settings.

6. Activate the top viewpoint viewport. Using the LINE command, draw the legs as shown in Figure 5.22.

Creating the Chair Back

7. Select the ELEV command and enter 1′5″ for the elevation and 2′ for the thickness. This will be used to place the back on the seat and give a thickness that will extrude above the seat. Do not use object snap. Object snap will override the elevation settings.

8. Activate the top viewpoint viewport. Using the PLINE command, draw the back as shown in Figure 5.23. (*Note:* Set the width of the polyline to 1′5″.)

Displaying a Hidden Line Removed Model

9. Use the ZOOM CENTER command in each viewport to set a matching scale. Try a scale factor of 5′.

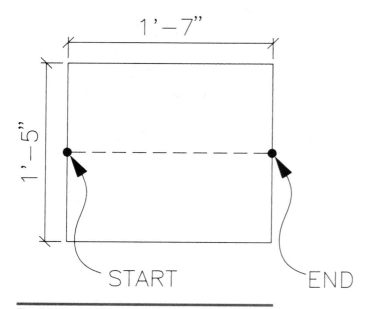

Figure 5.21
Top view of polyline chair seat

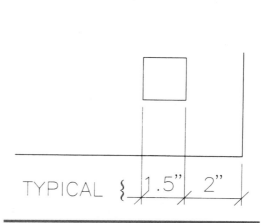

Figure 5.22
Top view of chair legs

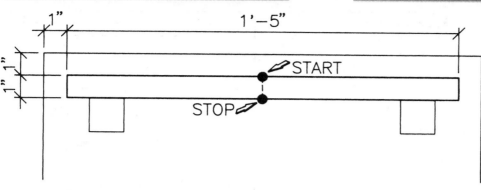

Figure 5.23
Top view of polyline chair back

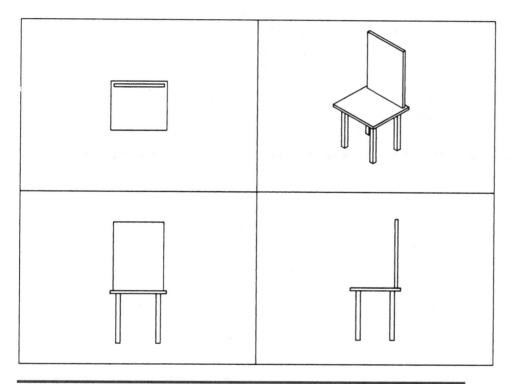

Figure 5.24
Viewports showing final model

10. Activate each viewport and use the HIDE command. Refer to Figure 5.24. Note that the seat and the back have surfaces.

Setting the Base Point

11. Because this model will be used later in Chapter 13, a new base point needs to be set. This base point should have an elevation of $0Z$, and the X and Y location should be in the center of the chair. Refer to Figure 5.25. To set a new base point:

   ■ Activate the top viewpoint viewport.
   ■ Select the BASE command.
   ■ Select the $.XY$ filter.
   ■ Select the object snap midpoint option.

Figure 5.25
Top view showing base point

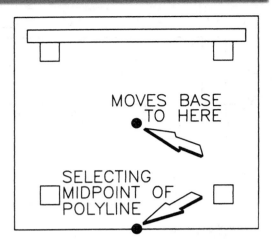

- Select the bottom width of the polyline of the seat.
- Enter 0 for the request of the Z coordinate.

A new base point has now been set.

12. Save the model as CHAIR.

13. Experiment with moving around the model using the VPOINT and the HIDE commands.

Questions

1. What two elements define the shape of an extrusion?

2. Explain the process of generating an extrusion.

3. Explain the process for altering the thickness of an entity that has already been created.

4. What is the significance of AutoCAD's thickness property compared to other CAD programs' extrusion capabilities?

5. How can the inclination of a line affect its extrusion?

6. What is the difference between a circle and an arc extrusion?

7. What is the difference between the extrusion of a polygon and the extrusion of a solid?

8. What are the two methods for accessing the Thickness option?

Assignments

Note: The prototype drawing 3DSET created in Assignment 1 of Chapter 3 is used in the following assignments.

1. Create a 3D model of a file cabinet using only extrusion. Refer to Figure 5.26. Save it as FCAB. (*Hint:* Use different elevations for the drawers or draw one and copy in a Z direction.) Use 3DSET for the prototype drawing. Use the HIDE command when finished to determine if any surfaces are missing. This model will be used again in Chapter 16, Assignment 2.

2. Generate a 3D model of a bookshelf using only extrusion. Refer to Figure 5.27. Save it as BSHEL. Use 3DSET for the prototype drawing. Use the HIDE command when finished and observe the results. This model will be used again in Chapter 16, Assignment 2.

Figure 5.26
File cabinet extruded model

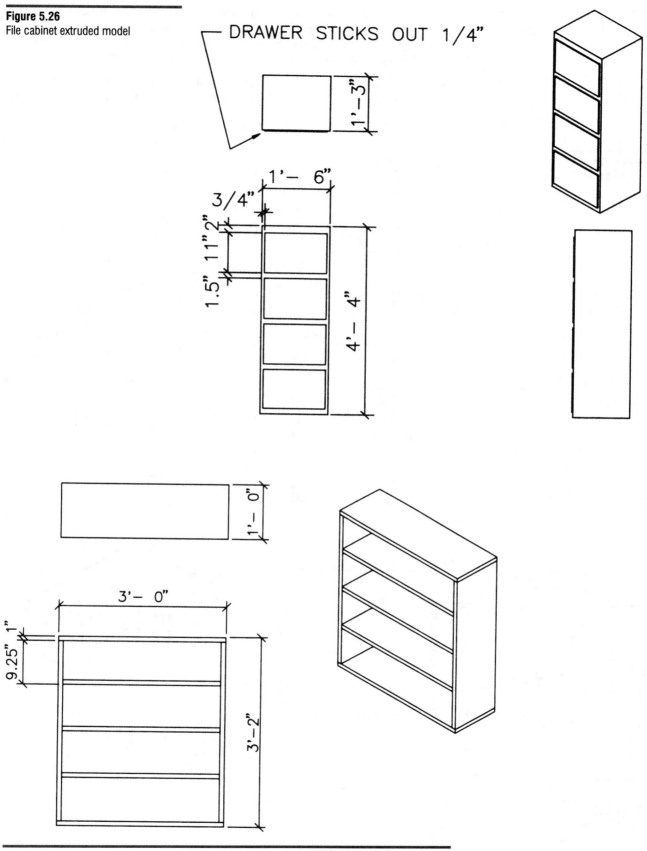

DRAWER STICKS OUT 1/4"

1'-3"

1'-6"

3/4"

2"

1.1"

1.5"

4'-4"

1'-0"

3'-0"

9.25"

1"

3'-2"

Figure 5.27
Bookshelf extruded model

3. Draw a length of an I-beam (structural member) using only extrusion. Refer to Figure 5.28. Use 3DSET for the prototype drawing. Use the HIDE command when finished and note, depending on whether lines, polylines, or solids are used, where there are no surfaces.

4. Referring to Figure 5.29, create an architectural floor plan. Use 3DSET for the prototype drawing. Experiment with the VPOINT and the HIDE commands.

Figure 5.28
I-beam extruded model

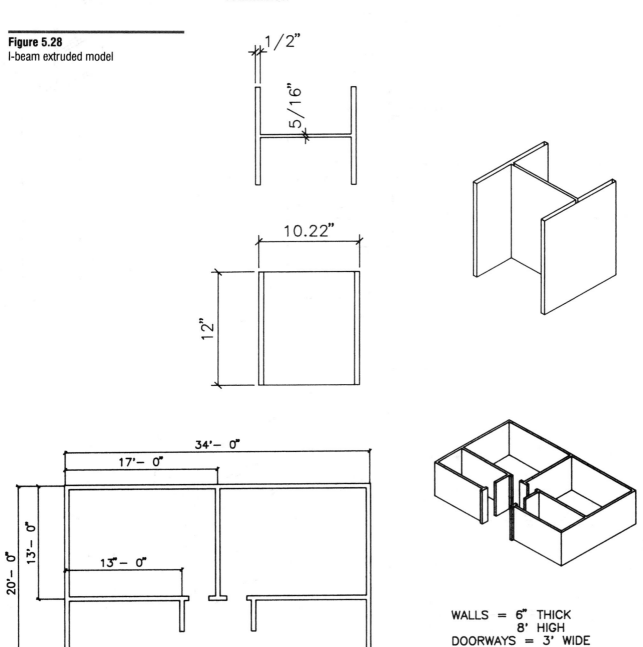

Figure 5.29
Floor plan extruded model

CHAPTER 6

Wireframe

Overview

This chapter explains the basic concepts you'll need to understand in order to generate true 3D models. Methods and applications mentioned in Chapters 3 and 4 are utilized here. For instance, in this chapter you will use working planes.

Concepts Explored

- What wireframe models represent
- The application of nodes
- The significance of coordinate filters
- The projection techniques required to solve model problems
- The behavior of true 3D entities
- The construction of wireframe models.

6.1 Introduction

The concept behind true three-dimensional modeling is that the start point and the finish point of any piece of geometry can have completely independent sets of coordinates. Because AutoCAD's line entity can start and stop at any location in three-dimensional space, it is considered a true three-dimensional entity. See Figure 6.1.

The initial method of model building using the concept of 3D modeling is wireframe construction. *Wireframe* means that lines are used to represent the boundary edge of any shape or model. Wireframes often serve as the skeleton of models. With some complex models, wireframes need to be constructed before surfaces can be formed. And surfaces are required before hidden line removal can be performed. Some of the AutoCAD automatic surface commands require that wireframe profiles be created before the surfaces are generated.

NODE points control the shape of the wireframe. Nodes are the intersection points of the various lines, or the vertices of polylines. Sometimes in the initial stages of model creation, the node points are the first entities to be added, followed by lines or surfaces defined by the node points. Figure 6.2 illustrates a model showing node points. Node points are further utilized in Chapter 23.

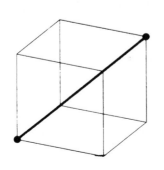

Figure 6.1
A cube showing a true 3D line

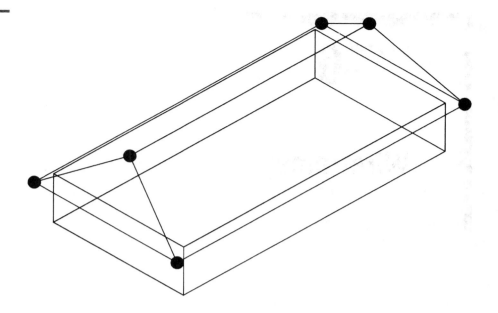

Figure 6.2
A model of a house showing NODE points

6.2 Coordinate Filters

When entering node points, it often is necessary to make use of geometry that has already been created, such as object end snap, or mid or intersection points. Sometimes it is necessary to use only part of the coordinates at the snap point instead of all three *X, Y, Z* axis points. Consider this typical scenario: A user needs the *X* and *Y* location of a point but wants the *Z* point at a different elevation. AutoCAD has foreseen this situation and has incorporated the Filters tool into the program. This option allows the user to extract any combination of points from a digitized location on a model and then to type in the missing coordinate. Two of the six filtering combinations (*.X, .Y, .Z, .XY, .XZ, .YZ*) are as follows. The other four combinations follow the same pattern.

FILTER	MEANING
.X	The user selects a point on the model. Auto-CAD extracts the *X* coordinate and asks the user to enter the *Y* and *Z* coordinates.
.XY	The user selects a point on the model. Auto-CAD extracts the *X* and *Y* coordinates and asks the user to enter the *Z* coordinate.

Figure 6.3 illustrates the use of the Filters option to enter 3D lines. Part A of the figure shows the original line drawn in 3D space. Part B shows the extrac-

Figure 6.3
Using the Filters option to draw a line

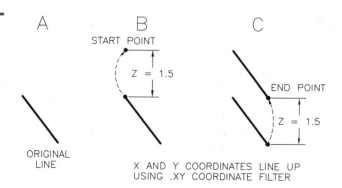

tion of the *XY* coordinate from one end of the original line and the input of 1.5 for the *Z* coordinate. Finally, part C shows the extraction of the *XY* coordinate from the other end of the original line and the input of 1.5 for the *Z* coordinate. The result is a new line whose *X* and *Y* coordinates match the first line but whose *Z* location is different. The following is the command procedure to create the new line from the original:

```
Command: LINE
From point: .XY  (this is used to extract the X and Y coordinates)
of ENDPOINT  (this is used to snap on to the end of the line)
of pick one end of the original line
(need Z) 1.5  (this is the distance along the Z axis)
To point: .XY
of ENDPOINT
of pick the other end of the original line
(need Z) 1.5
To point: press <Enter> to quit command
```

6.3 Projection Techniques

Projection is a very useful method of locating node points on a complex model. *Projection* refers to the technique of projecting lines along an axis until they intersect with lines projected along a different axis, resulting in a node point. A series of node points can then be used to generate a "line of intersection" outline where one object intersects another. Figures 6.4 to 6.7 illustrate how this technique is used for arc intersection.

FIGURE	DESCRIPTION
6.4A	The finished model of two arcs intersecting
6.4B	The initially created two planes
6.4C	The addition of arcs subdivided
6.4D	The projection of lines perpendicular to arcs
6.4E	The identification of intersection nodes
6.4F	The addition of 3D polyline through node points
6.5	The final model displayed in four viewports

Figure 6.4
Creating a line of intersection

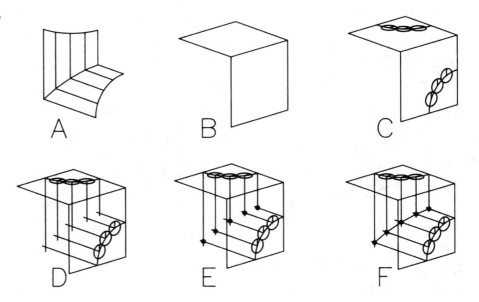

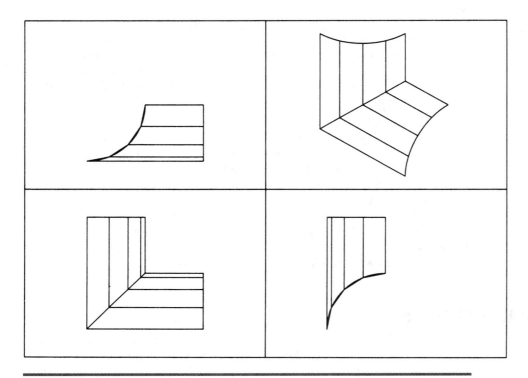

Figure 6.5
The final model in four viewports

Figures 6.6 and 6.7 illustrate how this technique is used for roof intersection:

FIGURE	DESCRIPTION
6.6A	The finished model of the two roofs intersecting
6.6B	The initially created planes
6.6C	The identification of intersection nodes
6.6D	The addition of lines through node points
6.7	The final model displayed in four viewports

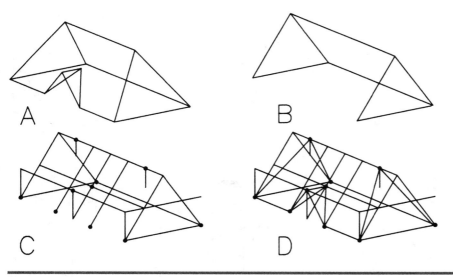

Figure 6.6
Creating intersecting roofs

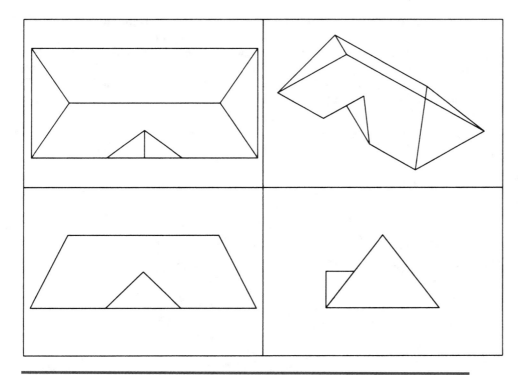

Figure 6.7
The final roof model in four viewports

6.4 2D Polyline Versus 3D Polyline

Although lines can be drawn along any axis at any time just by object snapping or by entering the 3D coordinates, the regular polyline is restricted to being aligned to wherever the working plane is currently set. The regular polyline can be thought of as a planar entity. Even if a user entered coordinates in an attempt to make the polyline nonplanar, the polyline would project the coordinates onto the working plane until the polyline became flat. To overcome this limitation, AutoCAD has established the 3D polyline. The 3POLY command creates a polyline that can run along any axis at any time, just like a line. Currently, however—and this is the only negative aspect—no width can be given to a 3D polyline. But it can have a thickness. Figure 6.8 illustrates a 2D polyline in the shape

Figure 6.8
A flat 2D polyline

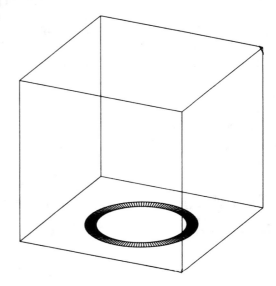

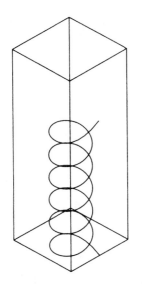

Figure 6.9
A helical 3D polyline

of a circle aligned to a plane. Figure 6.9 shows a 3D polyline in the form of a helical coil, illustrating that a polyline is indeed not limited to one plane.

Refer back to the 3D polyline shown in Figure 6.4F. There, the polyline follows the intersecting curve regardless of the coordinates. When creating models with irregular curves that lie in no particular plane, you'll find the 3D polyline extremely useful.

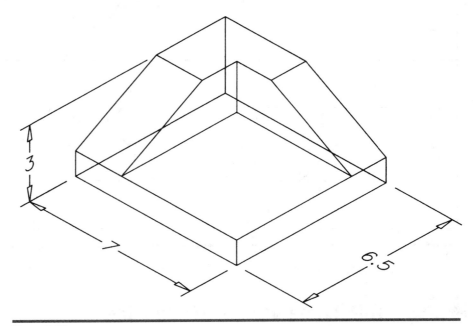

Figure 6.10
Angle plate wireframe model

Lab 6.A

Angle Block

Purpose

Lab 6.A will familiarize you with wireframe methods of model construction. You will create a wireframe model of an angle plate, emphasizing angular lines. The methods you'll be using will demonstrate AutoCAD's true 3D capabilities. This model will be used again in Chapter 7, where you will learn how to apply a surface to the wireframe skeleton.

Objectives

You will be able to:

- Construct a wireframe model.
- Display multiple viewpoints.

Primary Commands

ELEV–Elevation/Thickness
VPORTS
VPOINT
HIDE

Final Model

Figure 6.10 shows the final wireframe model you'll be constructing.

Procedure

1. Start a new drawing called ANGPLT (ANGle PLaTe) with the following settings. (*Note:* Use drawing file 3DSET from Assignment 1 of Chapter 3 for the prototype drawing. This will establish the initial settings and then proceed with the following lab-specific settings.)

Figure 6.11
Creating the orientation cube

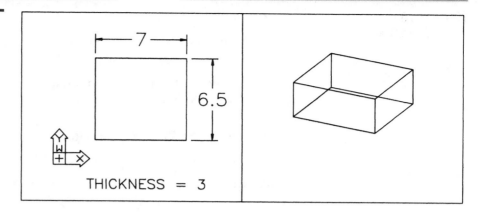

```
Units    =  decimal
Limits   =  −1,−1 to 8,8
Grid   =  1
Snap Incr  =  0.5
Current Layer  =  WIRE
Viewport Configuration  =  ORTHO1
```

Creating an Orientation Cube

When starting construction, it is useful to create a cube for initial orientation. This will give you some overall perspective while you're constructing, and will let you know if construction exceeds the boundary of the cube during the building process. (*Note:* The orientation shape isn't necessarily a true cube. The term *cube* is used as a standard name.)

2. Using the ELEV command, set the elevation to 0 and the thickness to 3.

3. Activate the top view viewport, and draw the box as shown in Figure 6.11. Observe the results in the other viewports.

Creating Working Planes

Three working planes are going to be created at this stage: the front, right side, and top. Another working plane will be created later.

4. Following Figure 6.12, create a working plane using the UCS command on the front of the cube. Make sure you use object snaps. Save the UCS as FRONT.

5. Create the working planes for the top and right side, giving them the names TOP and RSIDE. Make sure to use object snaps. Stop and save the model as ANGPLT.

Figure 6.12
Creating the FRONT working plane

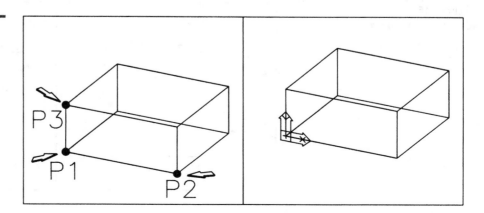

106 Lab 6.A
Angle Block

Drawing on the Front Plane

6. Restore the FRONT working plane.

7. Using the ELEV command, set the elevation to 0 and the thickness to 0.

8. Activate the front-view viewport, and draw the line shown in Figure 6.13. Observe the isometric viewport.

Drawing on the Right-Side Plane

9. Restore the RSIDE working plane.

10. Activate the right-side-view viewport, and draw the line shown in Figure 6.14.

Figure 6.13
Adding a line on the FRONT working plane

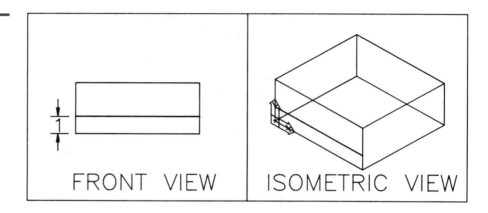

Figure 6.14
Adding a line on the RSIDE working plane

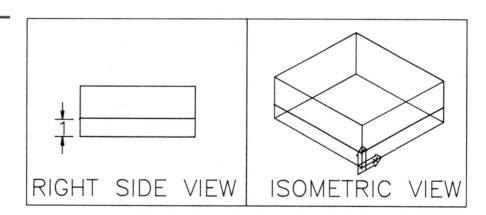

Figure 6.15
Creating on the TOP working plane

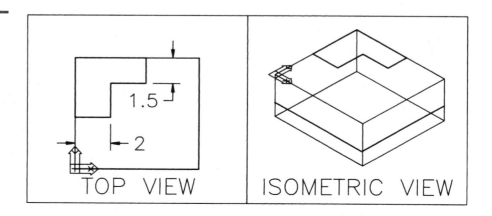

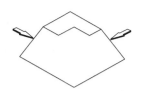

Figure 6.16
Adding sloped lines using object end-point snap

Drawing on the Top Plane

11. Restore the TOP working plane.

12. Activate the top-view viewport, and draw the profile (six lines in all) shown in Figure 6.15. Estimate the remaining dimensions. Stop and save the model as ANGPLT.

Drawing on an Incline

13. Activate the isometric viewport, and draw the lines indicated in Figure 6.16. It is very important to use object snap endpoint to ensure the lines are in the correct position.

14. With the use of the COPY command, create the parallel line B using line A and then create line D using line C. Refer to Figure 6.17.

Creating a New Working Plane

15. Referring to Figure 6.18, create a new working plane. Make sure you use object snaps. Save the UCS as TPLATE (Top of PLATE).

Figure 6.17
Adding sloped lines with COPY

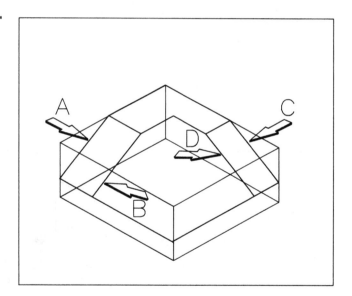

Figure 6.18
Creating a new working plane

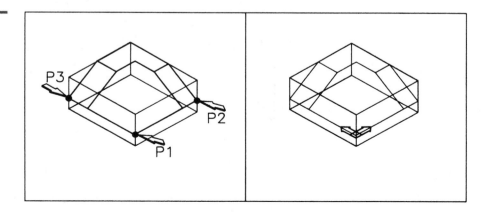

Figure 6.19
Adding lines to the top plate

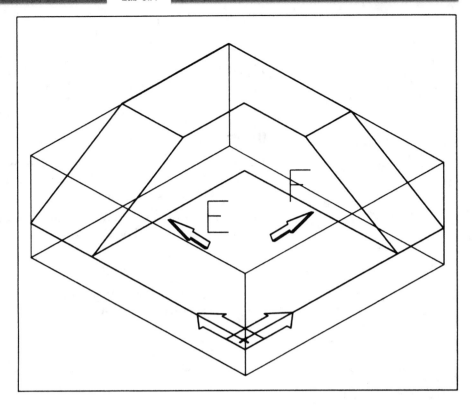

Figure 6.20
Adding a vertical line

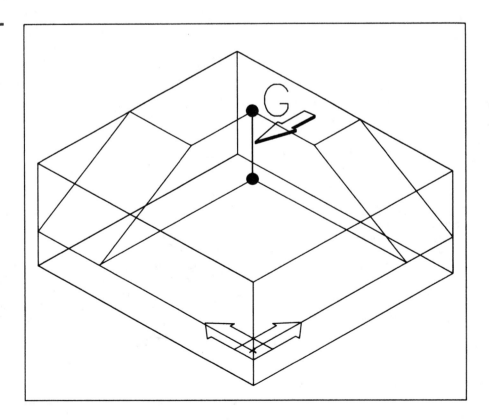

Figure 6.21
Returning lines to zero thickness

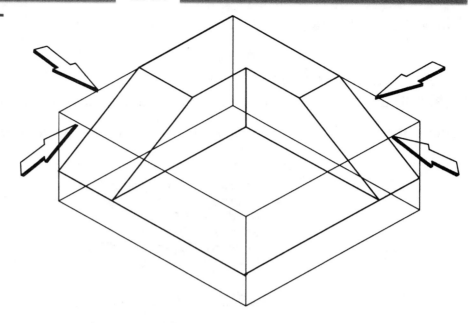

16. Keep the isometric viewport active, and add lines E and F, as shown in Figure 6.19.

17. Using object snap endpoint, draw in line G, as shown in Figure 6.20. Stop and save the model as ANGPLT.

Returning the Orientation Cube to Zero Thickness

18. Using the CHPROP command, set the original orientation cube lines back to 0 thickness, as shown in Figure 6.21. These lines will be used as part of the wireframe.

19. After observing the model in all the viewports, add the missing lines to finish the model. Refer back to Figure 6.10. (*Note:* Make sure to use object snap endpoint for this construction.)

20. Use the HIDE command and observe the results. Hidden line removal will only work with surfaces. Surfaces will be added to this model in the next chapter.

21. Save the model as ANGPLT.

Lab 6.B

Purpose

Objectives

Inca Structure

Lab 6.B will familiarize you with wireframe methods of model construction. You will create a wireframe model of an ancient Inca structure, emphasizing inclined lines. The methods you will be using will demonstrate AutoCAD's true 3D capability.

You will be able to:

- Construct a wireframe model.
- Display multiple viewpoints.

Primary Commands

```
ELEV—Elevation/Thickness
VPORTS
VPOINT
HIDE
```

Final Model

Figure 6.22 shows the final wireframe model you'll be constructing.

Procedure

1. Start a new drawing called INCA (INCA structure) with the following settings. (*Note:* Use drawing file 3DSET from Assignment 1 of Chapter 3 for the prototype drawing.)

```
Units  =  architectural
Limits  =  -10',-10' to 260',240'
Grid  =  10'
Snap Incr  =  10'
Current Layer  =  WIRE
Viewport configuration  =  ORTHO1
```

Creating an Orientation Cube

When starting construction, it is useful to create a cube for initial orientation. This will give you some overall perspective while you're constructing, and it will let you know if construction exceeds the boundary of the cube during the building process. (*Note:* The orientation shape is not necessarily a true cube. The term *cube* is used as a standard name.)

For this model, two orientation cubes will be constructed: one for the bottom pyramid shape and another for the top pyramid shape.

2. Using the ELEV command, set the elevation to 0 and the thickness to 60'.

3. Activate the top-view viewport, and draw the 240' square box as shown in Figure 6.23. Observe the results in the other viewports.

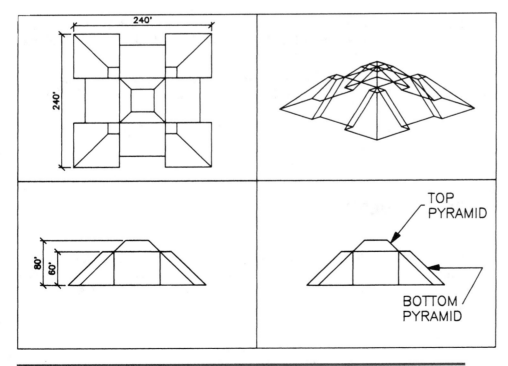

Figure 6.22
Inca structure wireframe model

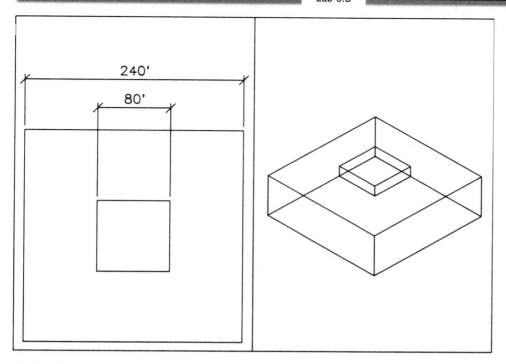

Figure 6.23
Creating two orientation cubes

4. Using the ELEV command, set the elevation to 60′ and the thickness to 20′. This will set the second cube on top of the first.

5. Activate the top-view viewport, and draw the 80′ square box as shown in Figure 6.23. Observe the results in the other viewports.

Creating Working Planes

Three working planes (one for each elevation point) are going to be created at this stage: level 1, level 2, and level 3.

6. Following Figure 6.24, create the three working planes using the UCS command. Save each working plane so that they may be restored any time. Call them LEVEL1, LEVEL2, and LEVEL3. Stop and save the model as INCA.

Figure 6.24
Creating three working planes

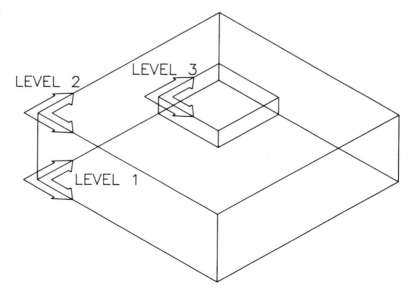

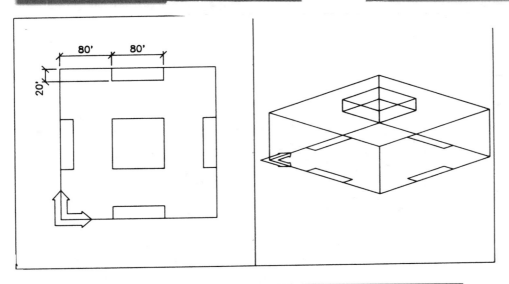

Figure 6.25
Creating on LEVEL1

Drawing on the LEVEL1 Plane

7. Restore the LEVEL1 working plane.

8. Using the ELEV command, set the elevation to 0 and the thickness to 0.

9. Activate the top-view viewport, and draw the lines shown in Figure 6.25. Observe the isometric viewport.

Drawing on the LEVEL2 Plane

10. Restore the LEVEL2 working plane.

11. With the top-view viewport still activated, draw the lines shown in Figure 6.26. Observe the isometric viewport.

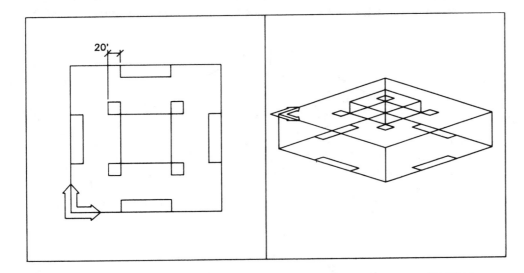

Figure 6.26
Creating on LEVEL2

Figure 6.27
Adding sloped lines using object snap endpoint

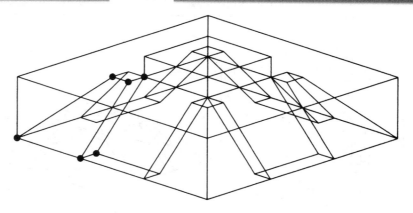

Figure 6.28
Returning lines to zero thickness

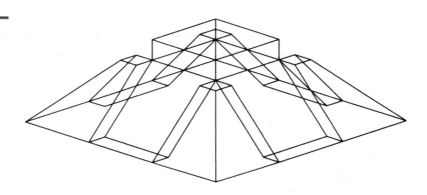

Adding the Inclined Lines to the First Pyramid

The inclined lines from level 1 to level 2 will now be added.

12. Activate the isometric viewport. Using object snap endpoint, add lines connecting the node points on level 1 with those on level 2. You will need to alter the viewpoint as lines are added around the model. Refer to Figure 6.27.

13. Using the CHPROP command, return the thickness of the bottom orientation cube to 0, as shown in Figure 6.28. Stop and save the model as INCA.

Drawing on the LEVEL3 Plane

14. Restore the LEVEL3 working plane.

15. Make sure the elevation and the thickness are set to 0.

16. Activate the top-view viewport, and draw the lines shown in Figure 6.29. Observe the isometric viewport.

Adding the Inclined Lines to the Second Pyramid

The inclined lines from level 2 to level 3 will now be added.

17. Activate the isometric viewport. Using object snap endpoint, add lines connecting the node points on level 2 with those on level 3. You may need to alter the viewpoint as lines are added around the model. Refer to Figure 6.30.

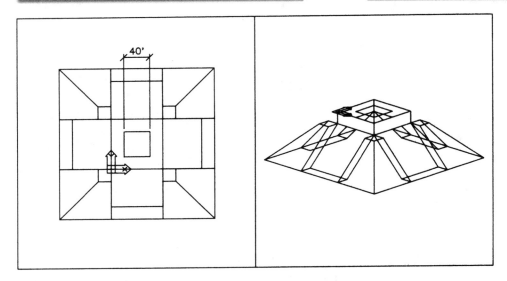

Figure 6.29
Creating on LEVEL3

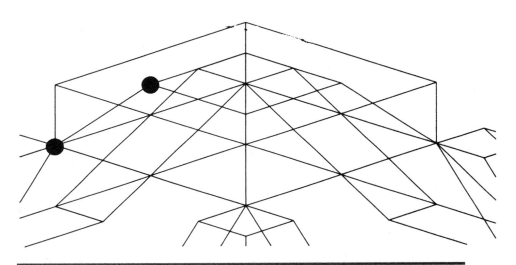

Figure 6.30
Adding sloped lines

18. Using the CHPROP command, return the thickness of the top orientation cube to 0 and use the TRIM command to remove lines at the base of the structure, as shown in Figure 6.31. Stop and save the model as INCA.

Altering the Viewpoint to Achieve a Better View

19. Activate the isometric viewport.

20. Using the VPOINT command, enter the coordinates (1,–2,3). This should generate a trimetric view, as shown in Figure 6.32. The trimetric view of this model should be more pleasing.

21. Use the HIDE command and observe the results. Because this is only a wireframe model and it has no surfaces, the HIDE command will have no effect.

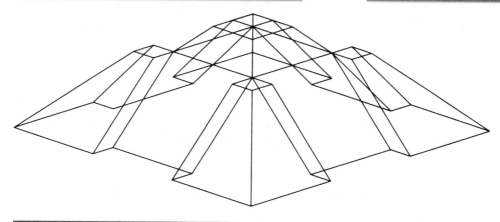

Figure 6.31
Trimming the model

Figure 6.32
Trimetric view of the model

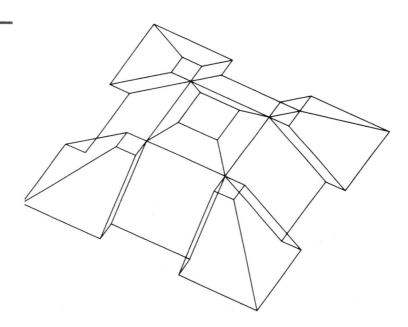

Lab 6.C

Using Projection to Solve a Problem

Purpose

Lab 6.C will demonstrate how to use projection to determine the line of inter-section between a sloped surface and an intersecting rectangular box. In this case, the sloped surface is a roof and the rectangular box is a chimney.

Objective

You will be able to use projection to solve a problem.

Primary Commands

UCS
LINE

Procedure

The Problem

1. Refer to Figure 6.33. It represents a rectangular chimney that intersects a sloped roof. You need to create the line of intersection that represents the

Figure 6.33
Chimney meets roof

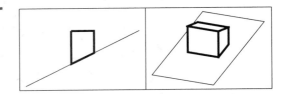

point at which the chimney and the roof surfaces meet. To solve this problem, use the projection techniques discussed in Section 6.3.

Initial Settings

2. Start a new drawing called INTERS (INTERSection) with the following settings:

```
Units  =  Architecture
Limits  =  -1',-1' to 10',11'
Grid  =  1'
Snap Inc  =  1'
UCS  =  WCS
UCSICON  =  ON, ORIGIN
```

Create the following layers:

LAYER NAME	DESCRIPTION
OCUBE	Orientation cube
ROOF	Roof surface
CHIM	Chimney surface
PROJ	Projection lines
INTERS	Line of intersection
PROF	Chimney profile

You may want to give a different color to each layer to help differentiate the geometry being shown at any time.

Creating an Orientation Cube

3. Make the OCUBE layer current and use ZOOM Extents to display the limits of the model.

4. Using the ELEV command, set the elevation to 0 and the thickness to 5', the height of the roof for this project.

5. Refer to Figure 6.34 and use the LINE command to draw the outline of the orientation cube. The geometry is 8' along the *X* axis, 10' along the *Y* axis, and 5' along the *Z* axis. The lower left corner should start at 0,0,0. (As with the previous labs, the orientation cube is not necessarily a cube. The term *cube* is used as a standard name.)

Creating the Chimney Surfaces

6. Set CHIM as the current layer.

7. With the elevation still set to 0 and the thickness to 5', use the LINE command to draw the outline of the chimney as shown in Figure 6.35. Because the chimney is drawn using lines with thickness, there are surfaces that represent the perimeter of the chimney.

Creating a Working Plane

You are going to create a working plane along the right side of the OCUBE. This requires that you display a trimetric view of the OCUBE.

8. Using the VPOINT command, set the view to 2,-3,1. It should look similar to Figure 6.36.

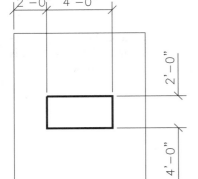

8'-0"

10'-0"

(0,0,0)

Figure 6.34
Orientation cube

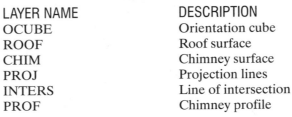

2'-0" 4'-0"

2'-0"

4'-0"

Figure 6.35
Chimney outline

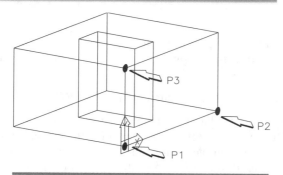

Figure 6.36
Creating the side working plane

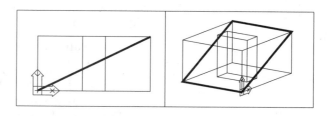

Figure 6.37
Sloped roof line

9. Using the 3Point option of the UCS command, create the new working plane by using the points indicated in Figure 6.36.

Creating Multiple Viewports

10. To allow better viewing, create two viewports side by side using the VPORTS command. The left viewport should display a plan view of the current UCS and the right viewport should display a trimetric view (2,–3,1).

11. Use the ZOOM command in each viewport with a scale setting of 0.8X. This will reduce the displayed geometry to 80% so that you can see the UCS icon better.

Creating the Sloped Roof

12. Set the current layer to ROOF.

13. Set the elevation to 0 and the thickness to –8′. This will give thickness that will stretch from the right to left side of the orientation cube.

14. Activate the right viewport and, using the LINE command, draw the sloped line as shown in Figure 6.37.

Observing the Results of the HIDE Command

15. Freeze the OCUBE layer.

16. Now use the HIDE command and observe the results. They should look similar to Figure 6.38. Notice that some of the chimney surfaces disappeared and you cannot tell where the chimney penetrates the roof. Unfortunately, the HIDE command does not work well on surfaces that pass through each other. Determining the line of intersection will correct the problem.

17. Thaw the OCUBE layer again.

Figure 6.38
Results of the HIDE command

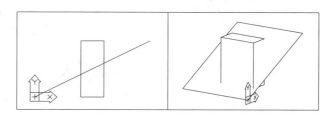

Creating Projection Lines

Creating various projection lines will produce intersection nodes so that you can create the line of intersection that represents where the chimney penetrates the roof.

18. Set elevation to 0, thickness to 0, and the current layer to PROJ.

19. Activate the left viewport that displays the plan view of the current UCS, as shown in Figure 6.39. Draw the two vertical lines by lining the cursor up with the chimney bottom. (Do not use object snap; instead use increment snap.) The vertical lines should extend so that they pass the slope of the roof.

20. Activate the right viewport that displays the trimetric view. This time use object snap endpoint to draw a line over the top of the roof line, as shown in Figure 6.39.

21. Use the COPY command to copy all three lines to the left side of the roof, as shown in Figure 6.40.

22. Using the 3Point option of the UCS command, create a working plane along the slope of the roof. Refer to Figure 6.41 for the three points.

23. Activate the left viewport and use the PLAN command to display the plan view of the current UCS.

24. In the left viewport, use the LINE command to draw two vertical lines that overlap the chimney lines. Refer to Figure 6.42 for their approximate lengths.

25. Activate the right viewport and use the VPOINT command to set the viewpoint to 3,–4,1. Once this is done use the ZOOM command and set the scale to 0.8X. This should give you a view similar to Figure 6.43 but without the extra lines.

26. Using intersect object snap, draw lines that extend across the roof, as shown in Figure 6.43.

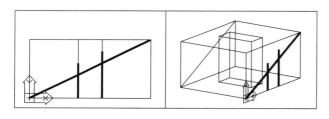

Figure 6.39
Two vertical lines and one sloped line

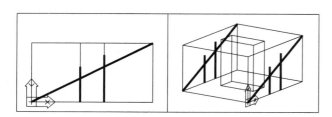

Figure 6.40
Copying the three lines from the right to the left side

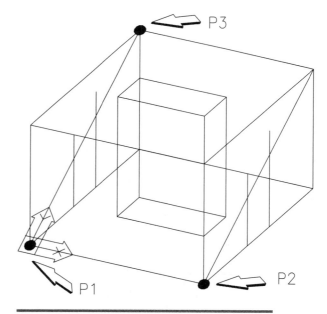

Figure 6.41
Creating a sloped UCS working plane

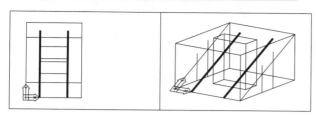

Figure 6.42
Adding lines to sloped surface

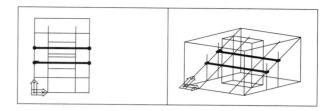

Figure 6.43
Adding horizontal lines across the roof surface

Generating the Lines of Intersection

You should now have the four main projection lines that lie on the roof surface and surround the chimney. You are going to use these lines that intersect at the four corners of the chimney to generate the line of intersection.

27. Set the current layer to INTERS. This will contain the lines of intersection. Freeze the OCUBE layer.

28. Using the intersect object snap, draw around the perimeter of the chimney where it penetrates the roof. Use the intersection nodes of the projection lines as your intersection snap points. Refer to Figure 6.44.

Creating a Wireframe Profile of the Chimney

You are now going to create a wireframe profile of the chimney portion that extends upward past the chimney.

29. Set the current layer to PROF.

30. Use the VPOINT command to set the viewpoint to 4,–5,1. This will make it easier to pick points on the chimney. Your view should look similar to Figure 6.45.

31. Using object snap, create lines that overlap the edges of the chimney surfaces, as shown in Figure 6.45.

Simulating the Hidden View

You are going to simulate what the hidden view of the extended chimney would be even though it will be shown in wireframe.

32. Freeze all layers, except for ROOF, CHIM, INTERS, PROF. Those layers should be thawed and visible.

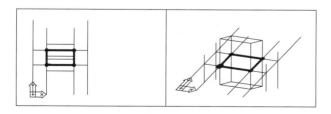

Figure 6.44
Adding the lines of intersection

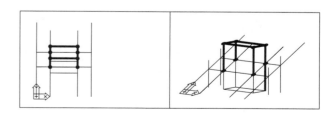

Figure 6.45
Adding wireframe lines to represent the chimney profile

Figure 6.46
Simulated hidden chimney lines

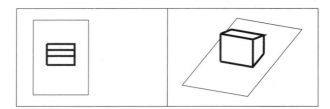

33. Using the VPOINT command set the viewpoint to 2,–3,1.

34. Use the HIDE command. Because the CHIM surface layer is still visible, AutoCAD used it in the hidden line calculations.

35. Freeze the CHIM layer. With the CHIM layer not visible you should only see the roof surface and the wireframe of the chimney and its penetration of the roof. The display should look similar to Figure 6.46.

36. Save your model.

Now, you have practiced one application of using intersections to solve a three-dimensional problem. Later, when you are able to create 3D faces, you may add them to represent the sides of the chimney.

Questions

1. What defines the true three-dimensionality of an entity?

2. Why are wireframe models constructed?

3. Explain the use of FILTERS in the entering of 3D coordinates.

4. Define *node* in the context of 3D modeling.

5. What advantage does a 3D polyline have over the regular 2D polyline? What disadvantage does it have?

6. Explain the projection technique of finding node points.

7. Explain the effect of the HIDE command on wireframe models.

8. What purposes does the orientation cube serve in the construction of models?

9. Basing your opinion on your experience with the labs so far, what might be the possible advantages of using multiple viewports? What disadvantages might there be?

Assignments

1. Produce the wireframe model illustrated in Figure 6.3. This requires the application of filters. The size of the model is not important. Save the model as SLOPE.

2. Draw the wireframe model illustrated in Figure 6.5.

3. Move on to the wireframe model illustrated in Figure 6.7. Can you produce this one? Save it as ROOF.

4. Generate the wireframe model of the structure shown in Figure 6.47. Save it as STRUC.

5. Keeping in mind that extrusion can be used for the circular base and the cylindrical center column, produce the wireframe model of the part shown in Figure 6.48. Use wireframe on the base and the four ribs. Save it as BPLATE.

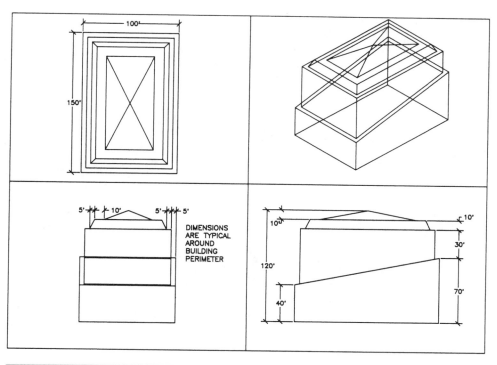

Figure 6.47
Wireframe building

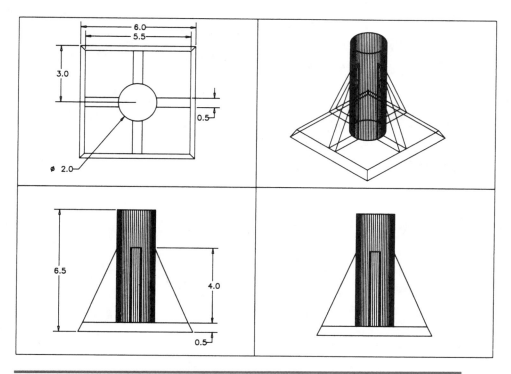

Figure 6.48
Wireframe baseplate

CHAPTER 7

Creation of a Shell

Overview

Now we're coming to the exciting stuff. In this chapter, for the first time, you will create a covered surface, add the possibility of texture and shade, and hide lines and entire objects. Your models will start having a truly 3D appearance. Most users, after reaching this point, begin to feel really accomplished. As the visual feedback becomes more satisfying, you'll begin to feel more confident in your use of 3D.

Concepts Explored

- The implications of adding surfaces to a model
- The area definition technique of creating surfaces
- How to create planar surfaces
- How to apply surface techniques to solve problems
- The creation of surface models.

7.1 Introduction

In Chapter 6, we explored the concept behind wireframe modeling. For construction purposes, wireframe is extremely important. However, trying to study a complex wireframe model can be quite confusing. But add a shell to cover the wireframe, and the model becomes much easier to perceive. And if you add shading, then the overall three-dimensionality of the model becomes obvious. Figure 7.1 illustrates how covering and shading a wireframe creates a more effective 3D model: Part A is a wireframe display, part B shows the same model with a shell, and part C shows the shell shaded.

Each planar area of a shell is referred to as a *surface*. To display a model with hidden lines removed or shaded, surfaces must be present. To create a surface, you can use entity thickness, which was explained in Chapter 5. As you will recall, thickness was cited as the easiest way to build a three-dimensional model. Another method used to create a surface is area definition, which is simply the defining of an area to be covered by a planar surface.

Sometimes area definition and extrusion can be combined. The three entities that make use of area definition are 2D polylines, 2D solids, and 3D faces.

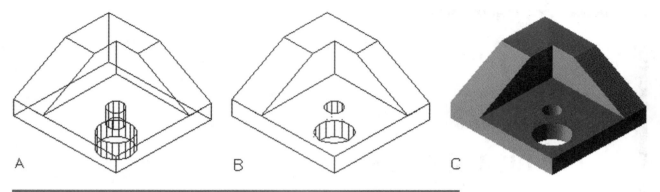

Figure 7.1
Wireframe model, with hidden lines removed and shaded

The first two entities use a combination of area definition and extrusion, but 3D faces use area definitions exclusively.

A fourth type of entity, called a region, can be used to cover an area with a surface. Its formation makes use of solid modeling commands, which are explained in more detail in Chapter 9. However, the region is mentioned here so that you may be aware, earlier in your creation, of its capabilities.

7.2 Polylines and Solids Revisited

We have already discussed how polylines and solids (not to be confused with solid modeling) are relevant to 3D construction. We know that each entity will allow extrusion of its respective form to create a 3D shape. But because both polylines and solids can acquire width or area, they also can form a surface over that area, regardless of their shapes.

Figure 7.2 shows some of the various forms that a 2D polyline with width can describe. Notice that each time the polyline changes direction, an edge bisects the width and separates the polyline into segments. Now look at Figure 7.3. Part A shows an area defined using the SOLID command. Whenever a new area is defined here, a line divides the two segmented areas, just like in the polyline. These dividing lines in both polylines and solids can be quite numerous, depending on the complexity of the area defined, and sometimes they result in a distracting surface. (Later, you will see how this problem can be overcome by using 3D faces.)

Solids are defined through a triangular process. Look at part B of Figure 7.3 and note the order of definition (or the order in which each area to be covered by a solid is defined). Figure 7.3C shows what happens if the wrong order is used.

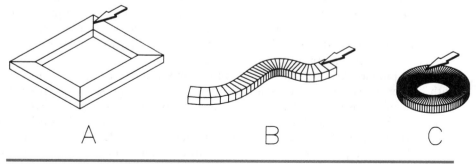

Figure 7.2
Polylines with width and thickness

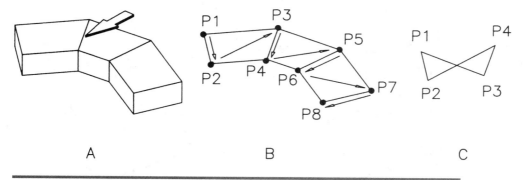

A   B   C

Figure 7.3
Solids showing order of creation

7.3   **3D Faces**

The 3D face uses area definition to form its shape by simply specifying the node points that define the perimeter of the desired area, and using 3D face forms to cover it. Refer to Figure 7.4. A 3D face is a true 3D entity because it is not bound by the current UCS working plane. You can pick node points at any 3D coordinates to form the face. Refer to Figure 7.5. Part A shows the four pick points used to create a 2D solid. Even though the points picked should create a sloped edge, the 2D solid is bound by the current UCS. Part B shows the creation of a 3D face. It is not bound by the current UCS. However, a 3D face is still a planar (flat) entity that uses only coordinates that will form a flat plane. Without these coordinates, the 3D face will become nonplanar and you may get unexpected results when hiding edges or rendering. In addition to this, remember not to add thickness to a 3D face. Its purpose is to cover an area, not to be extruded.

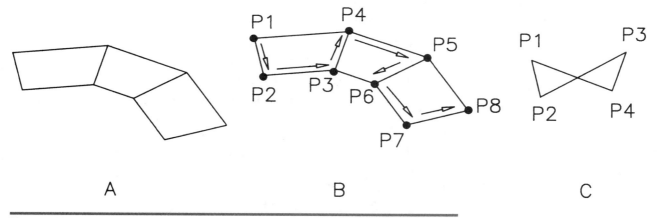

A   B   C

Figure 7.4
3DFACE command showing order of creation

3D Viewpoint

The HIDE Command and 3D Faces

Sometimes the HIDE command does not perform perfectly. It will leave behind dots on the screen where 3D faces meet or where entities intersect surfaces such as 3D faces. There is no immediate remedy to this; instead, you must use regions rather than 3D faces.

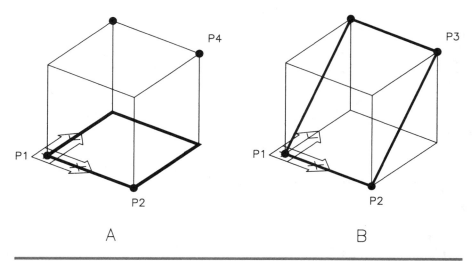

Figure 7.5
Defining a 2D solid versus a 3D face using 3D coordinates

3D Face Definition

The act of defining a 3D face is similar to that of defining a 2D solid: You specify node points around its perimeter. Looking back to Figure 7.3, notice that the definition of 2D solids requires a triangular pattern. Now refer to Figure 7.4 for the 3D face definition, which is a rectangular definition. If you specify the node points of a 3D face in a triangular pattern for four points, you produce the bow-tie shape shown in part C of Figure 7.4.

The following is the command to form the shape illustrated in part B:

```
Command: 3DFACE
First point: pick point P1
Second point: pick point P2
Third point: pick point P3
Fourth point: pick point P4 (If you press <Enter> instead of
picking a fourth point, a triangular 3D face is created.)
Third point: pick point P5 (The third and fourth pick points are
repeated allowing connected faces. Pressing enter at this point stops the
command.)
Fourth point: pick point P6
Third point: pick point P7
Fourth point: pick point P8
Third point: press <Enter> to exit from the command
```

3D Viewpoint

Order of Picking 3D Faces Points

When you pick the points to define a 3D face, you pick in a rectangular order. When you pick points to define a 2D solid, you pick in a triangular order.

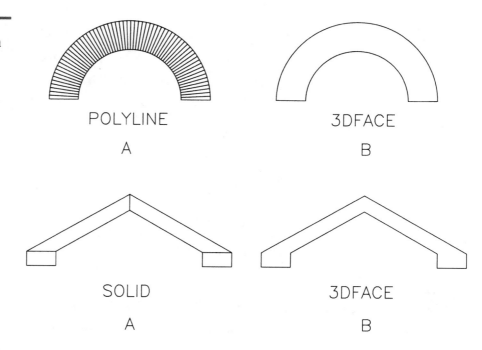

Figure 7.6
A polyline and a solid compared to a 3D face with invisible edges

POLYLINE
A

3DFACE
B

SOLID
A

3DFACE
B

7.4 3D Faces Invisible Edges

Unlike 3D polylines with width or 2D solids, the 3D face entity can have some or all invisible edges. Figure 7.6 shows a polyline and a solid in contrast to the same shape using 3D faces. By using invisible edges, an open, uncluttered area can be formed.

The procedure for making 3D face edges invisible usually occurs during the 3D face-creation stage. Just before picking the point that will start the invisible edge, select the Invisible option. Part A of Figure 7.7 shows the desired outcome and part B shows the pick points. Just before picking point P3, enter I for invisible and pick points P3 and P4. Then, before picking point P5, again enter I, and the pick points P5 through P8. The edges between points P3 and P4 as well as P5 and P6 would be invisible, as illustrated in part C. If you need to see the invisible edges temporarily, you can set the system variable SPLFRAME to 1 and REGEN the screen. All invisible edges will be displayed as shown in part D. To return to invisibility, set the variable back to 0 and REGEN.

To modify the edges of an already created 3D face, use the DDMODIFY command. You can move the node points and change the visibility of any edge.

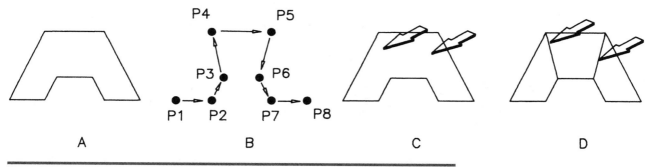

A

P4   P5

P3   P6

P1   P2   P7   P8

B

C

D

Figure 7.7
Creating a 3D face with invisible edges

3D Viewpoint

Forcing the Display of Invisible Edges

If the SPLFRAME variable is set to 1, invisible edges of 3D faces will be forced to be displayed. But don't forget to use the REGEN command after setting the variable to update the display.

In addition, an AutoLISP program, EDGE.LSP, is available that allows the user to change selectively the visibility of 3D face edges. To use EDGE.LSP, simply type EDGE on the command line; it will load and be ready to use. It will allow you to select the edges to turn invisible or visible by picking those edges on the screen.

7.5 A Special Application of Invisible Edges

One of the most cumbersome tasks in surface modeling is creating a hole in a surface. Figure 7.8A shows a desired model with a hole in the top surface. If the cube were created in the normal fashion, with lines or a polyline and two arcs added, the wireframe model would look acceptable, as Figure 7.8B shows. However, when hidden line removal is used, the model will either have no surface covering the top, as in Figure 7.8C, or have a surface that covers the entire top, obscuring the arcs, as shown in Figure 7.8D.

To create a hole, you must first create your model using a combination of 3D faces with invisible edges. Having to repeat the same steps every time you need to create a hole on a surface would be time consuming. Luckily, as Figures 7.9 and 7.10 illustrate, there is an initial hole model that, once created, can be used on any surface that requires a hole. It can be used in its entirety or in pieces to create half or quarter fillets. The actual procedure for creating this hole model is outlined in Lab 7.A.

Refer to Figure 7.9. Here you can see the various stages of display. Part A shows the entire hole model with the edges visible. Notice the square perimeter. This will give the model only four edges to the hole, instead of many around the arc. Part B shows the hole and the various marker points. The marker points will be used to snap to when additional 3D faces are created around the perimeter. Part C shows only the hole; the invisible edges are hidden and the marker points layer is frozen.

In Figure 7.10, you can see the various stages of applying the hole model to a surface. Part A shows the hole model, with the marker points showing, placed on the area to be covered. Part B shows the addition of four more 3D faces connecting onto the square perimeter of the hole model. These four new faces also have invisible edges. Part C shows the final model; the thickness given to the arcs completes the internal shape of the hole.

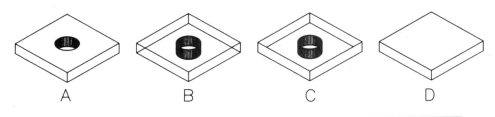

A   B   C   D

Figure 7.8
Difficulties in creating a hole

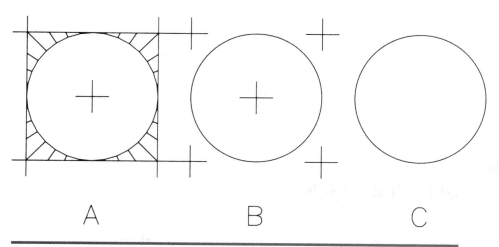

Figure 7.9
A hole model created with 3D faces

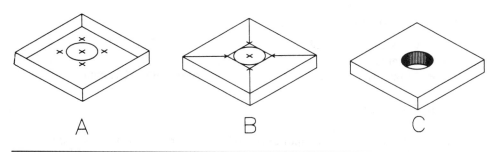

Figure 7.10
Application of the hole model

7.6 Creating Surfaces with Regions

Regions are two-dimensional enclosed areas that you create from a closed form such as a polyline or circle or lines that form a complete loop. Regions can be used in place of 3D faces to cover complex areas.

Prior to Release 13 of AutoCAD, regions were available only through the external AME (Advanced Modeling Extension) solid-modeling program. Now that 3D solids are an integral part of AutoCAD, regions are also available to be used. The same commands that are used to create complex composite 3D solids are used to create complex composite regions. Detailed explanations on the use of regions and 3D solids are explained in Chapters 9 through 12.

At this point, let's take a look at the basics of region creation. Refer to Figure 7.11. Part C of the figure shows the final desired model—a hole in an irregular shape. Part A shows the creation of a closed polyline, and part B shows the creation of a circle to represent the hole. Now the REGION command would be used to turn the polyline and the circle into separate regions. Once you generate regions, you can use the SUBTRACT command from solid modeling. It can also be used to subtract one region from another. In this case, pick the polyline region and then subtract the circle region from it. The result would be a composite region that would be a surface with a hole through it. If you want the hole to appear to extend into the model, you would need to add arcs with thickness, as you would with the 3D face method.

Figure 7.11
Creating a hole by using two regions

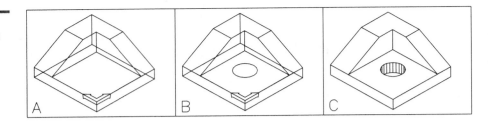

Lab 7.A

Surfaced Hole Model

Purposes

Lab 7.A will show you how to use surface modeling techniques to create a surfaced model of a hole. This model will be used again in the next lab. (*Note:* If you are going to use regions to create a hole instead of using 3D faces, you can proceed directly to Lab 7.B.)

Objectives

You will be able to:

- Construct a surfaced model.
- Create 3D faces.
- Make use of the Invisible Edge option of the 3DFACE command.

Primary Command

3DFACE—Invisible Edge

Final Model

Figure 7.12 shows the hole model you'll be creating with surfaces visible.

Procedure

1. Start a new drawing called HOLE with the following settings:

```
Units  =  decimal
Limits  =  −1,−1 to 2,2
Grid  =  .25 (ON)
Snap Incr  =  0.25 (ON)
Elevation  =  0
Thickness  =  0
Current Layer  =  MARKER
UCS  =  WCS
```

Figure 7.12
Hole model with surfaces visible

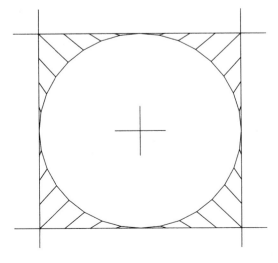

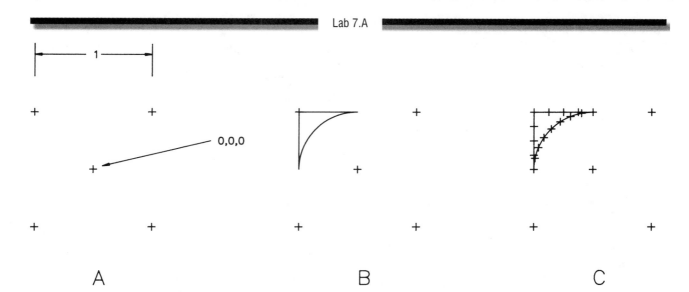

Figure 7.13
Initial creation steps

Creating Node Markers

2. First, place markers at the five snap locations on the hole model, as shown in Figure 7.13A. These markers will be needed when the hole is placed on a surface. Point entities will be used as markers.

Creating a Temporary Quarter Arc and Lines

3. Create a quarter arc and lines as shown in Figure 7.13B. These will be used for construction purposes only and will be deleted later.

Dividing Up the Temporary Geometry

4. Set the PDMODE to 2 so that + will mark the division points, and set the PDSIZE to 0.01.

5. Using the DIVIDE command, divide the arc into eight divisions and divide the lines into four divisions. Refer to Figure 7.13C.

6. Using the POINT command, place a point at each end of the arc.

7. Delete the lines and arc, but leave the node points.

Adding the Invisible 3D Faces

8. Create and make current a layer called HOLESURF.

9. Set system variable SPLFRAME to 1. At this point, it is desirable to see the invisible edges as they are created.

10. Using the 3DFACE command, create a 3D face in the order shown in Figure 7.14, parts A to D. Remember to use the Invisible option for the start of each edge on every 3D face. Then, use the MIRROR command to mirror the newly created surfaces.

11. Delete the construction nodes, except for the five original markers created in step 2 and the two that mark the ends of the arc.

12. Set system variable SPLFRAME to 0 and REGEN the screen. The surface should disappear, leaving only the markers.

Figure 7.14
Creating invisible 3D faces

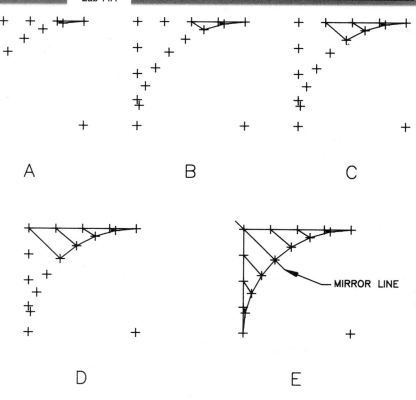

A   B   C

D   E

MIRROR LINE

13. Save the model at this point as HOLE4, a name that alludes to the fact that you will need to use this model four times to make a complete hole. HOLE4 will be used as a quarter of a hole, useful for fillets.

Mirroring to Make Half a Hole

14. Set system variable SPLFRAME to 1. Again, it is desirable to see the invisible edges as they are created.

15. Use the MIRROR command to mirror the quarter hole to make it a half hole. Refer to Figure 7.15.

16. Set system variable SPLFRAME to 0 and REGEN the screen. The surface should disappear, leaving only the markers.

17. Save the model now as HOLE2 (half a hole).

Mirroring to Make a Complete Hole

18. Set system variable SPLFRAME to 1. Once more, it is desirable to see the invisible edges as they are created.

19. Using the MIRROR command, complete the hole as shown in Figure 7.16.

20. Set system variable SPLFRAME to 0 and REGEN the screen. The surface should disappear, leaving only the markers.

21. Save the model now as HOLE1 (the "whole" hole).

At this point, you now have three hole models: HOLE1, HOLE2, and HOLE4. HOLE1 will be used in the next lab.

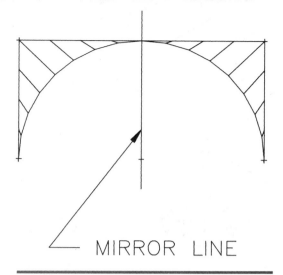

Figure 7.15
Mirroring the quarter-hole surfaces

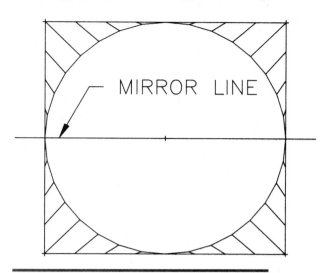

Figure 7.16
Mirroring the half-hole surfaces

Lab 7.B	# Surfaced Angle Plate

Purpose

Lab 7.B will show you how to use surface modeling techniques to add surfaces to the wireframe model created in Lab 6.A in Chapter 6.

Objectives

You will be able to:

- Create 3D faces.
- Make use of the Invisible Edge option of the 3DFACE command.

Primary Command

`3DFACE—Invisible Edge`

Final Model

Figure 7.17 shows the angle plate model with the surfaces you'll be adding.

Procedure

1. Open the model ANGPLT that was created in Lab 6.A. Use these settings:

```
Units  =  decimal
Limits  =  −1,−1 to 8,8
Grid  =  0.25
Snap Incr  =  0.25
Elevation  =  0
Thickness  =  0
Current Layer  =  SURFACE
UCS  =  WCS
Viewport Configuration  =  ISO1
Pdmode  =  2
Pdsize  =  0.125
```

Adding 3D Faces

2. Using the 3DFACE command, add faces to the areas shown in Figures 7.18, 7.19, and 7.20. (*Note:* The Invisible option must be used just before point P3 on Figure 7.19 is entered.)

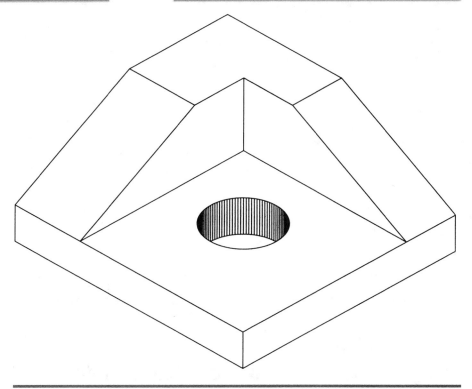

Figure 7.17
Angle plate model with surfaces

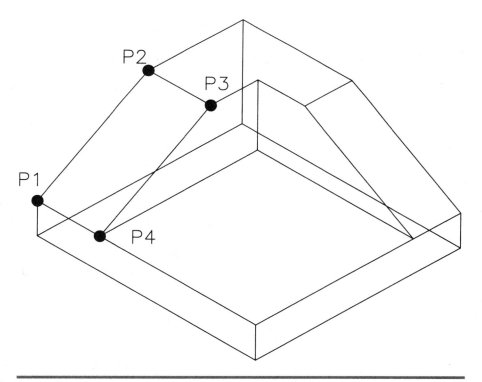

Figure 7.18
Sloped 3D face

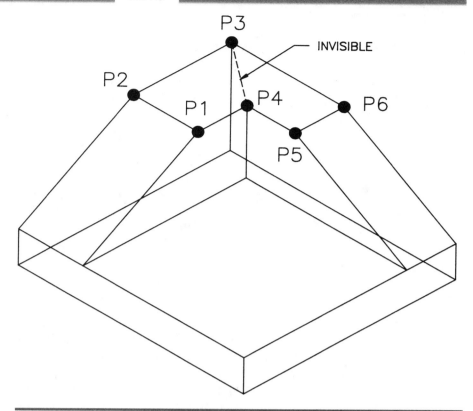

Figure 7.19
Top 3D face

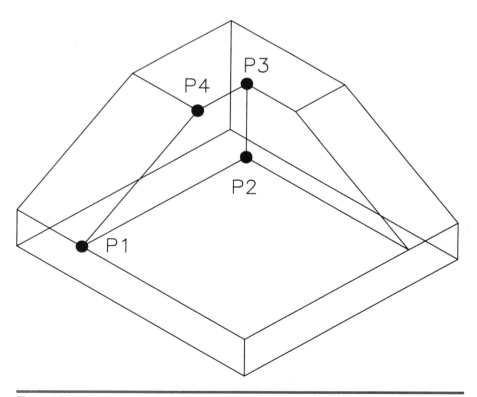

Figure 7.20
Upright 3D face

Figure 7.21
Side 3D face

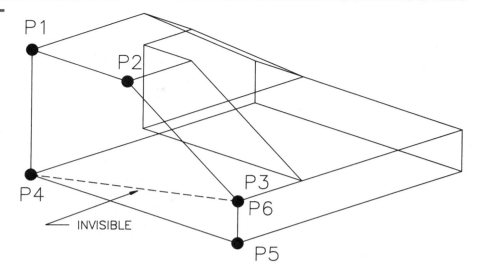

Changing the Viewpoint

3. Using the VPOINT coordinated command, enter the coordinates: –2, –2, 1.

4. Using the 3DFACE command, add a face as shown in Figure 7.21. (*Note:* The Invisible option must be used just before point P3 is entered.)
   Add 3D faces to other surfaces around the model except for the top and bottom where the hole is to be placed in step 5. Use the HIDE command periodically to determine missing faces.

Adding the Hole Model

The HOLE1 model from Lab 7.A will now be added to the top surface of the horizontal base plate. If you wish, attempt to use regions to create the hole surface as outlined in Section 7.6. If you use regions, replace steps 9 through 11 with the procedure outlined in Section 7.6.

5. Restore the working plane called TPLATE (created in Lab 6.A).

6. Split the screen into two equal viewports similar to Figure 7.22.

7. Activate the left viewport. Use the PLAN<UCS> command to display the top view.

8. Create a layer called HOLE, and make it current.

Figure 7.22
Inserting the HOLE1 model

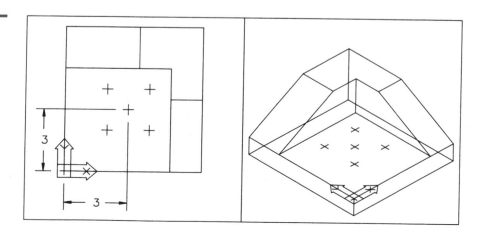

Figure 7.23
Adding the perimeter 3D faces

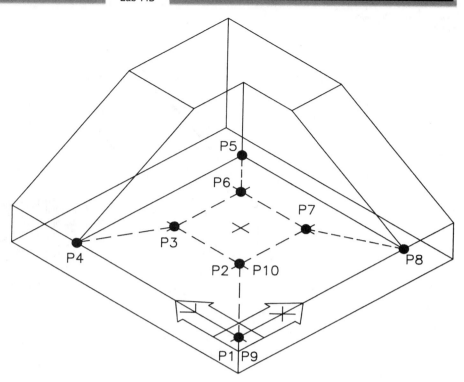

9. Keeping the top viewport active, use the INSERT command to insert the model called HOLE1. Place it as shown in Figure 7.22. Give it an *X* and *Y* scale factor of 2.

10. If the invisible edges of the hole are visible, set the system variable SPLFRAME to 0. Use the REGEN command.

Adding the Invisible-Edged 3D Faces

Invisible-edged 3D faces will now be added around the perimeter of the hole model.

11. Figure 7.23 shows the proper order for defining the areas of the 3D faces. Define the 3D face areas as outlined in Figure 7.23. When creating the 3D faces, you must follow these three considerations: *First,* use object snap endpoint to lock onto the corners of the plate. *Second,* use object snap node to snap to the four corner markers of the hole model. *Third,* use the Invisible option before digitizing every point—even the very first point (P1).

Adding the Arcs

Two arcs need to be added that will give an inside surface to the hole. The two arcs will have a negative thickness that goes from the top of the plate to the bottom. Create the arcs using the Center, Start, and End options.

12. Using the ELEV command, set the elevation to 0 and the thickness to –1.

13. Add the two arcs as shown in Figure 7.24. Both arcs should have a diameter of 2 to match the hole model.

14. Turn off or freeze the layer called MARKERS.

15. Restore the ISO1 viewport configuration.

Figure 7.24
Adding two arcs that have thickness

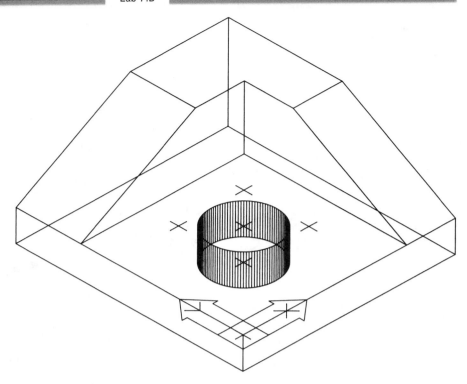

16. Return the variables PDMODE and PDSIZE to 0.

17. Use the HIDE command. The display should look similar to Figure 7.17.

    There are times when the HIDE command does not perform perfectly. It will leave behind dots on the screen. These usually are pieces of entities that show through surface joints. In the case of this model, some of the arcs with thickness may show through the 3D face joints.

18. Save the model as ANGPLT.

Lab 7.C

Surfaced Coffeemaker Model

Purpose

Lab 7.C will show you how to use surface modeling techniques to create a surfaced model of a coffeemaker. This model will be used again in Chapter 9.

Objectives

You will be able to:

- Construct a surfaced model.
- Create 3D faces.
- Make use of the Invisible Edge option of the 3DFACE command.

Primary Command

3DFACE—Invisible Edge

Final Model

Figure 7.25 shows the surfaced coffeemaker model you'll be creating.

Procedure

1. Start a new drawing called COFMK (COFfeeMaKer) with the following settings:

   ```
   Units  =  decimal
   Limits =  −1,−1 to 11,8
   ```

```
Grid     =  1
Snap Incr  =  1
Elevation  =  0
Thickness  =  12
Current Layer  =  OCUBE
UCS  =  WCS
```

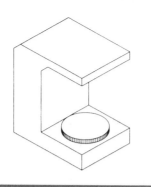

Figure 7.25
Coffeemaker model with surfaces

Creating an Orientation Cube

2. Split the screen into two equal viewports, as shown in Figure 7.26.

3. Activate the left viewport, and use the PLAN command to display a top view of WCS.

4. With the thickness set to 12, use the LINE command to draw the box, as shown in Figure 7.26.

Creating a Side Working Plane

5. Activate the right viewport, and use the VPOINT command to set the coordinates, 1, –1, 1.

6. Use the 3Point option of the UCS command and create a working plane, as shown in Figure 7.27. Name it FRONT. Display the plan view of the current UCS.

Adding Extruded Lines

7. Use the ELEV command to set the thickness to –7. Keep the elevation set to 0. Create a layer called SURF, and make it current.

8. Using lines, draw around the perimeter to create the profile shown in Figure 7.28. (Use increment snap, or relative, or polar coordinates, but not object snap.)

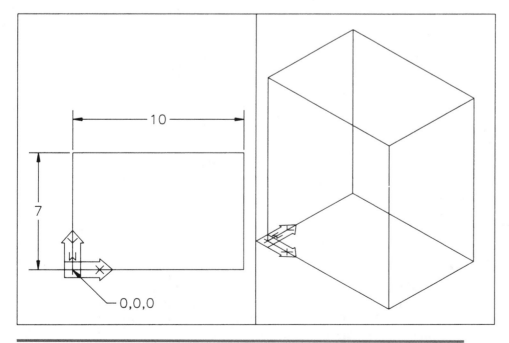

Figure 7.26
Orientation cube

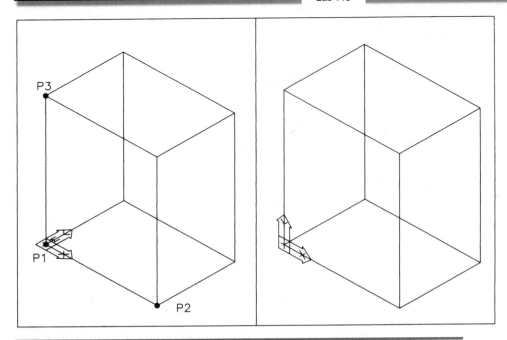

Figure 7.27
Defining the FRONT working plane

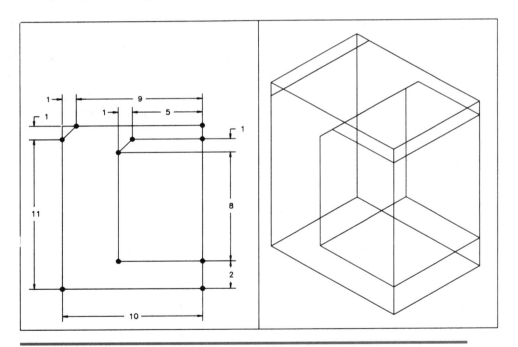

Figure 7.28
Adding extruded lines to create the profile

Adding the 3D Faces

9. Using the 3DFACE command, create faces, as shown in Figure 7.29. Follow the specific order shown. Use the Invisible option just before entering points P3, P5, and P7. (Use increment snap, or relative, or polar coordinates, but not object snap.)

10. Activate the isometric viewport and make the invisible 3D face edge visible by setting the SPLFRAME variable to 1. REGEN the screen.

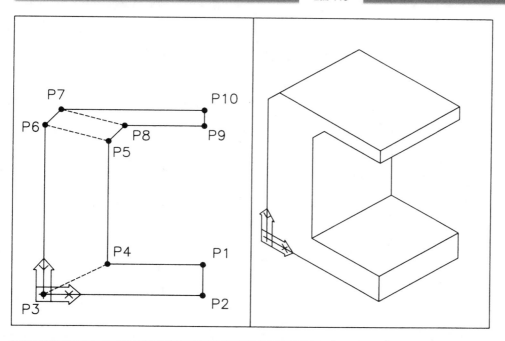

Figure 7.29
Adding the side 3D face

11. Copy the newly created 3D face to the other side of the profile, and then return the 3D face edges back to invisibility. Freeze layer OCUBE.

Creating a Lower Working Plane

12. Using the UCS command, create a working plane, as shown in Figure 7.30.

Adding the Warmer Plate

13. Using the ELEV command, set the thickness property to 0.5 and elevation to 0.

Figure 7.30
Creating the lower working plane

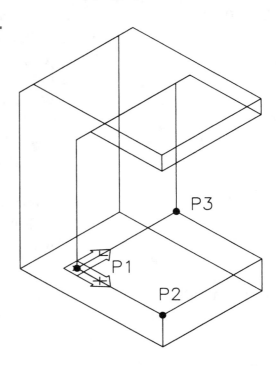

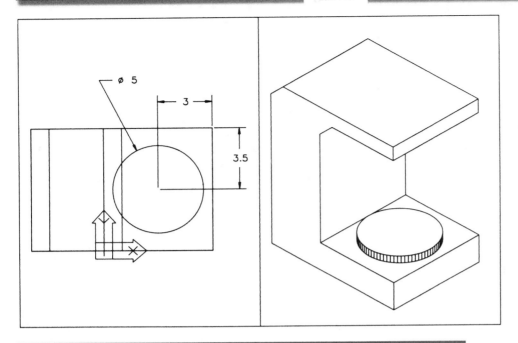

Figure 7.31
Adding the warmer plate

14. Activate the top-view viewport, and add a circle as shown in Figure 7.31.

15. Activate the isometric view, and use the HIDE command.

16. Save the model as COFMK.

Questions

1. What function do surfaces perform?

2. How can surfaces be created out of the properties of an entity?

3. What is the drawback of using 2D polylines and 2D solids to create surfaces?

4. What is the difference between the order of entering nodes for solids and the order of entering nodes for 3D faces?

5. What is the limitation of 3D faces?

6. How does the current UCS (working plane) control the creation of a 3D face?

7. Explain the procedure for creating invisible edges on 3D faces.

8. Describe the procedure for showing the invisible edges of 3D faces.

9. What is the benefit of using invisible edges when creating the hole model?

Assignments

1. Restore the BOLT model from Lab 5.A. Add a surface to the top of the bolt head. Invisible edges are required. Once the head has a surface on it, use the HIDE command and notice how different the model looks.

2. After restoring the INCA model from Lab 6.B, add surfaces over the wire-frame. Once that is done, use the HIDE command on the surfaced model.

3. Restore the model ROOF from Assignment 3 in Chapter 6 and add surfaces. Once that is done, use the HIDE command on the surfaced model.

4. Restore the model STRUC from Assignment 4 in Chapter 6 and add the missing surfaces. Once that is done, use the HIDE command on the surfaced model.

5. Create a NUT that will match the BOLT surfaced in Assignment 1. Refer to Lab 5.A for the size of the head of the bolt and use the same size for the nut. (*Hint:* The HOLE1 model is required to place a hole through a polygon or you can use 2 regions.) The BOLT and NUT models will be used again in Chapter 13.

CHAPTER 8

Elaborate Surfaces

Overview

In this final chapter of Part 3, you will create covered surfaces that either intersect or run parallel to each other, further enhancing the modeling you have been doing. What you learn in this chapter are the ideas and skills behind the ultimate in 3D modeling. The techniques presented here are used to model, for example, an automobile chassis, a 3D terrain for training simulations, a production for a commercial video presentation, and a cinematic special effect. Also included in this chapter are simple 3D geometric constructs that can be used as building blocks to create 3D models quickly.

Concepts Explored

- The timesaving methods that create elaborate surfaces through automatic means
- The creation and manipulation of 3D geometric constructs
- The various methods of generating 3D polygon meshes and how these methods are specialized
- How to construct surfaced models using polygon meshes.

8.1 Introduction

With the information that has been presented up to this point, you could, given time and patience, create any complex surface. However, you'll find the job of creating complex shapes much easier after you learn more of AutoCAD's commands. The commands presented here will allow you to create, in only a few steps, multiple planar surfaces to form meshes that can cover any type of area. These commands link together many or few polygons to create convoluted meshed shapes automatically. This ability to generate multiple surfaces makes the creation of irregular surfaces much less arduous and time consuming. All you need to do is create a wireframe or series of nodes to control the formation of the multiple polygons. Figure 8.1A shows the wireframe model used to generate the surface-covered form pictured in Figure 8.1B.

Some of AutoCAD's commands are more automatic than others, depending on the type of area to be covered. The area type also controls the number

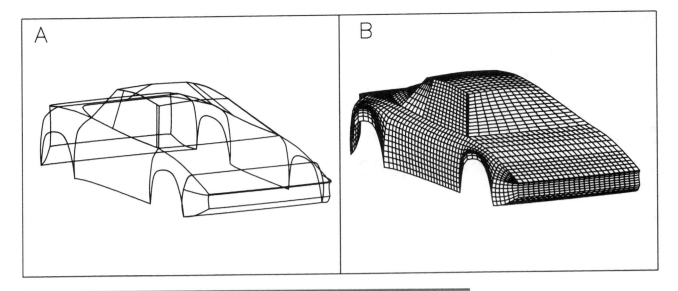

Figure 8.1
Wireframe model automatically covered with surfaces

of wires or nodes that may be required to achieve the desired shape. Area types may be cylindrical, conical, parallel, wave, or totally irregular, like terrain. Each multiple surface command has its own area of specialty, which we'll explain later.

8.2 3D Objects

Before we begin our exploration of mesh generation, we need to discuss an even simpler method of model creation. In the ways they are used and manipulated, 3D objects can be likened to building blocks. The constructs also are very similar in usage to their two-dimensional cousins; whereas the 2D user creates complex drawings by manipulating lines, circles, rectangles, polygons, and the like, the 3D user pieces together objects such as boxes, cones, and domes to form more complicated models. These 3D primitives, which can serve as the first step in the generation of complex shapes for the beginner or as a supplement for the advanced user, are really parts of a formulated program that AutoCAD uses to create a desired shape out of a series of 3D faces held together as a block (or mesh, as described by the software itself). With this program, the user simply fills in the missing data, such as length, height, or radius, and AutoCAD combines 3D faces to create a shape to the user's specifications. Once created, the new form is treated like a single object, even though it might be made of many separate3D faces.

Figure 8.2 lists the different 3D primitive objects and illustrates some of the shapes that can be made from them. The input data that these various 3D objects require from the user is given in the following list.

3D OBJECTS	REQUIRED INPUT
Box 3D	Corner/length/width or cube/height/rotation
Pyramid	1st base point/2nd base/3rd base/tetrahedron or fourth base/ridge (1st and 2nd) or top or apex point
Wedge	Corner/length/width/height/rotation
Mesh	1st corner/2nd corner/3rd corner/4th corner/mesh msize (2 to 256)/mesh nsize

Figure 8.2
3D primitive objects

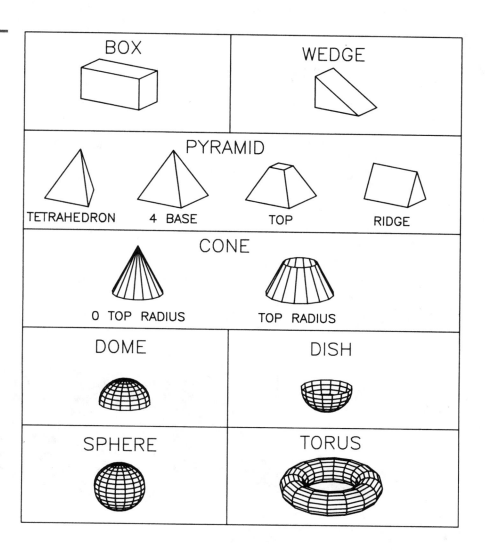

Cone	Base center/base diameter/top diameter/height/number of segments
Sphere	Center/diameter/number of longitudinal segments/number of latitudinal segments
Dome	Center/diameter/number of longitudinal segments/number of latitudinal segments
Dish	Center/diameter/number of longitudinal segments/number of latitudinal segments
Torus	Center/torus diameter/tube diameter

When using the cone, sphere, dome, dish, and torus, entering a limited number of segments can produce some interesting shapes. For example, if 16 segments are used with a sphere, the final curved shape will look moderately smooth, but if only four segments for the longitude and two for latitude are used, a crystal will be formed. Refer to Figure 8.3.

The 3D objects can be accessed from the sidebar (screen) menu or the pull-down menus. Once they have been loaded they can be used just by typing the shape name preceded by AI_ (for example, AI_BOX) at the command prompt. The purpose of the AI_ prefix is to differentiate the surface commands from the solids commands of the same name. To access the 3D objects from the pull-down menu, select Draw/Surfaces/3D Surfaces.

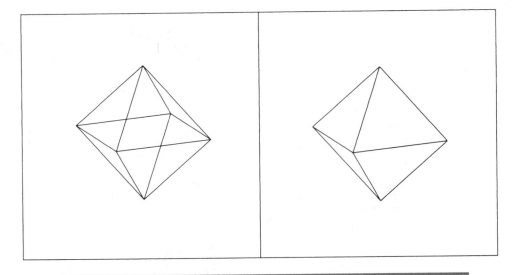

Figure 8.3
Generating a sphere with only eight surfaces

8.3 3D Polygon Meshes

To cover an area with a number of linked surfaces, AutoCAD uses what is called a *polygon mesh*. This mesh can form a flat surface or approximate a curved one. It is defined by the number of segments in an *M* and *N* direction. (These letters are used to ensure that there will be no confusion with the axis directions *X, Y,* and *Z.*) The number of mesh segments in any one direction controls the smoothness or roughness of the surface. AutoCAD uses two variables for this control: SURFTAB1 and SURFTAB2.

The SURFTAB variables control the number of faces created along each axis of the final form. The higher the number, the more faces created along the axis. Refer to Figure 8.6, shown later, for a demonstration of how the TABSURF command works. When using this command, faces are created around one axis. The SURFTAB1 variable controls the number of faces created. Refer to Figure 8.7, also shown later, for a demonstration of the REVSURF command. In that figure, faces are created in two axes and as a result both SURFTAB1 and SURFTAB2 variables are used. Try to limit the number of faces using the SURFTAB variable to the number necessary for your particular model. Using large values can create a large model and slow down some operations, such as hidden line removal and rendering. A value of 12 will be sufficient in most cases.

3D Mesh

The 3DMESH command will construct the most irregularly covered surface. It is used predominantly by outside programs to generate an irregular terrain.

SURFTAB1 and SURFTAB2 Variable Values

Because these variables control the number of surfaces created using commands such as REVSURF and EDGESURF, the best way to determine the number is to ascertain how close the viewer will be to the object. If the view is very close, a large number will give a smooth effect. If objects will be in the distance, then a lower number will suffice. A median starting value is 12 for each. When using REVSURF with polylines, each polyline segment will be divided by the SURFTAB1 or SURFTAB2 value, requiring a smaller SURFTAB value for polylines.

AutoCAD refers to the meshes generated as topologically rectangular polygon meshes. Basically, the area to be covered is divided into a number of nodes or vertices in the *M* and *N* directions. The minimum number of divisions in the *M* and *N* directions is 2, and the maximum is 256. Then, each vertex of the array is given a three-dimensional coordinate. After all the coordinates have been entered, AutoCAD constructs a mesh of polygons. The corners of the polygons are the coordinates that were just entered. See Figure 8.4.

The required input for the 3DMESH command is as follows.

```
Command: 3DMESH
Mesh M size: enter an integer from 2 to 256
Mesh N size: enter an integer from 2 to 256
Vertex (m,n): a three-dimensional coordinate is
required input
```

The Vertex input request is repeated until all the vertices have been given coordinates.

For a detailed application of 3DMESH, see Chapter 23.

The PFACE Command

The PFACE command is designed primarily for use with AutoLISP and ADS applications. It is similar to the 3DMESH command in that it requires vertex coordinates to be entered. But with the PFACE command, each face may have any number of vertices. As a result, entering the input required for this command can be a very time-consuming process.

Figure 8.4
3DMESH command

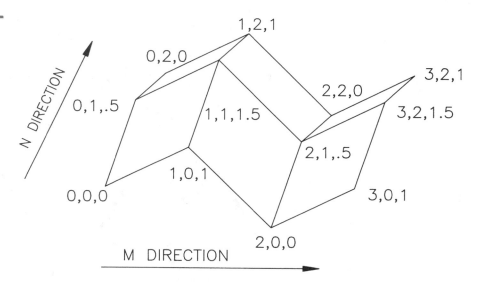

149

Ruled Surfaces

The RULESURF command is useful for generating a surface between two defining curves or lines. Each curve or line is divided based on the SURFTAB1 variable, and connecting polygon faces are formed along the divisions. The same number of divisions is used on both defining entities. However, since the size and shape of each defining entity may be different, each created polygon face twists and turns to accommodate both entities—starting on one defining entity and stretching to the other. The most common application of the RULESURF command is for radial development of conical or semiconical shapes. Examine Figure 8.5 for the creation of a semiconical form referred to as a transition piece (square to round). The required input for the RULESURF command follows:

```
Command: RULESURF
Select first defining curve: even though a curve is
requested, other entities can be selected
Select second defining curve: as above, lines,
points, arcs, circles, 2D or 3D polylines can be
selected
```

Extruded Surfaces

The TABSURF command is used to create a series of parallel polygon faces extruded over a desired area. A path for the polygons to follow and a direction/extrusion vector are required input. The number of faces is controlled by the SURFTAB1 variable. One common application of the TABSURF command is to produce a curve that defines the path of the faces to be generated and a line that travels obliquely to the curve that controls the length of the faces. Figure 8.6 shows such an application in the creation of an offset duct or pipe. The pipe is traveling along one axis but must be offset to avoid some obstacle. Both the starting and ending diameters are the same, but each has a different center location. Because each face created is parallel to the next, this method of surface creation is referred to as *parallel development*. Refer to Figure 8.6 for the method of creation, and see the next description of the TABSURF command's required input.

Figure 8.5
RULESURF command

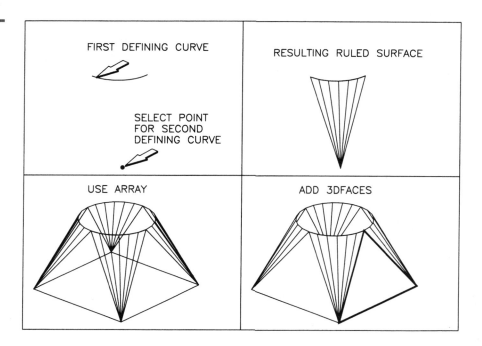

Figure 8.6
TABSURF command

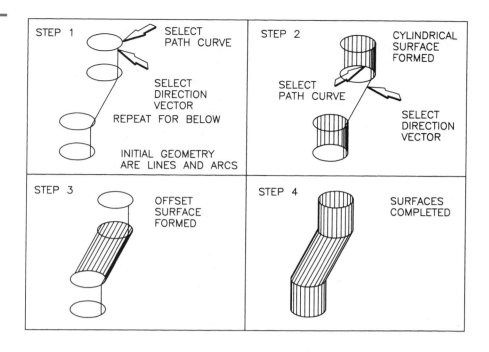

Command: **TABSURF**
Select path curve: **a line, arc, circle, or 2D or 3D polyline can be selected to control the path the polygons will follow**
Select direction vector: **the entity selected now will control the length of the polygons and the direction they will be pointing; only a line or open 2D or 3D polyline is acceptable as a direction vector**

Revolved Surfaces

The REVSURF command is used to generate surfaces that create circular forms such as light bulbs and soda bottles. A complete 360-degree form or a semicircular form can be created. Any type of profile can be swept around an axis to create the final shape; the only restriction is that the profile must be a single entity. To have a convoluted profile, a polyline is required. Depending on the application, it can be useful to apply the spline option of the PEDIT command to the polyline to smooth the sharp edges. The variables SURFTAB1 and SURFTAB2 are required for the REVSURF command. SURFTAB1 controls the number of surfaces around the axis, whereas SURFTAB2 controls the number of surfaces along the profile. Refer to Figure 8.7 for the application of the REVSURF command and note the following required input:

Command: **REVSURF**
Select path curve: **the entity selected now is the profile to be swept around an axis**
Select axis of revolution: **the entity selected now must be either a line or an open polyline; it controls the center axis of the final shape**
Start angle <0>: **this locates the position of the start of the surfaces**
Included angle (+=ccw -=cw)<Full circle>: **this sets the size of the surface in degrees**

Figure 8.7
REVSURF command

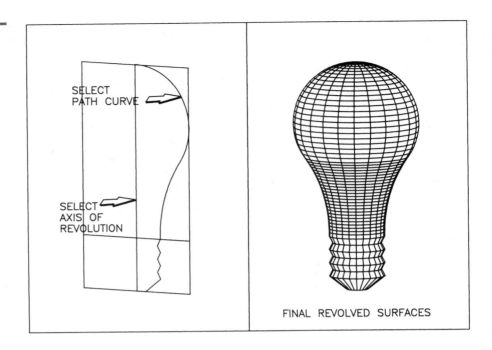

Edge Surfaces

The EDGESURF command is used to create a surface that is controlled by a boundary of four curves. A surface is interpolated between these four curves. The technical term for the surface is a *Coons surface patch*. The variable SURFTAB1 controls the number of divisions along the first curve picked and SURFTAB2 controls the density of the mesh in the other direction. *Note:* When creating the controlling curves, it is important to remember that they must form a completely enclosed area. If one of the corners is not closed, an error will result and AutoCAD will inform the user as to which edge is not touching.

Refer to Figure 8.8 for the application of the EDGESURF command. Its required input is listed next:

Figure 8.8
EDGESURF command

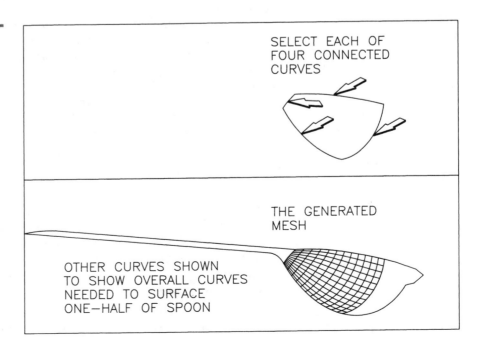

```
Command: EDGESURF
Select edge 1: select the first of the four connected
curves (lines, arcs, polylines can be used)
Select edge 2: select the second of the four con-
nected curves (lines, arcs, polylines can be used)
Select edge 3: select the third of the four connected
curves (lines, arcs, polylines can be used)
Select edge 4: select the fourth of the four con-
nected curves (lines, arcs, polylines can be used)
```

Modifying Meshes

Once a mesh has been created with any of the commands we have just discussed, it then can be modified to any desired shape. This is accomplished by
using the PEDIT command. This command, normally used to edit polylines,
can also edit meshes. When you use PEDIT, after you have identified the mesh
you wish to modify, you will be presented with various options that can be performed on the mesh, including vertex modification and mesh smoothing.

Note: You must be careful when modifying meshes because it is possible to
distort the surface mesh so much that it will affect hidden line removal and
rendering.

8.4 Surfaces Toolbar

The Surfaces toolbar can be used to create 3D objects and to access the various surface commands. The toolbar is displayed by checking the Surfaces box
from the Toolbars dialog box. The Toolbars dialog box is displayed by selecting
Toolbars from the View pull-down menu. If you move the cursor onto a tool
without picking it, a tooltip may appear. Tooltips are words that describe the
function of the tool. Tooltips can be turned on by checking the Show Tooltips
box in the Toolbars dialog box.

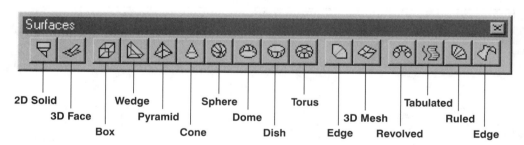

Lab 8.A

Coffeepot Surfaced Model

Purpose

Lab 8.A will show you how to use the REVSURF command to create a surfaced model of a coffeepot. This model will be used again in Assignment 1 in
Chapter 13.

Objectives

You will be able to:

■ Construct a surfaced model using the REVSURF command.
■ Create 3D faces.
■ Make use of the Invisible Edge option of the 3DFACE command.

Primary Commands

REVSURF
3DFACE—Invisible Edge

Final Model

Procedure

Figure 8.9 shows the coffeepot model you'll be creating.

Figure 8.9
Coffeepot model

1. Start a new drawing called COFPT (COFfeePoT) with the following settings. Use 3DSET as the prototype drawing.

```
Units  =  decimal
Limits  =  -3,-3 to 3,3
Grid  =  1
Snap Incr  =  0.25
Elevation  =  0
Thickness  =  0
Current Layer  =  PROFILE
UCS  =  WCS
Viewport Configuration  =  ORTHO1
```

Creating an Orientation Plane

With this model, it is better to use a single plane rather than a cube for orientation. The plane will represent the surface on which the profile to be swept will be drawn.

2. Use the ELEV command to set the thickness to 6.5.

3. Activate the top-view viewport, and draw a line 5.5 units long, as shown in Figure 8.10. The start point should be at -2.75, 0, 0.

Creating a Working Plane

4. Use the 3Point option of the UCS command to create a working plane that is aligned to the newly created orientation plane. Refer to Figure 8.11.

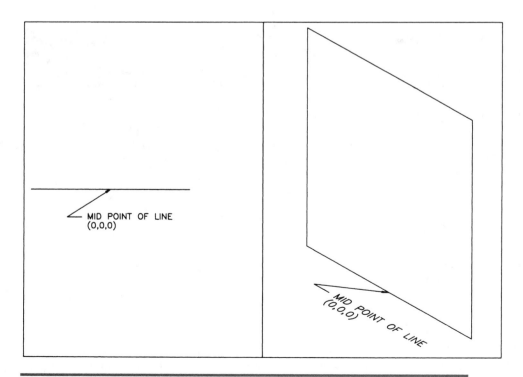

Figure 8.10
Creating an orientation plane

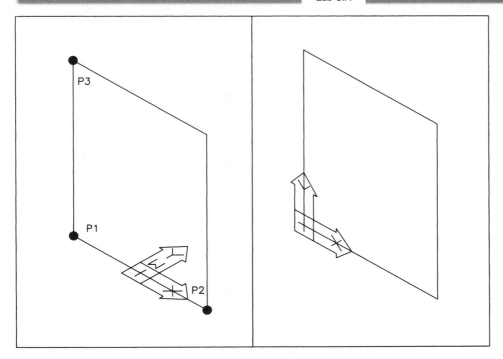

Figure 8.11
Creating a working plane

Drawing the Profile and Axis Line

5. Set the thickness back to 0.

6. Activate the front-view viewport.

7. Using PLINE, draw a profile to represent the edge of the pot. Figure 8.12 shows the node points and the final profile.

8. Using the LINE command, draw a center axis line, as shown in Figure 8.13. The length of this line is insignificant. Only its direction is important.

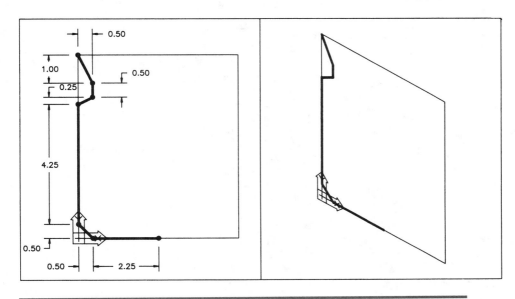

Figure 8.12
Nodes and profile

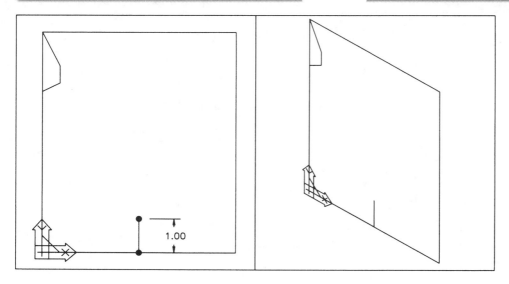

Figure 8.13
Center axis line

Creating the Surface of Revolution

9. Create a layer called SURF, and make it current.

10. Delete the orientation line, and turn FILL off.

11. Set the variables SURFTAB1 and SURFTAB2 to 20.

12. Use the REVSURF command to create a revolved surface.

```
Command: REVSURF
Select path curve: select the profile as shown in
Figure 8.14 (P1)
Select axis of revolution: select the center axis
line as shown in Figure 8.14 (P2)
Start angle <O>: press <Enter> to start the surfaces
at O degrees
Included angle (+=ccw -=cw)<Full circle>: press
<Enter> for a complete circle
```

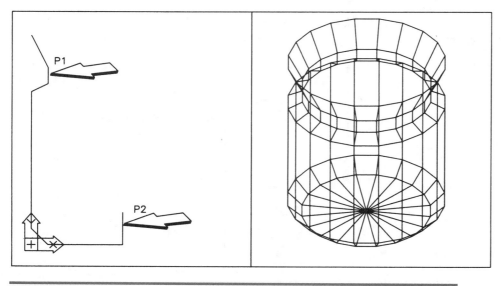

Figure 8.14
Creating a surface of revolution

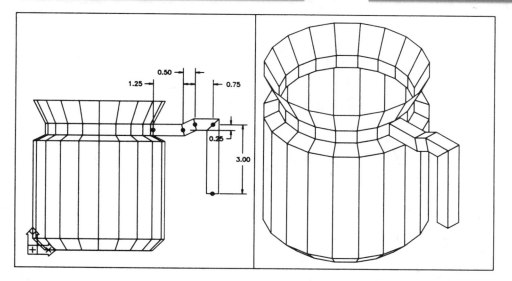

Figure 8.15
The handle with node points

Creating the Handle

13. Turn off **PROFILE** layer.

14. Activate the front-view viewport.

15. Set the elevation to 0.25 and the thickness to –0.5. These settings will place the handle in the center of the orientation plane.

16. With the **PLINE** command, draw the handle using the points shown in Figure 8.15. The polyline should have a width of 0.5.

17. Save the model as COFPT.

18. Use the **HIDE** command in the isometric view and observe the results.

Lab 8.B

Surfaced House Model

Purpose

Lab 8.B will show you how to use predefined 3D blocks to create a surfaced model of a house. This model will be completed in Lab 13.B in Chapter 13.

Objective

You will be able to construct a surfaced model using 3D objects.

Primary Commands

```
AI_BOX, AI_PYRAMID, and AI_CONE
CIRCLE—Extruded
```

Final Model

Figure 8.16 shows the house model you'll be creating.

Procedure

1. Start a new drawing called BDWELL (Basic DWELLing) with the following settings. Use 3DSET as the prototype drawing.

```
Units    =  architectural
Limits   =  −1′,−1′ to 137′,89′
Grid     =  10′
Snap Incr =  1′
```

Figure 8.16
House model

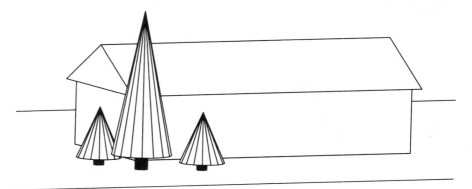

```
Elevation  =  0
Thickness  =  0
Current Layer  =  GROUND
UCS  =  WCS
Viewport Configuration  =  single
```

Creating the Ground

2. Using the 3DFACE command, draw a surface with the following coordinates.

P1 = 0, 0   P2 = 136′, 0
P3 = 136′, 88′ P4 = 0, 88′

This will be used as the ground plane.

Creating the Building

3. Create a layer called BUILDING, and make it current.

4. Using the 3D Objects AI_BOX command, draw the shape shown in Figure 8.17. (*Note:* The 3D Objects option needs to be loaded first; see Section 8.2.)

```
Command: AI_BOX
Corner of box: 40′, 30′, 0′
Length: 40′ (distance along the X axis)
Cube/<Width>: 20′ (distance along the Y axis)
Height: 9′ (distance along the Z axis)
Rotation angle about Z axis: 0
```

Creating the Roof

5. Create a layer called ROOF, and make it current.

6. Using the 3D Objects AI_PYRAMID command, draw the shape shown in Figure 8.18.

```
Command: AI_PYRAMID
First base point: 39′, 29′, 9′
Second base point: 81′, 29′, 9′
Third base point: 81′, 51′, 9′
Tetrahedron/<Fourth base point>: 39′, 51′, 9′
Ridge/Top/<Apex point>: R
First ridge point: 39′, 40′, 15′
Second ridge point: 81′, 40′, 15′
```

7. Save the model as BDWELL. Try the HIDE command and observe the results.

Figure 8.17
Creating the building with a box

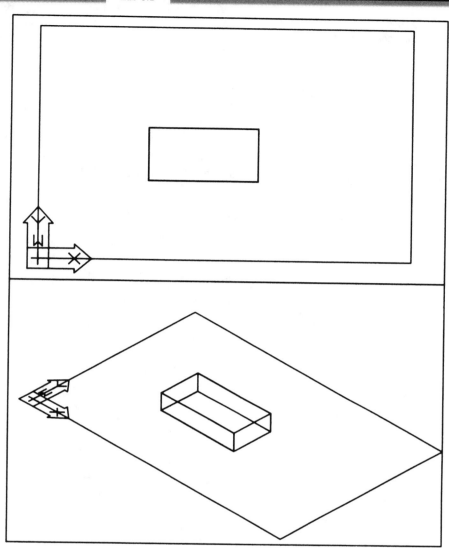

Creating the Trees

8. Create a layer called TREE, and make it current.

9. Using the ELEV command, set the thickness to 1′.

10. Using the CIRCLE command, draw the trunks of the small trees. They have a radius of 8″ and are at the following coordinates.

```
1st tree: 33′2″,26′6″,0′
2nd tree: 44′2″,17′4″,0′
```

Figure 8.18
Creating the roof with a pyramid

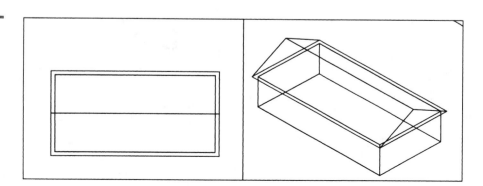

160 Lab 8.B
Surfaced House Model

11. Using the ELEV command, set the thickness to 2′.

12. Using the CIRCLE command, draw the trunk of the large tree. It has a radius of 10″ and is at the coordinates 36′6″, 20′0″, 0′.

13. Use the 3D Objects AI_CONE command to draw each tree. Refer to Figure 8.19.

```
       FIRST TREE
Command: AI_CONE
Base center point: 33'2",26'6",1'
Diameter/<radius> of base: 3'
Diameter/<radius> of top <0>: 0
Height: 7'
Number of segments <16>: 16

       SECOND TREE
Command: AI_CONE
Base center point: 44'2",17'4",1'
Diameter/<radius> of base: 3'
Diameter/<radius> of top <0>: 0
Height: 7'
Number of segments <16>: 16

       THIRD TREE
Command: AI_CONE
Base center point: 36'6",20',2'
Diameter/<radius> of base: 4'
Diameter/<radius> of top <0>: 0
Height: 20'
Number of segments <16>: 16
```

14. Save the model as BDWELL.

Setting the Viewpoint

15. Use VPOINT to display the model (which should be similar to Figure 8.16), and use the HIDE command.

16. If desired, use hatching to cover the walls with brick or siding and the roof with shingles. First, explode the 3D objects into 3D faces and set the UCS Working Plane to each surface to hatch.

17. Save the model as BDWELL.

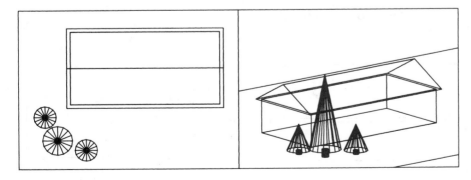

Figure 8.19
Adding the trees

Surfaced Automobile Head Model

Lab 8.C will show you how to use the EDGESURF command to create a surfaced model of an automobile hood.

You will be able to construct a surfaced model using the surface mesh commands.

EDGESURF
SURFTAB1, SURFTAB2
PLINE

Figure 8.20 shows the final surfaced model of the automobile hood.

1. Start a new drawing called CARH (CAR Hood) with the following settings. Use 3DSET as the prototype drawing.

   ```
   Units  =  architectural
   Limits  =  −1′,−1′ to 5′,5′
   Grid  =  3″
   Snap Incr  =  3″
   Elevation  =  0
   Thickness  =  0
   Current Layer  =  OCUBE
   UCS  =  WCS
   Viewport Configuration  =  ORTHO1
   ```

Creating the Orientation Cube

2. Activate the top-view viewport.

3. Set the thickness to 6″.

4. Using the LINE control, draw a 4′ square rectangle, as shown in Figure 8.21.

Creating the Working Planes

5. Using the UCS command, create three working planes: FRONT, REAR, and RIGHTSIDE. Save the working planes so that they may be restored by name.

Figure 8.20
Surfaced model of automobile hood

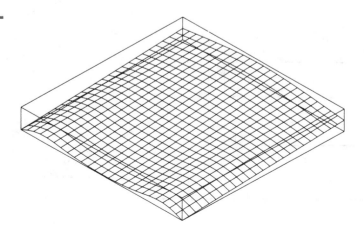

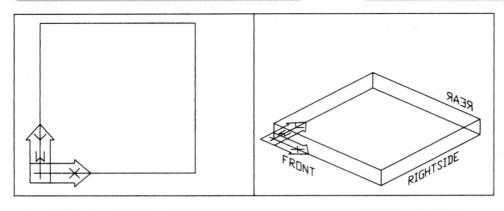

Figure 8.21
Orientation cube and working planes

Drawing the Front Profile

When you use EDGESURF, it is most important that the profiles you create touch at all four corners. If they do not meet, the surface will not be generated.

6. Create a layer called PROFILES, and make it current. Return the Thickness variable to 0.

7. Restore the FRONT working plane, and activate the front-view viewport.

8. Using the PLINE command, draw a polyline as shown in part A of Figure 8.22.

9. Use PEDIT to change the polyline into a spline, as shown in parts B and C of Figure 8.22.

Drawing the Rear Profile

10. Restore the REAR working plane, activate the front-view viewport, and display the PLAN UCS in that viewport.

11. Using the PLINE command, draw a polyline as shown in part A of Figure 8.23.

12. Use PEDIT to change the polyline into a spline, as shown in parts B and C of Figure 8.23.

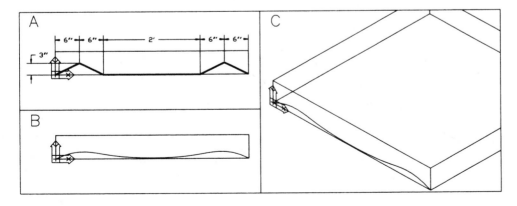

Figure 8.22
Front polyline

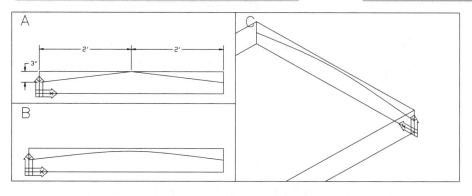

Figure 8.23
Rear polyline

Drawing the Side Profile

13. Restore the RIGHTSIDE working plane and activate the right-side-view viewport.

14. Using the PLINE command, draw a polyline, as shown in part A of Figure 8.24.

15. Use PEDIT to change the polyline into a spline, as shown in parts B and C of Figure 8.24.

16. Activate the isometric viewport, and copy the newly created polyline to the left side of the orientation cube.

Creating a Surface Mesh

17. Turn the OCUBE layer off.

18. Set variables SURFTAB1 and SURFTAB2 to 24.

19. Create a layer called SURF, and make it current.

20. Use the EDGESURF command and pick each profile. A surface should now be covering the defined area and the model should look similar to the one shown in Figure 8.20.

21. Save the model as CARH.

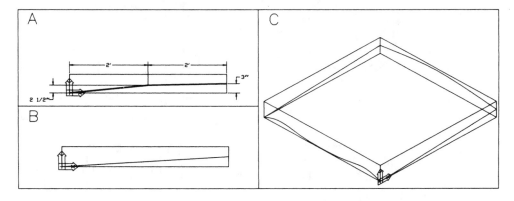

Figure 8.24
Right-side polyline

Questions

1. What previously constructed geometry (for instance, curves, lines, profiles, or points) is required to apply each of the following polygon mesh commands? What do you suppose the command names stand for?
   a. 3DMESH
   b. RULESURF
   c. TABSURF
   d. REVSURF
   e. EDGESURF

2. What function do the variables SURFTAB1 and SURFTAB2 serve?

3. In the creation of meshes, what do the letters *M* and *N* stand for?

4. Of what entities are AutoCAD's 3D objects comprised?

5. Explain the process for constructing AutoCAD's 3D objects.

6. List and describe the eight 3D objects.

7. What is a polygon mesh?

8. Of AutoCAD's six commands for generating a mesh-covered area, which would you use to create a wine glass?

9. Which command would you use to create a wavy sheet of metal?

10. Identify the surface-generating command that would be used to create a topographical map.

Assignments

1. Create a surfaced model of a coffee mug using REVSURF and PLINE. Refer to Figure 8.25. (*Note:* This model will be used in Assignments 1 in Chapters 13 and 14.)

   MUG STATISTICS
   Model Name   =   COFMUG

Figure 8.25
Coffee mug surfaced model

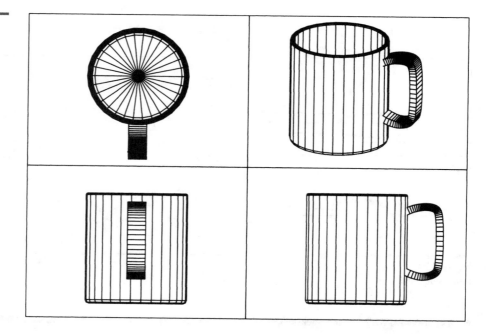

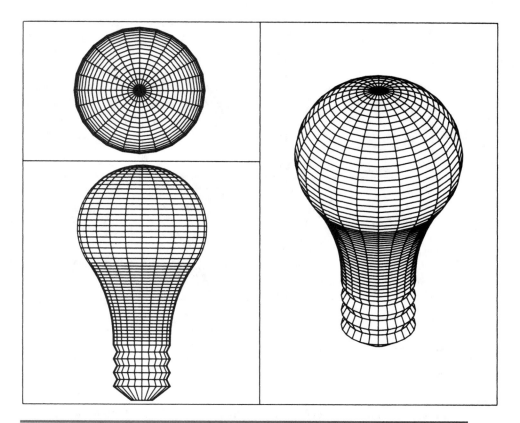

Figure 8.26
Lightbulb surfaced model

```
Diameter  =  3-1/2"
Height  =  4"
Wall Thickness  =  1/8"
Handle Width  =  5/8"
Handle Thickness  =  1/4"
BASE POINT  =  0, 0, 0 (mug bottom/center)
```

2. Generate a surfaced model of a lightbulb using REVSURF. Refer to Figures 8.26 and 8.7.

```
     LIGHTBULB STATISTICS
Model Name  =  LBULB
Bulb Diameter  =  2-1/4"
Bulb Height  =  3-1/4"
Base Diameter  =  1"
Base Height  =  1"
Overall Height  =  4-1/4"
```

3. Using the RULESURF command, draw a surfaced model of a transition duct. Refer to Figures 8.27 and 8.5.

```
     TRANSITION DUCT STATISTICS
Model Name  =  TDUCT
Top Diameter  =  4"
Base Square  =  6"
Height  =  4"
```

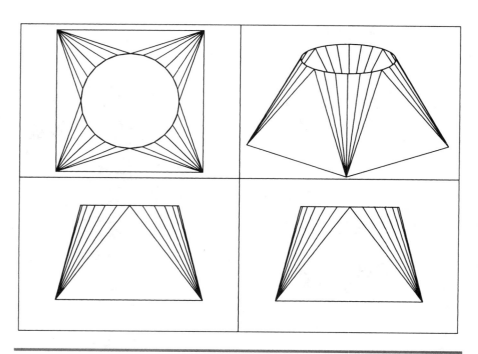

Figure 8.27
Transition duct surfaced model

4. Create a surfaced model of an offset duct using TABSURF. Refer to Figures 8.28 and 8.6.

      OFFSET DUCT STATISTICS
  Model Name = ODUCT
  Duct Diameter = 4″
  Offset Distance = 4″
  Length of Duct = 4″

5. Using EDGESURF, generate a surfaced model of a spoon. Refer to Figures 8.29 and 8.8. (*Note:* This model will be used in Assignment 1 in Chapter 13.)

      SPOON STATISTICS
  Model Name = SPOON
  Overall Length = 6″
  Dish Length = 2″
  Dish Width = 1-1/4″
  Dish Depth = 1/4″
  Handle Width = 1/2″
  BASE POINT = 0,0,0 (dish bottom)

6. Create a surfaced model of an automobile. Refer to Figure 8.30. The top part of the figure illustrates the wireframe that is used to create the surfaced model in the lower part. The entire body and window surfaces should be created using the EDGESURF command. The tires should be created using the REVSURF command. Save the model as CAR. It will be plotted in Assignment 4 of Chapter 16.

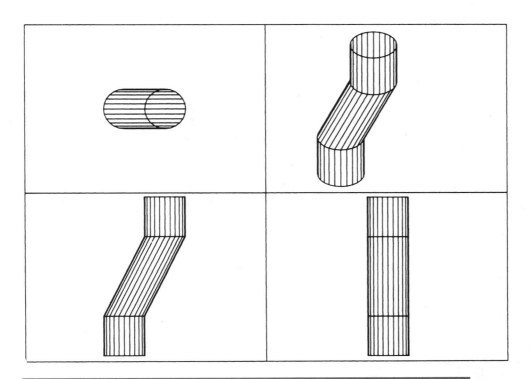

Figure 8.28
Offset duct surfaced model

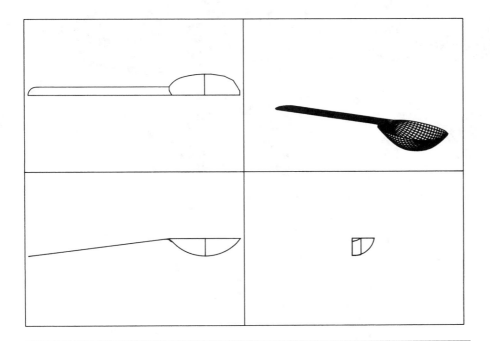

Figure 8.29
Spoon surfaced model

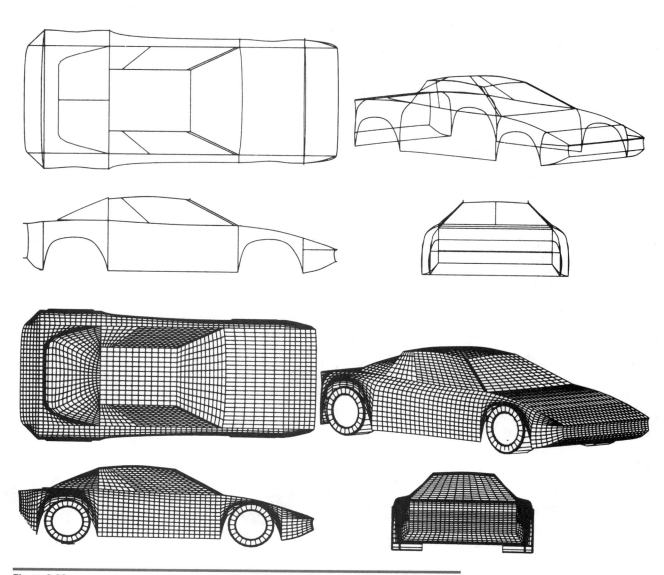

Figure 8.30
Automobile surfaced model

Solid Modeling

This part introduces AutoCAD's new integrated solid modeling. Here you will learn how to create actual solid models rather than surface-covered models. The concepts and basic techniques of solid modeling will be explored as you learn about solid primitive creation, how to build complex composite solids from these primitives, and how to display the models. The final chapter supplies two solid modeling projects that are more extensive than the usual end-of-chapter labs. The integration of solid modeling into AutoCAD is an exciting and new area, one that is becoming the focus of mechanical engineering.

CHAPTER 9

Concepts Behind Solid Modeling

9.1 Introduction

Solid modeling creates three-dimensional (3D) models with database properties, giving the models mass and density. The computer "believes" the model is a solid form, from the outside through to its inner core (refer to Figure 9.1), so capabilities that are unavailable with wireframe or surfaced modeling can be accessed with solid modeling. Think of yourself as a sculptor or a modeler of clay when you approach solid modeling. You start with a solid block, carve away a piece here, bore a hole there, or add a protrusion. This is how solid modeling works—by addition and subtraction. That is the basic process that you, as the user, need to understand. However, in the background, complex mathematical operations are taking place to accomplish the seemingly simple additions and subtractions. As more and more of these subtractions and additions are made, the mathematical intricacies and convolutions increase, which means, of course, that there is a price to pay. But the benefits in the model definition—especially in prototype generation and modification—can outweigh the disadvantage of extra calculation time.

Figure 9.1
Solid model of an apple

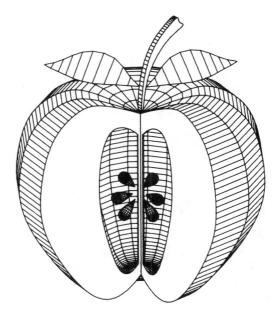

It is important to note that the benefits of wireframe and surfaced modeling are not lost by adding solid modeling. Each method has its own place and uses. There are, in fact, many situations in which solid modeling does not perform well, such as in terrain modeling. Solid modeling was not intended for that application; it is much more useful in the design of a mechanical component.

In addition, the techniques of model creation mastered up to this point were not learned in vain. They will remain as important in the creation of solid models as they were in the creation of wireframe and surfaced models. Solid modeling complements, rather than usurps, the other modeling methods. After some exploration of its techniques, you will soon locate the niche in which to place it.

9.2 Advanced Modeling Extension

Before release 13, AutoCAD made use of an extension program to create solid models; this was referred to as Advanced Modeling Extension, or AME. Entities created with AME were AME blocks. Solid modeling has now been totally integrated into the AutoCAD program and the entities created are now referred to as 3D solids. AME solids and 3D solids are totally different entities. Because of this, you must convert AME solids from previous releases to 3D solids. This can be accomplished with the AMECONVERT command. Because the new 3D solids are more accurate than the previous AME solids, you may see some differences in the converted AME model.

9.3 Solids and Regions

Two types of entities make use of solid modeling commands: 3D solids and regions. Three-dimensional solids are 3D objects that have solid properties. Regions can be thought of as flat solids (Figure 9.2); they have physical and material properties, but they have no thickness and are two dimensional (2D).

Complex 3D solids and regions can be created using the same commands, except that solids use 3D primitives, such as boxes and cylinders, and regions use 2D primitives, such as circles and polygons. Regions are composed of totally enclosed areas called *loops*. Loops can be combinations of lines, polylines, circles, arcs, ellipses, elliptical arcs, splines, 3D faces, traces, and solids (2D). These entities must form closed loops and be planar (on a flat plane) in nature.

To turn the basic entities into a region, use the REGION command. Once you have created region loops, you can make use of the solid modeling commands such as UNION or SUBTRACT to make more complex regions or use the EXTRUDE command to generate complex profiled 3D solids. In either case, you can use the MASSPROP command to extract information such as the calculated area and the perimeter of the region.

Note that, even though the same commands are used to form the complex shapes, 3D solids and regions cannot be combined. Because 3D solids are

Figure 9.2
A region

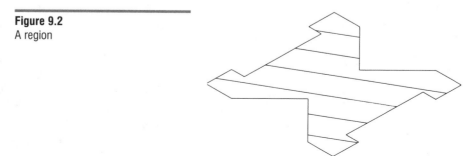

three dimensional and regions are two dimensional, 3D solids can combine with 3D solids and regions with regions but the two can never be mixed. However, a region can be made three dimensional, and a 3D solid two dimensional by means of a process that is explained later.

Note: For the sake of simplicity, and because solids and regions use similar techniques for creation, the discussion here focuses on 3D solids.

Construction and Display of 3D Solids

The primitives used by solid modeling to create final, complex forms can be viewed as building blocks that are added to or subtracted from each other to create the final form. (Note that 3D solids can also be created by extruding or revolving 2D objects.) The building blocks for 3D solids are boxes, wedges, cylinders, spheres, cones, and tori. Solid modeling can create these basic forms.

Once created, primitives can be combined in a number of ways to form what is called a *composite model*. A composite model is the final desired result of any combination of primitives or other composites. There are two types of composite models: composite 3D solids and composite regions. As is true of primitive 3D solids and regions, composite 3D solids and regions cannot be combined.

The composite model can be enhanced by special editing. Chamfering, filleting, slicing, and sectioning are types of 3D solid editing.

Like surface models, 3D solids can be displayed in four ways: wireframe, hidden line removed, shaded, and rendered. To control the display, 3D solids have some system variables that are particular to them. 3D solids also can provide graphic information to aid in the creation of 2D drafting drawings. These capabilities are explained in greater detail later.

Solid modeling keeps track of the material properties of 3D solids for use within AutoCAD in mass property calculations or outside AutoCAD for finite element analysis.

9.4 Primitive Creation

Six commands will create the six basic 3D solid primitives: BOX, WEDGE, CYLINDER, CONE, SPHERE, and TORUS. These commands have different options, to be used according to the primitive being created. However, their similarities allow for easy mastery. These primitives are very similar to the surfaced primitives discussed earlier. Figure 9.3 illustrates their various forms. The Solid tools are found under the Solids toolbar. The following explains each primitive creation command and its options:

BOX — Creates a 3D solid box by defining its diagonal corners, by defining its base and height, or by indicating its center and overall dimensions. A rubber band technique is used to visually determine sizes. It has two options. The Center option allows the user to define the center of the box. The Corner of Box option allows the user to define the corners of the box.

WEDGE — Creates a 3D solid wedge. Its parameters are identical to that of the BOX command. The base is parallel to the current working plane and the sloped face tapers along the X axis.

CYLINDER — Creates a 3D solid cylinder by defining its base and height. CYLINDER has two options. The Elliptical option allows the user to define the axis of the ellipse and the Center Point option allows the user to define the center of the cylinder.

CONE — Creates a 3D solid cone. Its parameters are identical to that of the CYLINDER command, except for references to the apex of the cone.

Figure 9.3
Primitive solids

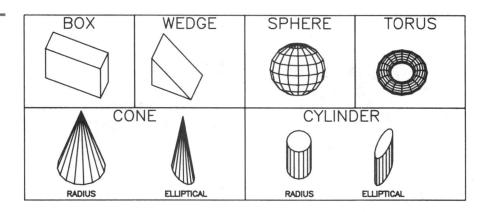

SPHERE   Creates a 3D solid sphere by defining its radius or diameter and its center.

TORUS   Creates a 3D solid torus, which is a donut shape, by defining two radii: one for the tube shape and one from the center of the torus to the center of the tube. If the radius of the tube is greater than the torus radius, a self-intersecting torus, resembling a football in shape, is formed.

3D Viewpoint

Number of Lines Used to Display a Curved Solid

The ISOLINES variable controls the number of tessellation lines used to display curves on a solid. This is explained in more detail in Chapter 11.

3D Viewpoint

Differentiating between 3D Solid Primitives and 3D Objects

3D objects are primitive surface objects, such as boxes and wedges. 3D solid primitives also come in boxes and wedges but are made of solids. The easiest way to tell if an object is a surface primitive or a solid primitive is to use the LIST command. If the object is composed of surfaces, it will be identified as a combination of polylines (polylines are used to display 3D surface objects). If the object is a solid, it will be identified as a 3D solid.

Primitives from 2D Entities

Two commands are used to create 3D solid primitives from 2D entities or regions: EXTRUDE and REVOLVE. The primitive 3D solids created by these commands are shown in Figure 9.4. The following subsections explain each command.

The EXTRUDE Command

The EXTRUDE command creates a 3D solid by extruding existing 2D entities or regions. You can select multiple objects on which to perform the extrusion. The extrusion always takes place perpendicular to the base of the entity, and it can have parallel or tapered sides. If you wish to create a sloped extrusion, base the

EXTRUDE

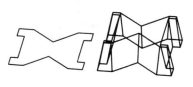

2D PROFILE EXTRUDED
INTO A SOLID

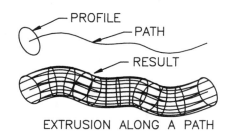

PROFILE
PATH
RESULT

EXTRUSION ALONG A PATH

REVOLVE

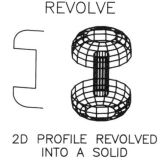

2D PROFILE REVOLVED
INTO A SOLID

Figure 9.4
Primitive solids from 2D entities

3D Viewpoint

Extruding 3D Solids

You cannot extrude 3D solids; the EXTRUDE command will work only on closed curves such as polylines, polygons, rectangles, circles, ellipses, closed splines, donuts, and regions.

taper on the angle measured in from the perpendicular sides of the extrusion. It must be greater than 0 and less than 90 degrees. It is also possible to extrude a profile along a 2D polyline path simply by picking the profile and the path.

The REVOLVE Command

The REVOLVE command creates a 3D solid by revolving a profile around an axis. This command is similar to the AutoCAD surface command REVSURF. Only one profile can be selected at a time, and only circles, polylines, polygons, ellipses, and region entities can be revolved. Blocks or 3D entities cannot be revolved.

9.5 Solids Toolbar

The Solids toolbar can be used to create primitive solid shapes and modify solids. The toolbar is displayed by checking the Solids box from the Toolbars dialog box. The Toolbars dialog box is displayed by selecting Toolbars from the View pull-down menu. If you move the cursor onto a tool without picking it, a tooltip may appear. Tooltips are words that describe the function of the tool. Tooltips can be turned on by checking the Show Tooltips box in the Toolbars dialog box.

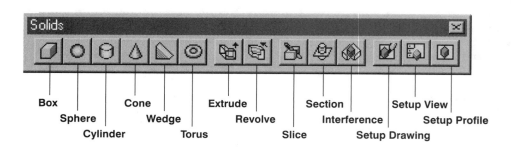

Introduction to Primitive Solids

This lab will introduce you to the basic commands for solid model creation. These commands will generate simple primitive solids. Further use will be made of this model in later labs.

Objective

You will be able to create primitive solids.

Primary Commands

BOX
WEDGE
ISOLINES

Procedure

Initial Settings

1. Start a model called PSOL1 (Primitive SOLids 1) with the following settings:

```
Units = decimal
Limits = -1,-1 to 6,6
Grid = 0.5
Snap Incr. = 0.5
Elevation = 0
Thickness = 0
UCS = WCS
Current Layer = SOLID
Display an axonometric view (VPOINT 0.5,-1,1)
```

Setting the Appearance of 3D Solids

2. The method used to control the appearance of 3D solids on the screen uses the ISOLINES command. This command is explained in more detail in Chapter 11, and its use is illustrated in labs in that chapter. However, it is desirable to set this variable now:

```
Command: ISOLINES
Wireframe mesh density<current>: 4
```

Creating a Solid Box

3. The procedure for creating solid primitives is very similar to the procedure for creating 3D surfaced objects. To create a solid box shape, use the following command:

```
Command: BOX
Center/<corner of box><0,0,0>: 0,0,0
Cube/Length/<Other corner>: L
Length: 3
Width: 2
Height: 1
```

You have created a solid box; the command is that simple.

Creating a Wedge

4. You will now create a solid wedge. In this step you will see that the different solid primitive creation commands are very similar.

```
Command: WEDGE
```

Figure 9.5
Creating two primitive solids

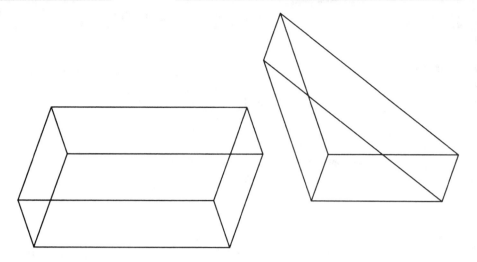

```
Center/<corner of wedge><0,0,0>: 4,1,0
Cube/Length/<Other corner>: L
Length: 2
Width: 1
Height: 3
```

Notice how the slope of the wedge lies along the *X* axis. This will always be the case. To align the wedge to a different orientation during creation, change the orientation of the UCS before creating the wedge.

The creation of the two primitives is illustrated in Figure 9.5.

5. Save the model as PSOL1.

6. Use the LIST command and pick the two solids. Refer to the displayed data about the objects. Note their entity names.

Lab 9.B

Creating Primitive Solids Through Extrusion and Revolution

Purpose

In this lab, you will use basic solid model creation commands to create solids from the extrusion and revolution of a 2D profile. Further use will be made of this model in later labs.

Objective

You will be able to create primitive solids from 2D profiles.

Primary Commands

```
ISOLINES
EXTRUDE
REVOLVE
```

Procedure

Initial Settings

1. Start a model called PSOL2 (Primitive SOLids 2) with the following settings:

```
Units = decimal
Limits = −1,−1 to 10,10
Grid = 0.5
```

```
Snap Incr. = 0.5
Elevation = 0
Thickness = 0
UCS = WCS
Current Layer = SOLID
Display a plane view
ISOLINES = 15
```

Creating the 2D Star Profile

2. Using the PLINE command, create the profile that is shown in Figure 9.6. Make sure you use the CLOSE command so that the profile is completely enclosed.

3. Copy the star profile 5″ to the right.

Extruding the Profile into a Solid

4. Display an axonometric view using a VPOINT setting of 1,–1,1.

5. Using the EXTRUDE command, select the profile of the first star. It will be extruded to a height of 3″.

Command: **EXTRUDE**
Select objects: **pick the first star**
Path/<Height of extrusion>: **3**
Extrusion taper angle <O>: **0**

The first star has been turned into a solid.

6. Using the EXTRUDE command, select the second profile of the second star. It also will be extruded to a height of 3″, but this time a taper will be added.

Command: **EXTRUDE**
Select objects: **pick the second star**
Path/<Height of extrusion>: **3**
Extrusion taper angle <O>: **5**

Setting the extrusion taper angle to 5 will cause the sides of the star to taper inward, toward the top. Now the second star has been turned into a solid, but with sloped sides. The two stars created in steps 5 and 6 are illustrated in Figure 9.7.

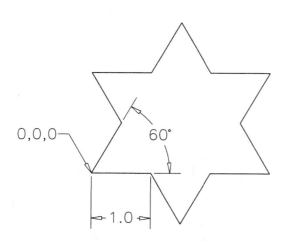

Figure 9.6
2D polyline profile

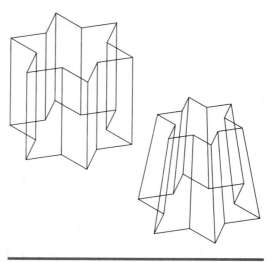

Figure 9.7
Solids created through extrusion

7. Save the model as PSOL2.

Creating a 2D Profile for Revolution

8. Revolve the UCS about the *X* axis so that the *Y* axis of the UCS matches the *Z* axis of the WCS:

```
Command: UCS
Origin/ZAxis . . . /X/Y/Z . . . /Del/?<World>: X
Rotation about X axis: 90
```

9. Display the plan view of the new UCS.

10. Create the profile shown in Figure 9.8 using the PLINE command. You could also use lines and arcs and turn them into a polyline loop using the PEDIT command. Remember that the polyline must be closed.

Creating the Revolved Solid

11. Display the axonometric view using the VPOINT –1,–1,1.

12. Using the REVOLVE command, select the polyline profile to turn into a revolved solid. Use the endpoints of the vertical line for the start and end axis endpoints.

```
Command: REVOLVE
Select objects: pick the polyline profile
Axis of revolution - X/Y/<Start point of axis>: pick
the top point of the vertical line using the endpoint
object snap
<Endpoint of axis>: pick the bottom of the vertical
line using the endpoint object snap
Angle of revolution <full circle>: press <Enter> to
create a 360-degree revolved solid
```

A solid in the shape of the revolved profile has now been created. Your model should look like the one shown in Figure 9.9.

13. Save the model as PSOL2.

Figure 9.8
Polyline profile

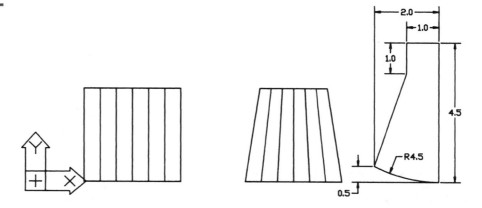

Figure 9.9
Revolved solid with extruded solid stars

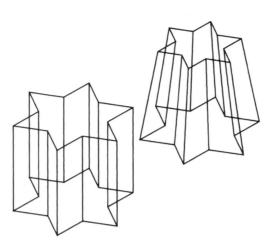
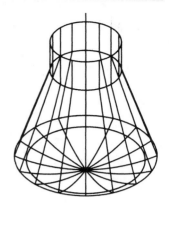

Questions

1. What is solid modeling?

2. What does AME stand for?

3. What is the difference between solids and regions?

4. Identify the six commands for creating solid primitives. What are the similar commands for creating surfaced objects?

5. Explain the purposes of the EXTRUDE and REVOLVE commands.

6. What AutoCAD surface command is similar to the REVOLVE command?

Assignments

1. Create each of the following primitive solids: cone, sphere, and torus.

2. Create a circular cylinder and an elliptical cylinder solid.

3. Create a torus with a tube radius that is greater than the torus radius. What is the outcome?

4. Come up with an interesting 2D profile that could be extruded into a solid using the taper option of the EXTRUDE command.

5. Generate a solid primitive of a soft drink bottle using the REVOLVE command.

6. Create a region from a closed polyline in the shape of a triangle by using the REGION command. Use the area command to determine the area of the triangle. Now draw a closed polyline of a more complex perimeter, turn it into a region, and calculate its area.

CHAPTER **10**

Composite Solids: Creation and Modification

10.1 Introduction

Chapter 9 introduced you to solid modeling and its method of creating simple primitive solids. Learning about those methods gave you in a good beginning for learning about creating truly functional solid models. To learn this, you need to know how to create composites.

A complex form, known as a composite, is created through the interrelationship of two primitives (solids with solids or regions with regions). Once the relationship is determined, a composite is formed. The process is very simple.

For example, to insert a hole through a rectangular plate, where the plate is a box solid, and the hole is a cylinder solid, identify the relationship between the box and the cylinder by subtracting the volume of the cylinder from the volume of the box. The final result is a plate with a hole through it, or a *composite* (see Figure 10.1).

Figure 10.1
Creating a hole in a solid plane

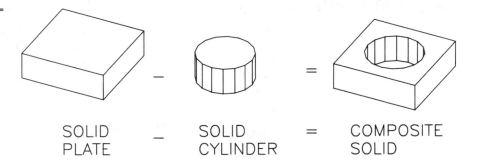

| SOLID
PLATE | _ | SOLID
CYLINDER | = | COMPOSITE
SOLID |

10.2 Relation Commands

Three commands are used to relate primitives to each other: UNION, SUBTRACT, and INTERSECT. UNION is used to add solids to each other; SUBTRACT is used to subtract solids from one another; and INTERSECT is used to create a composite from the intersection of two solids. Figure 10.2 illustrates the relationships between solids created by these three commands. You can repeat the relationship commands with any two solids, composite or primitive, to create as complex a solid object as desired. The tools for relating solids can be found under the Modify II toolbar.

Figure 10.2
Relationships between solids

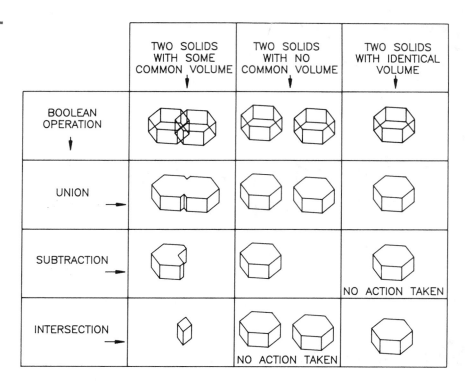

	TWO SOLIDS WITH SOME COMMON VOLUME ↓	TWO SOLIDS WITH NO COMMON VOLUME ↓	TWO SOLIDS WITH IDENTICAL VOLUME ↓
BOOLEAN OPERATION ↓			
UNION →			
SUBTRACTION →			NO ACTION TAKEN
INTERSECTION →		NO ACTION TAKEN	

3D Viewpoint

Combining Solids That Do Not Overlap

It is possible to use the UNION command to combine solids that do not overlap. The solids that are combined are then treated as one solid and can be moved or acted on as one solid.

10.3 Modifying Composites

To further enhance your composite model, use the standard modify commands, CHAMFER and FILLET, and the 3D solid command SLICE. Because you are modifying 3D solids, the CHAMFER and FILLET commands behave slightly differently than they do when used on 2D entities. The following is an explanation of the three commands.

The CHAMFER Command

To produce a chamfer of a solid, use the CHAMFER command. It will automatically subtract the solid area defined by the CHAMFER settings. To use the command, refer to Figure 10.3 and follow this procedure:

```
Command: CHAMFER
(TRIM mode) Current chamfer Dist1 = 0.5000 Dist2 =
0.5000
Polylines/Distance/Angle/Trim/Method/<Select first
line>: pick edge to be chamfered
Select base surface: select the base surface from
which to start the chamfer
```

Figure 10.3
The CHAMFER command

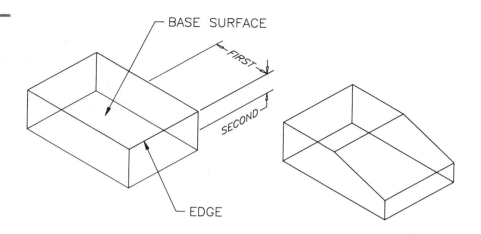

Next/<OK>: **one of the two surfaces adjoining the selected edge is highlighted; either OK it to be used as the base surface or use the Next option to move to the next surface**
Enter base surface distance: **enter the distance in from the edge of the base surface that will represent the first edge of the chamfer**
Enter other surface distance: **enter the second distance along the adjacent surface**
Loop/<select edge>: **pick as many edges that surround (are adjacent to) the base surface**

The FILLET Command

To create a fillet along the edge of a solid, use the FILLET command. It creates an internal or external arc (concave or convex) along selected edges of a solid. Refer to Figure 10.4 and the following procedure:

Command: **FILLET**
(TRIM mode) Current fillet radius = 0.5000
Polyline/Radius/Trim/<Select first object>: **pick an edge of the solid to fillet**
Enter radius <0.5000>: **enter the desired radius of the fillet**
Chain/Radius/<Select edge>: **pick the edges to be filleted**

Figure 10.4
The FILLET command

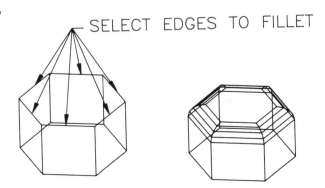

SELECT EDGES TO FILLET

Slicing a Solid in Two

AutoCAD has the ability to take a solid and slice it into two pieces along a user-defined plane. This ability is accessed with the SLICE command. You can find the SLICE tool in the Solids toolbar. Once the slice has been made, both new solids or only one may be retained. The options for defining the slicing plane are Object, ZAxis, View, XY, YZ, ZX, and 3Points. Refer to Figure 10.5 and the following procedure:

```
Command: SLICE
Select objects: pick the solid to be sliced
Slicing plane by Object/Zaxis/View/XY/YZ/ZX/<3
points>: enter the desired method for specifying the
slicing plane
Both sides/<Point on the desired side of the plane>:
press <Enter> to identify the desired side to retain
or enter Both to keep both sides
```

The following are descriptions of the slicing plane options:

Object	Aligns the slicing plane with an object such as a circle, ellipse, circular or elliptical arc, 2D spline, or 2D polyline segment.
Zaxis	Defines the slicing plane by a specified point on the Z axis of the XY plane.
View	Aligns the slicing plane with the current viewport's viewing plane.
XY	Aligns the slicing plane with the current UCS XY plane.
YZ	Aligns the slicing plane with the current UCS YZ plane.
ZX	Aligns the slicing plane with the current UCS ZX plane.
3Points	Defines the slicing plane by identifying three points on the plane.

Figure 10.5
The SLICE command

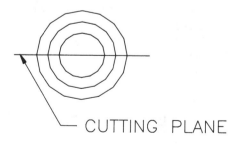

CUTTING PLANE

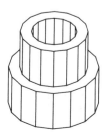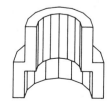

Union | Intersect
Subtract

10.4 Modify Toolbar

The Modify II toolbar contains various tools to perform modifications on solids. The toolbar is displayed by checking the Modify II box from the Toolbars dialog box. The Toolbars dialog box is displayed by selecting Toolbars from the View pull-down menu. If you move the cursor onto a tool without picking it, a tooltip may appear. Tooltips are words that describe the function of the tool. Tooltips can be turned on by checking the Show Tooltips box in the Toolbars dialog box.

Lab 10.A

Relating Solids to One Another

Purpose

This lab uses actual models to illustrate how solids relate to each other. The relationships formed will serve as building blocks for the creation of complex composite solids. In later labs you will apply this knowledge to create more complex models.

Objectives

You will be able to

- Create primitive solids.
- Form relationships between solids to create composite solids.

Primary Commands

ISOLINES
CYLINDER
UNION
SUBTRACT
INTERSECT

Procedure

Initial Settings

1. Start the model called RELSOL (RELation of SOLids) and enter the following settings:

```
Units = decimal
Limits = −1,−1 to 4,4
Grid = 0.5
Snap Incr. = 0.5
Elevation = 0
Thickness = 0
UCS = WCS
Display an axonometric view (VPOINT 0,−1,1)
Current layer = SOLID
ISOLINES = 15
```

Creating Solid Primitives

2. Using the CYLINDER command, create two cylinders. Refer to part A in Figure 10.6.

```
Command: CYLINDER
Elliptical/<Center point>: 0,0,0
Diameter/<Radius>: .5
Height of cylinder: .5
Command: CYLINDER
Elliptical/<Center point>: .75,0,0
Diameter/<Radius>: .5
Height of cylinder: .5
```

Relating Solids by Union

3. Relate the two solids by uniting them with the UNION command. This adds the mass of the two solids to create the final composite solid.

```
Command: UNION
Select objects: pick the two
```

AutoCAD will calculate the union of the two cylinders and then display the results. The screen should look similar to part B of Figure 10.6. Notice that the composite solid is a single object and that the geometry does not overlap each other. AutoCAD calculated what was unique mass and what was identical mass and produced the composite solid.

Separating Solids

4. There is no special command for separating solids. The AME utility does have a command called SOLSEP to separate solids, but this command is not part of the integrated solid modeling. To separate solids that have just been related, use the UNDO command, or U. Proceed to undo the UNION command, so that the two distinct solids are visible.

Relating Solids by Subtraction

5. Relate the two solids by subtraction with the SUBTRACT command. This command will subtract the mass of one of the solids from the mass of the other solid to create the final composite.

```
Command: SUBTRACT
Select solids and regions to subtract from . . .
Select objects: pick the left cylinder
Select solids and regions to subtract . . .
Select objects: pick the right cylinder
```

Figure 10.6
Relating solids by union

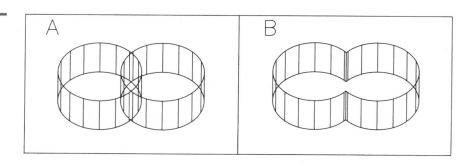

Figure 10.7
Relating solids by subtraction

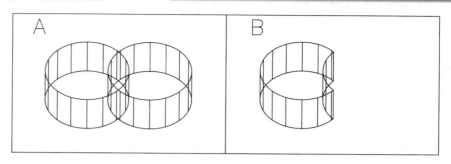

AutoCAD will calculate the subtraction of the right cylinder from the left cylinder and then display the results. The screen should look similar to part B of Figure 10.7. Notice how the composite solid has a piece subtracted from it. AutoCAD calculated the overlapping mass of the right cylinder and produced the composite solid.

Separating Solids

6. Use the UNDO command to undo the SUBTRACT command, so that the two distinct solids are visible.

Relating Solids by Intersection

7. Relate the two solids by intersection by using the INTERSECTION command. This command will take the overlapping masses of the two solids to create the composite.

```
Command: INTERSECT
Select objects: pick the two cylinders
```

AutoCAD will calculate the intersection and then display the results. The screen should look similar to part B of Figure 10.8. Notice how only the overlapping mass of the two cylinders remains.

Separating Solids

8. Use the UNDO command to undo the INTERSECT command, so that the two distinct solids are visible.

9. Save the model as RELSOL.

You have now created composite solids from primitives. Remember that you can relate composite solids to each other in the same ways you related primitives in this lab. Thus, the possible final complex solids you can create are unlimited. You will be creating more complex composites in the labs in Chapters 11 and 12.

Figure 10.8
Relating solids by intersection

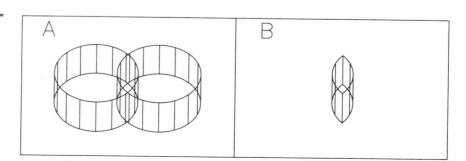

Modifying Solids

Purpose

This lab will introduce you to the use of modify commands to alter the shape of solids.

Objectives

You will be able to

- Fillet and chamfer solids.
- Slice solids in two.

Primary Commands

```
FILLET
CHAMFER
SLICE
```

Procedure

1. Open the model PSOL1.

2. Use the SAVEAS command to save it as MODSOL (MODifying SOLids).

3. Set the VPOINT to 0.75,–1,1.

Filleting a Solid

4. Using the FILLET command, round the top edge of the wedge, as shown in Figure 10.9:

```
Command: FILLET
(TRIM mode) Current fillet radius = 0.5000
Polyline/Radius/Trim/<Select first object>: pick top
edge
Enter radius <0.5000>: 0.25
Chain/Radius/<Select edge>: press <Enter> to accept
edge picked earlier
```

The top edge should now be filleted with a 0.25 radius.
    The first time you picked the edge, you identified the solid object; the second time, you identified the edge to fillet. You could have picked more edges at this point if you wanted to add more fillets at the same time.

Chamfering a Solid

5. Using the CHAMFER command, add a 45-degree bevel to the top edges of the solid box:

```
Command: CHAMFER
```

Figure 10.9
Modifying solids

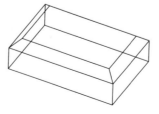

```
(TRIM mode) Current chamfer Dist1 = 0.5000 Dist2 =
0.5000
Polylines/Distance/Angle/Trim/Method/<Select first
line>: pick a top edge
Select base surface
Next <OK>: enter OK if top surface is highlighted or
enter Next until top surface is highlighted, then
enter OK
Enter base surface distance: 0.25
Enter other surface distance: 0.25
Loop/<Select edge>: pick each edge around the top of
the box and press <Enter>
```

All the top edges of the box should now have a 45-degree bevel.

Slicing a Solid in Two

6. Set VPOINT to 0.5,–1,0.75.

7. Using the CYLINDER command, create two solid cylinders, one inside the other. The top surface of the inside cylinder will coincide with the top surface of the outside cylinder.

```
Command: CYLINDER
Elliptical/<Center point>: 1.5,4.5,0
Diameter/<Radius>: 2
Height of cylinder: 2
Command: CYLINDER
Elliptical/<Center point>: 1.5,4.5,1
Diameter/<Radius>: 1
Height of cylinder: 1
```

8. Using the SUBTRACT command, subtract the inside cylinder from the outside cylinder. You should now have a composite cylinder with a hole in its top.

9. Using the SLICE command, slice the composite cylinder into two halves (Figure 10.10):

```
Command: SLICE
```

Figure 10.10
Slicing a solid in half

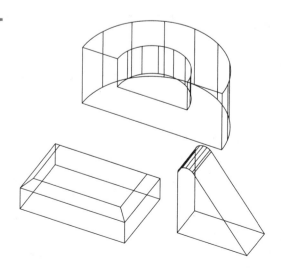

```
Select objects: pick the composite cylinder
Slicing plane by Object/Zaxis/View/XY/YZ/ZX/<3
points>: ZX
Point on the ZX plane <0,0,0>: 0,4.5,0 (4.5 is the center of
the cylinder.)
Both sides/<Point on the desired side of the plane>:
0,5,0
```

The composite cylinder has now been sliced into two halves, and only one half has been retained.

10. Save the model as PSOL1.

Questions

1. Identify and explain the commands used to create solid relationships.

2. Explain the command that is used to cut a solid in two.

3. Explain the two commands used to bevel and round edges of a solid.

Assignments

1. Create a solid of the 1/4″ machine nut shown in Figure 10.11. (*Hint:* To achieve the chamfer on the edge of the nut, relate a chamfered solid cylinder to a hexagon solid by intersection.)

2. Generate a solid model of the 1/4″ wrench socket shown in Figure 10.12.

3. Examine the chess piece illustrated in Figure 10.13. Produce a model of this solid.

4. Create a solid model of a wooden pencil. This will be a composite: use cones, an extruded hexagon, and a revolved profile of the eraser end.

5. Create an apple shape. Now, take a bite out of it, graphically speaking.

Figure 10.11
Solid model of a machine nut

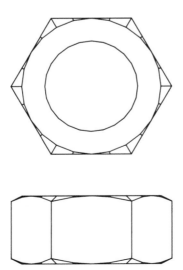

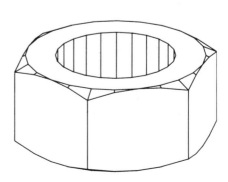

Figure 10.12
Solid model of a wrench socket

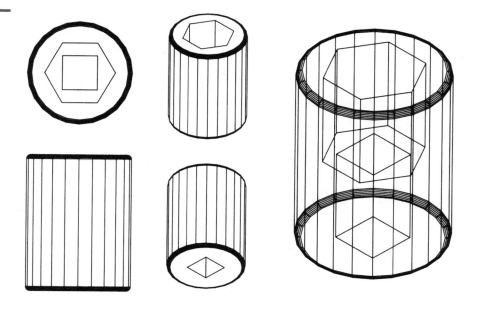

Figure 10.13
Solid model of a rook chess piece

CHAPTER 11

Solid Display and Inquiry

11.1 Introduction

The solid model utilities of AutoCAD are powerful—not only can you construct a composite model quickly and accurately, but you can also utilize a variety of methods to display it, in both 3D and 2D, and extract information about its properties. This chapter explores these abilities, discussing the various methods of representing a solid model and the methods of inquiring about the model's characteristics.

11.2 3D Representation

A solid model can be displayed as wireframe, hidden lines removed, shaded, and rendered. However, there are two variables that have a direct effect on those types of displays: the ISOLINES and FACETRES variables. The ISOLINES variable controls the number of tessellation lines that are used to define the curved features of the model in wireframe. Tessellation lines are the parallel lines used to define the curve of a surface for easier visualization. The FACETRES variable controls the resolution of the facets that are created when you perform a hidden line removed, shaded, or rendered display of a solid. You may enter an integer value from 0 to 2047 for the number of isolines per surface of a solid. The higher the value, the greater the number of isolines. You may enter a value from 0.01 to 10.0 for the facet resolution. The higher the value, the more facets that are created and the smoother the resultant figure.

The Effect of ISOLINES and FACETRES Settings on a Sphere

Look at the sphere shown in Figure 11.1, part A. This sphere was created with an ISOLINES value of 5. Only a few lines are used to define the curved surfaces. Now refer to parts B, C, and D of Figure 11.1. The sphere in part B is shown in wireframe with an ISOLINES setting of 1. Because of the higher number, more isolines are drawn, giving a clearer view of the sphere. However, it takes longer to manipulate the view of the model with a higher ISOLINES setting. Finally, refer to the last two spheres, hidden lined removed and with FACETRES settings of 0.25 and 0.5. You can see that the ISOLINES and FACETRES variables are independent of each other.

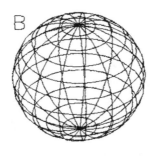

ISOLINES = 5

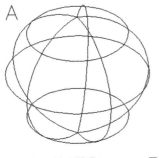

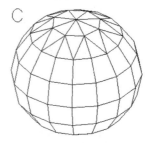

ISOLINES = 1

FACETRES = .2

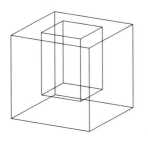

FACETRES = .50

Figure 11.1
Wireframe and hidden displays

You can change the ISOLINES and FACETRES variables at any time to increase or decrease the number of lines and facets when representing the solid model. Use the least number of isolines that you can and still be able to manipulate the solid. Use the least number of facets possible when creating initial settings for rendering and then increase the number for the final render.

If you don't want to see all the various facet faces on the 3D solid when you hide it, you can set the variable DISPSILH to 1. This setting shows only the silhouette of the solid when using the hide command or hiding when plotting. To see the faces again, set DISPSILH to 0.

3D Viewpoint

Rendering Solids

If you are going to use the Smooth option of the RENDER command, you will not need to have as many facets on a solid. The Smooth option blends edges together to give a smooth curve. You can then reduce the FACETRES variable before rendering and consequently reduce the rendering time.

11.3 2D Representation

You can create 2D objects from a 3D Solid model using several commands: SECTION, SOLPROF, SOLVIEW, and SOLDRAW. Using these commands you can create 2D drawings that can be dimensioned. SECTION works with

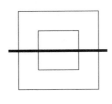

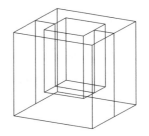

MOVED FOR CLARITY

ORIGINAL
SOLID MODEL

DEFINE CUTTING PLANE
USING SECTION COMMAND

RESULTING SECTION PROFILE

Figure 11.2
Creating a section view

TILEMODE set to 1 or 0. The others require you to have TILEMODE set to 0 and be working in paper space. Section 16.4 of Chapter 16 explains the details of paper space.

You can also lay out 2D drawings using the Designer add-on program; this is explained in Chapter 24.

Creating Sections with SECTION

The Section command will create section view objects automatically by specifying the cutting plane. It works very much like the SLICE command. But instead of slicing the model, it creates a profile outline of the cut area. Refer to Figure 11.2 and the following procedure:

```
Command: SECTION
Select objects: pick the solid to be sectioned
Section plane by
Object/Zaxis/View/XY/YZ/ZX/<3 points>: enter the
desired method for specifying the sectioning plane
```

Solid Profiles Using SOLPROF

The SOLPROF command is used to create a projected 2D profile view of a solid. This works only from a floating viewport created in PAPERSPACE (Section 16.4).

The following is the procedure for using the command:

1. Create the 3D solid.
2. Set TILEMODE to 0.
3. Make sure you are in paper space by using the PS alias command for PAPERSPACE.
4. Create a floating viewport using the MVIEW command.
5. Enter into MODELSPACE using the MS alias.
6. Pick in the floating viewport to activate it.
7. Using the VPOINT, set the desired view, either orthographic or axonometric.
8. Use the SOLPROF command. You will be asked to

   Pick the objects to project;
   Display hidden profile lines of separate layers;
   Project profile lines onto a plane;
   Delete tangential edges.

   You normally answer *yes* to the previous requests. The profile objects are then created. They are created on new layers with the prefixes PV and PH. The layer name is followed by the handle name of the viewport itself. PV stands for Profile Visible (visible lines), and Profile Hidden stands for hidden lines. You may have to load the HIDDEN linetype and assign it to the proper layer.
9. To see the profile you need to freeze the original 3D solid in that viewport only.
10. These profiles are designed to be seen from paper space. If you switch back to TILEMODE 1, you will see the profile objects in 3D space. The profiles are actual objects added to your drawing.

Solid Profiles Using SOLVIEW and SOLDRAW

The SOLVIEW and SOLDRAW commands are used together to create 2D views of a 3D solid. As with the SOLPROF command, these commands will work only with TILEMODE set to 0 and in PAPERSPACE. The SOLVIEW command sets up the floating viewports and views based on a primary view.

Figure 11.3
Extracting a 2D profile view

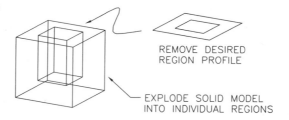

REMOVE DESIRED
REGION PROFILE

EXPLODE SOLID MODEL
INTO INDIVIDUAL REGIONS

3D Viewpoint

Exploding a Solid

When you explode a solid, it breaks down into individual regions (and sometimes an entity called a body). If you explode the region, you will end up with polylines or lines. You can then extract as many of the resulting entities as you need.

The SOLDRAW command updates the viewports created using SOLVIEW with the proper visible and hidden profiles.

The following is the procedure the SOLVIEW and SOLDRAW commands:

1. Create the 3D solid.
2. Set TILEMODE to 0.
3. Make sure you are in paper space by using the PS alias command for PAPERSPACE.
4. Create a primary floating viewport using the MVIEW command. This viewport is used to create and position the other viewports.
5. Enter into MODELSPACE using the MS alias.
6. Pick in the floating viewport to activate it.
7. Using the VPOINT, set the desired orthographic view, such as the top view.
8. Switch back to PAPERSPACE using PS.
9. Use the SOLVIEW command. You will be asked to

    Set the type of view, such as orthographic or auxiliary;
    Pick the side of the primary viewport to project;
    Pick the location of the view's center and hit return;
    Pick the corners that set the size of the floating viewport;
    Enter the unique name of the view.

    The viewport and profile are created. Special layers are created with the prefix of the unique name of the view and followed by VIS, HID, and DIM. As with SOLPROJ, these layers are used to store the separate profiles for visible and hidden lines as well as dimensions you add. You may have to load the HIDDEN linetype and assign it to the proper layers.

10. Once you have created the views, use the SOLDRAW command to update each viewport you pick. If you use the ALL option to select objects, you can update all the SOLVIEW viewports at once.
11. These profiles are designed to be seen from paper space. If you switch back to TILEMODE 1, you will see the profile objects in 3D space. The profiles are actual objects added to your drawing.
12. If you modify your 3D solid, use the SOLDRAW command to update the viewports to reflect the changes.

Exploding a Solid

If you explode a solid, it breaks down into individual region and body entities. From these entities, you can extract the surface area profiles to help create a 2D drawing (Figure 11.3).

Using a DXB Plot File

You can create a projected view of your model by plotting a view to a DXB file and then importing the resultant DXB file back into your drawing. This will allow you to assemble a 2D view of any view of a model. However, the DXB plot file converts all arcs into lines.

11.4 Extracting Solid Model Information

As with regular AutoCAD entities, you can inquire and receive information about the model you are constructing. You can inquire about area as well as mass properties.

Area Calculations

The AREA command displays the calculated surface areas of selected solids and regions. You can use the Add option of the AREA command to total the areas of several individual solids.

Mass Property Calculations

You can extract mass properties from solids and regions. This is accomplished with the MASSPROP command by selecting the solid model from which you wish to extract the mass property information. The MASSPROP tool is found in the Standard toolbar under the List flyout. Refer to the following data for the sample mass properties of a 2″ cube:

```
SOLIDS
Mass:              8.0000
Volume:            8.0000
Bounding box:  X:  0.0000 – 2.0000
               Y:  0.0000 – 2.0000
               Z:  0.0000 – 2.0000
Centroid:      X:  1.0000
               Y:  1.0000
               Z:  1.0000
Moments of     X:  21.3333
inertia:       Y:  21.3333
               Z:  21.3333
Products of   XY:  8.0000
inertia:      YZ:  8.0000
              ZX:  8.0000
Radii of       X:  1.6330
gyration:      Y:  1.6330
               Z:  1.6330
Principle moments and X-Y-Z directions about centroid:
               I:  5.333 along [1.0000 0.0000 0.0000]
               J:  5.333 along [0.0000 1.0000 0.0000]
               K:  5.333 along [0.0000 0.0000 1.0000]
```

Definitions of Mass Property Terms

Here are brief definitions of the terms used for the solid modeling mass property calculations as given by AutoCAD:

Mass   The measure of inertia of a body. Because Auto-
                               CAD uses a density of one, mass and volume have
                               the same value.

Volume	Amount of space occupied by the selected object.
Bounding box	A 2D or 3D rectangular box that encloses the object and upon which the calculations are performed.
Centroid	Center of the selected object.
Moments of inertia	Amount of force required to rotate the selected object about its various axes.
Products of inertia	Values used in determining the forces causing the motion of an object.
Radii of gyration	Radial distance from the point of rotation at which the total mass must be concentrated.
Principal moments	*X-Y-Z* directions about centroid values derived from products of inertia; the first value is the axis through which the moment of inertia is the highest, the second is the axis through which the moment of inertia is the lowest, and the third lies between the highest and the lowest.

Indication of Solid Interferences

It is possible to exhibit the interferences between solids with overlapping masses. The INTERFERE command finds the interference of two or more solids and highlights the pairs that interfere. You can turn the interference volume into a separate solid if you desire. The command allows you to create two selection sets and compare the first set to the second. However, if you only select the first set, the solids in that set will be compared to one another.

Lab 11.A

Displaying a Solid and Extracting the Solid's Information

Purpose

This lab demonstrates the different methods for controlling the display of a solid model. You will alter the variables that control the display and observe the results. You will also learn how to extract solid property information about your model.

Objectives

You will be able to

- Change the representation of a solid in wireframe.
- Change the representation of a solid in hidden line removal.
- Extract solid property information.

Primary Commands

```
ISOLINES
FACETRES
CYLINDER
MASSPROP
```

Procedure

Initial Settings

1. Start the model called DISSOL (DISplay of SOLids) and enter the following settings:

```
Units = decimal
Limits = −3,−3 to 3,3
```

```
Grid = 0.5
Snap Incr. = 0.5
Elevation = 0
Thickness = 0
UCS = WCS
Display an axonometric view (VPOINT 0.5,-1,0.5)
Current layer = SOLID
```

2. Set the ISOLINES variable to 4.

Creating a Solid Cylinder

3. Using the CYLINDER command, create a cylinder with a center at 0,0,0, a radius of 2, and a height of 3. The resulting model should look similar to part A in Figure 11.4.

Increasing the Number of Tessellation Lines

4. Increase the value of the ISOLINES variable to 15 and then REGEN the screen. The screen should look similar to part B of Figure 11.4. Notice the greater number of lines defining the curves. This helps with visualization but slows down the display of AutoCAD. You will have to decide on a "happy medium" between speed and number of lines.

Setting the Resolution of Solid Facets

5. Set the FACETRES variable to 0.5 and then use the HIDE command. Refer to part C of Figure 11.4. The cylinder is shown with hidden lines removed, but it is slightly rough looking along the curves.

Smoothing a Surface

6. Increase the FACETRES variable to 1 and then use the HIDE command. Refer to part D of Figure 11.4. Notice how there are now more facets than before and that the curved edge is smoother. Similar to the ISOLINES

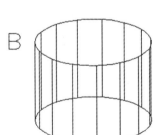
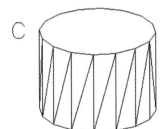
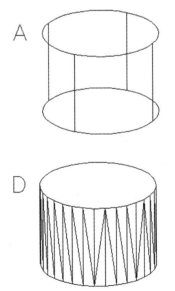

Figure 11.4
Altering the display of a cylinder

200   Lab 11.A
Displaying a Solid and
Extracting the Solid's
Information

variable, you need to decide how many facets you require to display a model. The more facets, the more time needed to display the model.

Now set the variable DISPSILH to 1 and try the HIDE command again. This variable controls whether you see the faces of a solid or just the silhouette. Return the variable to 0 if you want to see the faces.

Performing Mass Property Calculations

7. Using the MASSPROP command, select the cylinder to display the mass properties of the cylinder. Note three items:

   the volume of the cylinder,
   the bounding box, and
   the centroid.

   You can easily identify the volume of a cylinder of these proportions, the rectangular bounding box the cylinder fits within, and where the center of the mass of the cylinder is located.

Questions

1. What is the purpose of the ISOLINES variable?

2. What is the purpose of the FACETRES variable?

3. How can you extract a sectional view from a solid?

4. How can you extract mass property information from a solid?

Assignments

1. Experiment with the solid models created in Labs 9.A, 10.A, and 10.B using the ISOLINES and FACETRES variables.

2. Use the MASSPROP command on the solid models created in Labs 9.A, 10.A, and 10.B. Note the results.

CHAPTER **12**

Solid Modeling Projects

12.1 Introduction

The purpose of this chapter is to present more extensive solid models and the step-by-step method needed to create them. This should help reinforce the theory gained in the previous solid modeling chapters through more practical application. Additional complex solid model assignments are given at the end of this chapter.

Lab 12.A

Purpose

Solid Model of Socket Head Cap Screw

This lab introduces you to more basic solid model creation commands during the modeling of a socket head cap screw. You will use the commands to extrude 2D profiles, generate simple primitive solids, and form complex composite solids by interrelating primitives.

Objectives

You will be able to

- Create primitive solids.
- Create composite solids.
- Create solids for 2D profiles.
- Perform modifications to solids.

Primary Commands

ISOLINES
EXTRUDE
CYLINDER
SUBTRACT
UNION
CHAMFER

Final Model

Figure 12.1 is the final solid model of the socket head cap screw.

Lab 12.A
Solid Model of Socket
Head Cap Screw

Figure 12.1
Solid model of socket head cap screw

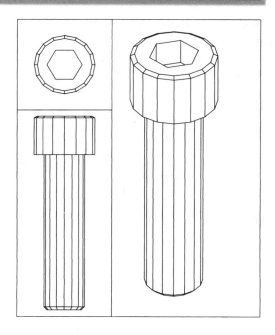

Procedure

Initial Settings

1. Start the model called SOCSOL (SOCket head cap screw SOLid) and
   enter the following settings:

   ```
   Units = decimal
   Limits = -1,-1 to 2,2
   Grid = 0.5
   Snap Incr. = 0.5
   Elevation = 0
   Thickness = 0
   UCS = WCS
   Display an axonometric view (VPOINT 1,-1,1)
   Current layer = SOLID
   ISOLINES = 15
   ```

Creating a Solid Cylinder

The body and the head of the screw will be created first, using the CYLIN-
DER command. The top of the body will be at 0,0,0 and the rest of the body
will extend in a negative Z direction. The head will sit on top of the body and
extend in the positive Z direction.

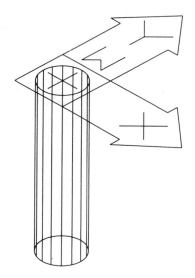

Figure 12.2
Solid model of cylinder body

2. Using the CYLINDER command, create the body of the screw as shown
   in Figure 12.2:

   ```
   Command: CYLINDER
   Elliptical/<Center point>: 0,0,0
   Diameter/<Radius>: .125
   Height of cylinder: -1
   ```

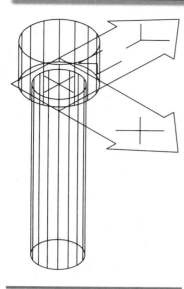

Figure 12.3
Adding the head to the body

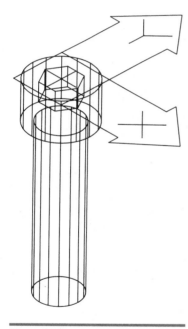

Figure 12.4
Adding the hexagon socket

3. Using the CYLINDER command, create the head of the screw, as shown in Figure 12.3:

```
Command: CYLINDER
Elliptical/<Center point>: 0,0,0
Diameter/<Radius>: .1875
Height of cylinder: .25
```

Creating a 2D Profile and Extruding It

4. Using the POLYGON command, draw a hexagon that will represent the socket in the head of the screw (Figure 12.4):

```
Command: POLYGON
Number of sides: 6
Edge/<Center of polygon>: 0,0,.25
Inscribe in circle/Circumscribe about circle (I/C): C
Radius of circle: 0.9375
```

5. Using the EXTRUDE command, select the hexagon and give it a height of –0.120 with no taper angle:

```
Command: EXTRUDE
Select objects: pick hexagon
Path/<Height of extrusion>: -0.120
Extrusion taper angle <0>: 0
```

The final results should look similar to Figure 12.4.

Chamfering Solids

The top of the head and the bottom of the body will each have a different chamfer. Both will make use of the CHAMFER command.

6. Using the CHAMFER command, create a chamfer along the top edge of the head of the screw, as shown in Figure 12.5:

```
Command: CHAMFER
(TRIM mode) Current chamfer Dist1 = 0 Dist2 = 0
Polylines/Distance/Angle/Trim/Method/<Select first
line>: pick a top edge of head
Select base surface
Next <OK>: enter OK if top surface is highlighted or
enter Next until top surface is highlighted, then
enter OK
Enter base surface distance: 0.019
Enter other surface distance: 0.019
Loop/<Select edge>: pick each edge around the top of
the head and press <Enter>
```

7. Repeat the CHAMFER command for the bottom of the body, as shown in Figure 12.6:

```
Command: CHAMFER
(TRIM mode) Current chamfer Dist1 = 0 Dist2 = 0
```

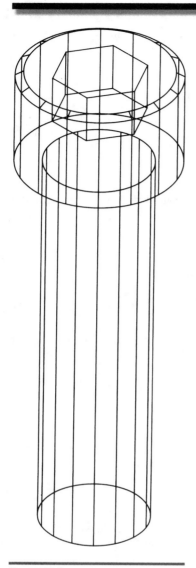

Figure 12.5
Chamfer of the head

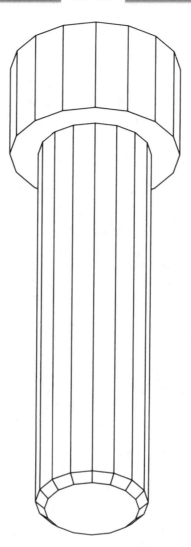

Figure 12.6
Chamfer of the body

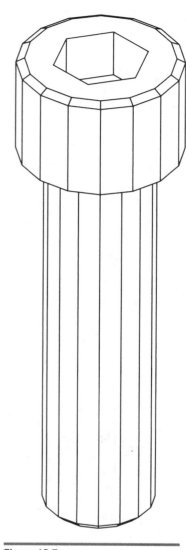

Figure 12.7
The final composite model

```
Polylines/Distance/Angle/Trim/Method/<Select first
line>: pick a bottom edge of body
Select base surface
Next <OK>: enter OK if bottom surface is highlighted
or enter Next until bottom surface is highlighted,
then enter OK
Enter base surface distance: 0.019
Enter other surface distance: 0.010
Loop/<Select edge>: pick each edge around the bottom
of the body and press <Enter>
```

Relating the Primitives to Each Other

At this point, the head, body, and hexagon are all separate solids. Now they will be related to each other to create the complex composite solid illustrated in Figure 12.7.

8. Using the SUBTRACT command, subtract the solid hexagon from the solid head:

```
Command: SUBTRACT
Select solids and regions to subtract from . . .
Select objects: pick the head solid
Select solids and regions to subtract . . .
Select objects: pick the hexagon solid
```

9. Using the UNION command, add the body and the head:

```
Command: UNION
Select objects: pick the body and the head
```

10. Save the model as SOCSOL.

11. Use the HIDE command and observe the results. Try different FACETRES variable values and the HIDE command to see the effect on the model.

Lab 12.B

Solid Model of Split Pillow Block

Purpose

In this lab, you will use the more advanced solid model creation commands to create a solid model of the split pillow block. This lab will illustrate the ease of constructing a solid model compared to a surfaced model and highlight the characteristics and abilities of solid models not found in surfaced models. You will need to allocate more time for the completion of this lab.

Objectives

You will be able to

- Create primitive solids.
- Create composite solids.
- Create solids for 2D profiles.
- Perform modifications to solids.
- Slice a solid into separate parts.

Primary Commands

```
ISOLINES
EXTRUDE
CYLINDER
SUBTRACT
FILLET
SLICE
```

Final Model

Figure 12.8 shows the final solid model of the split pillow block.

Figure 12.8
Solid model of split pillow block

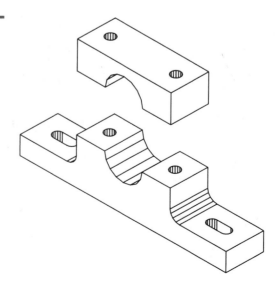

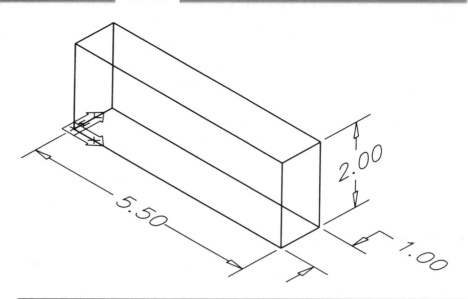

Figure 12.9
Orientation cube

Procedure

Initial Settings

1. Start the model called SPSOL (Split Pillow block SOLID) and enter the following settings:

```
Units = decimal
Limits = -1,-1 to 6.2
Grid = 0.125
Snap Incr. = 0.125
Elevation = 0
Thickness = 2
UCS = WCS
Display a plan (top) view (VPOINT 0,0,1)
Current layer = OCUBE
ISOLINES = 15
```

Creating the Orientation Cube

2. Using the LINE command, draw the orientation cube shown in Figure 12.9. The cube is 5.5″ along the X axis, 1″ along the Y axis, and 2″ along the Z axis. The lower left corner starts at 0,0,0.

Creating the 2D Profile

3. Using the UCS command, create a working plane on the front face, as shown in Figure 12.10.

4. Create a layer called PROFILE and make it current. Display a plan view of the current UCS. Set the thickness to 0.

5. Using the PLINE command, draw a completely closed polyline representing the profile shown in Figure 12.10.

Figure 12.10
Setting the UCS and creating the 2D profile

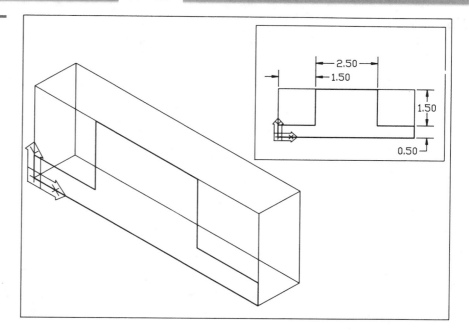

Extruding the Profile into a Solid

The 2D profile will be turned into a 3D solid by means of the EXTRUDE command.

6. Using the VPOINT command, display an axonometric view (1,–1,1).

7. Using the EXTRUDE command, select the profile to be extruded:

```
Command: EXTRUDE
Select objects: pick the polyline profile
Path/<Height of extrusion>: –1
Extrusion taper angle <O>: O
```

The command will turn the profile into a 3D solid, as illustrated in Figure 12.11.

Creating a Hole Through the Solid

8. Using the CYLINDER command, create a solid cylinder that starts on the front face of the solid and extends to the rear of the solid (Figure 12.12):

Figure 12.11
A 3D solid from the 2D profile

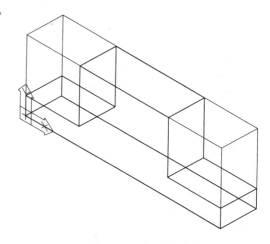

Lab 12.B
Solid Model of Split Pillow
Block

Figure 12.12
Subtracting the cylinder from the body

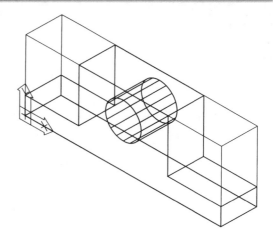

```
Command: CYLINDER
Elliptical/<Center point>: 2.75,1.25,0
Diameter/<Radius>: .5
Height of cylinder: —1
```

9. Using the SUBTRACT command, subtract the cylinder from the main body:

```
Command: SUBTRACT
Select solids and regions to subtract from . . .
Select objects: pick the main body as the source solid
Select solids and regions to subtract . . .
Select objects: pick the cylinder
```

The display may not change but the cylinder was subtracted from the body. Try the HIDE command to test the results. Your screen should look like Figure 12.13 when the OCUBE is frozen.

10. Freeze the OCUBE layer and save the model as SPSOL.

Adding Two Top Bolt Holes

11. Using the UCS command, set the working plane to the top of the model, as shown in Figure 12.14.

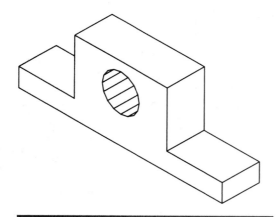

Figure 12.13
The hidden model showing the hole

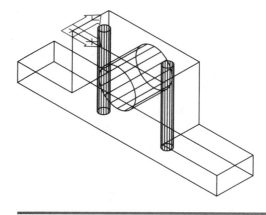

Figure 12.14
Subtracting the two cylinders from the body

Figure 12.15
Creating the 2D profile

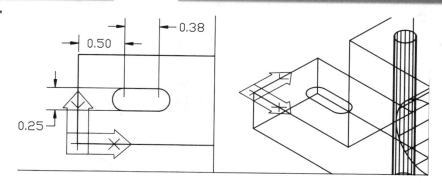

12. Using the CYLINDER command, place two cylinders inside the model, extending from the top to the bottom. Each cylinder has a radius of 0.125 (Figure 12.14).

```
Command: CYLINDER
Elliptical/<Center point>: .375,.5,0
Diameter/<Radius>: .125
Height of cylinder: −2
Command: CYLINDER
Elliptical/<Center point>: 2.125,.5,0
Diameter/<Radius>: .125
Height of cylinder: −2
```

13. Using the SUBTRACT command, subtract the two newly created cylinders from the body.

Adding Slots to the Base Using Extrusion

14. Using the UCS command, set the working plane to the top of the base of the body (see Figure 12.15) and display the plan view of the current UCS.

15. Set both the elevation and the thickness to 0.

16. Using the PLINE command, draw a closed polyline profile, as shown in Figure 12.15.

17. Using the EXTRUDE command, extend the polyline profile into the base and turn it into a 3D solid as shown in Figure 12.16:

```
Command: EXTRUDE
Select objects: pick the slot profile
Path/<Height of extrusion>: −.5
Extrusion taper angle <0>: 0
```

18. Copy the slot solid to the other side of the base, as shown in Figure 12.17.

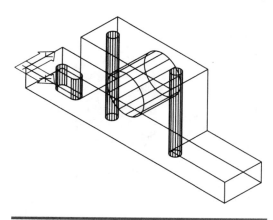

Figure 12.16
Creating a solid slot from a 2D profile

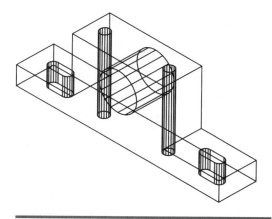

Figure 12.17
Copying the solid slot

Figure 12.18
Using the FILLET command to create fillets

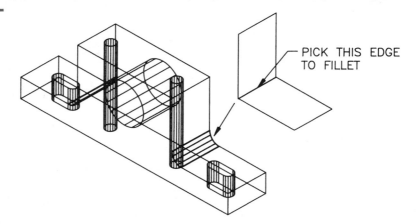

PICK THIS EDGE
TO FILLET

19. Using the SUBTRACT command, subtract the slots from the body in order to create slotted holes in the body.

Adding Fillets to the Body

20. Display the previous axonometric view (1,–1,1).

21. Using the FILLET command, create fillets that run along the edge of the body (Figure 12.18):

```
Command: FILLET
(TRIM mode) Current fillet radius = 0
Polyline/Radius/Trim/<Select first object>: select
the edge as shown in Figure 12.18
Enter radius <0>: .25
Chain/Radius/<Select edge>: select the edges to fillet
```

Slicing the Solid in Two

The solid body will be cut into two pieces: the upper yoke and the lower yoke. The cut is accomplished with the SLICE command.

22. Using the UCS command, set the UCS to equal the WCS and then move the origin to 0,0,1.25. This will set the working plane so that it intersects the body 3/4″ from the top, which is where the slice will take place. The working plane will be used as the slicing plane (Figure 12.19).

23. Using the SLICE command, slice the single solid into two pieces:

```
Command: SLICE
```

Figure 12.19
Slicing the solid along the working plane

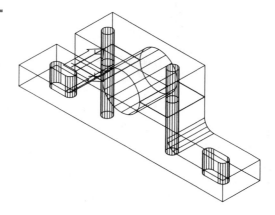

Figure 12.20
Separating the two solids

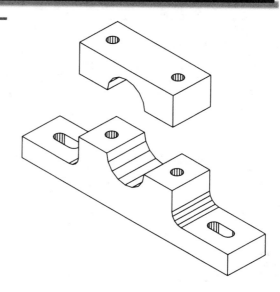

```
Select objects: pick the solid body
Slicing plane by Object/Zaxis/View/XY/YZ/ZX/<3
points>: XY
Point on the XY plane <0,0,0: 0,0,0
Both sides/<Point on the desired side of the plane>: B
```

Separating the Two Solids

24. Using the MOVE command, separate the two solids. Move the top solid 1.5″ in the Z direction (Figure 12.20).

25. Use the HIDE command to observe your finished model.

26. Save the model as SPSOL.

27. Experiment by reassembling the upper and lower yokes and adding the socket headed cap screw from Lab 12.A.

Assignments

1. Create the solid model of a strap clamp shown in Figure 12.21.

2. Create the solid model of a die base shown in Figure 12.22.

3. Examine the solid model of a miniature pneumatic cylinder body, as shown in Figure 12.23. Generate it.

4. Research the works of the British sculptor Henry Moore. Create a solid model that is similar in style to one of his sculptures.

Figure 12.21
Solid model of a strap clamp

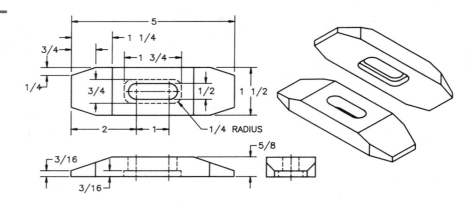

Figure 12.22
Solid model of a die base

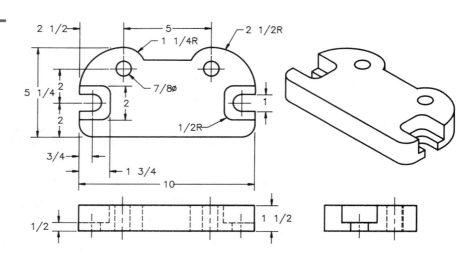

Figure 12.23
Solid model of a miniature pneumatic cylinder

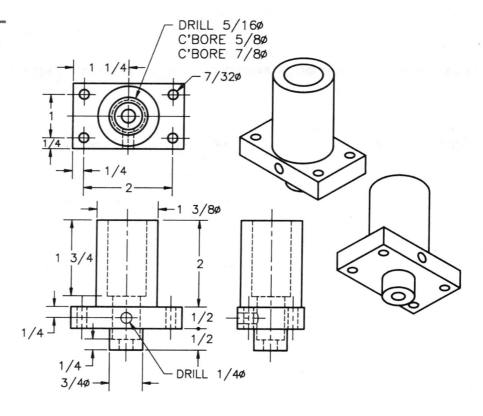

Enhancing the Use of 3D

The chapters in this part will give you some helpful tips, tricks, shortcuts, and timesaving hints for generating 3D models. Experienced users eventually discover these helpers on their own. But they are usually unknown and inaccessible to beginners. Too frequently left out of manuals, these helpful tips will add to your growing experience with 3D CAD. This "wisdom" is incorporated in two chapters: Chapter 13, which focuses on the creation of three-dimensional libraries, and Chapter 14, which covers parametric design.

CHAPTER 13

Three-Dimensional Libraries

Overview

This chapter provides instruction on the creation of repetitious libraries of models. It also explains how to modify the elements within these libraries. For the architect, these elements might be window or door styles; for the mechanical engineer, they might be various nuts, bolts, or structural members. Thus, the elements contained within libraries will differ from discipline to discipline, but the timesaving nature of the libraries themselves is a constant. This chapter also describes three movement commands that aid in the orientation of 3D objects.

Concepts Explored

- The process of creating 3D symbols and the factors that control their creation
- The scaling characteristics of 3D symbols
- Timesaving techniques in the use of 3D symbols
- The proper orientation for the insertion of 3D symbols
- Differences between blocks and external reference files.

13.1 Introduction

As you probably know, 2D users employ blocks to speed up the drawing process. Blocks are of no less importance to 3D users. In fact, blocks have new applications in the 3D realm. Not only can 3D users scale, rotate, and position 3D blocks to suit the models being constructed, but also they can extrude the forms—stretch the blocks three dimensionally—to make connections, such as those needed in piping, structural, or wood construction.

Because it is now possible to add external files to drawings by either inserting blocks or attaching external reference files (Xrefs), we'll refer to the original term *block* by a new term, *symbol*. A symbol is any group or association of entities that creates a single object, whether it is a block or an Xref. The differences between blocks and Xrefs are explained in Section 13.6, which also explains how Xrefs can be substituted for blocks. Before we do that, however, let's consider how symbols are created and used.

13.2 Creation Considerations

The 3D symbol is much the same as the 2D symbol, except of course for the obvious third dimension. The process of constructing a 3D symbol is virtually the same as that of constructing any three-dimensional model. But when a model is being constructed to be used as a symbol, some construction factors become especially important. The addition of the third dimension affects not only the shape of an object, giving it a three-dimensional form, but also the base point and the insertion process.

The orientation of the model during construction has a direct bearing on how it can be oriented when it is inserted into another model. Currently, Auto-CAD allows insertion rotation in the *X* and *Y* directions only. A model cannot be rotated in the *Z* axis during the insertion process. Thus, during initial construction, the orientation of the model in the *Z* direction must be considered.

The positioning of the base point in the application of 2D symbols is an easy task. But with three-dimensional models, the *Z* location must be considered because the new location of the base point will have an effect on its placement when inserted. When a base point is moved from the 0*Z* location on a model, AutoCAD informs the user, "Warning, *Z* insertion base is not zero." This is nothing to be worried about, only something to note. When entering the base point, the *Z* axis can be entered as a third coordinate (as in 34, 21, 8) or it can be set automatically by object snapping onto an existing three-dimensional entity.

13.3 Insertion and Working Planes

When inserting a 3D model, it is (obviously) important to orient the model. This orientation usually is controlled by the current model's presently active UCS working plane. The user simply activates the working plane on which the 3D symbol is to be inserted. When inserting a 3D symbol, however, orientation is affected by the alignment of the WCS and UCS during the creation of that symbol.

Symbols can be created in two ways—as an original model file or with the use of the BLOCK command inside another model file. Each creation method affects the orientation of the model during insertion differently.

If the model is a separate external file that is to be inserted into a target model, the external file's WCS aligns itself with the target model's active UCS (refer to Figure 13.1). Therefore, the user must choose the desired alignment

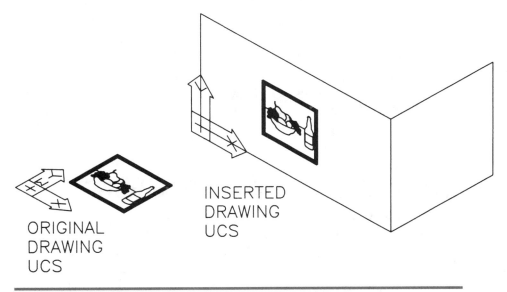

ORIGINAL
DRAWING
UCS

INSERTED
DRAWING
UCS

Figure 13.1
WCS of an external file aligns itself to the active UCS of the current model upon insertion

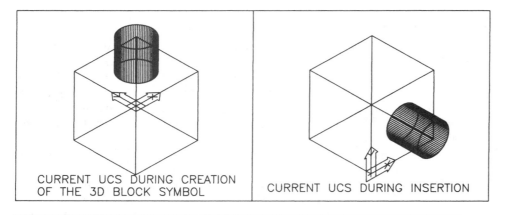

Figure 13.2
UCS of block aligns itself to the active UCS of the current model upon insertion

3D Viewpoint

Inserting Blocks and the UCS
Always remember to set the UCS to the correct working plane before insertion takes place to ensure proper alignment of the symbol.

based on the WCS *before* the symbol model is created. During symbol creation the user must realize that whichever plane on the symbol model is aligned to the WCS will also be aligned to the UCS of the current model when the symbol is inserted.

If the 3D symbol is created using the BLOCK command, then the UCS working plane that was active during the block creation will align itself to the current model's active UCS working plane during insertion (refer to Figure 13.2). In this case, during creation the user must realize that whichever plane on the symbol model is aligned to the UCS when the block is made will be aligned to the current UCS on insertion.

13.4 Scaling the 3D Symbol

A 3D symbol can be scaled upon insertion in the same manner as a 2D symbol, with the additional option of scaling in the Z direction.

Note the input for this INSERT command:

```
Command: INSERT
Block name (or ?): NUT
Insertion point: 3, 11, 4
X scale factor <1>/Corner/XYZ: here the user can
enter the X factor as usual or can enter XYZ.
```

AutoCAD responds to this command with the scale factor for Z as well as those for X and Y:

```
X scale factor <1>/Corner: .375
Y scale factor <default=X>: press <Enter> to default
Z scale factor <default=X>: now the user can enter a
scale for the Z direction
```

Figure 13.3
Scaling a 3D symbol in any axis

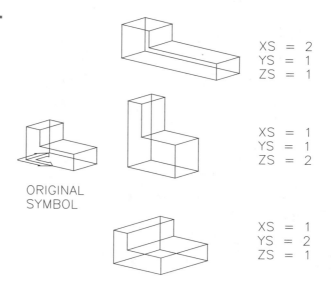

ORIGINAL SYMBOL

XS = 2
YS = 1
ZS = 1

XS = 1
YS = 1
ZS = 2

XS = 1
YS = 2
ZS = 1

This allows the 3D symbol to be scaled independently in all three axes, as shown in Figure 13.3. Keep in mind that if the scaling factor of all three axes is not equal, the user cannot explode the block.

Rotation angle <O>: **enter the appropriate rotation angle here**

13.5 Simple Versus Complex Symbol Models

We all know that three-dimensional models can get quite complex in form. A complex model that is going to be used as a symbol can become cumbersome to manipulate on the screen. And, depending on the model's complexity, it can significantly slow the computer's processing speed. To overcome both of these problems at once, we can use the technique of 3D symbol replacement, which uses a complex symbol or series of symbols to define a whole model. The 3D symbol replacement technique simply involves having two definitions of a symbol type—a simple symbol and a complex symbol. The complex symbol is the completed, fully detailed model. The simple symbol is constructed of rectangular forms that outline the area of the symbol and is used for insertion and manipulation in the model. Both symbols should be created as individual drawing files. The entire model is laid out using the simple symbols. Once the planning and placement are accomplished and the overall model is complete, the simple symbols in the current workfile are quickly replaced with the complex, fully detailed ones from external files. This is accomplished using AutoCAD's ability to update symbols with the use of the equal (=) sign during the insertion process. Figure 13.4 illustrates the use of 3D symbol replacement. It shows a layout for a grocery store checkout counter. During the initial construction phase, a simple symbol called CHECKS (CHECKout counter Simple) is inserted into the desired locations. Once construction is complete, the INSERT command is used to replace the simple symbol with the completed complex symbol called CHECKC (CHECKout counter Complex):

Command: **INSERT**
Block name (or ?): **CHECKS=CHECKC**
Block CHECKS redefined.
Insertion point: **press CTRL C**

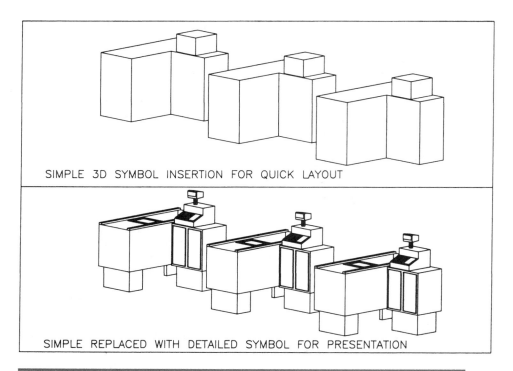

Figure 13.4
Replacing a simple symbol with a complex one

Now all occurrences of CHECKS in the current workfile are replaced (redefined) by the external file CHECKC. (*Note:* The name of the symbol in the model remains CHECKS, but the symbol itself appears as CHECKC.)

Using simple symbols first can save time and make the manipulation process easier. Because a simple symbol does not have as many entities as a complex one, the computer does not have to process as much information. Therefore, movement of the symbols—simply zooming in—is accomplished much more easily and quickly.

13.6 Xrefs and Blocks

As mentioned earlier, entities that are grouped or associated into a single object are known as blocks. The process that allows many entities to be manipulated as one in a variety of applications, which has always been and continues to be useful and efficient, now relates both to blocks and external referenced files (Xrefs). Blocks and Xrefs behave in a similar fashion; they both can be attached (inserted), scaled, and rotated. But there are differences, too. Once blocks are created or inserted from external files, the entities are stored in a library inside the drawing file, from which they can be recalled at any time. This internal library retains the original form of the block, regardless of what happens to the original external file. This is an important facet of blocks, and it is the main difference between them and Xrefs.

Xrefs differ from blocks in another, related way: in their referenced form, Xrefs are not physically part of the drawing. They are like a projection of the external file onto the current workfile (referencing file). The Xref entities are not added to an internal library, only the name and path of the referenced file are kept in the current workfile. The Xrefs can be seen, but not modified. However, when the original external file is changed, these changes automatically appear in the Xrefs. When a change is made to the referenced files, then that same change is made to the referencing file. Whenever the referencing file is opened in the drawing editor or if the XREF/RELOAD command is used, that file is automatically updated to match the external file.

Because the Xrefs are not actually part of the workfile, they can handicap the workfile in one respect. Although it saves disk space when a workfile storing only the names and not the entities of referenced files is saved, what happens when that disk is given to someone who does not have access to the referenced files? Either the external files have to be given as well or they have to be permanently attached to the referencing file.

You'll need to determine which symbol best suits the needs of each of your models. Use a block symbol when you do not want the block symbol to be altered if the original external file is modified. For example, you would not want the parts (symbols) of a completed design to suddenly change when the external file is updated in some way, so you would use blocks as the symbols in that design. (Should you need to insert revised block symbols in a completed design, you can do so manually by reinserting the block symbols as outlined in Section 13.5.) Use Xrefs when symbols are constantly changing and you want the model to reflect those changes automatically. When you so desire, you can permanently attach an entire external referenced file to a model by using the XREF/BIND command. The XBIND command allows you to partially attach an Xref to a model. Basically, these commands turn Xrefs into blocks.

Note: The labs in this chapter use blocks, but you can and should experiment with Xrefs in order to become versatile in using both kinds of symbols.

Automatic Revisions

What makes the Xref so valuable is its ability to affect automatic revisions in the drawing that references it. Whenever a drawing is opened, it automatically recalls the external drawing information from the Xrefs. If one of the externally referenced drawings has been revised, the revision is automatically shown in the newly opened drawing. In this way, you can assemble a complex drawing from individual external referenced drawings and have the main drawing automatically updated whenever changes are made to the individual drawings. A drawing of a mechanical assembly can have its parts updated whenever a change is made to an individual part. A complex building drawing, which might contain architectural, electrical, and mechanical systems, can have each discipline's drawing externally referenced. Whenever a change is made to one of the discipline's drawings, the main drawing will reflect the change.

Xref Do's and Don'ts

As mentioned earlier, Xrefs are very similar to blocks but there are some differences. Here are some things they can do, as well as some things they can't:

- You can manipulate the layers of an Xref but you cannot draw on an Xref layer. Layers added using Xref have the name of the Xref added to the layer name, separated by a vertical bar (|).
- You can object snap to Xref entities but cannot directly change the Xref entities.
- You can see Xref blocks that have been inserted in the Xref drawing, but you cannot use the Xref blocks directly. Blocks of an Xref drawing are called dependent blocks because they are dependent on the Xref drawing of which they are a part.

3D Viewpoint

Blocks and Xrefs

You cannot Xref a file into a drawing where the file has already been inserted as a block. You must erase all occurrences of the block and purge the drawing of the block before you can Xref the file.

Attaching and Detaching

To reference a drawing externally, use the Attach option of the XREF command and select the name of the file to attach. If it was already attached, then all occurrences of the Xref in the drawing are updated and another copy is made to be placed in the drawing. If a block of the same name has already been inserted into the drawing, the command is aborted and an error message is displayed. Note that you cannot attach a drawing that is already a block. An example of the command follows:

The following is the procedure to attach an Xref to a drawing:

1. Command: XREF
2. The External Reference dialog box appears as shown in Figure 13.5A.
3. Pick the Attach button and the Attach Xref dialog appears as in Figure 13.5B.
4. Pick the Browse button and the Select File to attach dialog box appears as shown in Figure 13.5C.
5. Select file and Open.
6. Specify parameters, as shown in Figure 13.5D.
7. Place Xref if Specify On-screen was checked.

To remove all occurrences of an Xref in a drawing, use the Detach option of the XREF command.

Updating an Xref

To update the definition of an Xref in a currently open drawing, use the Reload option of the XREF command and highlight the files. This command is useful if you suspect that an Xref drawing was modified while you were working on the current drawing.

Binding and the XBIND Command

You may want to attach Xrefs permanently to the master drawing when giving the complete drawing to someone outside the drawing network or to prevent automatic, and perhaps unintentional, revisions. There are two ways to go about this. If you use the Bind option of the XREF command, the entire Xref drawing is then changed into a block and added permanently to the drawing (you can still erase the block and purge). If you would like to add part of an Xref drawing, use the XBIND command. In the case of XBIND, you can add blocks, dimension styles, layers, linetypes, and text styles from an Xref without adding the entire Xref drawing. Any parts of an Xref that are added to the current drawing are named with the Xref drawing name, except now the name is separated by a number sandwiched between two dollar signs (0). If the name already exists, the number is increased (1).

Figure 13.5
Dialog boxes used to attach and Xref

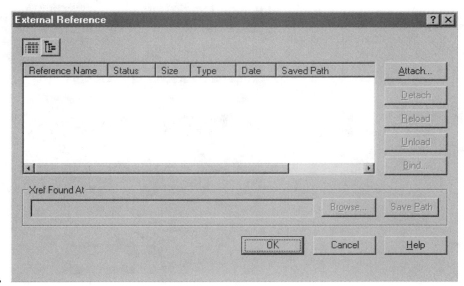

A.

B.

C.

Attach Xref

Xref Name

Browse...   HEXACYL

Path: D:\AutoCAD R14\hexacyl.dwg

Reference Type
- (●) Attachment   ( ) Overlay

Parameters

At: 0,0,0   ☑ Specify On-screen

X Scale Factor: 1.00   ☐ Specify On-screen

Y Scale Factor: 1.00

Z Scale Factor: 1.00

Rotation Angle: 0   ☐ Specify On-screen

OK
Cancel
Help

☑ Include Path

D.

Path Names

When you attach a drawing, the location of the file (or path) is also stored with the name so that when loading the master drawing, the program knows where to find the Xref drawings. If you change the location of an Xref drawing, you must change its referenced path in the master drawing with the Browse/SavePath options of the XREF command.

Using the Overlay Option

The Overlay option references a drawing into the current drawing. If the current drawing is Xref'ed into an additional drawing, the overlay will not appear. Title blocks commonly use the overlay.

13.7 3D Movement Commands Useful for Moving Blocks

There are three 3D movement commands, ALIGN, ROTATE3D, and MIRROR3D, that can be invaluable in the manipulation of 3D symbols as well as any three-dimensional geometry.

The ALIGN Command

The ALIGN command is used to align existing entities to specified 2D or 3D planes. The command performs a rotation and a movement in one command. Refer to part A of Figure 13.6 and the following demonstration of the command:

```
Command: ALIGN
Select Objects: pick the objects you want to move
Specify 1st source point: pick a point on the objects
(P1)
Specify 1st destination point: pick the point to
which you want the first point to travel (P2)
```

Figure 13.6
Using the ALIGN command

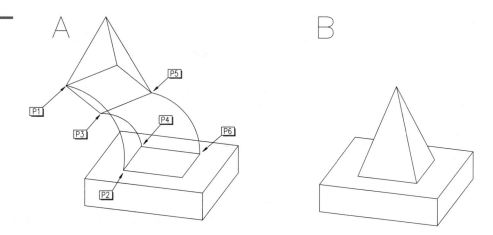

Specify 2nd source point: **pick a second point on the objects (P3)** (This point, in combination with the first point, defines a source axis on the objects.)
Specify 2nd destination point: **pick a second destination point (P4)** (This point, in combination with the first destination point, defines the destination axis.)
Specify 3rd source point or <continue>: **pick a third source point (P5)** (This point is used with the first and second source points to form a source plane.)
Specify 3rd destination point: **pick a third destination point (P6)** (This point is used with the first and second destination points to form a destination plane.)
Scale objects to alignment points?[yes/no]<no>:

The source plane is aligned with the destination plane, causing the objects to move and rotate in 3D space, into the new position as shown in part B of Figure 13.6.

The ROTATE3D Command

The ROTATE3D command is used to rotate existing entities about a three-dimensional axis that you define with the Object, Last, View, Xaxis, Yaxis, Zaxis, or 2points options. Figure 13.7 illustrates the use of the ROTATE3D command using the Entity option:

Command: **ROTATE3D**
Select Objects: **pick the objects to rotate**

Figure 13.7
Using the ROTATE3D command

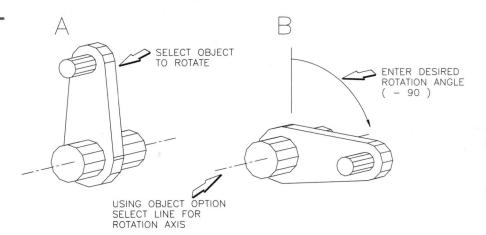

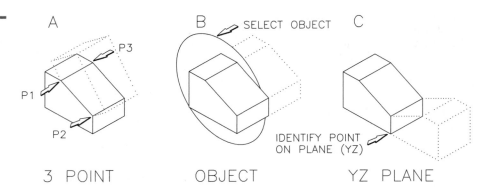

Figure 13.8
Using the MIRROR3D command with
various options

```
Axis by Object/Last/View/Xaxis/Yaxis/Zaxis/<2points>:
Object
Pick a line, circle, arc or 2D-polyline segment: pick
object to use as the rotation axis
<Rotation angle>/Reference: enter the desired rota-
tion angle
```

OPTION	DEFINITION
Object	Aligns the axis of rotation with an existing object
Last	Uses the last specified axis of rotation
View	Aligns the axis of rotation with the viewing direction of the current viewpoint and a specified point
Xaxis, Yaxis, Zaxis	Aligns the axis of rotation with one of the X, Y, or Z axes and a specified point
2Points	Aligns the axis of rotation through two specified points.

The MIRROR3D Command

The MIRROR3D command allows the user to mirror an object about an arbitrary three-dimensional plane defined with the Object, Last, Zaxis, View, XY, YZ, ZX, or 3point options. Refer to Figure 13.8 and the following for a demonstration of the command:

```
Command: MIRROR3D
Select objects
Plane by Object/Last/Zaxis/View/XY/YZ/ZX/<3points>:
enter 3point
1st point on plane: enter a point (P1)
2nd point on plane: enter a point (P2)
3rd point on plane: enter a point (P3)
Delete old objects? <N>: enter Y to erase the origi-
nal copy or N to keep it
```

The MIRROR3D command works similarly to the MIRROR command, except that the former requires a mirror plane defined in three dimensions.

Lab 13.A

Purpose

House Symbols

Lab 13.A will familiarize you with the creation of 3D symbols. In this lab, you will create a symbol of a window, a door, and a fence section. These symbols will be used again in Lab 13.B.

Objective

You will be able to construct 3D symbols.

Primary Commands

PLINE
BASE

Final Model

Figure 13.9 shows the 3D symbols you'll be creating.

Procedure

1. Start a new drawing called W4X3-6 (Window 4′ by 3′6″) with the following settings. Use 3DSET as the prototype drawing.

   ```
   Units = Architectural
   Limits = -1",-1" to 5',10'
   Grid = 1'
   Snap Incr. = 1"
   Elevation = 0
   Thickness = 1"
   Current Layer = 0
   UCS = WCS
   Viewport Configuration = ORTHO1
   Fill = off
   ```

Creating the Window

2. Activate the plan-view viewport.

3. Using the PLINE command, draw the window frame as shown in Figure 13.10. Use a width of 2″ for the polyline. The coordinates for the polyline are

   ```
   P1 = 0,0,0          P2 = 0,3'8"
   P3 = 4'2",3'8"      P4 = 4'2",0
   ```

   Close the polyline.

Figure 13.9
3D symbols of a window, a door, and a fence section

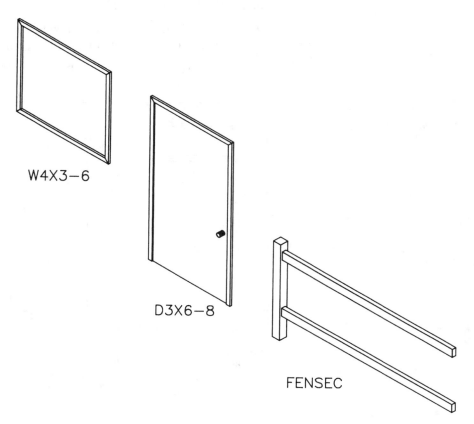

W4X3—6

D3X6—8

FENSEC

Figure 13.10
Window symbol

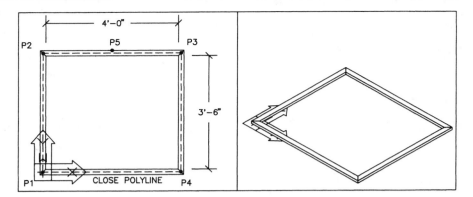

4. Use the BASE command to set the base insertion point of P5. Enter the coordinate 2'1", 3'9", 0. This will place the base insertion point at the top rear of the window frame.

   If desired, other features can be added to the model before it is saved.

5. Save the model as W4X3-6.

Creating the Door

6. Erase the window entity.

7. Using the PLINE command, draw the door frame as shown in Figure 13.11. Use a width of 2" for the polyline. The coordinates for the polyline are

P1 = 0,0,0	P2 = 0,6'9"
P3 = 3'8",6'9"	P4 = 3'8",0

   Do not close the polyline.

8. Set the Thickness to 0.5".

9. Using the PLINE command, draw the door as shown in Figure 13.12. The polyline will have a width of 3'6". The coordinates for the polyline are

   P1 = 1'10",0,0   P2 = 1'10",6'8"

Figure 13.11
Door frame symbol

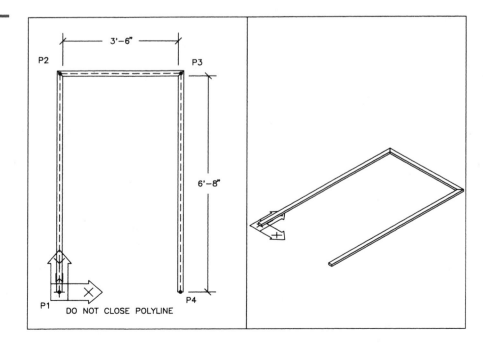

Figure 13.12
Door symbol

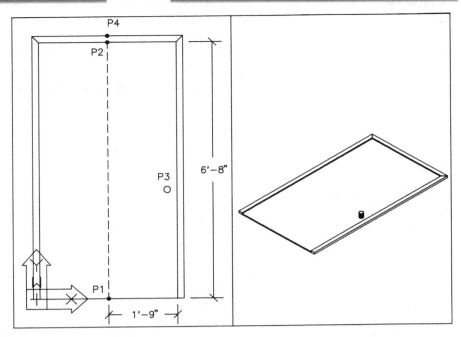

10. Draw a circle with a thickness of 2.5″ and a diameter of 2″ at the coordinates 3′4″, 2′10″, 0.5″. Refer to Figure 13.12 for P3.

11. Use the BASE command to set the base insertion point of P4. Enter the coordinates 1′10″, 6′10″, 0. This will place the base insertion point at the top rear of the door frame.

12. Save the model as D3X6-8.

Creating the Fence Section

13. Erase the door entities.

14. Use the PLINE command to draw the post. Refer to Figure 13.13. The polyline will have a width of 4″, a thickness of 4′, and an elevation of 0. Draw the polyline from 0,0 to 4″,0.

Figure 13.13
Fence section symbol

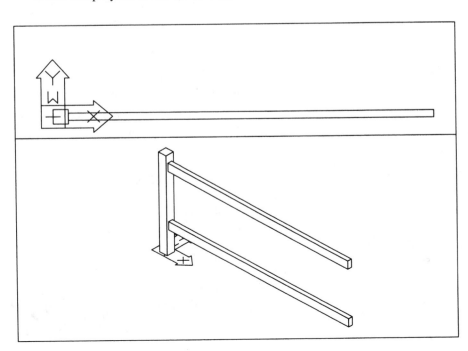

15. Use the PLINE command to draw the fence boards as shown in Figure 13.13. The polyline will have a width of 2″, a thickness of 4″, and a length of 8′. The bottom elevation of the board is 3′4″.

16. Use the COPY command to copy the top board to the lower location. The bottom elevation of the lower board is 1′.

17. Use the BASE command to set the insertion point on the fence section to the coordinates 0,0,0.

18. Save the model as FENSEC (FENce SECtion).

Lab 13.B

Purpose

Symbol Insertion

Lab 13.B will show you how to manipulate 3D symbols. In this lab, you will insert the symbols of the window, door, and fence section you created in Lab 13.A into the BDWELL model you created in Lab 8.B in Chapter 8.

Objective

You will be able to insert and manipulate 3D symbols.

Primary Commands

UCS
INSERT

Final Model

Figure 13.14 shows the 3D house model you'll be creating.

Procedure

1. Restore the BDWELL model created in Lab 8.B. Use these settings:

```
Grid = 1'
Snap Incr. = 1"
Elevation = 0
Thickness = 0
Current Layer = 0
UCS = WCS
Viewport Configuration = ORTHO1
TREE layer = frozen
Fill = off
```

Inserting the Door

2. Create a layer called DOOR, and make it current.

3. Using the UCS command, create a working plane on the front of the building, as shown in Figure 13.15.

4. Activate the front-view viewport.

5. Use the INSERT command to insert the door (D3X6-8), as shown in Figure 13.15. The scale is kept at 1 (full size). Notice how the door is aligned to the wall.

Figure 13.14
3D house model

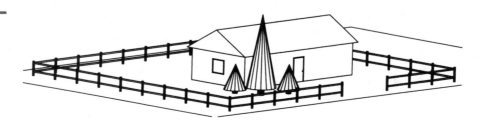

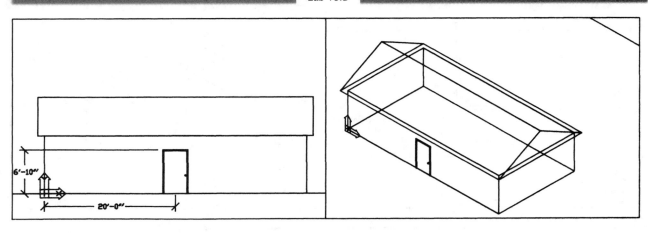

Figure 13.15
Inserting the door

Inserting the Window

6. Create a layer called WINDOW, and make it current.

7. Using the UCS command, create a working plane on the left side of the building, as shown in Figure 13.16.

8. Activate the right-side viewport and use the PLAN/UCS command to display the left-side view.

9. Use the INSERT command to insert the window (W4X3-6), as shown in Figure 13.16. The scale is kept at 1 (full size). Notice how the window is aligned to the wall.

Inserting the Fence Section

10. Create a layer called FENCE, and make it current.

11. Using the UCS command, set the UCS to the WCS.

12. Activate the plan-view viewport.

13. Use the INSERT command to insert the fence section (FENSEC) at the coordinates 68'8", 5'2", 0. Refer to Figure 13.17.

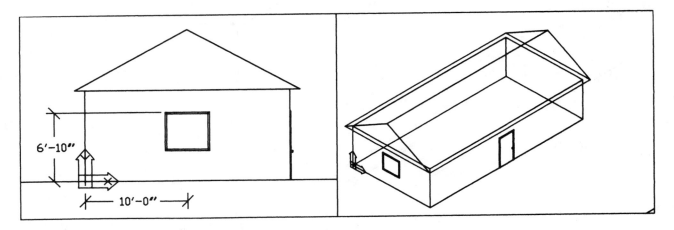

Figure 13.16
Inserting the window

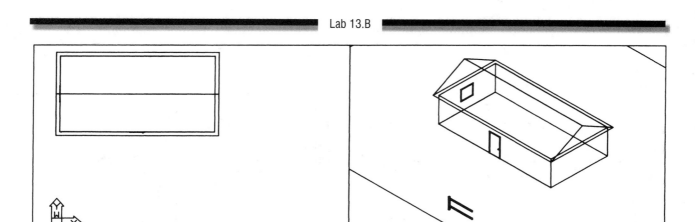

Figure 13.17
Inserting the fence section

Copying the Symbol

14. Use the ARRAY command to copy the fence section along the front to the left, as shown in Figure 13.18. The distance between the posts is 8′4″. The array has one row and three columns.

15. Repeat the insert and copy procedures to form the fence around the lot perimeter. Refer to Figure 13.19.

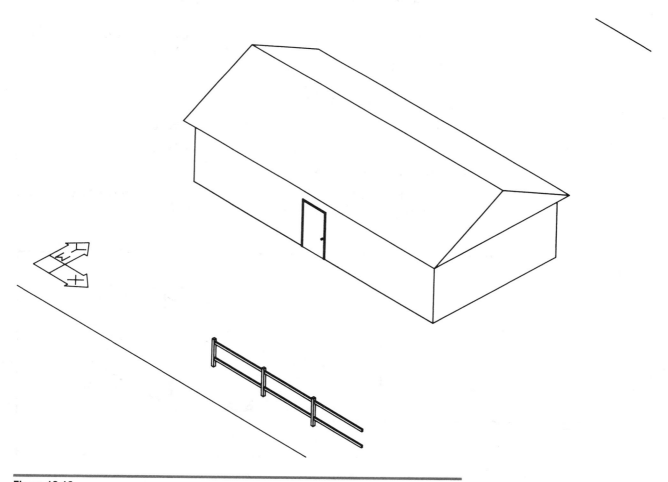

Figure 13.18
Copying the fence along the front

Figure 13.19
Layout of the fence perimeter

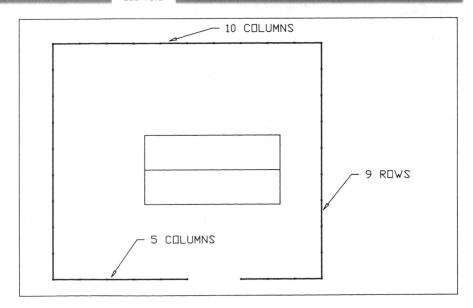

16. Use PLINE to add the missing fence post.

17. Thaw the TREE layer and use the VPOINT command to display a view similar to that shown in Figure 13.14. Use the HIDE command and observe the results.

18. Save the model as BDWELL.

Lab 13.C

Simple Versus Complex Blocks and Xrefs

Purpose

Lab 13.C will demonstrate how to insert simple blocks in a model and then replace them with complex blocks when the layout is complete. You will also practice the application of Xrefs to revise a model automatically. This lab makes use of the models created in Chapter 5, Labs 5.B and 5.C, the Table and Chair models. It will also make use of the 3D floor plan from Assignment 4 in Chapter 5.

Objectives

You will be able to

- Use simple and complex blocks.
- Use Xrefs to revise a model automatically.

Primary Commands

INSERT
XREF

Procedure

Part A: Simple and Complex Blocks—Simple Table

1. Start a new drawing called TBSIM (TaBle SIMple) with the following settings:

```
Units = Architectural
Limits = −1',−1' to 6',4'
Grid = 1'
Snap Incr. = 1'
UCS = WCS
UCSICON = ON, ORIGIN
```

Figure 13.20
TBSIM model

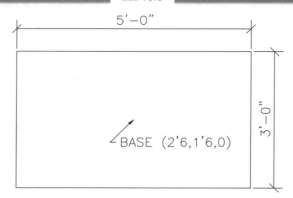

2. Refer to Figure 13.20, and create the 3D rectangle using the AI_BOX command. This will represent a simplified version of the TABLE model.

```
Command: AI_BOX
Corner of box: 0,0,0
Length of box: 5'
Cube/<width>: 3'
Height: 2'5"
Rotation angle about Z axis: 0
```

3. Using the BASE command, set the base insertion point to 2'6",1'6",0. This is the center of the box in the *X* and *Y* axes. This point must match the complex TABLE model.

4. Save the drawing as TBSIM.

Simple Chair

5. Start a new drawing called CHSIM (CHair SIMple) with the following settings:

```
Units = Architectural
Limits = -1',-1' to 3',2'
Grid = 1"
Snap Incr. = 1"
UCS = WCS
UCSICON = ON, ORIGIN
```

6. Refer to Figure 13.21, and create the model using a line and an arc with a 3'5" thickness. This will represent the simplified version of the CHAIR model.

7. Using the BASE command, set the base insertion point to 9-1/2",8-1/2",0. This is the center of the model in the X and Y axes. This must match the complex CHAIR model.

8. Save the drawing as CHSIM.

Simple Layout

9. Start a new drawing called BHALL (Banquet HALL) with the following settings:

Figure 13.21
CHSIM model

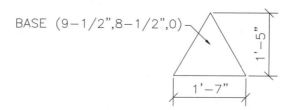

Figure 13.22
Simple layout

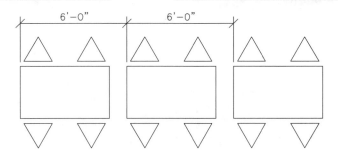

```
Units = Architectural
Limits = -1',-1' to 19',7'
Grid = 1'
Snap Incr. = 6"
UCS = WCS
UCSICON = ON, ORIGIN
```

10. Insert the simple blocks of the table (TBSIM) and the chair (CHSIM) to create the layout shown in Figure 13.22. Remember to rotate the chair when required.

11. Save the model as BHALL.

Replacing the Simple with the Complex

12. Display an axonometric view $(1,-1,1)$.

13. Using the INSERT command, replace the simple table with the complex one:

```
Command: INSERT
Block name (or ?)<current>:TBSIM=TABLE  (The TABLE model
was created in Lab 5.B.)
Block TBSIM redefined
Regenerating Drawing
Insertion point: CTRL C  (Cancel the insertion.)
```

The complex table should now be displayed in the scene, as shown in Figure 13.23.

14. Repeat the INSERT command, now replacing the simple chair with the complex one:

```
Command: INSERT
Block name (or ?)<current>:CHSIM=CHAIR  (The CHAIR model
was created in Lab 5.C.)
```

Figure 13.23
Model with complex tables and simple chairs

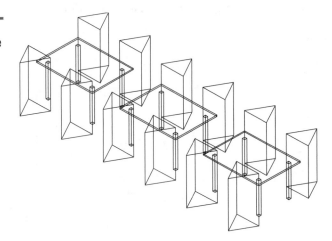

Figure 13.24
Complete replacement

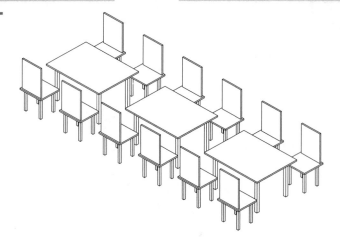

```
Block CHSIM redefined
Regenerating drawing
Insertion point: CTRL C (Cancel the insertion.)
```

The scene now shows the complex tables and chairs illustrated in Figure 13.24.

15. Save the model as BHALL.

Reversal

16. Using the INSERT command once more, return the tables and chairs to their simple forms. Use the following commands:

```
Command: INSERT
CHSIM=CHSIM
```

and

```
Command: INSERT
TBSIM=TBSIM
```

It is that easy to switch from simple to complex blocks and back again.
Quit this drawing.

Part B: Using Xrefs

17. Make a copy of the complex table and chair models. Name the copies TBOFF (TaBle OFFice) and CHOFF (CHair OFFice), respectively.

18. Open the 3D floor plan from Assignment 4 in Chapter 5. Turn the FILL variable off.

19. Display a plan view, as shown in Figure 13.25.

Figure 13.25
Plan view and isometric view

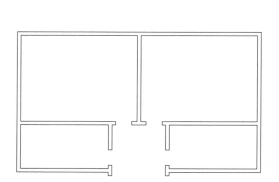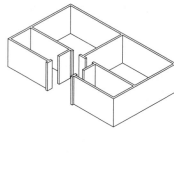

Figure 13.26
Attaching the TBOFF Xref

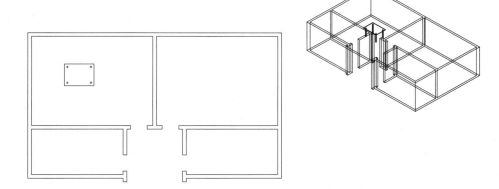

20. Using the XREF command, attach the TBOFF model, as shown in Figure 13.26.
    The table should have a scale of 1 and a rotation of 180 degrees.

21. Using the XREF command, attach the CHOFF model, as shown in Figure 13.27.
    The chair should have a scale of 1 and a rotation of 180 degrees.

22. Repeat to fill the office as shown in Figure 13.28.

23. Save the model as OFFICE.

Figure 13.27
Attaching the CHOFF Xref

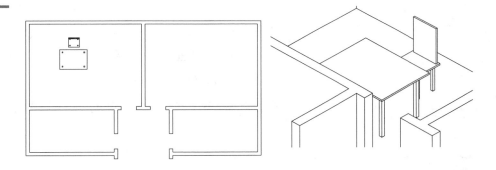

Figure 13.28
Office with desks and chairs inserted

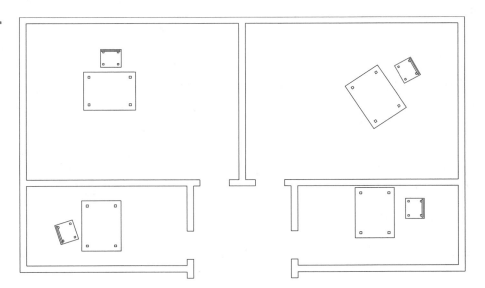

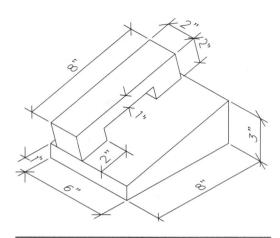

Figure 13.29
PHONE drawing

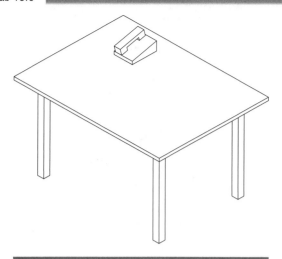

Figure 13.30
Inserting the PHONE on the table

24. Start a new drawing called PHONE with the following settings:

```
Units = Architectural
Limits = -1",-1" to 7",9"
Grid = 1"
Snap Incr. = 0.5"
UCS = WCS
UCSICON = ON, ORIGIN
```

25. Create the model shown in Figure 13.29 using lines and 3D faces.

26. Set the BASE point to one of the corners of the phone.

27. Save the model as PHONE.

28. Open the TBOFF model.

29. Using the INSERT command, place the PHONE model on the table, as shown in Figure 13.30.

Figure 13.31
The final outcome of the Xrefs

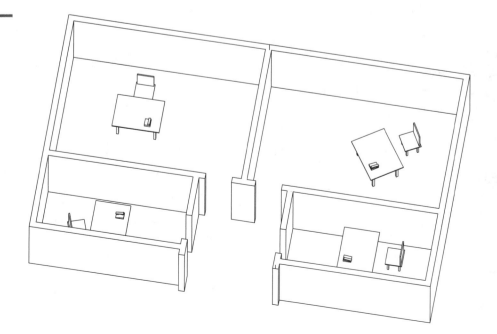

30. Save the model as TBOFF.

31. Open the OFFICE file and watch the results. The PHONE model has been added automatically to every table in the office. The orientation of the phones may be incorrect based on the orientation of the tables with which they were first attached using XREF. To correct the orientation, use the ROTATE command to swing the tables around as needed. Refer to Figure 13.31 for the final layout.

Questions

1. How does the orientation of a symbol model in its own model file affect its orientation when it is inserted into another model?

2. How does the orientation of a symbol model when it is made into a block affect its orientation when it is inserted?

3. What option allows scaling of a 3D symbol independently in all three axes?

4. What is the benefit of using simple 3D symbols and then replacing them with more complex ones?

5. What is the procedure for replacing 3D symbols in a model?

6. Why is it convenient to use polylines to construct window frames?

7. You must take into consideration one extra factor when using the BASE command to create 3D symbols. What is it?

8. What must you always remember to do just before inserting a 3D symbol?

9. What 3D movement commands assist in the movement of objects in three-dimensional space?

Assignments

1. Use the previously created models given in the following list to assemble the kitchen table shown in Figure 13.32. Save the model as BKIT. It will be used in Chapter 14, Assignment 1; in Lab 15.C in Chapter 15; and in Chapter 17, Assignment 2.

3D SYMBOL	SOURCE
TABLE	Lab 5.B
CHAIR	Lab 5.C
COFMK	Lab 7.C
COFPT	Lab 8.A
COFMUG	Chapter 8, Assignment 1
SPOON	Chapter 8, Assignment 5

2. Assemble a nut and bolt, as shown in Figure 13.33. Use the previously created models given in the following list. Save the model as NBOLT. Remember to set the BASE point of the symbol during the creation stage.

3D SYMBOL	SOURCE
BOLT	Chapter 7, Assignment 1
NUT	Chapter 7, Assignment 5

3. Create a 3D symbol of a hexagon bolt head. Refer to Figure 13.34. The model should fit within a 1-unit cubic area. Remember to add a 3D face to

Figure 13.32
Kitchen table layout

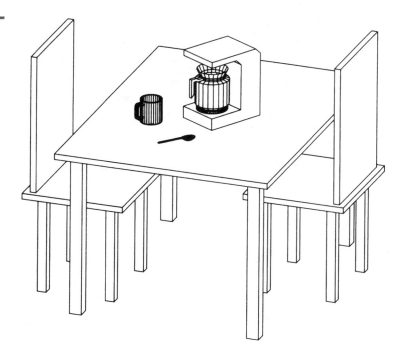

the top of the hexagon. Save it as BHEAD. This will be used in Chapter 14, Assignment 3.

4. Generate the two common architectural models shown in Figure 13.35. Use 3D objects, such as the box and the pyramid, to perform the construction. Create the models using the full-size dimensions they would have if used on a house. Assume the lamppost would be placed beside a driveway and the coach light would be placed beside the exterior entrances. Save the lamppost as LPOST and the coach light as COLIT.

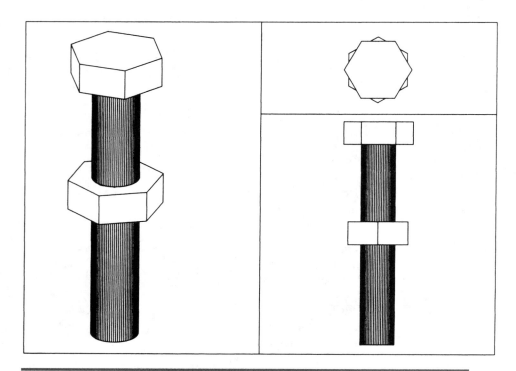

Figure 13.33
Nut and bolt assembly

Figure 13.34
Hexagon bolt head symbol

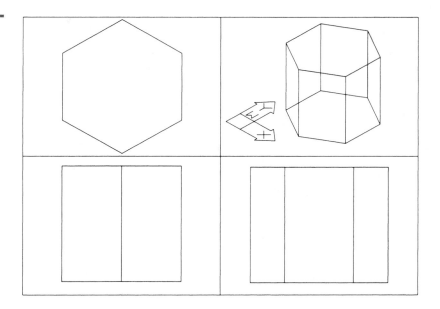

5. Construct a grocery store checkout in a manner similar to Figure 13.4. Create a simple 3D symbol and perform the initial layout. Then, create the fully detailed checkout symbol and replace the simple symbol with the complex 3D symbol. Once you have completed the layout, try switching the symbols back and forth.

Figure 13.35
Lamppost and coach light models

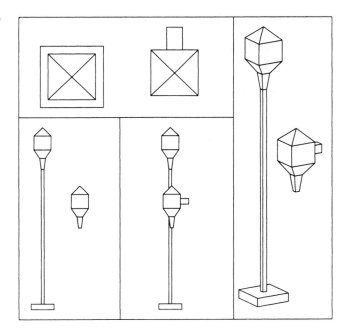

CHAPTER **14**

3D Parametric Design

Overview

This chapter discusses parametric design as it relates to 3D models. It is always useful to have on hand a model that can be used in several applications. In this chapter, we'll show how to create a model whose shape can be altered to suit various applications and we'll give specific examples of 3D parametric models.

Concepts Explored

- A description of parametric design
- The three parametric symbol types, their differences, and their uses
- Object snapping in the setting of the parametric parameters
- How to create and apply parametric symbols.

14.1 Introduction

Parametric design creates a standard design that can be applied to differing sets of parameters. The standard design, then, is capable of changing and conforming to new parameters. The process followed during the creation of the standard design gives the model its parametric properties.

As Chapter 13 explained and illustrated, 3D symbols are extremely useful devices for saving time and labor. Here, in Chapter 14, we'll see how giving 3D symbols parametric properties makes their usefulness infinitely greater. We'll illustrate how parametric design techniques can be applied to 3D symbols, and we'll explain the process for creating 3D symbols that allows different parameters to be applied to them.

14.2 Parametric Symbol Types

The essence of parametric symbol design is AutoCAD's ability to scale 3D blocks independently in all three axes upon insertion. This ability creates three parametric symbol types: The first will be referred to as 3ES, for three Equal axes Scaling; the second will be referred to as 3US, for three Unequal axes Scaling; and the third will be referred to as 2ES, for two Equal axes Scaling.

Figure 14.1
3ES parametric symbols

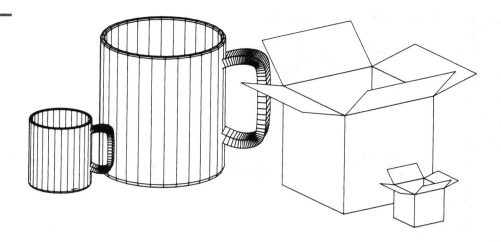

The parameters of a type 3ES parametric symbol allow it to be scaled uniformly in all three axes. Basically, the symbol can get larger or smaller, but its overall proportions remain the same. Because the scaling is equal, any complex symbol can be used, such as a large mug versus a small mug or a large carton versus a small carton, as shown in Figure 14.1. Once created, the model can be used over and over again at any size desired as long as each axis scaling remains equal. If a 3ES parametric symbol is inserted and the scaling is not equal, a distorted symbol will result. While this result might be desirable in certain cases, keep in mind that the 3ES parametric symbol was designed for equal scaling in all three axes.

The second parametric symbol type, 3US, allows unequal scaling in all three axis directions. This ability means the symbol is much more versatile, but its shape is restricted. Because of its need to be scaled unequally in all three axes without distortion, the 3US parametric symbol must be shaped without features, like a box. At first glance, one may doubt that a featureless box can be of any use. In fact, however, the uses of a 3D symbol that can be stretched in any direction are almost endless. Refer to Figure 14.2. You can form the box into blocks of any size or shape. You can stretch it into sheets of any thickness. You can use the box to create planks or posts of wood in any length simply by specifying different scales in each of the three axes. It is up to the user's need to define this symbol's boundaries.

Two of the scaling axes of our third parametric symbol type, 2ES, must remain equal, whereas the third can be any size. The 2ES is a combination of

Figure 14.2
3US parametric symbols

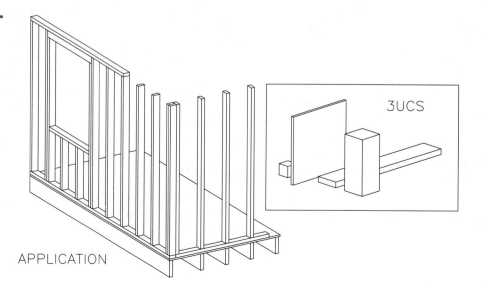

Figure 14.3
2ES parametric symbols with third
axis remaining constant

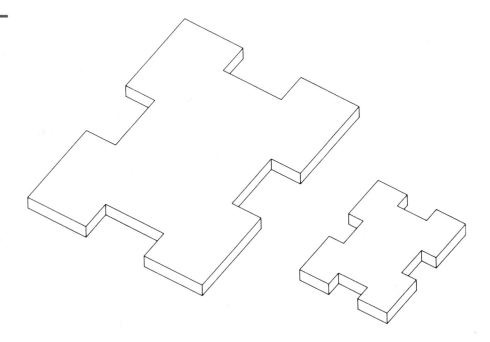

the 3ES and the 3US parametric symbol types. As a result, it can have a complex shape along two axes and be extruded or stretched along the third. This compromise between the 3US and the 3ES symbol types allows the 2ES symbol to take on unique shapes (like a 3ES) while retaining the ability to be stretched (similar to the 3US). The 2ES parametric symbol can be categorized according to how the third axis functions. In one category are 2ES symbols with a constant third axis. The two axes that define the profile of this kind of 2ES symbol are enlarged or reduced while the third axis remains constant or at the same thickness (see Figure 14.3). This type of 2ES symbol has limited applications.

In the other category is a much more versatile kind of 2ES symbol. Its two profile axes remain the same, whereas its third axis controls the transformation. Like the thickness property, this allows the user to take a profile and extrude it to any length, but with 2ES the user has more control and maneuverability. The profile can be any complex form, such as structural members, pipe of any diameter, and complicated moldings that are used in extruded aluminum window and door frames, and the complex profile can be extruded to any length, thereby allowing for quick construction of any model. Refer to Figure 14.4.

Whenever you are going to create a 3D symbol, you should first categorize it by its parametric type. Give some thought to how you are going to apply it and how it could be best utilized before you create it. In this way, you'll design a more efficient and versatile 3D symbol. As always, remember that blocks that have unequal scaling cannot be exploded into their original entities.

Figure 14.4
2ES parametric symbols with extrusion along the third axis

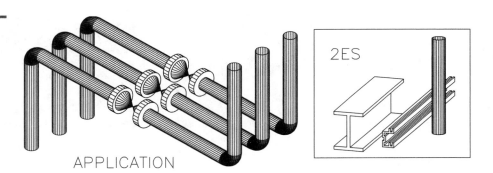

APPLICATION

2ES

Object Snap and Scaling

Once you have created a parametric symbol in 3D, you can scale it by snapping to an existing entity to set the scaling distance along a particular axis. All that is required when using this simple technique is to have some type of entity to snap to, so that the axis scaling can be set. Then you literally need only indicate the start and the end, and the 3D parametric symbol astonishingly stretches to conform to the indicated length. You'll find this technique extremely helpful when using 2ES symbols where lengths of materials are required. Items such as pipe, wood, or structural members can be assembled easily using this method.

Refer now to Figure 14.5, where the scaling method is illustrated. Part A of the figure shows two 3D symbols already in place. In this example, the symbols are two I-beams. The UCS is aligned to the face of one of the symbols. The faces of both the symbols are parallel and in line with each other.

In part B of Figure 14.5, the 3D parametric type 2ES symbol of an I-beam is inserted and is snapped onto the midpoint of the face of the lower I-beam. In part C, the inserted I-beam symbol is scaled in the Z axis to conform to indicated length by snapping to the midpoint of the upper I-beam's face. Thus, as Figure 14.5 shows, the actual steps from insertion to scaling are few.

The following labs give direct hands-on experience in the creation and application of two parametric symbols. You should be able to apply what you practice in these labs to the creation of other parametric symbols, whatever their type (3US, 3ES, or 2ES) and abilities.

Figure 14.5
Scaling a 3D symbol using snap points

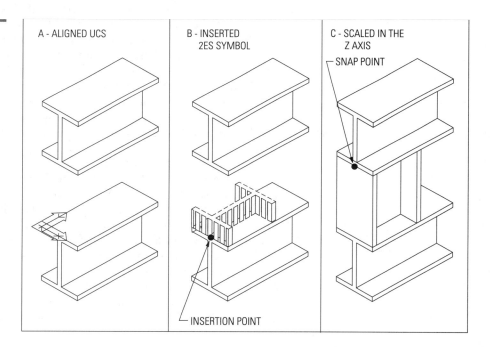

A - ALIGNED UCS

B - INSERTED 2ES SYMBOL

C - SCALED IN THE Z AXIS

SNAP POINT

INSERTION POINT

3D Viewpoint

UCS and Scaling

The orientation of the UCS working plane is crucial for proper stretching along the Z axis. Stretching of 2ES parametric symbols usually occurs along the Z axis so it is particularly important to determine in which direction the Z axis is pointing during the scaling.

Parametric Cube and Deck

Purpose

Lab 14.A will show you how to create a type 3US parametric symbol. After you create a symbol of a cube, you will learn how to use it as a 3US parametric symbol to create a wooden deck.

Objectives

You will be able to:

- Construct a type 3US parametric symbol.
- Apply the parametric symbol in the creation of a model.

Primary Commands

```
INSERT—XYZ
BASE
```

Final Model

Figure 14.6 shows both the type 3US parametric symbol and the final model you'll be creating.

Procedure

1. Start a new model called PCUBE (Parametric CUBE) with the following settings:

```
Units = architectural
Limits = —1",—1" to 1",1"
Grid = 1"
Snap Incr. = 1"
Elevation = 0
Thickness = 1"
Current Layer = 0
UCS = WCS
Fill = off
```

Creating the Parametric Cube

In this case, there is no need to create an orientation cube because the piece of geometry that the user is constructing is a cube.

2. A 3D surface object is going to be used for this symbol.

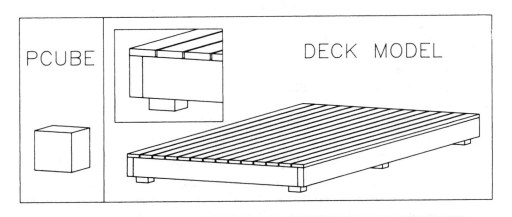

Figure 14.6
Type 3US parametric symbol and the final model

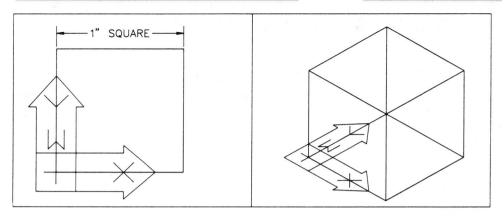

Figure 14.7
PCUBE model

3. Use the AI_BOX command to create a surface model that is a 1″ cube (1 × 1 × 1), as shown in Figure 14.7.

4. Set the BASE point to 0.5,0,0 so that it is halfway along the *X*-axis cube.

5. Save the model as PCUBE.

Constructing the Deck

You are going to create a wooden deck using 4 × 4s, 2 × 6s, and 1 × 4 decking. The sizes used for the lumber are the nominal sizes as opposed to the actual sizes (see following list). This makes it easier to construct the deck at this point. Although you could use actual lumber sizes, you would have to change the lengths and positions accordingly. The deck itself is 10′ long, 4′11-1/4″ wide, and a total of 9″ high.

NOMINAL SIZE	ACTUAL SIZE
4 × 4	3-1/2 × 3-1/2 construction lumber
2 × 6	1-1/2 × 5-1/2 construction lumber
1 × 4	1 × 3-1/2 decking

6. Start a new model called DECK with the following settings:

```
Units = architectural
Limits = -1',-1' to 11',6'
Grid = 1'
Snap Incr. = 1/4"
Elevation = 0
Thickness = 8"
Current Layer = OCUBE
UCS = WCS
Fill = off
```

Creating the Orientation Cube and Division Line

7. Using the LINE command, draw a box, as shown in Figure 14.8. The start should be at 0,0,0, and the box should be 10′0″ by 4′11-1/4″. This will allow the deck boards to cover the area evenly.

8. Set the elevation to 5″ and the thickness to 0. This will allow a line to be drawn around the orientation cube at the height of 5″ above the ground.

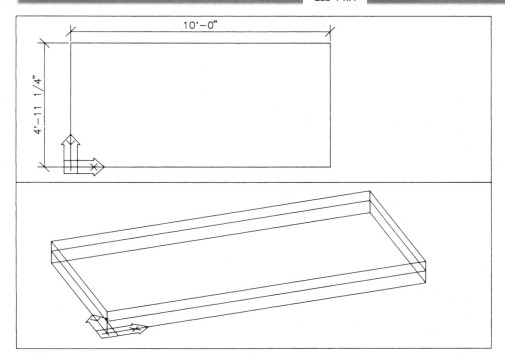

Figure 14.8
Orientation cube and division line

This line, which we'll call the division line, will be used to insert the PCUBE model.

9. Using the LINE command, draw a line around the perimeter of the orientation cube. This is the division line.

Using PCUBE for the Leg Columns

Now you are going to create a leg column that is 4″ square and 8″ high. Refer to Figure 14.9.

Figure 14.9
Inserting the PCUBE to create legs

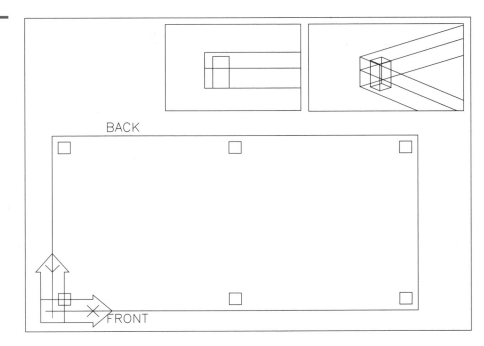

10. Create a layer called LEG, and make it current.

11. Set the elevation to 0 and the thickness to 0.

12. Using the INSERT command, insert the PCUBE model:

```
Command: INSERT
Block name (or ?): PCUBE
Insertion point: 4",2",0
X scale factor <1>/Corner/XYZ: XYZ
```

AutoCAD will respond with the scale factor for *Z* as well as for *X* and *Y*.

```
X scale factor <1>/Corner: 4
Y scale factor <default=X>: 4
Z scale factor <default=X>: 8
Rotation angle <0>: 0
```

13. Copy the newly created leg to the other three corners and the two center positions.

14. Save the model as DECK.

Using PCUBE to Create Support Joists

Now you are going to create supports that are 2″ × 6″ boards. To place the boards and set the length, use the division line to snap to.

15. Create a layer called SUPPORT, and make it active.

16. Display an axonometric view (–1,–1,1) similar to the view in Figure 14.10. This will make it easier to place the supports.

17. Create a working plane that runs along the inside of the right side of the orientation cube with the *Z* axis pointing toward the left side of the cube. This will allow for the placement of the PCUBE and the desired stretching along the *Z* axis. Refer to Figure 14.10. Save this working plane/UCS as

Figure 14.10
Using PCUBE to create supports

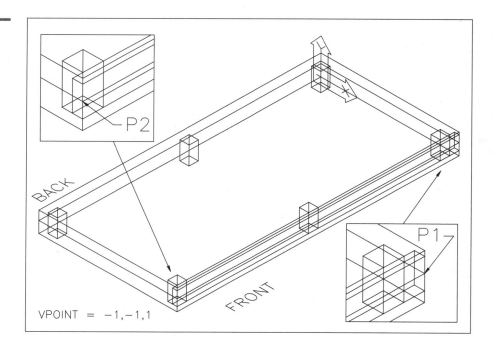

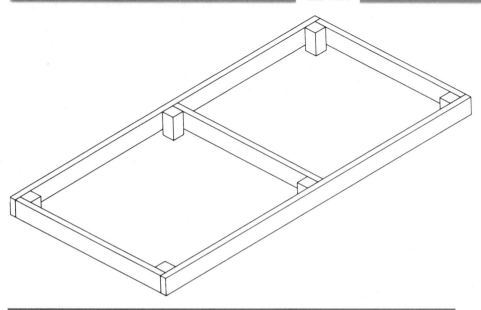

Figure 14.11
Adding the remaining supports

IRIGHT (Inside RIGHT side). The correct placement of this working plane is crucial for proper stretching along the Z axis.

18. Use INSERT to add and form PCUBE into the front support member. (*Note:* The orientation of the PCUBE model during insertion will affect the direction of the Z scaling.)

```
Command: INSERT
Block name (or ?): PCUBE
Insertion point: enter an R to rotate the block 90
degrees
Enter rotation angle: 90
Insertion point: endpoint snap to the point labeled
P1
X scale factor <1>/Corner/XYZ: XYZ
```

AutoCAD will respond with the scale factor for Z as well as for X and Y.

```
X scale factor <1>/Corner: 6
Y scale factor <default=X>: 2
Z scale factor <default=X>: endpoint snap to the
point labeled P2
```

The length of the member is automatically entered based on points P1 and P2.

19. Add the remaining supports using the procedure just listed. Refer to Figure 14.11 for the locations.

20. Save the model as DECK.

Using PCUBE to Create the Decking

Now it is time to add the decking, which will be 4″ wide and 1″ high. Refer to Figure 14.12.

21. Create a layer called DECKING, and make it active.

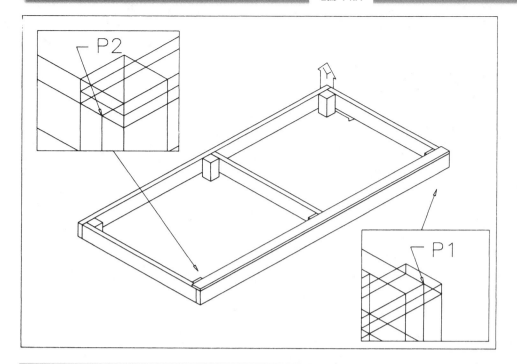

Figure 14.12
Using PCUBE to create the decking

22. Restore the IRIGHT working plane.

23. Using the INSERT command, insert the PCUBE model to use in the creation of the decking:

```
Command: INSERT
Block name (or ?): PCUBE
Insertion point: endpoint snap to the point labeled
P1
X scale factor <1>/Corner/XYZ: XYZ
```

AutoCAD will respond with the scale factor for *Z* as well as for *X* and *Y*.

```
X scale factor <1>/Corner: 4
Y scale factor <default=X>: 1
Z scale factor <default=X>: endpoint snap to the
point labeled P2
Rotation angle <O>: 0
```

The length of the member is automatically entered based on points P1 and P2.

24. Use the ARRAY command to create the rest of the decking. The decking will have a 1/4″ gap between each plank.

```
Command: ARRAY
Select the objects: pick the newly created deck mem-
ber
Rectangular or Polar array (R/A): R
Number of rows (---)<1>: 1
Number of columns (|||)<1>: 14 (14 decking boards)
Unit cell or distance between columns (|||): -4.25″
```

The distance of 4.25 will give a gap of 1/4″ between the decking boards.

25. Save the model as DECK.

26. Turn off the OCUBE layer. Use the HIDE command and observe the model. It should be similar to the one shown in Figure 14.6.

You have just created an entire model from parametric 3D symbols. As you have seen, using parametric symbols makes construction tasks much easier. Remember to note that Lab 14.A used a 3US symbol, allowing unequal scaling in all three axes.

Lab 14.B

Parametric Pipe and Piping

Purpose

Lab 14.B will show you how to create a 3ES parametric symbol of a pipe elbow and a symbol of a pipe that will be used as a 2ES parametric 3D symbol. You will create a small piping system using the 3ES elbow and 2ES pipe symbols.

Objectives

You will be able to:

- Construct a 2ES parametric symbol.
- Construct a 3ES parametric symbol.
- Apply the parametric symbols in the creation of a model.

Primary Command

INSERT—XYZ

Final Model

Figure 14.13 shows the 2ES and 3ES parametric symbols and the final model you'll be creating.

Procedure

1. Start a new model called ELBOW (piping ELBOW) with the following settings:

   Units = decimal

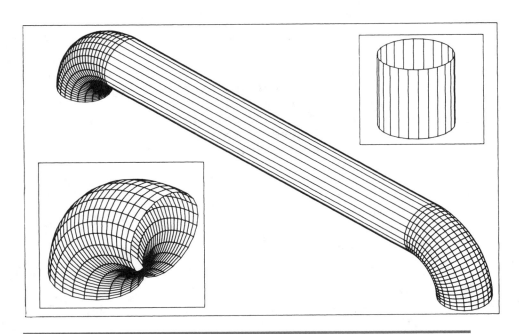

Figure 14.13
2ES and 3ES parametric symbols and the final model

251

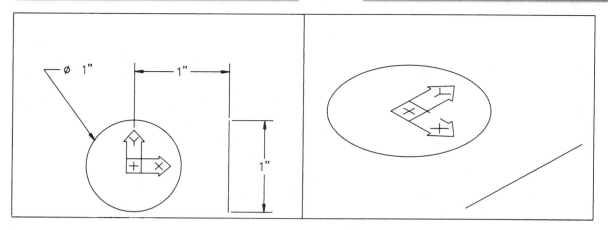

Figure 14.14
Profile of a circle and a line

```
Limits = -1",-1" to 2",2"
Grid = 0.5"
Snap Incr. = 0.5"
Elevation = 0
Thickness = 0"
Current Layer = PROFILE
UCS = WCS
Fill = off
```

Creating the Elbow Model

2. Using a circle and a line, draw the entities shown in Figure 14.14. The circle's center should be 0,0,0 and have a radius of 0.5". The line should start at 1,–0.5,0 and end at 1,0.5,0.

3. Set the SURFTAB1 and SURFTAB2 variables to 24.

4. Create a layer called SURF, and make it current.

5. Using the REVSURF command, construct the model shown in Figure 14.15.

```
Command: REVSURF
Select path curve: select the profile as shown in
Figure 14.15 around an axis (P1)
Select axis of revolution: select the center axis
line as shown in Figure 14.15 (P2)
Start angle <0>: press <Enter> to start the surfaces
at 0 degrees
Included angle (+=ccw -=cw)<Full circle>: enter-90
for a quarter of a circle
```
(*Note:* This angle may be –90 or +90, depending on how the axis line was created and which end you pick.)

Changing the Thickness

The thickness of the line that was used as the axis of revolution must be changed to 1.5". It will be used as a working plane.

6. Using the CHPROP command, change the thickness of the line to 1.5", as shown in Figure 14.16.

7. Create a working plane on the face of the extruded line, and set the current layer to PROFILE.

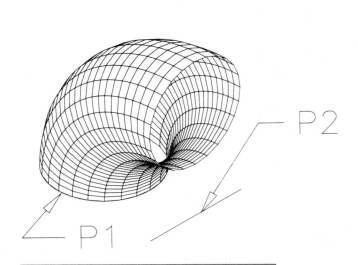

Figure 14.15
Creating a surface of revolution

Figure 14.16
Adding a line to the elbow face

8. Draw a line 2.5″ long on the working plane, from the center of the elbow's circular face, as shown in Figure 14.16. Later in the lab, this line will be used as a snap point when adding the pipe symbol.

9. Set UCS to equal the WCS, and save the 3ES model as ELBOW.

Creating the 2ES Pipe Symbol

10. Start a new model called PIPE with the following settings:

```
Units = decimal
Limits = -1",-1" to 2",2"
Grid = 0.5"
Snap Incr. = 0.5"
Elevation = 0
Thickness = 0"
Current Layer = PROFILE
UCS = WCS
Fill = off
```

Creating the Pipe Model

The pipe model will be only one unit high and one unit long. This will allow the scaling that is required during insertion.

11. Using a circle and a line, draw the entities shown in Figure 14.17A. The circle's center should be at 0,0,0 and have a radius of 0.5″. The line should start at 0.5,0,0 and end at 0.5,0,1.

12. Set SURFTAB1 and SURFTAB2 variables to 24.

13. Create a layer called SURF, and make it current.

14. Using the TABSURF command, construct the model shown in Figure 14.17B:

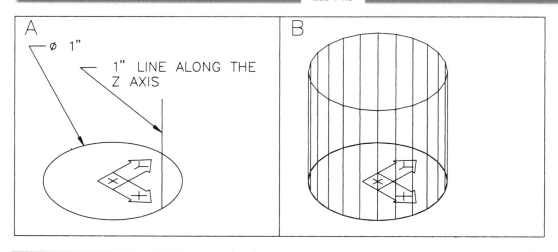

Figure 14.17
Creating the surfaced pipe

```
Command: TABSURF
Select path curve: select the circle to control the
path the polygons will follow
Select direction vector: select the line to control
the length of the polygons and the direction they
will be pointing; pick line near the end that touches
the circle
```

The end of the line that was selected controls the direction of the surfaces. If the surfaces are generated in the wrong direction, delete them and repeat the command. This time, however, select the other end of the line.

15. Make sure the BASE is set to 0,0,0 and save this 2ES model as PIPE.

Creating a Piping Model

Now you are going to assemble the two 3D symbols ELBOW and PIPE into a piping model. Remember, ELBOW is a 3ES parametric symbol, and PIPE is a 2ES parametric symbol.

16. Start a new model called PIPES with the following settings:

```
Units = decimal
Limits = -1",-1" to 10",10"
Grid = 0.5"
Snap Incr. = 0.5"
Elevation = 0
Thickness = 0"
Current Layer = ELBOW
UCS = WCS
Fill = off
```

Inserting the Elbow Model

17. Insert the model called ELBOW at the locations shown in Figure 14.18. Remember to use the Rotate option for one of the elbows.

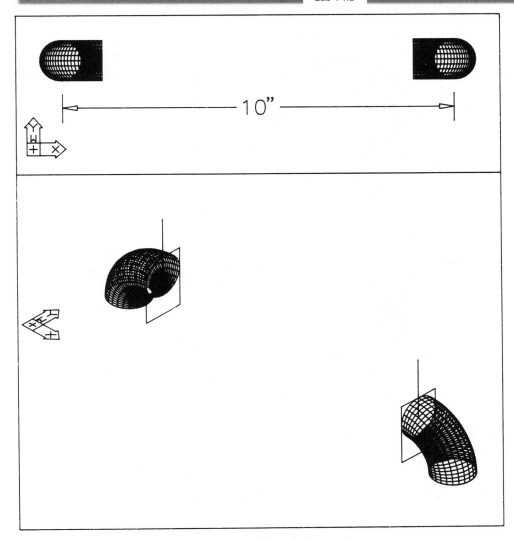

Figure 14.18
Inserting the 3ES symbol ELBOW

Inserting the Pipe Model

18. Create a working plane on the elbow, as shown in Figure 14.19.

19. Insert the 2ES symbol called PIPE:

```
Command: INSERT
Block name (or ?): PIPE
Insertion point: endpoint snap to the lower endpoint
of the line labeled P1 in Figure 14.19
X scale factor <1>/Corner/XYZ: XYZ
```

AutoCAD will respond with the scale factor for *Z* as well as for *X* and *Y*.

```
X scale factor <1>/Corner: 1
Y scale factor <default=X>: 1
Z scale factor <default=X>: endpoint snap to the
lower endpoint point of the line labeled P2 in Figure
14.20
Rotation angle <O>: 0
```

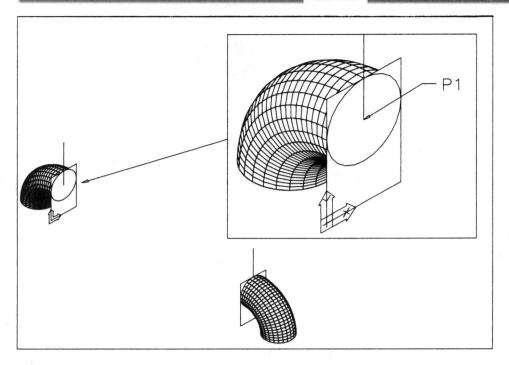

Figure 14.19
Inserting the 2ES symbol PIPE

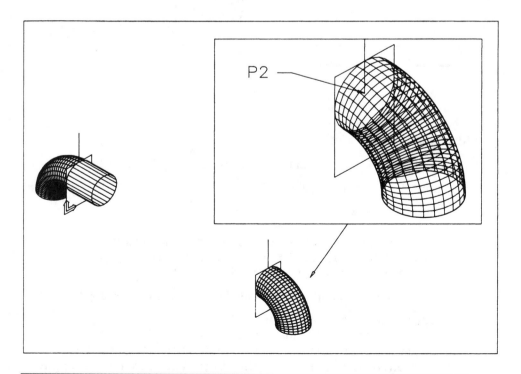

Figure 14.20
Scaling the length to point P2

Figure 14.21
The final length of pipe

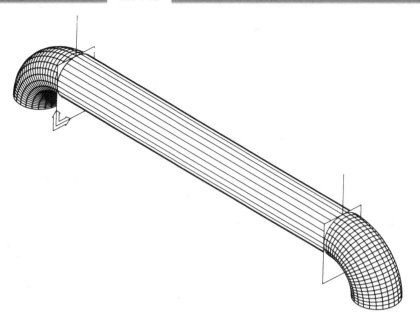

The length of the pipe is automatically entered based on points P1 and P2 and should look like the final length shown in Figure 14.21.

20. Freeze the layer called PROFILE.

21. Save the model as PIPES.

22. Use the VPOINT and the HIDE commands to move about the model and observe the display after it has the hidden edges removed.

Questions

1. Explain what a parametric design represents.

2. What is a 3ES symbol?

3. What is the advantage of a 3US parametric symbol over a 3ES parametric symbol? What is the disadvantage?

4. What is the main feature of a 2ES parametric symbol?

5. How is snapping to existing entities an aid in the setting of parametric parameters when inserting a parametric symbol?

6. What option is used to allow independent scaling along the three axes when inserting a 3D symbol block?

Assignments

1. Create a carton, like the one illustrated in Figure 14.1, that is large enough to contain the mug model created in Chapter 8, Assignment 1 (COFMUG). This carton model is a 3ES parametric symbol. Save the model as CARTON. Now, restore the kitchen model created in Chapter 13, Assignment 1, called BKIT. Insert the 3ES symbol CARTON at an XYZ scale of 0.75 and place it on the table top. Then insert the mug model, COFMUG, into the box. It will also be XYZ scaled to 0.75. Save this scene as BKIT2. Display a view looking toward

Figure 14.22
A small mug in a small carton

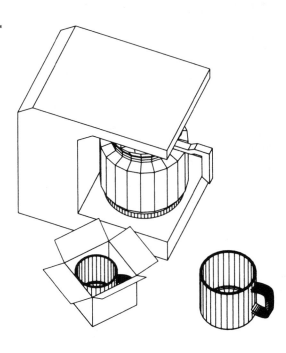

the open box so that the mug can be seen, and use the HIDE command. Refer to Figure 14.22 for an illustration of the final scene. (*Note:* All the 3D models in this scene are actually 3ES parametric symbols. They must be scaled equally in all three axes so that they retain their shapes and proportions.)

2. Generate a stud wall as shown in Figure 14.23. The entire wall should be constructed out of 2 × 4s (nominal size = 2 × 4, actual size = 1-1/2 × 3-1/2) and make use of the 3US symbol PCUBE, created in Lab 14.A.

3. Draw the flange/bolt assembly shown in Figure 14.24. Use the model of the bolt head, BHEAD, created in Chapter 13, Assignment 3. The BHEAD model is a 2ES symbol. When inserting the BHEAD parametric symbol, be sure the XY scale is 1.125. This gives a size of 1-1/8″ across the flats. Use a Z

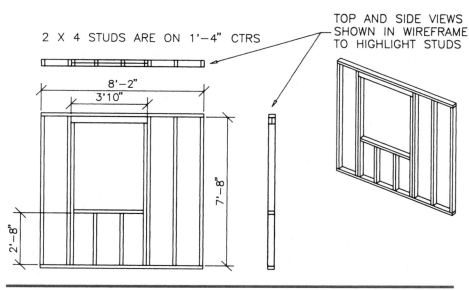

Figure 14.23
Stud wall

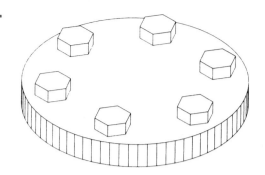

Figure 14.24
Flange/bolt assembly

scale of 0.5 to give a head thickness of 1/2″. The flange should be created using a circle of 8″ and a thickness of 1″.

4. Design a structure that could make use of the 3US parametric symbol PCUBE. Sketch the design first on paper, outlining where the parametric symbol can be used. Then create a 3D model using the parametric symbol.

5. Research to identify some 2ES parametric symbols and their applications. Undertake to create these 2ES symbols in AutoCAD.

6. Restore the model BKIT2 from Assignment 1 in this chapter. Try to put the entire kitchen table into a carton using a procedure similar to that used in Assignment 1. Orient the view so that the table can be seen inside the box.

Presentation

Now that you can create a 3D model and visually move it about on the screen, it's time to study the various aspects of presentation. The presentation techniques we'll discuss in this part relate to both the appearance of the model on the video screen and the resultant hard copies. We'll also explore the enhancement features available within AutoCAD and the other software available to enhance the presentation of your model.

15

Display of 3D Models for Presentation

Overview

In this chapter, we'll explore techniques that are not necessarily important in model creation but will enhance the viewing of the model on the screen and prepare it for final presentation. For instance, you will learn how to create a camera's view of the model, which results in a picture that is closer to those images the human eye is accustomed to seeing. In addition, we'll explain techniques for clipping away unwanted features.

Concepts Explored

- The importance of perspective views, the principles behind them, and how they differ from axonometric views
- How the DVIEW command relates to an SLR camera
- The operation of the DVIEW options
- The way in which different lenses distort an image
- How to remove obstructing entities
- How to recognize a new form of the UCS icon
- How to create various perspective views.

15.1 Introduction

Up to this point, we have viewed models axonometrically. This type of viewing is extremely important in the construction stage. It is easier to tell if the model is drawn correctly when the lines that create the model are parallel to each other. But when we want to display a model, especially if it is something large like an architectural structure, axonometric display is less than visually pleasing. It is much more appealing to have the model displayed in a perspective view. An image with perspective is the ultimate in pictorial drawing. There is no substitute for a picture that depicts what the viewer's eyes would actually see, as Figure 15.1 shows. To compare the two ways of viewing, look at Figures 15.2 and 15.3. Figure 15.2 shows the axonometric view of a house model, and Figure 15.3 illustrates the way the human eye would perceive the same model.

Figure 15.1
Perspective display of a 3D model of a house

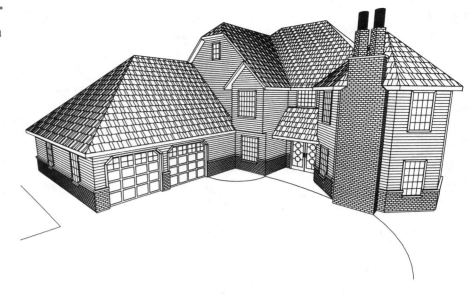

Figure 15.2
Axonometric display of a house

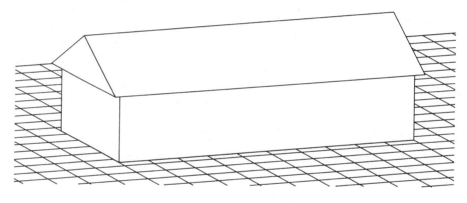

Figure 15.3
Perspective display of a house

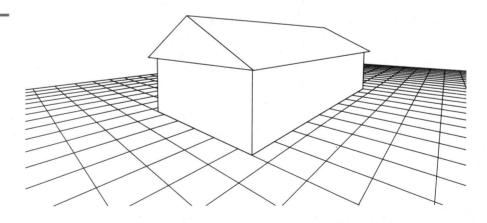

15.2 Perspective Versus Axonometric Views

Axonometric (including isometric) drawings make use of parallel lines to generate a picture or 3D view of an object. Because the lines along one of the three axes are parallel to each other, the displayed view of the object remains uniform, regardless of the viewing distance. Obviously, although the overall displayed size can change, the proportional distance from each entity remains the same. Axonometric views are created using the AutoCAD command VPOINT, which is explained in Chapter 3.

Figure 15.4
How the human eye perceives objects

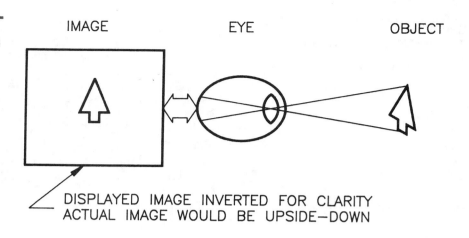

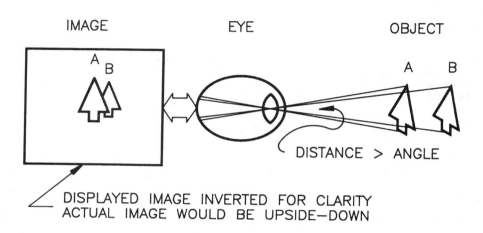

Perspective drawing is different. Perspective drawing attempts to simulate the view of a human's eye (refer to Figure 15.4). Because lines converge toward the eye as they pass the lens, an angle is formed from the extent of the object viewed. As the object's distance away from the eye increases, the extent angle decreases, as Figure 15.4 illustrates. Eventually, the angle is too small for the human eye to discern. This point is referred to as the *vanishing point.*

Thus, in perspective viewing, the farther an object is from the viewer, the smaller it appears, until it eventually blends into a dot. AutoCAD simulates this type of view with the command DVIEW, which stands for dynamic viewing.

15.3 Center of Interest and the Station Point

When creating any perspective view, whether by drafting manually or by using CAD, you need two key points—the center of interest and the station point. The center of interest is the most important feature or component of the object or model. In other words, it is the part in an entire scene that draws your eye, such as the front door of a house. The station point represents where the viewer is standing, and it may be close, far away, or above or below. Refer to Figure 15.5.

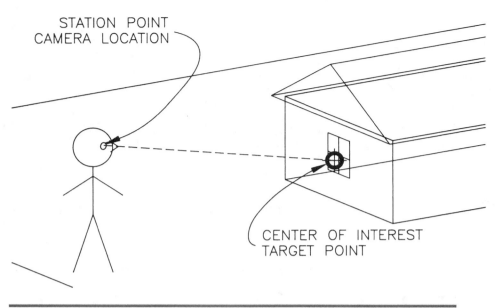

STATION POINT
CAMERA LOCATION

CENTER OF INTEREST
TARGET POINT

Figure 15.5
The center of interest and the station point

The DVIEW Command

DVIEW, AutoCAD's command for generating a perspective view of a three-dimensional model, has many features similar to those of a camera. Let's investigate how it works and what it can do.

The Camera and DVIEW

Consider the operation of a 35-mm single-lens reflex (SLR) camera. When using an SLR camera with a 50-mm lens (similar to the human eye), you look at an object from a set distance, as in Figure 15.6. If you are too far away, you can either move closer to decrease the distance or use a telephoto (zoom) lens (such as a 200-mm lens) to magnify the picture. If the view is larger than the frame, as in Figure 15.7, then you can use a wide-angle lens, such as a 35-mm lens. And if you want to change your viewing angle, you can simply turn the camera in your hand, as Figure 15.8 illustrates.

All these features of a regular 35-mm SLR camera can be simulated with AutoCAD's DVIEW command. AutoCAD refers to the center of interest as the *target point* and the stationary point as the *camera point*. Using DVIEW, the distance away from the model to be viewed can be set, and any length of telephoto lens can be selected. The camera can even be twisted, much like turning a hand-held camera. And there are other features in DVIEW not found on a regular camera, such as the Clip option. Clip can remove unwanted obstructions from the viewed picture. Wouldn't that be a wonderful feature to find on a regular camera? It would eliminate that large thumb in the foreground of your breathtaking shot of the Grand Canyon!

DVIEW's Camera-like Options

Using the DVIEW command allows you to display a preview of a model. Once you have achieved the desired preview, you can apply the view to the entire model. A similar feature is DVIEW's Drag option. The standard Drag option

Figure 15.6
50-mm lens image versus 200-mm
lens image

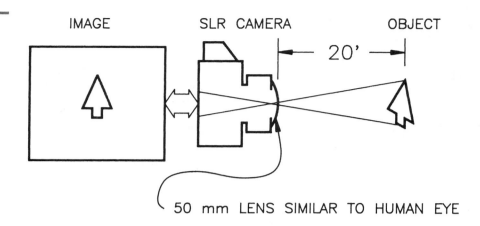

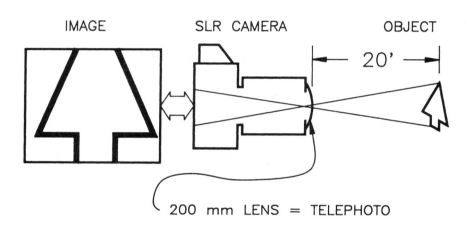

of most of the modifying commands allows you to see the entities' movements while modification is actually taking place. The Drag option of DVIEW allows you to view the model three dimensionally while selecting the desired view. You can see the model rotate, enlarge, shrink, twist, or turn.

With the Drag option, as with the DVIEW Camera, Target, and Pan options, you move the cursor/crosshairs attached to the object in question. However, the DVIEW options that control Zoom and Distance also have slider bars that produce feedback on the bar to inform you of the desired values to be entered. The slider bar is shown in Figure 15.9. Depending on where the cursor is on the bar, the desired effect is applied to the image displayed. You can override the slider bar by entering values on the command line.

Selecting an Object

As mentioned previously, to apply the DVIEW options to a model, you must select a preview. You may do this using the Preview Selection Set. If desired, you may select the entire model or only those items that give definition to the model. For example, consider the finished house model illustrated in Figure 15.10, containing the dwelling walls, roof, showing windows, and doors. This entire model could be selected for dynamic manipulation, but the dynamic movement would be slow, especially if the computer being used is not very fast. Instead, only the entities that define the model need to be selected. These entities could be some of the walls and perhaps the roof and

Figure 15.7
50-mm lens image versus 35-mm lens image

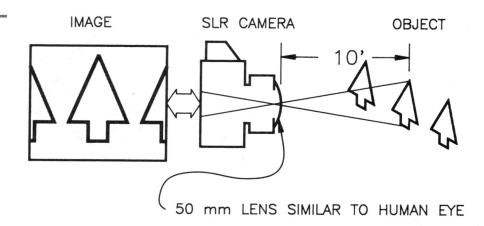

IMAGE   SLR CAMERA   OBJECT

10'

50 mm LENS SIMILAR TO HUMAN EYE

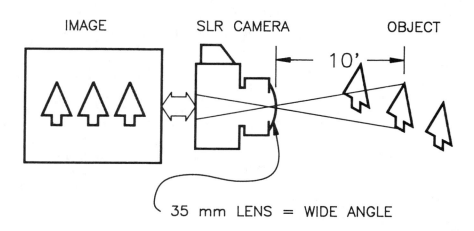

IMAGE   SLR CAMERA   OBJECT

10'

35 mm LENS = WIDE ANGLE

Figure 15.8
Turning the camera on an angle

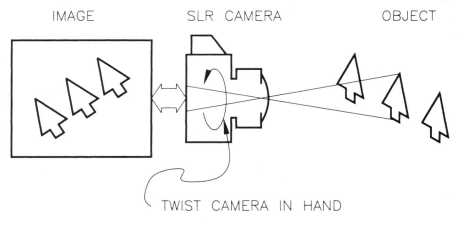

IMAGE   SLR CAMERA   OBJECT

TWIST CAMERA IN HAND

Figure 15.9
The vertical and horizontal slider bars

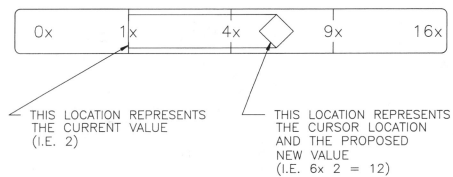

0x   1x   4x   9x   16x

THIS LOCATION REPRESENTS
THE CURRENT VALUE
(I.E. 2)

THIS LOCATION REPRESENTS
THE CURSOR LOCATION
AND THE PROPOSED
NEW VALUE
(I.E. 6x 2 = 12)

Figure 15.10
Entire house model

the front door, as Figure 15.11 shows. When selecting entities, choose the ones that would enable you to recognize the house's orientation when it is dynamically shifted.

As an alternative to the Preview Selection Set, AutoCAD has a built-in feature for manipulating the DVIEW environment. It is called the DVIEW-BLOCK, and Figure 15.12 shows this three-dimensional block that can be manipulated within DVIEW. AutoCAD supplies a block model of a simple house for the DVIEWBLOCK command. However, if desired, you can create a new three-dimensional block and name it to replace the original DVIEW-BLOCK. The only restriction to the block you create is that it must fit within a one-unit cube. The DVIEWBLOCK is activated by pressing the <Enter> key when the prompt to select objects for DVIEW appears. Then the DVIEW-BLOCK is displayed and can be manipulated. Once you complete the preview manipulation, you can apply it to the actual model.

Figure 15.11
Selected entities for the Preview Selection Set

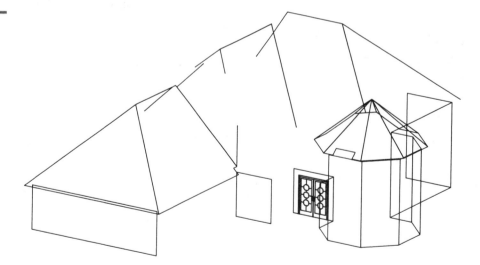

Placing the Camera

As soon as the selection set is complete, depending on the previous settings, the model is displayed in the DVIEW environment. The first option of the DVIEW command to be activated is the Camera option. Here, use the cursor/crosshairs to swing the model around its horizontal axis first and then around its vertical axis next. Either move the cursor device or type the appropriate angle on the command line to accomplish these swings. It is possible to toggle between angles by using the T suboption of the Camera option, which has the effect of switching from one angle to the other.

Figure 15.12
The DVIEWBLOCK command

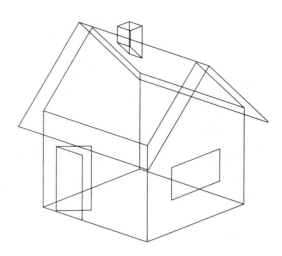

Selecting a Center of Interest

When you enter the DVIEW environment for the first time, the camera distance and the center of interest are selected automatically. To change the center of interest, use the Target option. This option is similar to the Camera option, except that moving along the cursor with the Target option causes the center of interest to swing about the camera location. The camera location becomes the pivot point. There is an easy way to think of the difference between the Camera and the Target options (refer to Figure 15.13). The Camera option gives a view similar to what you see when walking around an object while focusing on one spot of the object. The Target option gives a view similar to what you see when standing still but turning to look around from that stationary position.

Activating the Perspective View

The perspective view is activated by using the Distance option, which changes the distance from the target point to the camera point, or how far the viewer is away from the center of interest. As soon as the Distance option is used, the view changes to perspective. You can tell if the perspective view has been acti-

Figure 15.13

The Camera option versus the Target option

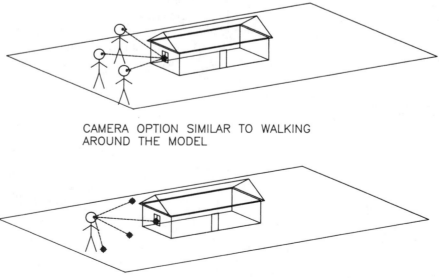

CAMERA OPTION SIMILAR TO WALKING
AROUND THE MODEL

TARGET OPTION SIMILAR TO LOOKING
AROUND IN ONE SPOT

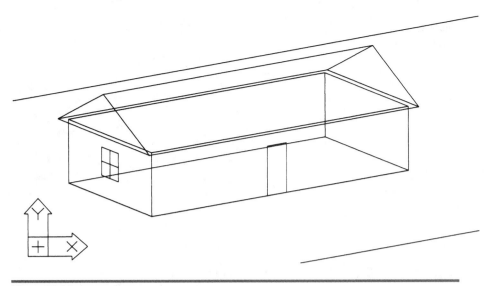

Figure 15.14
Axonometric UCS icon

vated by looking at the UCS icon: Instead of the usual L-shaped symbol (see Figure 15.14), it has changed to a perspective box (see Figure 15.15).

The Distance option moves along the axis of vision, which runs along an imaginary line that passes through the camera point (stationary point) and the target point (center of interest). It is possible to have a distance that is too close to the object viewed. If the model suddenly disappears, it is likely that the distance setting is too close to the object.

When using this option, it is easier to enter the distance away from the object at the command line than to use the slider bar. If the operator was looking at a house, it may be desirable to set the distance preliminarily to 100' or if the model to be viewed happens to be the size of a coffee mug, the preliminary distance could be 12".

The slider bar uses a multiplicative factor with the Distance option. This means that whatever distance was previously set is multiplied by the slider bar the next time the Distance option is used. If the previous distance was 100' away from the target point, the next time the slider bar is set to 2X, then the distance becomes 200'.

It is possible to reduce or enlarge a model without turning on the perspective. This is accomplished by using the Zoom option, which works as long as the Distance option has not been used.

The perspective can be turned off by using the Off option of the DVIEW command.

Figure 15.15
Perspective icon

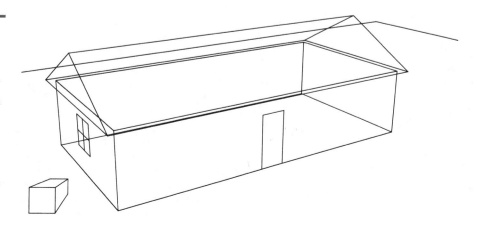

Turning Off Perspective Viewing

Perspective viewing is created with the DVIEW command. To turn a perspective view off, use the Off option of the DVIEW command but remember to use the Save option of the VIEW command to save your DVIEW settings before you turn the view off, so that you can restore them later.

Choosing the Proper Lens

Once you have decided how far the viewer will be standing away from the model, your next step is to choose the proper lens with which to view the model. To do this, use the Zoom option. Activate the slider bar, and use it to adjust the camera's lens length. The 50-mm lens simulates what an unassisted human eye would see of the model at the set distance. An actual camera has set lens lengths, but the distance is variable with DVIEW. If the view is too small, then increase the lens length, thereby increasing the magnification. If the view does not show enough of the model and its surroundings, then choose a smaller lens length. Keep in mind, however, that using too small a lens length can greatly distort the display of the model, as Figure 15.16 shows. If this happens—and it is not desirable—the distance from the camera to the target and the lens length should be increased. By alternating the Distance and Zoom options, you can achieve the most pleasing view.

Simultaneous Moving of the Camera and the Target

It is possible to move the camera and the target together. This is accomplished with either the Pan or the Twist option. The Pan option moves the camera and the target in a sliding fashion. The distance or the angle of view does not change. The Pan option used here functions much the same as the standard PAN command used outside of DVIEW. Using the Twist option has the same effect as manually turning a camera; it twists about the axis of vision.

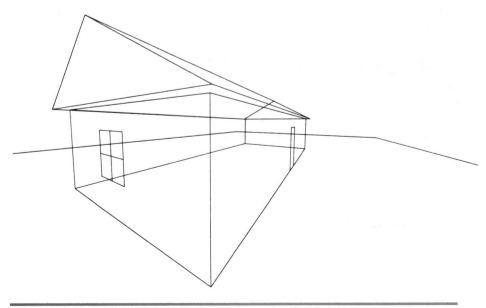

Figure 15.16
Model display distorted by too close a camera distance and too small a lens size

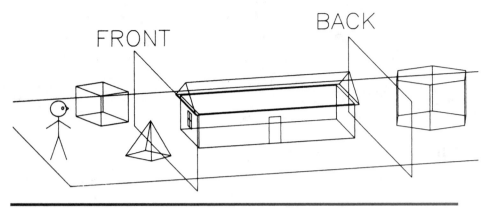

Figure 15.17
Removing obstructions with the Clip option

Getting Rid of Unwanted Objects

Often, when model construction is finished and the desired view has been set, there is some part of the model that is obstructing the view of the center of interest. To alleviate this problem, the Clip option can be utilized. Its purpose and operation are quite simple. There are two clipping planes—front and back. These planes move along the axis of vision, parallel to the graphics screen. Whatever is in front of the front clipping plane toward the viewer is hidden from the display. Whatever is behind the back clipping plane away from the viewer is hidden from the display. See Figures 15.17 and 15.18. Both the front and back planes of the Clip option can be turned on and off, and they can be set any distance from the target point. Positive distances are in front of the target, and negative distances are behind the target.

Another use for the Clip option is to "cut" through surfaces, which you may need to do when you want to see inside a model, such as a house or a mechanical assembly. When a clipping plane cuts through a surface, the edge that cuts through the surface is displayed as a line. This makes it easy to tell where the "cut" is taking place. This cutting affects only what is on display, not the actual construction of the geometry.

Locating the Camera and Target Exactly

When a specific view is desired (for instance, "I want to stand at the top of the stairs and look down into the entrance hall"), it can be achieved using the Points option. This option allows the user to pick or enter exact X,Y,Z point locations of both the camera and the target. Filters and object snaps are func-

Figure 15.18
The display after the clipping planes have been applied

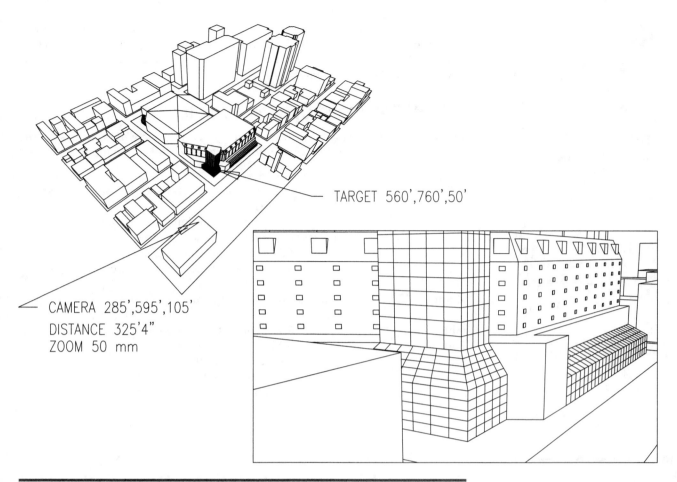

TARGET 560',760',50'

CAMERA 285',595',105'
DISTANCE 325'4"
ZOOM 50 mm

Figure 15.19
Locating the camera and target

tional, even when perspective is on. When the option is selected, perspective viewing is turned off to allow the user to specify a target point and a camera location. To ensure the proper view, you need to enter the distance option. Its default will be changed to the distance between the camera and target. Remember to set the proper zoom lens. Refer to Figure 15.19, which shows a city model (created in the application project of Chapter 19). In this case, the target is the roof of the main entrance (560',760',50') and the camera is located on the roof of a nearby building (285',595',105'). The calculated distance 325'4" and a 50-mm lens were used. You can see the resulting view, just as if you were standing on the roof looking at the entrance.

Hiding the Preview

To generate a hidden line removal of the Preview Selection Set, select the Hide option while in the DVIEW command. The Hide option will apply only to those surfaces that were selected for the DVIEW command.

Applying the Preview to the Entire Model

Once the desired view and effects have been achieved with the Preview Selection Set, you only need to exit from the DVIEW command. Then, all the effects, except the Hide option, are applied to the model. After exiting from the DVIEW command, you can invoke the HIDE command.

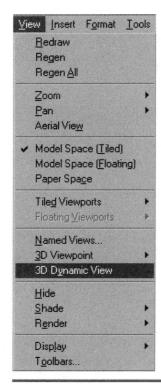

Figure 15.20
The View/3D Dynamic View
pull-down menu

DVIEW settings can be stored for later recall by saving the current view.

Note that there are some limitations when the perspective view is active: The ZOOM, PAN, and SKETCH commands do not function, and the pointing device cannot be used to enter coordinates.

DVIEW Command Options Summarized

Figure 15.20 illustrates the pull-down menu that provides access to the DVIEW command. The various options of the DVIEW command follow:

OPTIONS	DESCRIPTION
\<Enter\>	Pressing enter at the "Select objects" prompt activates the DVIEWBLOCK
CAmera	Places the camera in relation to the target
TArget	Places the target in relation to the camera
Distance	Sets the distance from the camera to the target
POints	Places the camera and the target using coordinates
PAn	Shifts the display
Zoom	Changes the size of the displayed view
TWist	Turns the camera
CLip	Temporarily removes unwanted features
Hide	Removes hidden lines
Off	Turns perspective view off
Undo	Reverses the effects of the last DVIEW operation
eXit	Leaves DVIEW and applies settings

Lab 15.A

Dynamic Viewing with Exterior Perspective

Purpose

Lab 15.A will show you how to create a perspective view of the exterior of a model. The basic dwelling model created in Lab 8.B, Chapter 8, will be your tool.

Objectives

You will be able to:

- Create an exterior perspective view of a model.
- Understand the manipulation of the DVIEW command's options.
- Save the perspective view settings for later retrieval.

Primary Commands

DVIEW—Camera, Distance, Zoom
VIEW—Save

Procedure

Initial Setup

1. Open the basic dwelling drawing that was created in Lab 8.B in Chapter 8. The file name is BDWELL.

2. Align the UCS to the WCS, and turn on the UCS icon.

3. Display an isometric view using the VPOINT command:

   Command: **VPOINT**
   Rotate/\<View point\>\<current\>: **1,−1,1**

Creating the Preview Selection Set

4. Activate the DVIEW command:

Figure 15.21
Selecting the Preview Selection Set

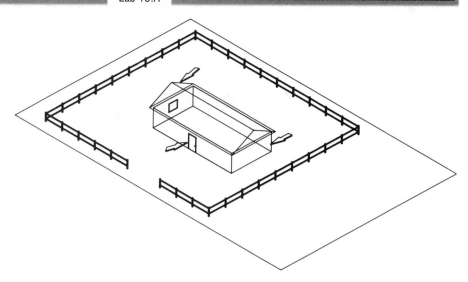

```
Command: DVIEW
Select objects:
```

5. Select the entities for the Preview Selection Set. Refer to Figure 15.21.

Using the Camera Option

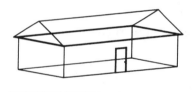

Figure 15.22
Selecting the desired camera view

6. Now activate the Camera option. Move the cursor up and down and notice how the preview model pivots about a horizontal axis. This is the angle from the *X–Y* plane.

7. Move the cursor from left to right until the display is similar to that shown in Figure 15.22. Press the pick button at the desired location. (*Note:* The Camera option can be used as many times as necessary to achieve the desired view.)

Setting the Camera Distance

8. To choose the distance of the viewer from the model, use the Distance option. When you select this option, a slider bar will appear, controlling the distance the camera is from the target. Move along the slider bar, observing the reduction and enlargement of the displayed model. Instead of using the slider bar to set the distance, however, enter the distance of 100' at the command prompt:

```
Command:
CAmera/TArget/Distance/ . . . /CLip/Hide/OFF/Undo/
<eXit>: D
New camera/target distance<current>: 100'
```

Notice how the UCS icon has changed. Whenever the Distance option is selected, the view of the model changes from an axonometric view to a perspective view.

Using the Zoom Option to Get a Better Picture

9. The display now shows the view as it would appear to a person standing 100' away from the model. To allow a closer look, you must change the type of lens used to view the model, which is accomplished with the Zoom option. When you select the Zoom option, a slider bar will appear. Move the cursor along the bar. Notice how the image gets larger or smaller. The

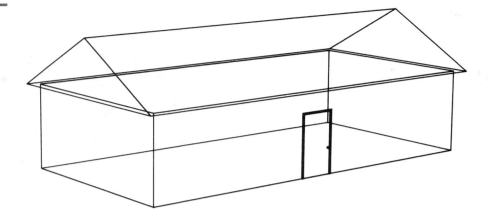

distance from the model has not changed, only the size of the lens used to view the model has changed. As the size of the lens increases, the picture will appear to be closer; as the size of the lens decreases, more of the overall model will be seen. Set the lens length to 75 mm. When you're done, the display should look like Figure 15.23.

```
Command:
CAmera/TArget/Distance/ . . . /CLip/Hide/OFF/Undo/
<eXit>: ZOOM
Adjust lens length <50 mm>: 75 (You may have to adjust the
```
value, depending on your graphics card, to achieve the same view as Figure 15.23.)

Applying the Preview to the Entire Model

10. Select the eXit option and observe the results. The display should look like Figure 15.24, where the manipulated DVIEW options have been applied to the entire model, achieving the desired perspective view. If the view on your screen is radically different than Figure 15.24, reenter DVIEW and adjust the settings as necessary.

Saving the Perspective Settings

11. It is always useful to save the settings of DVIEW, because they can be unique and hard to duplicate if lost. To save these settings, use the standard Save option of the VIEW command. Save the view under the name

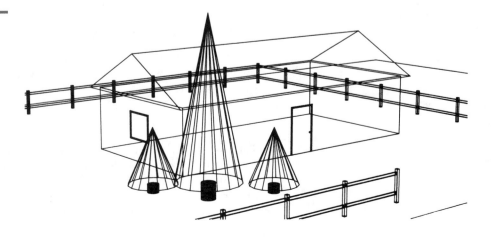

PERSP1. The exact view with the DVIEW settings will be recalled if you use the Restore option of the VIEW command.

12. Save the model as BDWELL. Then, return to the DVIEW command and experiment with the options used in this lab.

Lab 15.B

Dynamic Viewing with Removal of Obstructing Objects

Purpose

Lab 15.B will show you how to remove temporarily objects that are obstructing the best view of the model. The basic dwelling model created in Lab 8.B, Chapter 8, will be your tool.

Objectives

You will be able to:

- Create an exterior perspective view of a model.
- Temporarily remove obstructing geometry from the model.
- Save the current perspective view for later retrieval.

Primary Commands

DVIEW—Camera, Distance, Zoom, Clip
VIEW—Save

Procedure

Initial Setup

1. Open the basic dwelling drawing that was modified in Lab 15.A. The file name is BDWELL.

2. Align the UCS to the WCS, and turn on the UCS icon.

3. Display the perspective view from Lab 15.A by restoring the view PERSP1:

   Command: **VIEW**
   ?/Delete/Restore/Save/Window: **R**
   View name to restore: **PERSP1**

Creating the Preview Selection Set

4. Activate the DVIEW command:

   Command: **DVIEW**
   Select objects:

5. Select the entities for the Preview Selection Set. Select the roof, the walls, and the trees, as shown in Figure 15.25.

Figure 15.25
Selecting the Preview Selection Set

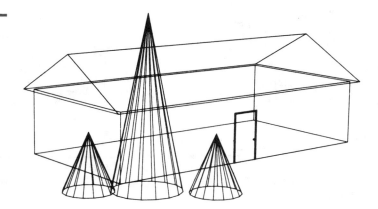

Using the Camera Option

6. Since the previous settings were restored when the view was restored, there is no need to move the camera.

Setting the Camera Distance

7. To achieve more of a perspective effect, select the Distance option and set the distance to 72'. You may have to adjust the distance depending on your screen. The value may be between 65' and 75'.

Using the Zoom Option to Get a Better Picture

8. Select the Zoom option, and set the lens length to 25 mm. The display should look like Figure 15.26.

Removing Obstructing Features

9. Notice how the trees would be obstructing the view of the window. Use the Clip option to remedy this problem. Select the Clip option:

```
Command:
CAmera/TArget/Distance/POints/ . . . /CLip/Hide/OFF/
Undo/<eXit>: CL
Back/Front/<off>: F
Eye/ON/OFF/<Distance from target> <1.0000>: follow the
next paragraph
```

Move the cursor along the slider bar and observe the results. Objects will disappear or appear as the cursor moves. An imaginary clipping plane is being moved forward and backward over the model. Anything that lies between the plane and the view is temporarily hidden from the view. Set the plane so that the trees disappear from the model, as shown in Figure 15.27. If desired, you can use the back clipping plane to remove the objects that lie on the side of the plane away from the viewer.

Applying the Preview to the Entire Model

10. Select the eXit option. The display should look like Figure 15.28, where the Clip option of the DVIEW command has been applied to the entire model, achieving the desired perspective view. Notice how both part of the fence, as well as all of the trees, have been clipped away.

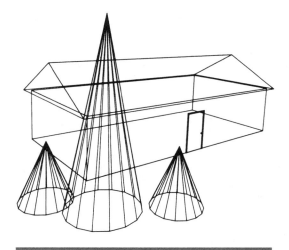

Figure 15.26
Achieving more of a perspective effect with new Distance and Zoom settings

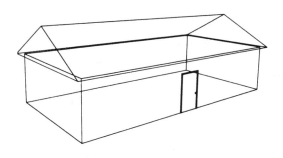

Figure 15.27
Using the Clip option to remove the trees

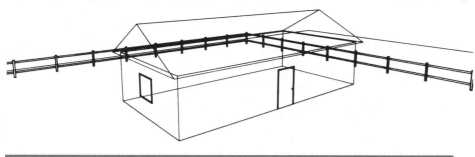

Figure 15.28
Applying the Clip feature to the entire model

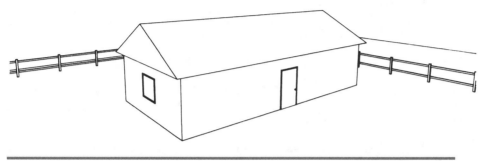

Figure 15.29
Using hidden line removal on the entire model

Saving the Perspective Settings

11. Use the Save option of the VIEW command to save the current view, including the DVIEW settings. Save under the name PERSP2.

12. Save the model as BDWELL. Then, use the standard HIDE command on the model, and observe the results. They should be similar to Figure 15.29.

Lab 15.C

Dynamic Viewing with Interior View

Purpose

Lab 15.C will show you how to create an interior view and use a wide-angle lens to widen the pictured view. The basic kitchen model created in Assignment 1, Chapter 13, will be your tool.

Objectives

You will be able to:

- Create an interior perspective view of a model.
- Pan the displayed image.
- Make use of a wide-angle lens.
- Use the Hide option.

Primary Commands

DVIEW—Camera, Distance, Pan, Zoom, Hide
VIEW—Save

Procedure

Initial Setup

1. Open the basic kitchen drawing that was created in Assignment 1 in Chapter 13. The file name is BKIT.

2. Align the UCS to the WCS, and turn on the UCS icon.

Figure 15.30
Selecting the Preview Selection Set using the Window option

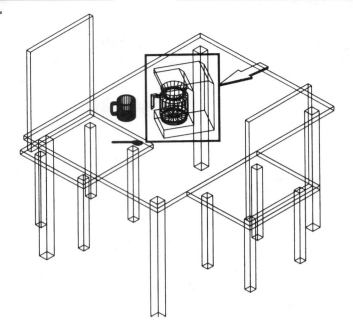

3. Display an isometric view using the VPOINT command:

```
Command: VPOINT
Rotate/<View point><current>: 1,-1,1
```

Creating the Preview Selection Set

4. Activate the DVIEW command:

```
Command: DVIEW
Select objects:
```

5. Select the entities for the Preview Selection Set. Use the Window option to place a window around the coffeemaker, as shown in Figure 15.30.

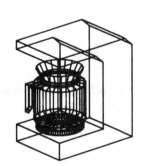

Figure 15.31
Getting the desired view by using the Camera option

Using the Camera Option

6. Now activate the Camera option. Use the cursor to place the angular location of the camera, as in Figure 15.31.

Picking a New Target

7. To select a new target point, use the Pan option. Pick the center of the coffeepot as the base point and the center of the screen as the new location. Now, the coffeemaker is the new target location. This will enable closer viewing of that particular area.

Setting the Camera Distance

8. Select the Distance option, and set the distance to 2'. The view is now very close, and it is difficult to make out features.

Using the Zoom Option to Get a Better Picture

9. Select the Zoom option, and set the lens length to 20 mm. This is a wide-angle lens, so it provides a larger viewing area. The display should look like Figure 15.32.

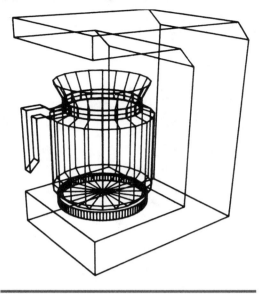

Figure 15.32
Using a distance of 2′ and a lens of 20 mm

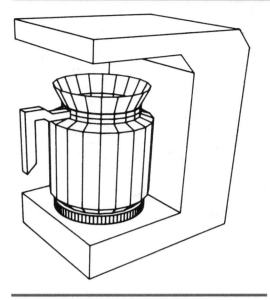

Figure 15.33
Using the Hide option within the DVIEW environment

Using the Hide Option while in DVIEW

10. When it is desirable to view the Preview Selection Set with hidden line removal, use the DVIEW command's Hide option. Select the Hide option now and observe the results. Your screen should be similar to that of Figure 15.33.

Applying the Preview to the Entire Model

11. Select the eXit option. The display should look like Figure 15.34.

Saving the Perspective Settings

12. Use the Save option of the VIEW command to save the current view as PERSP1.

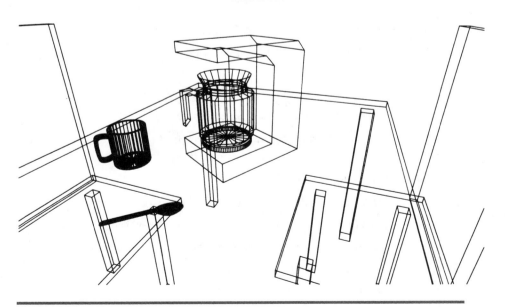

Figure 15.34
Applying the DVIEW settings to the entire model

Figure 15.35
Display showing the entire model with hidden lines removed

13. Save the model as BKIT. Then, use the standard HIDE command on the model and observe the results. They should be similar to Figure 15.35.

Questions

1. What is the difference between an axonometric view and a perspective view?

2. In a perspective view, what effect does moving objects farther and farther away from the viewer have on the displayed view?

3. What causes the effect described in Question 2?

4. Explain the relationship between the center of interest and the station point.

5. What does the command DVIEW stand for? To what other AutoCAD feature is it similar?

6. Explain the purpose of slider bars and how they operate.

7. Explain the purpose of the Preview Selection Set.

8. Why might it be important to limit the items used in the Preview Selection Set?

9. Explain the function of the DVIEWBLOCK.

10. Which DVIEW options do you use to cause the perspective effect?

11. What happens to the UCS icon when a perspective view is being displayed?

12. How does the Distance option affect the location of the viewer?

13. What is the significance of the Zoom option?

14. Explain how the Clip option can be of use.

15. Identify the limitations of some of AutoCAD's commands when the perspective view has been activated.

Assignments

1. Create two lines of posts parallel to each other. Each line should be 10′ apart. In each line, there should be at least twenty 12′-high posts, 6′ apart from each other.

   First, display an axonometric view. Save the view as AXONA. Now, use the DVIEW command to create a view similar to the axonometric view, but make it a perspective view. Save this view as PERSPB.

   Split the screen into two horizontal viewports. Display the view AXONA in one view port and the view PERSPB in the other. Compare the two views.

2. Using the file BDWELL, which was saved in Lab 15.B, create a perspective worm's-eye view of the house.

3. Insert the BKIT model (used in Lab 15.C) into the inside of the house model BDWELL (from Lab 15.B). Use the Clip option and a wide-angle lens to cut through the walls and view the kitchen scene. Use the HIDE command to enhance the effect.

4. Open the model NBOLT created in Chapter 13, Assignment 2. Use the Clip option of the DVIEW command to section the assembly.

5. Open the INCA model surfaced in Chapter 7, Assignment 2. Display a perspective view as if someone were standing close to the model and looking up, toward its top.

CHAPTER 16

Plotting

Overview

In this chapter, you'll learn the techniques for making hard copies of wireframe and more complex models. (*Note:* The labs in this chapter have been designed so that you will be able to do them whether or not you have access to a plotter.)

Concepts Explored

- The importance of model plots
- How to create wireframe and hidden line removed plots
- The differences between axonometric and perspective plots
- What paper space represents
- How to work within paper space
- The creation of paper space viewports
- The creation of two-dimensional drawings from three-dimensional models
- How to plot three-dimensional models in single and multiple views.

16.1 Introduction

Many experts believe that we are progressing toward a paperless society, where everyone will have access to computer monitors and be able to call up virtually anything for viewing. This may sound appealing and very efficient, but in most areas of industry today paper copies are still very much a necessity.

For instance, plots of 3D models are very effective presentation tools. If you can quickly generate multiple views of a model or even display what-if scenarios, illustrating different modifications to the model, then you can provide your client with a thorough and impressive presentation. But doing this on screen usually isn't possible. Even though the screen does provide for on-the-fly changes during client-requested viewing, screens of a size that can be seen by many at one time are still very expensive. However, plotting the various views and scenarios onto large sheets is relatively cheap by comparison and still enables you to make impressive presentations.

Illustrators and artists also need paper copies. An illustrator creates a model—perhaps of a mechanical part or a commercial building—displays a

Figure 16.1
Multiview plot

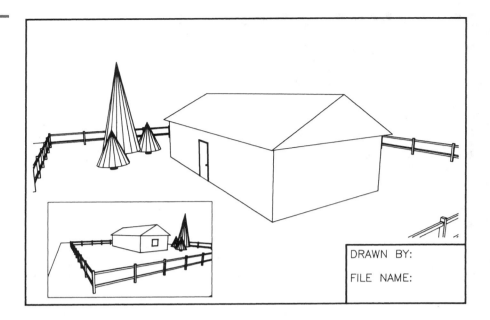

desirable view, turns it into a perspective, and then plots it onto a sheet of paper. The illustrator then uses this plot as a guide when creating a manually drawn and painted rendering. The model does not have to be as complex as the final rendering; it merely has to have enough detail to give the illustrator a basis for the rendering.

Plots can be produced in a number of ways—using wireframe, hidden line removal, or axonometric, perspective, or multiple views (Figure 16.1). All these techniques are discussed in this chapter. In addition, paper space, which greatly reduces the complexity of these techniques, is introduced.

16.2 Wireframe Versus Hidden Line Removal

The quickest way to display a model on the screen is in wireframe. Similarly, when plotting a model, leaving it in wireframe produces the fastest plot. However, this type of model is not the most desirable for presentation purposes. In most cases, hidden line removal is the most effective way to present a model illustration. Producing a plot of a wireframe representation requires no special settings. When running through the PLOT command, a user will check the Hide lines box if hidden line removal is desired. If the Hide lines box is not checked, a wireframe representation is generated. Note that the user does not have to do hidden line removal on screen before doing a plot. This is taken care of automatically when the user specifies that hidden lines be removed in the Plot Configuration. (Paper space plot requirements are a little different; we'll discuss them later.) Also, recall that frozen layers are not used in the calculation of hidden line removal. So, to speed up hidden line removal during display or plotting, remember to first freeze layers that are not going to be shown.

3D Viewpoint

Hollow Arrowheads During Plotting
If you have arrowheads on your model and you plot the model with the Hide Lines option, the arrowheads will appear to be hollow.

16.3 Axonometric Versus Perspective Representations

Axonometric representations of a model are to scale. This means that the entities are proportional to each other. The model can be dimensioned and plotted to a particular scale when it is generated as hard copy. On the other hand, perspective representations of a model are not to scale. This means that each entity is not proportional to the other and that when entities are closer to the viewer they appear larger than when they are farther away from the viewer. Although this is what gives the representation its realistic look, it means that a perspective view cannot be dimensioned as such and is to no particular scale when plotted. Because of these differences between axonometric and perspective representations, the scaling of their plots is done differently.

Scaling a Single-View Plot

Plotting an axonometric representation in 3D is basically the same as 2D plotting. You select the desired view, and activate the PLOT command. When a specific scale is desired, you simply enter a scale in much the same way as for a 2D drawing (that is, 1 = 2 or 1/4″ = 1′, for example).

When plotting a perspective representation, you use the Scaled to Fit option. The view is then scaled to fit a particular area of the drawing. In this way, the size of the final plot is based on the sheet area that you predefine.

16.4 Paper Space

In Release 11 and later releases, there are two working environments within any drawing—model space and paper space. Model space is used for construction purposes. This is where the 3D model is built. The paper space environment is used to arrange multiple viewing areas on an imagined two-dimensional sheet of paper. Paper space can be thought of as an electronic cut-and-paste environment. In paper space, the viewports (floating) represent various pictures of the model. Each picture can be scaled, rotated, or written on, just as if the user had cut out various details and arranged them on a piece of paper.

Multiviews and Paper Space

Until Release 11, multiple-viewport displays could not be plotted as one unit. And, although not impossible, it was cumbersome to generate multiple views. Then came the introduction of paper space in AutoCAD. With paper space, you can create a layout of your desired views, set their scale, identify which views will be wireframe and which will be hidden, and, if desired, specify borders or labels for any or all of the views. You can also surround the entire layout with a border, such as a title block. Then, you can simply plot the layout without any complicated settings. The paper space layout stays with the drawing so that it can be used at any time.

Accessing Paper Space

The two working environments created originally with Release 11 are accessed through the system variable TILEMODE. A TILEMODE setting of 1 is the standard setting. It allows the creation of tiled viewports using the VPORTS command. It allows construction to take place only in model space. This common mode was available in earlier versions of AutoCAD. The newer TILEMODE setting of 0 opens the door to paper space and model space together.

To use paper space properly, you must create individual floating viewports that will display the various desired views of your model. When you first switch

TILEMODE to 0 and access paper space for the first time, no viewing areas exist yet. To create a viewport, use the MVIEW command. This command will work only when TILEMODE is set to 0. MVIEW stands for "Make VIEWport," which is exactly what it does. By selecting the various options, you can create any combination of viewports. These areas can be any size and can display any view of a model. Once you have placed the viewing areas, you can annotate and detail them in any fashion. As you might imagine, these floating viewports are very similar to the tiled viewports, except that each viewport created in paper space is considered an individual entity. They can be any size, and they can overlap each other, hence the term floating. The border lines identifying their boundaries can be turned on or off. (Refer to the later section on initial paper space layout and plotting for information on the size of the model and the viewport border when plotting.)

You may add any type of entities in paper space, but these entities will only be present in the paper space environment; they are not added to the actual model. When you switch to TILEMODE = 1, any entities you created in paper space will not be shown. Then, when you switch back to paper space, with TILEMODE set to 0, the paper space entities will reappear.

PSPACE Versus MSPACE

The power of paper space is increased by its ability to enter into any of the newly created floating viewports and alter the model contents in any way, such as changing the viewpoint, exactly as if you had switched back to the TILEMODE = 1 setting. Once TILEMODE is set to 0, you can toggle back and forth between paper space and model space through the use of the MSPACE and PSPACE commands. To access a viewport when TILEMODE is set to 0, use the MSPACE command. This command switches to model space within the paper space environment, allowing you to digitize any viewport and make actual changes to the model. To exit this environment, use the PSPACE command, which switches back to the paper space environment. Note that PSPACE and MSPACE commands do not work with TILEMODE set to 1. They are designed to be used when TILEMODE = 0 only.

PSPACE Versus MSPACE Identification

You can identify which "space" you are in while TILEMODE is set to 0 in three different ways. First, you can watch the behavior of the cursor. If the cursor extends to the length of the screen, you are in paper space. If the cursor extends only to the limit of a particular viewport, then you are in model space. However, if the viewport fills the screen, this can be difficult to distinguish.

Second, you can look at the UCS icon. When you are in paper space, the icon takes on a new form, as illustrated in Figure 16.2. It is a good idea to keep the icon turned on when working within paper space. This will allow you to identify quickly the "space" mode in which you're working.

Third, check the status line. When in paper space, a "P" appears on the status line.

3D Viewpoint

Accessing Floating Viewports
If a floating viewport lies completely within another floating viewport, you may find it impossible to access. To access it, you must turn off the larger viewport with the MVIEW command.

Figure 16.2
Model space icon versus paper space icon

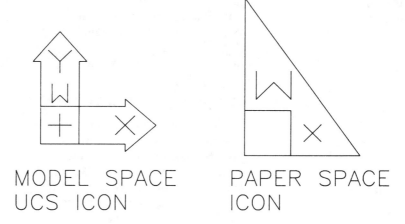

Exiting the Paper Space Environment

When you set TILEMODE back to 1, you exit the paper space environment entirely and return to the common construction mode of model space. The screen will return to the settings originated before you entered paper space. The paper space settings and entities are not lost; they are simply stored until you return to paper space by again setting TILEMODE to 0. Any changes made to the model when TILEMODE is set to 1 will be reflected in the viewports of paper space, even though they are turned off. When you return to paper space, you will be able to see the changes you made while in model space. At any time, you can switch back and forth between TILEMODE settings 0 and 1, effectively switching between the two environments.

Initial Paper Space Layout and Plotting

The following outlines a method for setting up a paper space layout and plotting a model. This method could be used for any model.

1. The model has been constructed at this point.
2. Set the TILEMODE variable to 0 to switch into the paper space environment. The paper space icon should be visible. *Warning:* Your model will disappear from the screen temporarily until viewports are created in step 4.
3. Because the paper space environment is a 2D environment and can be thought of as a flat piece of paper, insert a border that represents the sheet of paper onto which the model will be plotted. This could be a standard title block and border. Most often, the scale of a paper space layout is plotted as 1:1, so the border should match the sheet at a scale of 1 to 1. The title block can be filled in now or later.
4. Within the border, use the MVIEW command to create viewports that will display the various views that are desired. Remember that the viewports can be any size and can overlay each other. If the viewports are placed on their own layers, the border of a viewport can be turned off simply by turning off the layer on which its viewport was placed. When a layer the viewport is on is turned off, the border disappears and will not plot. However, the contents of the viewport will not be affected—they will still be visible and will plot.
5. Switch to model space with the MSPACE command and, using the various display commands, display the desired viewpoint and orientation. The scale of the model in the viewport needs to be set at this point. A special ZOOM option is available to do this. It is called XP. It will scale the model in relation to the paper space plot scale. Because you normally plot the

paper space layout on a 1 = 1 scale, the XP scale will be in proportion to that. For example, if you wanted a floor plan at a scale of 1/4″ = 1′ (1 = 48), then the XP scale value would be 1/48. conversely, if a view is to be plotted at a scale of 2 = 1, the XP scale would be 2. To use this option, enter the desired viewport and type the following command:

```
Command: ZOOM
All/Center/Dynamic/Extents . . . /<Scale(X/XP)>: 1/48XP
```

This model would be scaled to 1/4″ = 1′ when the paper space layout was plotted at a scale of 1 = 1. (*Note:* The XP option will only work when the TILEMODE variable is set to 0.)

6. While still within MSPACE, the layers in each viewport are independent. This means you can freeze different layers in different viewports, giving you any combination of displayed or not displayed layers. The command that controls the layers in the currently active viewport is called VPLAYER. You also can use the much more visual Layer Control dialog box from the Settings pull-down menu or type DDLMODES at the command prompt to freeze layers. First, highlight the layers you wish to modify, and then pick the Cur VP: Frz button. Each of the highlighted layers will be frozen in the currently active viewport.

7. Switch to paper space with the PSPACE command and finish annotating the layout, such as adding text labels and so forth.

8. Use the MVIEW command to set which viewports will be plotted with hidden line removal. To do so, type the following command:

```
Command: MVIEW
ON/OFF/Hideplot/Fit/2/3/4/Restore/<First Point>: H
Hideplot ON/OFF: ON
Select objects: pick the edge of each viewport and
then press <Enter>
```

This selection ensures that the contents of each viewport will be plotted with hidden lines removed. (*Note:* The viewport border needs to be visible when this option is selected, but it does not have to be visible for plotting. Before plotting, turn the layer off that contains the viewport, and the viewport border will no longer be visible.)

9. Save the file with the paper space layout.

10. Use the PLOT command to alter the plot configuration. When in paper space, you can alter the plot configuration as you normally do, except the plot scale should be 1 = 1 and the Hide lines option will have no effect because you will have already set it using the MVIEW command.

Once you have mastered the use of paper space—a process that should not take long—you will appreciate its power in setting up a drawing sheet. You might even wish to use paper space for all your construction and drawing, whether in 2D or 3D. Paper space is a very powerful feature; don't underestimate its uses. And remember its benefits! Paper space and the creation of independent viewports allow you to set up all plot scales directly within a drawing, and also to identify which detail will have hidden lines removed. When plotting from now on, you only need to plot to a scale of 1 = 1 and not worry if hidden line removal is turned on or off in the plot configuration.

16.5 Turning a 3D Model into a 2D Drawing

There are times when it is useful to have a 2D drawing of a 3D model. For instance, sometimes users require several plots of the same view of a model with hidden lines removed. In 3D, you have to wait for AutoCAD to go through the process of calculating the removal of hidden lines each time you plot a model. A 2D drawing of the 3D model, however, can be plotted again and again without having to go through the hidden line removal process.

Consider another example: The creator of a model needs to give an electronic copy of the picture of the model to someone (the client perhaps). The creator can give a 2D drawing of the model rather than the precious model itself. Then the recipient can plot that file, while the creator retains the original model.

Finally, a 2D drawing of a model is useful because it can be enhanced more easily than a 3D model. Sometimes the hidden line removal process does not generate the perfect picture, usually because of intersecting surfaces. Unwanted lines appear and mar the final drawing. But a user can easily edit a 2D drawing of a model to remove and fix unwanted geometry before producing the plot, with no one the wiser.

From 3D to 2D with a Plot File

AutoCAD's File Output Format plotter option allows the generation of a binary file from a plot. This binary file can, in turn, be read into an AutoCAD drawing with the use of the DXBIN command. This process makes it very simple to turn a 3D model into a 2D drawing with the assistance of the PLOT command. The steps for doing so are as follows:

1. From AutoCAD's command prompt, enter CONFIG to configure Auto-CAD.
2. Select the option to add a printer configuration.
3. Select "AutoCAD file output formats (pre 4.1)—by Autodesk" as the printer type and add DXBOUT as the description.
4. Select AutoCAD DXB file as the output option.
5. Leave maximum X plot size as 11. This sets the X length, but it can be changed if desired. Because the imported plot can be scaled when it is made into a drawing, there is no need to set the size at this time.
6. Leave plotter steps as 1000. If smoother curves are required, the number may be increased up to a maximum of 2900.
7. Leave maximum Y plot size as 8.5 (for the same reason given in step 5).
8. Respond to the rest of the questions as you have learned in previous plot setups.
9. Plot the model as always, only this time select DXBOUT instead of a regular plotter as the device for output and add a name to the plot file. The binary information will be stored here instead of going to a plotter. The extension of the file will be DXB. For example, a plot file named ANGPLT would end up with a name of ANGPLT.DXB. This is the file that will be imported into an AutoCAD drawing file.
10. Start a new drawing.
11. Use the DXBIN command to import the binary file into AutoCAD. When asked for the file name, respond with the name that was given for the plot file in step 10.
12. Once the plot file has been imported, it can be modified in any way. Remember that it is now a flat 2D drawing.
13. Save the imported plot file as a drawing using the standard file SAVE command.

Once you have completed steps 1 to 8, you can plot as many DXB files as necessary. When it is time to plot to an actual plotter, set the output device back to the usual plotter instead of DXBOUT.

Working Drawings of Models

Once created, a model usually will either be prepared for final presentation (see Chapter 15) or used to create working drawings. A working drawing is a completely annotated 2D drawing that is used for the production of the modeled component. To add notes and text to a model is a simple process; you just create a paper space environment (see the 10-step procedure outlined earlier). The dimensioning of the 3D model is a more difficult process.

The easiest way to create a working drawing is to create 2D orthographic views of the model, put each view on its own layer, and then dimension those views. To create a 2D view of a surface model, you can use the method that creates a DXB plot file (see the 13-step procedure outlined earlier). Once you have created a drawing of the DXB file, you can modify it to turn it into a working drawing. The problem with this method is that the resultant drawing file is made up entirely of lines. Even the curves have been translated into lines. You would have to replace the curved line shapes with actual arcs and circles.

The second method for creating orthographic views involves the generation of a solid model using the Designer program. This is a separate application program from Autodesk. Its purpose is to enhance the creation of 3D solid models through the use of parametric design. One of its features is the automatic creation of 2D drawings from a solid model (refer to Chapter 24).

Lab 16.A

3D Model to 2D Plot

Purpose

Lab 16.A will show you how to use the plotter configuration to create a two-dimensional drawing from a three-dimensional model. If you do not have access to a plotter, you will still find this and the following labs helpful. However, instead of creating a hard copy, you will create an electronic image of the plot.

Objectives

You will be able to:

- Set the plotter configuration to the ADI plot driver.
- Create a DXB plot file.
- Import a DXB plot file into a drawing.

Primary Commands

```
Config (Autocad Configuration, Plotter Configuration)
PLOT
DXBIN
```

Final Drawing

Figure 16.3 shows the final 2D drawing of the coffeepot model.

Procedure

1. Open the COFPT model created in Chapter 8, Lab 8.A.

2. Using the VPOINT command, display a view similar to the one shown in Figure 16.3.

3. Save the model as COFPT. Set the CMDDIA variable to 1 so that the Plot dialog box will appear.

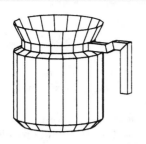

Figure 16.3
Two-dimensional drawing of the coffeepot model

Configuring the Plotter Output

4. At AutoCAD's command prompt, enter CONFIG to configure AutoCAD.

5. The current settings of AutoCAD's configuration should now be displayed. Observe them and note how the plotter is configured. Press <Enter> to continue.

6. From the configure menu, select the option that adds plotter configurations.

7. You should now be presented with a listing of various plotters. Pick the one that indicates "AutoCAD file output formats (pre. 4.1)—by Autodesk."

8. Now you will be prompted for the type of output required. Here, pick the AutoCAD DXB file option.

9. When asked for the X length of the plot, the number of plotter steps, and the Y length, respond with 11, 1000, and 8.5, respectively.

10. Now you will be asked the usual plot configuration questions. Answer all those prompts—except for the plot scale—in the desired format. Unless an actual scale needs to be plotted, the usual plot scale is set to FIT. This means the model plot will scale to fit an area 11 × 8.5 inches, as set in step 9.

11. Finally, you will be asked for the description of the plotter. Enter DXBOUT as the new plotter configuration name, and save the AutoCAD configurations.

Creating the Plot File

12. Type PLOT at the command prompt.

13. When the dialog box is presented, select the Device and Default Selection option, and then select DXBOUT as the device.

14. Make certain the Plot To File box has a check mark showing and enter COFPT for the file name to plot.

15. Set the plot configuration settings as usual. For the plot scale, checkmark the Scaled to Fit box. Checkmark the Hide lines box. Pick OK to start the plot.

16. At this point, you should now have a DXB file called COFPT.DXB. This is the file that is going to be imported into a drawing.

Importing the DXB File

17. Start a new blank drawing file and call it COFPT2.

18. Using the DXBIN command, answer COFPT to the prompt for the name of the plot file to import. The drawing of the coffeepot model (as shown in Figure 16.3) should now appear on the screen. It is a 2D version of the 3D model.

19. Save the drawing as COFPT2. Then, using the VPOINT command, confirm that it is indeed a flat 2D drawing by displaying an isometric view. In this state, the drawing is like any ordinary 2D drawing and can be modified as such.

Paper Space Plot

Purpose

Lab 16.B will familiarize you with the paper space environment and help you to appreciate how easy it is to lay out a multiple-view plot. You will make use of the ANGPLT model created in Chapter 7, Lab 7.B.

As mentioned in Lab 16.A, if you do not have access to a plotter you can still do this lab. Watch for the note referring you back to Lab 16.A and providing you with the necessary information for creating an electronic image of the plot.

Objectives

You will be able to:

- Lay out a multiview plot in paper space.
- Select which viewports will be plotted with hidden lines removed.
- Switch back and forth between MSPACE and PSPACE.

Primary Commands

TILEMODE
MVIEW
PSPACE
MSPACE
PLOT

Final Plot

Procedure

Figure 16.4 shows the multiview plot of the angle plate model you'll be laying out.

1. Create a title block as shown in Figure 16.5. This will be inserted into the paper space layout. Save the drawing as PSTB (Paper Space Title Block).

2. Open the ANGPLT model surfaced in Chapter 7, Lab 7.B.

Switching into the Paper Space Environment

3. Using the TILEMODE command, enter the number 0. The screen will go blank. This is perfectly normal. The screen is blank because no paper

Figure 16.4
Multiview plot of the angle plate model

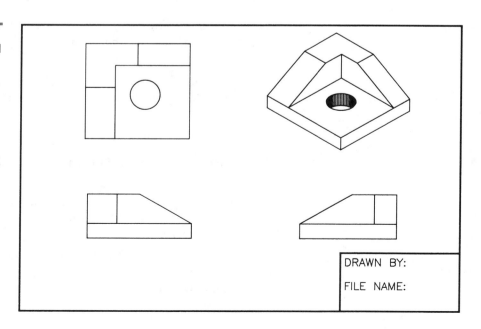

DRAWN BY:

FILE NAME:

Figure 16.5
Title block named PSTB

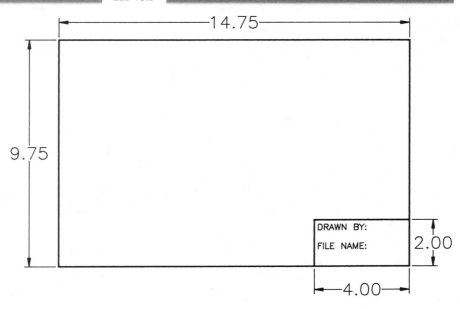

space viewports have been created yet. If you have turned on the UCS icon, the paper space icon should be visible in the lower left corner of the screen.

Switching Back to the Model Space Environment

4. Using the TILEMODE command again, enter the number 1. The angle plate model should appear again, because you are back in the model space environment again. Recall that both environments are kept intact when you switch from one to the other.

5. Switch back to paper space by setting TILEMODE = 0.

Inserting the Title Block in Paper Space

6. Create a layer called TBLOCK, and make it current.

7. Using the INSERT command, place the title block with its lower left corner at 0,0 and fill it in with the appropriate information. Refer to Figure 16.6.

Creating Paper Space Viewports

8. Create a layer called VPORTS, and make it active.

9. Using the MVIEW command, create a four-viewport configuration:

```
Command: MVIEW
ON/OFF/Hideplot/Fit/2/3/4/Restore/<First Point>: 4
Fit<First Point>: 0.5,1.5 (Refer to Figure 16.7, P1.)
Second point: 14.5,9.5 (Refer to Figure 16.7, P2.)
```

If you use a different title block and border, use the appropriate P1 and P2. Refer to the figure for proper locations.

You should now have four viewports, each displaying the last active viewport from model space, as shown in Figure 16.7.

Figure 16.6
Title block inserted into paper space

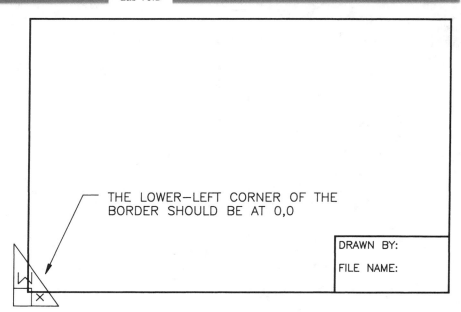

THE LOWER—LEFT CORNER OF THE
BORDER SHOULD BE AT 0,0

DRAWN BY:

FILE NAME:

Figure 16.7
Four paper space viewports

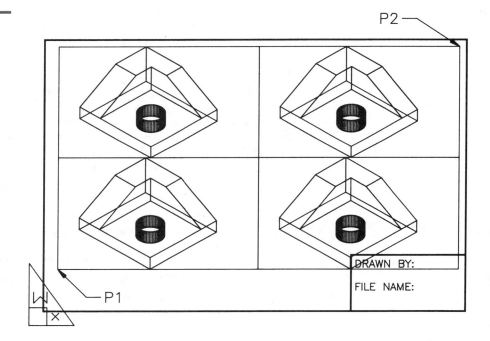

Using MSPACE to Display Desired Viewpoints

To change the displayed view in any of the viewports, you must use the MSPACE command. This command switches to model space *within* the paper space environment, and allows access to the contents of the viewports.

10. Using the MSPACE command, enter into model space. Notice how the cursor switched into one of the viewports. This is the currently active viewport.

11. Using the VPOINT command, display the standard orthographic views—top, front, right-side, and axonometric. Refer to Figure 16.8.

Setting the Scale

12. While still in MSPACE, go into each viewport by digitizing in the viewport, and set the scale using the XP option of the ZOOM command:

Figure 16.8
Multiviews in paper space set to 0.5XP

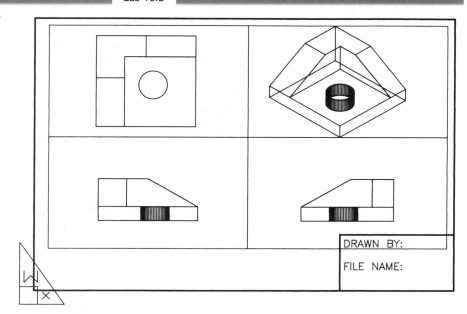

```
Command: ZOOM
All/Center/.... Window/<Scale>(X/XP)>: .5XP
```

This will set the scale of the views at 1 = 2 when the paper space layout is plotted at a scale of 1 = 1 (see Figure 16.8).

Freezing the Viewport Entity

Viewports created in paper space are considered entities. This means they can be scaled, stretched, or frozen when the layer they are on is frozen.

13. Enter paper space, and make layer 0 current.

14. Using the LAYER command, freeze the layer called VPORTS. Notice how the outline of the viewport disappears, but the contents of the viewport do not. Remember, you can choose not to display the viewport border by freezing the layer that contains the viewport entities.

15. Thaw the VPORTS layer to display the viewport border again.

Removing Hidden Lines

To plot with hidden line removal in paper space, you must tell AutoCAD which viewports will be plotted with hidden lines removed. Use the MVIEW command to do this.

16. Using the MVIEW command, select all four viewports for hidden line removal:

```
Command: MVIEW
ON/OFF/Hideplot/Fit/2/3/4/Restore/<First Point>: H
Hideplot ON/OFF: ON
Select Objects: pick the edge of each viewport and
then press <Enter>
```

Because of this selection, the contents of each viewport will be plotted with hidden lines removed.

17. Freeze the layer called VPORTS

18. Save the model as ANGPLT.

Plotting the Paper Space Layout

Note: If you do not have access to a plotter, you can follow Lab 16.A to create a drawing of this lab's paper space layout. Refer to step 9 of Lab 16.A: the *X* length should be 17″ and the *Y* length should be 11″. In the later steps, substitute ANGPLT as the model file, ANGPLT as the plot file name, and ANGPL as the 2D drawing into which the ANGPLT plot file will be imported. The final drawing should look like Figure 16.4.

If you do have access to a plotter, complete the following steps:

19. Set up the plotter in the usual fashion.

20. From AutoCAD's main menu, select the option to plot a file.

21. Set up the Plot Configuration. (Recall that the Hide lines option has no effect when plotting in paper space because you identify which viewport will be plotted with hidden line removal during the layout stage.) Also, be sure to plot this layout at a scale of 1 = 1.

22. Your final plot should look like Figure 16.4. Notice how the text in the title block stayed the same size, whereas the model views plotted at half their actual size. This happened because the text was added in paper space and the model views were scaled using the XP option of the ZOOM command.

Lab 16.C

Paper Space Layout with Insert

Purpose

Lab 16.C will familiarize you with the process of manipulating viewports in paper space and show you how paper space viewports can overlap each other. You will be using the BDWELL model from Chapter 8, Lab 8.B, again.

As mentioned in Lab 16.A, you do not have to have access to a plotter to do this lab. Watch for the note referring you back to Lab 16.A, and providing you with the information you'll need to create an electronic image of the plot.

Objectives

You will be able to:

- Lay out a master viewport with an overlapping viewport in paper space.
- Select which viewports will be plotted with hidden lines removed.
- Switch back and forth between MSPACE and PSPACE.

Primary Commands

TILEMODE
MVIEW
PSPACE
MSPACE
PLOT

Final Plot

Figure 16.9 shows the final multiview perspective plot of the basic dwelling model.

Procedure

1. Open the model BDWELL created in Chapter 8, Lab 8.B.

2. Using the DVIEW command, display a perspective view similar to that shown in Figure 16.10.

Switching into the Paper Space Environment

3. Using the TILEMODE command, enter the number 0. The screen will go blank. This is perfectly normal. The screen is blank because you have

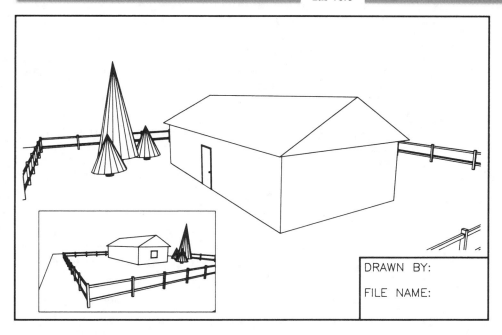

DRAWN BY:

FILE NAME:

Figure 16.9
Multiview perspective plot of the basic dwelling model

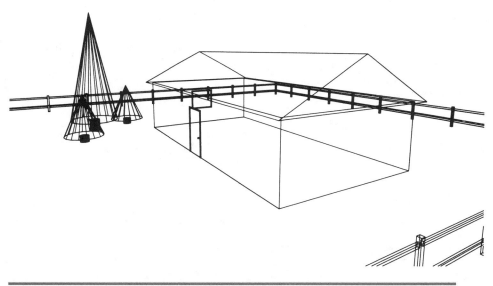

Figure 16.10
Perspective view of the basic dwelling

not created any paper space viewports yet. If you have turned on the UCS icon, the paper space icon should be visible in the lower left corner of the screen.

Inserting the Title Block in Paper Space

4. Create a layer called TBLOCK, and make it current.

5. Using the INSERT command, place the title block that was created in Lab 16.B (PSTB from step 1) with its lower left corner at 0,0, and fill it in with the appropriate information.

Creating Paper Space Viewports

6. Create a layer called VPORT1, and make it active.

7. Using the MVIEW command, create one viewport that fits within the title block area, as shown in Figure 16.11.

   ```
   Command: MVIEW
   ON/OFF/Hideplot/Fit/2/3/4/Restore/<First Point>: 1/4",
   2-1/4" (Refer to Figure 16.11, P1.)
   Second point: 1'2-1/2", 9-1/2" (Refer to Figure 16.11, P2.)
   ```

   If you use a different title block and border, use the appropriate P1 and P2. Refer to the figure for proper location.

8. Create a layer called VPORT2, and make it current.

9. Using the MVIEW command, create one viewport that overlaps the first viewport, as shown in Figure 16.12.

   ```
   Command: MVIEW
   ON/OFF/Hideplot/Fit/2/3/4/Restore/<First Point>: 3/4",
   1/4" (Refer to Figure 16.12, P3.)
   Second point: 6-1/4", 3-1/2" (Refer to Figure 16.12, P4.)
   ```

Switching to Model Space

10. Using the MSPACE command, switch to model space.

11. Make the small viewport active. The best way to do this is to digitize it in the nonoverlapping area. Otherwise, AutoCAD does not know which viewport you are activating.

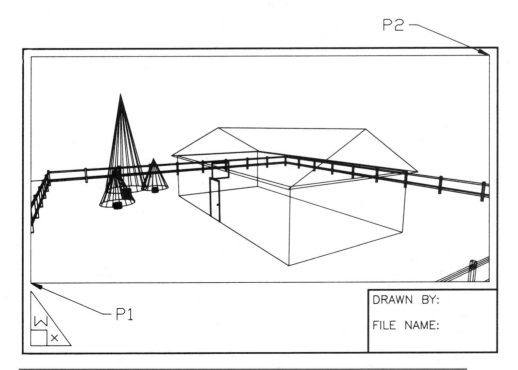

Figure 16.11
Single paper space viewport

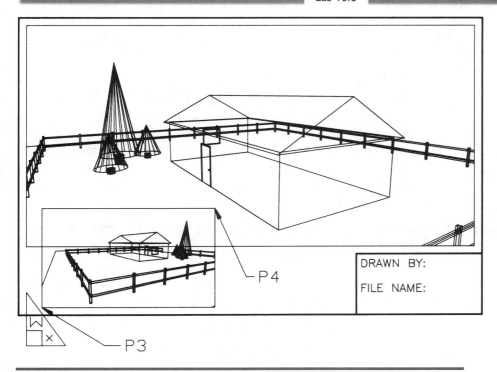

Figure 16.12
A small viewport overlapping onto a larger viewport

12. Using the DVIEW command, display a rear perspective view of the dwelling similar to the one shown in Figure 16.9.

13. Using the PSPACE command, switch back to paper space.

Removing Hidden Lines

To plot with hidden line removal in paper space, you must tell AutoCAD which viewports will be plotted with hidden lines removed. Use the MVIEW command to do this.

14. Using the MVIEW command, select both viewports for hidden line removal:

```
Command: MVIEW
ON/OFF/Hideplot/Fit/2/3/4/Restore/<First Point>: H
Hideplot ON/OFF: ON
Select Objects: pick the edge of each viewport and
then press <Enter>
```

Because of this selection, the contents of each viewport will be plotted with hidden lines removed.

15. Freeze layer VPORT1 so that the border around the viewport will not be plotted.

16. Save the model as BDWEL2.

Plotting the Paper Space Layout

Note: If you do not have access to a plotter, you can follow Lab 16.A to create a drawing of this lab's paper space layout. Refer to step 9 of Lab 16.A: the *X* length should be 17″ and the *Y* length should be 11″. In the later steps, substitute BDWEL2 as the model file, BDWEL2 as the plot file name, and

302 Lab 16.C
Paper Space Layout with
Insert

BDWEL3 as the 2D drawing into which the BDWEL2 plot file will be imported. The final drawing should look like Figure 16.9.

If you do have access to a plotter, complete the following steps:

17. Set up the plotter in the usual fashion.

18. From AutoCAD's main menu, select the option to plot a file.

19. Set up the Plot Configuration. (Recall that the Hide lines option has no effect when plotting in paper space because you identified which viewport will be plotted with hidden line removal during the layout stage.) Also, be sure to plot this layout at a scale of 1 = 1.

20. The final plot should look like Figure 16.9.

Questions

1. In what way do artists make use of 3D model plots?

2. How do you activate hidden line removal when plotting?

3. In what way do frozen layers affect hidden line removed plots?

4. How is scaling affected by axonometric and perspective plots?

5. What does the system variable TILEMODE control?

6. What are the various functions of the MVIEW command?

7. Can the MVIEW command be used in model space?

8. What are the various functions of the MSPACE and PSPACE commands?

9. What is DXB, and what is its application?

Assignments

You'll be creating a hardcopy plot or a 2D drawing file using a DXB file in each of the following assignments.

1. Using the model scene BKIT (Basic KITchen) assembled in Chapter 13, Assignment 1, produce a paper space layout illustrating (a) the entire kitchen layout in perspective and (b) an overlapping view showing a close-up of the coffee maker. Use MVIEW to make all the viewports plot with hidden lines removed. Save the model plus the layout as BKIT. Then, plot the layout or create a 2D drawing using DXBIN.

2. Create an office layout using the models from Chapter 5 given in the following list. Use paper space to lay out several viewports looking around the scene. Use MVIEW to make all the viewports plot with hidden lines removed. Save the model plus layout as OFFC (OFFiCe layout). Then, plot the layout or create a 2D drawing using DXBIN.

3D SYMBOL	SOURCE
TABLE	Lab 5.B
CHAIR	Lab 5.C
FCAB	Chapter 5, Assignment 1
BSHEL	Chapter 5, Assignment 2

3. With the duct models created in Chapter 8 (see following list), create an assembly. Use paper space to lay out four viewports that display the top, front, right-side, and isometric views. Use MVIEW to make all the view-

ports plot with hidden lines removed. Save the model plus layout as PIPA (PIPing Assembly). Then plot the layout or create a 2D drawing using DXBIN.

3D SYMBOL	SOURCE
TDUCT	Chapter 8, Assignment 3
ODUCT	Chapter 8, Assignment 4

4. Create a paper space layout of a perspective view and an overlapping orthographic view of the side of a car, using the CAR model created in Chapter 8, Assignment 6. Use MVIEW to make all the viewports plot with hidden lines removed. Save the model and layout as SCAR (Sports CAR). Then plot the layout or create a 2D drawing using DXBIN.

5. Restore the ANGPLT model plotted in Lab 16.B. Turn off the paper space layer called VPORTS created in that lab and create a new layer, called VPORT2. On this new layer, create a paper space layout that has two viewports that are side by side. Display the same axonometric view in each. Set the left viewport to use hidden line removal and the right one to remain as a wireframe model. Save the model and new layout as ANGPLT. Then plot the layout or create a 2D drawing using DXBIN.

CHAPTER 17

Rendering

Overview

In this chapter, we explore the use of light, shadow, materials, and preferences in final renderings. The techniques for presenting drawings in enhanced fashions are explained, and the additional rendering procedures necessary for these effects are noted.

Concepts Explored

- The process involved in CAD rendering
- The Render utility and the different types of rendering
- Choosing and placing lights
- Attaching materials
- Applying mapping projection
- Setting preferences.

17.1 Introduction

For AutoCAD users, rendering presents a design in an artistic form; it generates an image that gives a more representative view of their creations. In CAD, rendering is the process of taking an image made basically of lines and adding tones across the surfaces between those lines, which produces a more realistic form of the design. The tones range from light to dark and may be in black and white or a combination of other colors. Because the chances of selling the resulting product improve as the prototype design becomes more appealing, rendering is often the finishing touch that ensures the sale. An example of a rendered image is shown in Figure 17.1.

Performing renderings with three-dimensional models is an art in and of itself. Producing photorealistic images is a long process, but it no longer requires access to expensive hardware. This chapter introduces you to the range of possible rendering techniques and helps make your first attempt at rendering relatively easy. Here, you'll only get your feet wet, but you'll be able to see what you can accomplish with rendering given skill and opportunity. New terms that apply to rendering and various rendering types are discussed in the chapter.

Figure 17.1
A rendered image of an automobile

17.2 AutoCAD and Rendering

The Render utility is used to create basic to photorealistic images. It is more powerful than the Shade utility because it gives you control of lighting and the addition of materials. With the integrated enhancements of Release 14 of AutoCAD, each light type can cast shadows, and materials can make use of bitmap images.

There are three rendering types: Render, Photo Real, and Photo Ray-Traced. Render is the fastest but does not show material maps or shadows. The next is Photo Real, which does show shadows and material maps. The third, Photo Ray-Traced, shows reflections, refractions, and more precise shadows.

Render Toolbar

The Render toolbar can be used to access all the commands related to rendering. The toolbar is displayed by checking the Render box from the Toolbars dialog box. The Toolbars dialog box is displayed by selecting Toolbars from the View pull-down menu. If you move the cursor onto a tool without picking it, a tooltip may appear. Tooltips are words that describe the function of the tool. Tooltips can be turned on by checking the Show Tooltips box in the Toolbars dialog box.

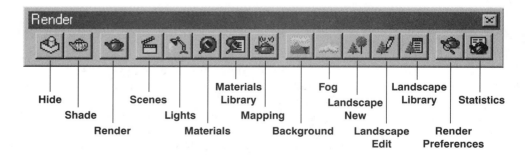

Rendering Procedures Outlined

To make rendering a relatively easy task, follow the procedure outlined next. Once you have committed the procedure to memory, you'll find the task of rendering to be a pleasurable experience. The outline of the procedure identifies major areas that will be explained in the text that follows.

1. Open the desired model to be rendered.
2. Create the desired pictorial views, whether axonometric or perspective. These should be stored under the VIEW command.

3. Specify (place) the desired number and type of lights to illuminate the view using the LIGHT command. Although it is possible to create a rendering without specifying lights (AutoCAD would then use default settings to create the rendering), placing lights will give you more control over the final rendering.

4. Load materials to be used with the RMAT command. First, however, you must extract materials from a material library that can be accessed through the RMAT command or the MATLIB command.

5. Assign material properties to objects, colors, or layers (to add highlights and bitmap images to the model) using the RMAT command.

6. Assemble scenes that contain the desired view and lights utilizing the SCENE command.

7. Set the rendering preferences, such as rendering type, background fog, and so on, using the RPREF command.

8. Select the desired scene, use the RENDER command, and pick the render button. The screen should display the model in a rendered form.

9. Save the image on disk using the SAVEIMG command so that it may be replayed at a later time.

10. Replay an image using the REPLAY command.

17.3 Creating the Pictorial View

You will need to manipulate the view of the model on the screen until the desired position is attained. When creating pictorial views of small components, it is often best to display them as axonometric views. When viewing an actual physical model, the human eye usually does not discern vanishing points on small, close objects. The simplest method for creating axonometric views is by using the VPOINT command (refer to Chapter 3).

When creating renderings of large objects, such as buildings or large machinery, where vanishing points are readily discernible, display them as perspective views. Use the DVIEW command to generate perspective views (see Chapter 15).

Regardless of the viewpoint chosen, store the views so that they may later be selected to be placed into scenes. Both axonometric and perspective views can be stored using the VIEW command.

17.4 Choosing the Lights

The addition of lights varies the tones of the rendered image. When used in combination with materials, lights will also create highlights and even cast shadows for an increasingly dramatic effect.

When lighting a scene, it is important to remember that the brightness of a surface is controlled by its relation to the light source. The closer the face is to being perpendicular to the source of the light, the brighter the surface will be. Two other factors govern the brightness of a surface—reflection and roughness. These are explained later, when we discuss material properties.

The four light types are ambient, distant, point, and spot. The ambient light type is referred to as background light. It creates an illumination that is all around the model and that lights every surface evenly. There is no specific source to ambient light, but you assign an intensity that controls the overall level of brightness. Referring to part A in Figure 17.2, note that an ambient setting of 1.0 illuminates the area uniformly. Ambient light is useful to brighten or darken a scene uniformly.

The distant light type simulates a light source that is a great distance from the model, such as the sun. Because the light source is treated as if it is far away, its light rays are projected parallel with each other. The distance away from the model has no effect on the light. Only the direction in which the light type is pointing and its intensity affect the lighted model. Referring to part B of Figure 17.2, you can see that, with the addition of a distant light source, there is a distinct difference in the effect of lighting on the surfaces.

The point light type radiates light out from its source location, in an effect similar to that of a lightbulb. The distance that the point light is away from the model affects the amount of light reaching the model. This phenomenon is referred to as *falloff* and is controlled by using the inverse linear and inverse square settings of the point light options. If it is set to "none," the point light will not fall off and will be the same level of brightness regardless of the distance from the light to the surface. The Inverse Linear setting causes the light to diminish with distance, and Inverse Square causes it to diminish at a greater rate. The greater the amount of light that falls off, the farther the point light is from a surface. Light from point sources passes through surfaces and does not cast shadows. This light type illuminates a large space and is useful for accenting an area, emphasizing a feature, or adding highlights. Part C of Figure 17.2 shows the effect of a point light when light falloff is turned on. The point light

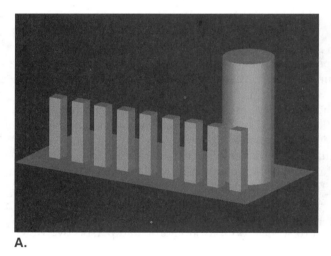

A.

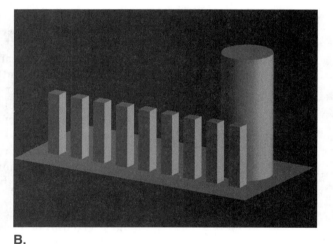

B.

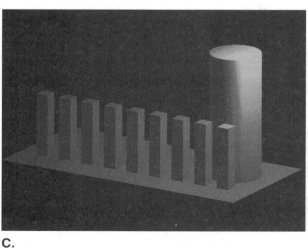

C.

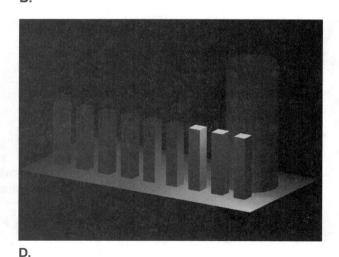

D.

Figure 17.2
Behavior of light types

source is at the right, so the surfaces of objects going toward the left become darker with increasing distance.

The spotlight type simulates the effect of spotlights to create brightly lit areas. The spotlight's purpose is to generate a cone of light projecting from a source and falling on a particular area. Its intensity falls off as the distance from the source increases; therefore, it is particularly useful in highlighting areas or casting shadows. Refer to Part D of Figure 17.2.

Shadow Casting

The three main light types—Point, Distant, and Spot—each have shadow-casting capabilities. Each light type dialog box has a check box to turn on shadow casting. Refer to Figure 17.3, which shows the shadow-casting effect.

Placing the Lights

In a scene to be rendered, it is important to place lights in a way that will cause changes in the surfaces to be lighted or shadowed. This is what makes the model stand out. A model can be rendered without placing any lights, but this usually results in a flat-toned image. It is best to include at least one light in any scene to be rendered.

When placing lights, direct a light to shine diagonally on the model from the left or right top of the screen. This produces a most desirable effect because it causes at least three tone levels. The first level, and the brightest one, appears on the surfaces that are closest to being perpendicular to the light. The other two levels are not as bright because they appear on surfaces that are more parallel and less perpendicular to the light source.

If the model is large, such as a house, more lights may be needed in order to accent areas. By casting more light, you can increase the contrast between light and dark in the scene. Light surfaces appear to project toward the viewer, and dark surfaces recede from the viewer. Ultimately, it is up to you to decide how much lighting best suits the model, but remember: The more contrast between light and dark, the more the model will stand out.

Figure 17.3
Shadow casting

You may place a light type in one of three ways: select Lights from the Render pull-down menu, select LIGHT from the Render sidebar menu, or type LIGHT at the command prompt. Any of these three methods will display the Lights dialog box, which is shown in Figure 17.4A. Note that the LIGHT command cannot be used in paper space.

Looking at Figure 17.4A, notice that on the right side of the Lights dialog box are the Ambient Light settings. The intensity can be adjusted at any time.

The procedure to place a new light is as follows:

1. Pick one of the three light types: point, distant, or spot.
2. Select NEW from the Lights dialog box.
3. Now a New Light dialog box appears depending on which type of light you chose. Now give a name to the light type. Give a unique name for each placement of light. Also, enter the Intensity. A value of 0 turns the light off. For point and spotlights, the value can be any real number. For distant lights, the value can be any real number between 0 and 1.

The following are some unique settings for each light type:

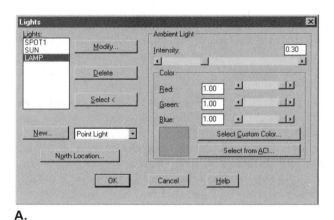

A.

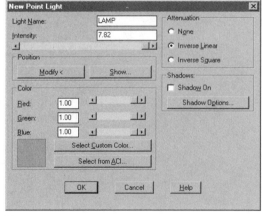

B.

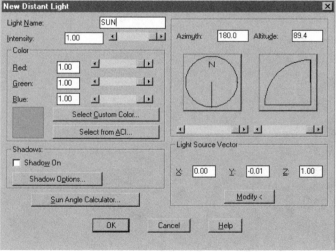

C.

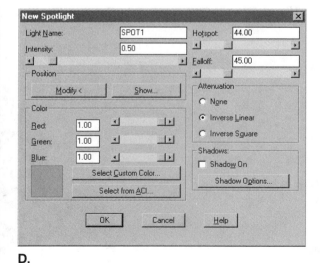

D.

Figure 17.4
Lighting dialog boxes and the light blocks

POINT	The point light dialog box contains an Attenuation area (refer to Figure 17.4B), which controls the point light falloff, the rate at which the point light intensity decreases as the distance from the light source increases. If you do not wish any decrease in light intensity, select the None box; if you want a gradual decrease, select the Inverse Linear box; and if you want a rapid decrease, select the Inverse Square box. To place the point light, use the Modify button and to check its location, use the Show button.
DISTANT	The distant light is normally used to simulate the sun. To assist in its placement, use image boxes to define the Azimuth and Altitude (refer to Figure 17.4C). To identify the location toward which the sun is shining, use the Modify button.
SPOTLIGHT	The spotlight is used to highlight areas and cast shadows. To define the area on which the light falls, use the Hotspot and Falloff values (refer to Figure 17.4D). The Hotspot defines the area of the brightest and most definite shadow, whereas the Falloff value defines the area where the shadow gradually fades away. Like the point light, use the Modify and Show buttons to place the light by identifying the light location and the direction in which its pointing.

4. To accept the light type settings and place the light, select the OK button. When a light is placed, a block with the light's unique name appears at the given coordinate location. The size of the block is governed by the Icon Scale setting in the Rendering Preferences dialog box (RPREF).

5. To modify a currently placed light, you can either pick the light name from the list or use the Select option to select the light block required. This is done from the Lights dialog box.

Note: A file may have up to 500 lights contained in it.

17.5 Material Properties

Material properties control the way light is reflected from or absorbed by a surface. These properties can be attached to specific objects, colors, or layers. Refer to Figure 17.5, which shows a tire on a car. The tire itself has a low reflection value and a high roughness value, giving it a flat, uniform tone. The hub cap has a high reflection value and a low roughness value, giving it a very shiny, polished look.

You can create your own material types or select previously created ones from a material library. Each material has a set of attributes that control the behavior of light and color or the application of a bitmap image.

Using Materials

The creation and attachment of materials is performed from the Materials dialog box (see Figure 17.6A). The following is the procedure used to access and attach a material:

1. Use the RMAT command to display the Materials dialog box.
2. If materials were already included in the drawing, select them from the Materials list on the left side of the Materials dialog box. But if the drawing is new, you must import materials into the drawing. To do this, pick the Materials Library button. You are presented with the Materials Library dialog box shown in part B of Figure 17.6.

Figure 17.5
Flat and shiny surfaces

Figure 17.6
Material dialog boxes

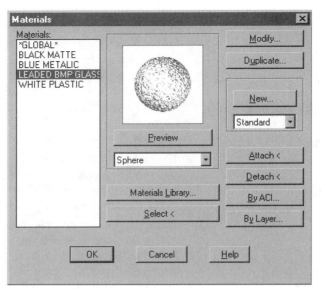

A

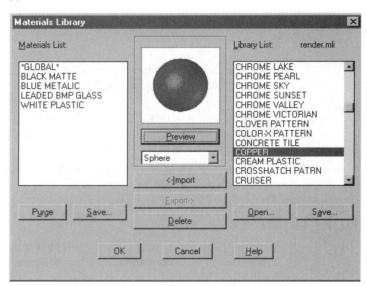

B.

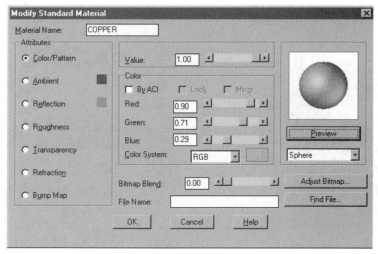

C.

3. Along the right side of the box is the Library list. Normally, it displays the default library, RENDER.MLI. Scroll through the list and highlight the desired materials to bring into your drawing. When you have highlighted the ones you want, pick the Import button and these materials are brought into your drawing.

4. You can preview any single material that you highlight, either from the Materials list or the Library list.

5. You can save a drawing's Material list to its own library with the Save button. It allows you to create a library file with the extension .MLI that you can use in other drawings by opening it as a library.

6. Once you have created your materials list, use the OK button to return to the Materials dialog box.

7. Then, highlight the material you want to assign and pick either the Attach, By ACI, or the By Layer buttons. The Attach button allows you to attach the material to a specific object. The By ACI button allows you to assign a material to a color in the drawing. The By Layer button allows you to assign a material to a specific layer.

8. If you select the Modify or New button, you are presented with a dialog box similar to that of Figure 17.6C. This allows you to create your own materials or to modify existing ones.

Modifying Materials

The following is a description of the different areas of the Modify Standard Material dialog box, as shown in part C of Figure 17.6.

Each material is given a unique name. Once you have created a new material or modified a previously created one, you can export it to the currently active library so that you may use it with other models.

Attributes

There are seven different attributes that control the rendering of a material.

Color/Pattern	Controls the main color of the material. It is often referred to as the Diffuse color. This area is in the light, and you must set the color to match the color you wish the material to be. You can also apply a bitmap image to the attribute to take the place of the color.
Ambient	Controls the color of the material that is in shadow. Usually a darker tone of the main color is used.
Reflection	Controls the color of the material that is in the brightest light. It is often referred to as the highlight, or specular, color. You can also apply a bitmap image to the attribute to take the place of the color.
Roughness	Controls the size of the highlight portion of the Reflection attribute. A low value means the material is highly reflective, and the highlight is small and intense. A high value means the material is rougher, and the highlight is spread over a larger surface.
Transparency	Controls the transparency of a material and the object to which it is attached. You can also apply a bitmap image to the attribute.
Refraction	Adjusts how refractive a material is. This attribute will function only if Photo Ray-Traced rendering is used.
Bump Map	Applies a bitmap image that causes the material surface to appear bumpy based on the bitmap. Light portions of the image appear to be raised above the surface.

Value

This area is used to adjust the strength of the associated attribute. To use the value, pick the attribute and then adjust its strength value. For example, if you select the Transparency attribute, you can adjust how transparent the material will be by adjusting its value.

Color

You can adjust the color value of the three color attributes: main, ambient, and reflective.

By ACI	When this box is checked, the colors match the color of the object when it was created.
Lock	This setting locks the attribute colors to the main color.
Mirror	This setting applies to the Reflection attribute only and is used to create actual mirror images on the attached object.
Color System	This value determines what type of color system is to be used: RGB or HLS. RGB uses red, green, and blue to adjust the color. HLS uses hue, saturation, and lightness to adjust the color.
Color Swatch	The color swatch displays a dialog box needed to adjust the levels of the color system.

Bitmap

The Bitmap area controls the application of a bitmap image to one of these four attributes: Color/Pattern, Reflectivity, Transparency, and Bump Map.

Bitmap Blend	This value controls the strength of the image. The image is not shown at a value of 0 and is the strongest at 1.
File Name	The name of the bitmap image is stored here.
Adjust Bitmap	This setting is used to adjust the scale and orientation of the image.
Find File	This value is used to locate a bitmap image. You have six different file types from which to choose: tga, bmp, tif, gif, jpg, and pcx.

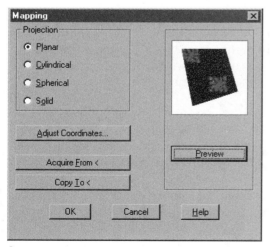

A.

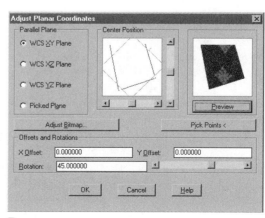

B.

Figure 17.7
Mapping dialog box and Adjusting Coordinates dialog box

Preview

You can see a preview of the current material using either a sphere or a cube.

Material Mapping

When you use a material that contains an image map, you need to make sure the object has the appropriate mapping projection applied. This is accomplished using the SETUV command. When you use the command, you are requested to select an object and then you are presented with a dialog box, as shown in part A of Figure 17.7.

Projection

Planar   Projects map parallel to the surface. Used on flat surfaces.
Cylindrical   Wraps map around a single axis. Used on cylindrical surfaces.
Spherical   Wraps map around all three axes. Used on spherical surfaces.
Solid   Special application used for materials having solid properties.

Adjust Coordinates

This area is used to make adjustments to the selected projection type so that you may change the orientation. Refer to part B of Figure 17.7. You can alter the location of the planes or axes. By using the Picked Plane radio button or Pick Points button, you can identify the plane or axis on the object itself.

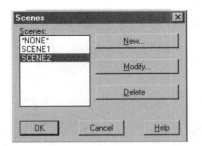

A.

Scenes

Scenes are combinations of desired views, light types, and their placements that are stored under a scene name that can be restored at any time prior to rendering.

Creating Scenes

To create a scene, enter the Scenes dialog box shown in Figure 17.8A. The following procedure is used to create scenes:

B.

Figure 17.8
Scene dialog boxes

1. Select New from the Scenes dialog box and the New Scene subdialog box will appear, as shown in Figure 17.8B.
2. Enter a unique name for the new scene.
3. From the list of presaved views, highlight the single desired view.
4. From the list of preplaced lights, highlight as many lights as you desire.
5. Select the OK button on the New Scene dialog box to return to the Scenes dialog box.
6. To use a scene, highlight its name and then select the OK button. When you use the RENDER command, the indicated scene will be rendered.

17.6   Rendering Preferences

By making use of the options in the Rendering Preferences dialog box, you can control the rendering type, destination, edge smoothness, material, and more. There are default values to help speed up the rendering process. Settings that are subject to constant use should be recorded here. Part A of Figure 17.9 shows the Rendering Preferences dialog box. The following lists some of the options available:

Rendering Type   Sets the rendering type: Render, Photo Real, or Photo Ray-Traced. Render is the fastest but does not use shadows or material maps. Photo Real uses materials and shadows, whereas Photo Ray-Traced is the same as Photo Real but creates sharper shadows and makes use of refraction.

Rendering Procedure	Selects individual objects, identifies a rendering window, and skips the Render dialog box.
Scene to Render	Sets the scene to render from a list of previously created scenes.
Rendering Options	Controls the render display with various on/off toggles for smoothing, materials, shadows, and so on.
Destination	Sets where the final rendered image will be sent: viewport, render window, or file. With the file setting you can adjust the file type and image resolution.
Sub Sampling	Sets the level of pixel rendering and the speed of the rendering. At 1:1, every pixel is rendered, making it the most detailed and the longest procedure. At 8:1, only every 1 in 8 pixels is rendered. This gives the least detail but is the fastest way to check a sample rendering.
Background	Sets the type of background to use: solid, gradient, image, or merge. Refer to part B of Figure 17.9.

Figure 17.9
The Rendering Preferences and Background dialog boxes

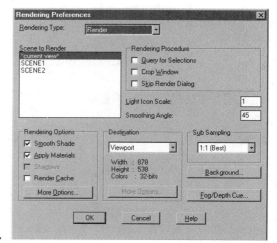

A.

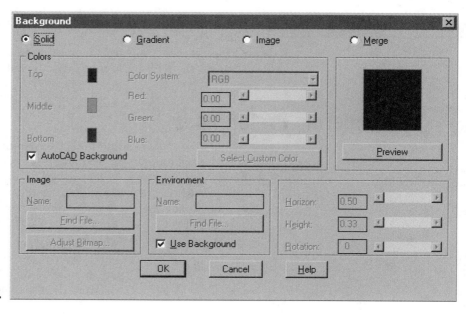

B.

Fog/Depth Cue	Enables the application of fading to simulate fog or depth cue. Fog traditionally uses a white color and depth cuing uses black. However, you can use any color. Use Near and Far settings to establish where the fog starts and stops as well as the density of the fog.

17.7 Rendering the Model

The Render command will render a selected scene or the current display if no scene is selected. Figure 17.10A shows the Render dialog box. It is identical to the Render Preference dialog box so that you can make any changes to the next render. If the Skip Render dialog is checked, either in the Render Preferences dialog box or the Render dialog box, the Render dialog box will not appear the next time the Render command is used. To reset this, use the RPREF command.

If the image is rendered in a viewport, you can save the image to an external file by using the SAVEIMG command. Refer to Figure 17.10B, which shows the Save Image dialog box. To redisplay an image, use the REPLAY command. Refer to Figure 17.10C, which shows the Replay dialog box.

If you render to the Render Window, the image is displayed in a separate window, as shown in Figure 17.11. This new window can be used to save the image as a BMP file or copy the image to the Windows clipboard. You can also

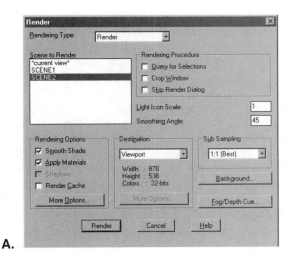

A.

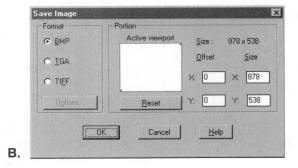

B.

C.

Figure 17.10
The Render, Save Image, and Replay dialog boxes

Figure 17.11
The Render Window

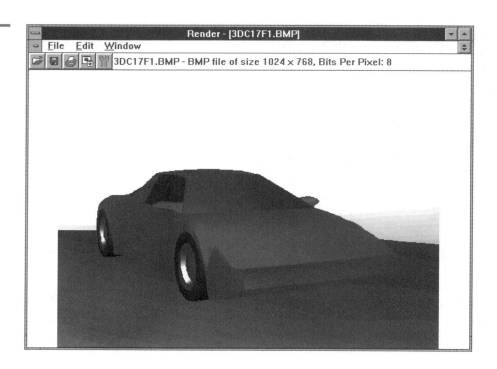

display previously saved BMP images, print them, and resize the image using the Windows options.

If you intend to render to a file, you can set the image size and file time before engaging the Render.

17.8 Landscape Objects

A landscape object is extended-entity geometry with an image mapped onto it that you can place in model scene. Basically, you place a simple geometric object in the model, and when you render the scene, it is replaced with a bitmap image. If you place a tree object, you will see simple lines to represent the tree; however, when you render the scene, the simple lines are replaced by a picture of a tree.

The LSNEW command is used to add a landscape object to your scene. Refer to Figure 17.12, which shows the Landscape New dialog box. You can select from a list of objects, pick the type geometry, and position the object. View aligned is useful with objects such as trees.

The LSEDIT command is used to edit an existing landscape object. You can adjust its geometry and height.

The LSLIB command is used to access the landscape libraries that contain the objects. Refer to Figure 17.13. You can modify landscape objects or create your own.

Creating photorealistic renderings requires a great deal of time and experience, but such renderings can be very rewarding when the project is presented to others. Creating shaded images or basic renderings, on the other hand, is relatively easy, and these can be effective presentation tools as well. The following labs will give you enough hands-on experience in the rendering of models to show you that rendering does not have to be an intimidating process.

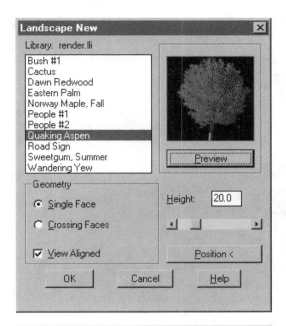

Figure 17.12
Landscape New dialog box

Figure 17.13
Landscape Library dialog box.

Lab 17.A	# Rendering with AutoCAD

Purpose

Lab 17.A will show you how to render a model using the RENDER utility. You will be rendering the BDWELL model created in Lab 8.B in Chapter 8.

Objectives

You will be able to:

- Select views and place lights.
- Assemble a view and lights into a scene.
- Display various model representations.
- Save a rendered display and recall it.

Primary Commands

```
LIGHT
SCENE
RPREF
SAVEIMG
REPLAY
```

Final Shaded Model Procedure

Figure 17.14 shows the initial rendered basic dwelling model.

Initial Setup

1. Open the BDWELL model from Lab 13.B, Chapter 13.

2. Using the DVIEW command, display a perspective view similar to that shown in Figure 17.15. Use a Zoom lens of 25 mm.

3. Save the view settings by using the VIEW/Save command. Give it the name PERSP2.

Figure 17.14
Rendering of the basic dwelling model

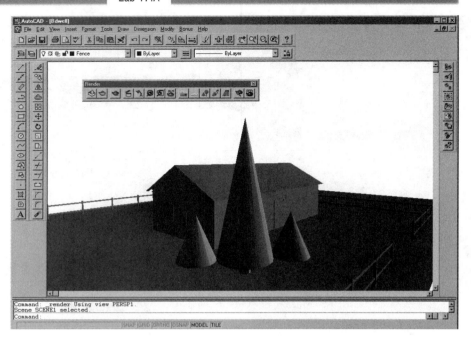

Placing the Sun

4. Select the Light option from the View/Render pull-down menu. The Lights dialog box should appear on the screen.

5. Select Distant Light from the pop-up list. Pick the New button, and the New Distant Light dialog box should appear.

6. Select the Light Name box, and enter the name of the light as SUN. This light will represent a dawning sun shining on the dwelling. Enter an intensity of 1.

7. Select the Light Source Vector Modify button, and place the light at the following coordinates:

```
Enter light direction to <current>: 80', 30', 15'
Enter light direction from <current>: 130', -9', 30'
```

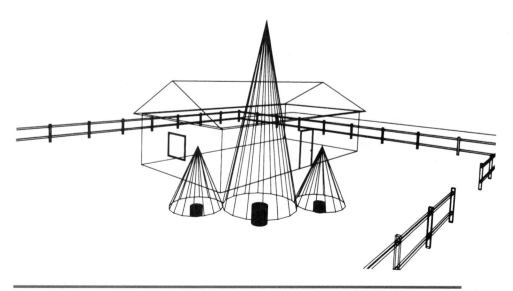

Figure 17.15
Perspective view of the basic dwelling model

The screen will return to the dialog box.

Check Shadow Casting box.

8. Select OK on the New Distant Light dialog box to return to the Lights dialog box. Do not exit from this box.

Placing Accent Lighting

9. Select Point Light from the pop-up list. Pick the New button, and the New Point Light dialog box should appear.

10. Select the Light Name box, and enter the name of the light as ACCENT. This light will add some accent lighting to the side of the dwelling on which the sun does not shine, which will bring out the features on that wall. Enter an intensity of 2.

11. Select the Position Modify button, and place the light at the following coordinates:

```
Enter light location <current>: 39', 40', 5'
```

The screen will return to the dialog box.

12. Select OK on the New Point Light dialog box to return to the Lights dialog box. Set the ambient light to 0.6 to brighten the scene. Select OK to exit from the Lights dialog box.

Observing the Placement of the Light Blocks

13. Display a plan view of the model. You should be able to see the newly placed light blocks.

14. Window in closer to see the names that are attached to the lights. These should match the names you gave them when creating the light types. (*Note:* The scale of these icons is controlled in the Render Preferences dialog box.)

Putting a Scene Together

15. Select Scene from the View/Render pull-down menu. The Scenes dialog box should appear.

16. Select New from the Scenes dialog box. The New Scene dialog box should appear.

17. Enter SCENE1 for the scene name.

18. Highlight PERSP2 as the View, and highlight both SUN and ACCENT for the lights.

19. Select OK to exit the New Scene dialog box and return to the Scenes dialog box.

20. Make sure that scene SCENE1 is highlighted, and then select OK to exit from the Scenes dialog box.

Checking the Rendering Preferences

21. Select Preferences from the View/Render pull-down menu. The Rendering Preferences dialog box should appear.

22. Check the following:

Render Type:	Render
Rendering Procedure:	Skip Render dialog is checked.
Rendering Options:	Leave Smooth Shade and Apply Materials checked.
Destination:	Viewport
Icon scale:	200 (This enlarges the viewing size of the light blocks.)

23. Select OK to exit from the dialog box.

Rendering the Scene

24. Select Render from the View/Render pull-down menu. The screen should be rendered as shown in Figure 17.14. If you are using full screen rendering, use the space bar to return to the drawing editor screen.

Saving the Image

25. Select Tools/Display Image/Save from the Tools pull-down menu. The Save Image dialog box should appear.

26. Select the appropriate format for the graphics of the computer you are using. Normally, GIF should work.

27. Enter IMAGE1 as the image name, and select Save to save the image. The image is saved as a separate file with the extension dependent on the graphics format selected. If you selected BMP, then the extension would be BMP.

Replaying the Image

28. Select Tools/Display Image/View from the Tools pull-down menu. The Replay dialog box should appear. You may have to specify *.GIF as a pattern.

29. Highlight the IMAGE1 file, and select OPEN. The Image Specification dialog box should now appear. Select OK at this dialog box, and the rendered image should reappear on the screen.

30. Save the model as BDWELL.

Changing the Rendering Type

31. Using the RENDER command, set the Render Type to Photo Real and render the scene. The image should look like Figure 17.16. Notice that the shading is more uniform.

32. Using the RENDER command, check the Shadows box so that it is on, and render the scene. The image should look like Figure 17.17. Notice that the addition of shadows makes the scene more realistic.

33. Save the model as BDWELL. In the next lab you will add materials to the building for a rendering that looks even more realistic.

You may want to experiment with the light intensities to achieve a more desirable combination, or you could add more lights for different effects. Getting the best looking picture is all up to you. Have fun!

Figure 17.16
Rendering using Photo Real

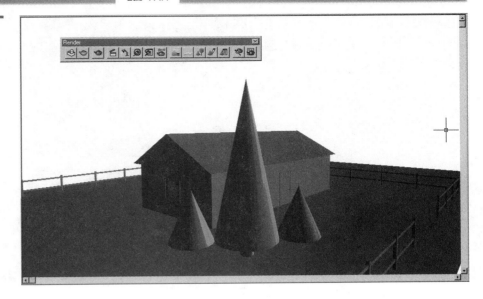

Figure 17.17
Rendering using Photo Real with Shadows on

Adding Materials

Purpose

Lab 17.B will show you how to add materials to the surfaces in your model. You will use the model BDWELL from Lab 17.A.

Objectives

You will be able to:

- Import materials from the material library.
- Attach material to objects.
- Adjust the mapping projection on an object.
- Add landscape objects.

Primary Commands

RMAT
SETUV
LSNEW

Figure 17.18
Materials dialog box

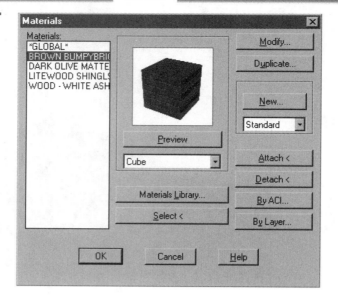

Procedure

Initial Setup

1. Open the BDWELL model from Lab 17.A and display an isometric view using the VPOINT command.

Attaching a Material

2. Use the RMAT command to display the Materials dialog box, as shown in Figure 17.18.

3. Select the Materials Library button and import the materials shown in Figure 17.18.

4. In the Materials dialog box, highlight the BROWN BUMPY BRICK material and, using the Attach button, attach it to the rectangular box that represents the walls of the house.

Figure 17.19
Rendered image with material streaks showing

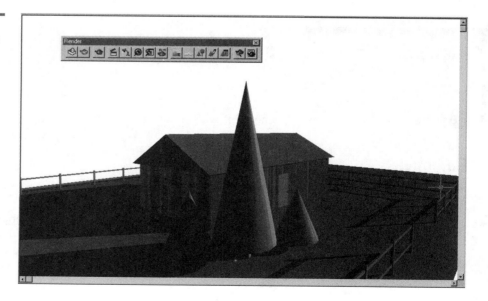

5. Using the Render command, render SCENE1 with materials on. The resulting image should look like Figure 17.19. Notice the streaks on the object. The material did not render well because you need to set the mapping projection to each surface of the object.

Setting the Mapping Projection

6. Use the Explode command to break the box that represents the wall into individual surfaces.

7. Use the SETUV command. Pick the front wall of the building and press enter. The Mapping dialog box will appear, similar to Figure 17.20. Make sure the Planar Projection radio button is checked.

8. Pick the Adjust Coordinates button to display the Adjust Planar Coordinates dialog box, as shown in Figure 17.21.

9. In the Parallel Plane area of the dialog box, check the WCS XZ plane radio button. This matches the plane to the plane of the front wall. You should now see the outline of the wall in the Center Postion viewing box.

10. Pick the Preview button and you should see the wall rendered with brick. The image is small, so don't expect to see much detail.

11. Pick the Adjust Bitmap button to display the Adjust Object Bitmap Placement dialog.

12. Set the U and V scales to 3. This will reduce the size of the bitmap image of the brick, making it look more realistic on the wall.

13. Click OK to move out of all the dialog boxes. The mapping project is now set for the front wall.

14. Use the RENDER command again. The results should be similar to Figure 17.22.

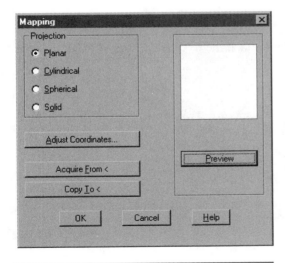

Figure 17.20
Mapping dialog box

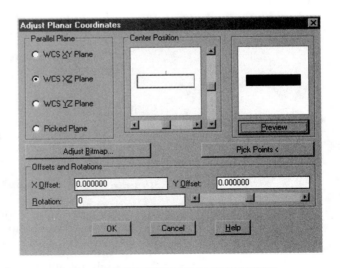

Figure 17.21
Adjust Planar Coordinates dialog box

Figure 17.22
Rendered image with mapping project applied to front wall

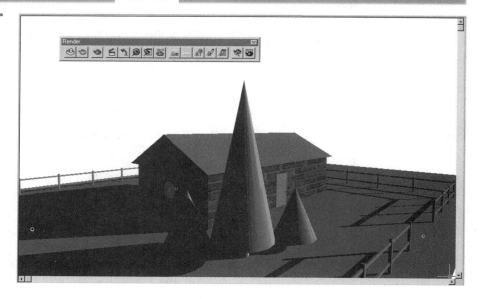

Adding Wall Materials

15. Attach the brick material to other walls and then use the SETUV command each time to match the mapping plane to the plane of the wall, as in steps 7, 8, 9, 10, 11, and 12.

Adding Roof Materials

16. Explode the roof object into individual surfaces.

17. Attach the LITEWOOD SHINGLES material to the sloped surfaces.

18. Using the SETUV command, set the planar coordinates for the roof. When adjusting the planar coordinates you will have to use the Pick Points button. You will then be asked to pick the three points that represent the plane of the roof. Don't forget to use object snap endpoint. Set the U and V scales of the bit map to 5.

Adding Lawn Material

19. There is no lawn material, but attach the DARK OLIVE MATTE material to the lawn.

Adding Fence Material

20. Using the RMAT command, add the WOOD-WHITE ASH material to the fence blocks.

Rendering with Mapping Coordinates

21. Render the scene now that you have set the mapping projection. The image should look similar to Figure 17.23.

Adding Landscape Objects

22. Display a world plan view of the scene and set the UCS to World.

23. Erase the tree and trunk objects from the scene.

Figure 17.23
Rendered image with other materials applied

24. Use the LSNEW command to display the Landscape New dialog box, as shown in Figure 17.24.

25. Select the Dawn Redwood landscape object and pick the Preview button to see what it looks like. Make sure the boxes are checked as shown in Figure 17.24 and that the scale is set to 300.

26. Using the Position button, place the tree at approximately: 29′5″, 34′8″, 0′0″ and click OK to leave the dialog box.

27. Render the scene again, making sure that you use the Photo Ray-Traced rendering type. The image should look similar to Figure 17.25.

28. Save the model as BDWELL2.

Figure 17.24
Landscape New dialog box

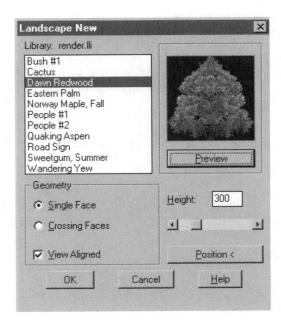

Figure 17.25
Rendered image showing tree landscape object

Questions

1. What is meant by CAD rendering?
2. How is rendering accomplished within AutoCAD?
3. List the four light types and explain their differences.
4. What is the purpose of assigning materials and how do you create them?
5. Why create scenes?
6. How are images saved and recalled?
7. What is the difference between the SHADE and RENDER commands?
8. If a material were created with a high reflection value and a low roughness value, what would the surface be—flat or reflective?

Assignments

Note: To achieve a more favorable effect on any rendering, the colors you set for different elements of a model should differ. It would be wise to set the various colors before rendering the model.

For these assignments, do the following:

- Shade the scene within AutoCAD. Use a 256-color setting, if available.
- Render the scene within AutoCAD. You'll need to create a scene and a view and place lights.
- Compare the results.

1. Create a scene by assembling a coffee maker (use the COFMK model created in Lab 7.C, Chapter 7) and a coffee pot (use the COFPT model created in Lab 8.A, Chapter 8).

2. Create a scene using the kitchen model BKIT (created in Assignment 1, Chapter 13).

3. Add a shiny material to the nut and bolt assembly NBOLT (created in Assignment 2, Chapter 13).

4. Recall the DECK model created in Lab 14.A, Chapter 14, and generate the various rendered images.

5. Assign different materials to the pipe assembly model (PIPES) created in Lab 14.B, Chapter 14, to create the various rendered images.

1

Application Projects

This part of the text will provide you with practical techniques for and pictorial information on effectively applying the concepts you have learned up to this point. Now a competent 3D user, you will apply 3D commands and techniques to specific disciplines. This part is an excellent tool for the teacher who wants to show students how to apply 3D CAD to a number of disciplines.

The following chapters take the form of self-contained projects and, as such, they do not have associated exercises or questions. However, they are easy to extend and will thoroughly explain the basic skills you need to be able to design a similar project on your own. The first project, found in Chapter 18, is extremely directed, allowing you to make few choices. In later chapters, the projects become increasingly complex and you will be making more and more decisions.

The projects in this part deal with wireframe, surface, and solid modeling.

Architectural Project: Residential Dwelling

Overview

This chapter walks you through the creation of a model of a residential dwelling, starting with the organization of the basic plan and then adding the various individual elements and library symbols until the final 3D rendering is complete. This residential dwelling project is not intended to teach the concepts involved in the design or the construction of a house; instead, it is meant to illustrate the techniques and procedures in the construction of a 3D model of a house. At the conclusion of this step-by-step project, you will be able to apply all the basic elements learned here to many more complex creations.

Concepts Explored

- Application of the AutoCAD features presented in the previous chapters
- Creation of a complex 3D model of a residential dwelling
- Generation of 3D symbols for insertion into the main model
- Production of ideally located perspective views
- Generation of shaded and rendered images.

18.1 Introduction

In this chapter, we create an exterior model of a residential dwelling, as illustrated in Figure 18.1. The parameters of the dwelling have already been determined to allow easy construction of the model. However, new values (or even a new dwelling) can easily be substituted for the ones given in this project, allowing you to create a model of your own choosing. Also, although this project focuses on the construction techniques used in the creation of the exterior of the dwelling, it would not be more difficult (just more time-consuming) for you to complete the inside of the model as well.

When this model is finished, you should be able to view the house from any angle and look through the windows into the house. In addition, you should be able to hide the walls and roof at will, enabling you to see into the interior.

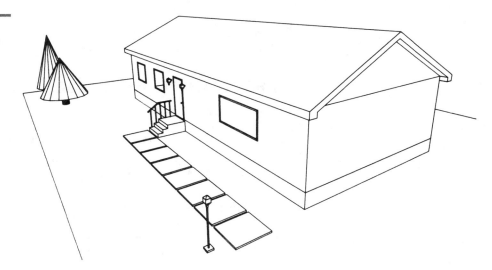

Figure 18.1
Perspective display of the residential dwelling project

Project Stages

In this project, as in all CAD projects, it is important to organize the model before attempting any creation. The first step in organizing a model is determining the stages of model development. Some of these stages are necessary in all model creation, but others are unique to each model type. The order in which the stages are performed is usually unique to each model type as well.

PROJECT STAGES
1. Division of the architectural model (into foundation, roof)
2. Layer designations (for elevations)
3. Initial settings (for units, base)
4. Initial architectural plan layout (for plan extrusion)
5. Initial complex surface generation (for roof peak)
6. 3D symbol creation (for windows, doors, concrete steps)
7. Insertion of symbols
8. Complex surface generation (for window openings)
9. Exterior features (steps, walkways)
10. Presentation display (creating a perspective view, rendering).

Stage 1: Division of the Model

At this point in the learning process, you are creating more complex models. To make creation more manageable, complex models need to be broken down into sections. This holds true for our residential dwelling model, and because this is an architectural project there are some obvious section divisions, as listed here:

- The foundation, which includes footings and the foundation wall
- The first floor, including all exterior walls
- The roof, including the soffits and fascia
- The windows, including trim and sills
- The doors, including the treads and handles
- The external features that would be attached to a house, such as steps and lights
- The temporary entities that facilitate model construction.

Other divisions, such as extra floors or gabled windows, would be created depending on the type of house model to be constructed.

The name of the master model should be determined at this point. In this project, the master model will be called DWELL. Start a new drawing with this name.

Stage 2: Layer Designations

It is very important that layer designation takes place in the early stages of development. The ability to make entities visible or invisible is one of the most powerful features of CAD, and we want to utilize it in our 3D construction. The separation of layers will facilitate both the construction and the display of the final model. Most of the layers will be named now, but some layers will not be created until a need for them becomes apparent during the actual 3D creation.

Before we create the layers, let's recall two important pieces of information that, if not utilized in advance of the modeling, will cost us too much time to correct. First, as anyone who has used the HIDE command to view a model with hidden features removed knows, the more complex the model, the longer it takes to remove the hidden features. Second, to alleviate this problem, Auto-CAD will ignore entities on a layer that is frozen during the process of hidden line removal. To make use of these two important facts, we'll divide the model in this project into viewing directions. Any view of the exterior of the house will normally show only two sides of the house as well as the roof section.

Viewing sides can be named either for compass directions (north, south, east, west) or for hand directions (left side, right side, front, rear). For this model, we'll use the hand directions. The geometry will be broken into viewing sides so that any combination of sides can be frozen at any time. This will simplify the construction of the model and greatly speed up the HIDE routine. Here are the designated abbreviations for the viewing sides:

ABBREVIATION	VIEWING SIDE
FR	front
RE	rear
RI	right
LE	left

When naming layers, remember that, even though the name of the layer can have as many as 31 characters, only the first 8 characters of the layer name are visible on the status line. Taking this into consideration for our model, we'll use the first 8 characters of each layer as an abbreviation and the rest as a longer explanation of the layer.

The layers to be designated at the start of the model creation are as follows:

LAYER NAME	LAYER DESCRIPTION
LOT	Ground line and lot area
FR-FOUND	Front foundation
FR-1FLOR	Front first floor
FR-ROOF	Front roof
FR-WINDO	Front window
FR-DOOR	Front door
FR-FEATU	Front feature attached to wall
FR-TMPOR	Temporary front (for construction)
RE-FOUND	Rear foundation
RE-1FLOR	Rear first floor
RE-ROOF	Rear roof
RE-WINDO	Rear window
RE-DOOR	Rear door
RE-FEATU	Rear feature attached to wall
RE-TMPOR	Temporary rear (for construction)
RI-FOUND	Right foundation

RI-1FLOR	Right first floor
RI-ROOF	Right roof
RI-WINDO	Right window
RI-DOOR	Right door
RI-FEATU	Right feature attached to wall
RI-TMPOR	Temporary right (for construction)
LE-FOUND	Left foundation
LE-1FLOR	Left first floor
LE-ROOF	Left roof
LE-WINDO	Left window
LE-DOOR	Left door
LE-FEATU	Left feature attached to wall
LE-TMPOR	Temporary left (for construction)

Note: A quick way of either freezing/thawing or turning on/off layers can be accomplished by using wild card characters. Wild card characters are inserted in place of letters or groups of letters. The wild card question mark (?) can be substituted for any individual character and the wild card asterisk (*) can be substituted for any group of characters. Here is an example of combining the question mark and the asterisk in one command. The two question marks replace the first two characters in the layer name (FR, RE, RI, LE). The single asterisk replaces all the remaining characters after "-1FLOR":

```
Command: LAYER
?/Make/Set/New/ON/OFF/Color/Ltype/Freeze/Thaw: F
Layer name(s) to Freeze: ??-1FLOR*
```

This command would freeze all the first floor layers.

Wild cards also can be used to add color designations for the various layers after all the layers have been created. For the purposes of our model construction, each section type will be given its own separate color. At this point, it is not important which color goes with each section type; we simply want to give each a separate color to make it easier to distinguish what is on each layer. The section types and their colors are as follows:

```
SECTION TYPE        COLOR
FOUNDATION          1 (red)
1ST FLOOR           2 (yellow)
ROOF                3 (green)
WINDOW              4 (cyan)
DOOR                5 (blue)
FEATURE             6 (magenta)
TEMPORARY           7 (white)
LOT                 12 (this might appear as blue-gray)
```

Now create the layers listed previously and assign each its appropriate color. *Note:* It is customary to use continuous linetype for all construction of 3D models.

Stage 3: Initial Settings

The following is a list of settings that need to be entered before modeling can take place:

```
    SETTINGS
Units = Architectural
Limits = 0',0' to 100',100'
Grid = 1'
Snap Incr. = 2"
Initial Elevation Thickness = 0'
Initial Thickness = 0'
```

```
UCS = WCS
UCSICON = on and set to ORIGIN
```

Remember to ZOOM All, so that the display shows the set limits.

There may be other settings that you would like to set. If so, now is the time to set them, before we enter stage 4.

Stage 4: Initial Architectural Plan Layout

Review the plan and elevation views shown in Figures 18.2 and 18.3, respectively. Then, proceed through the steps of this stage. REMEMBER TO SAVE YOUR DRAWING PERIODICALLY TO AVOID TIME LOSS!

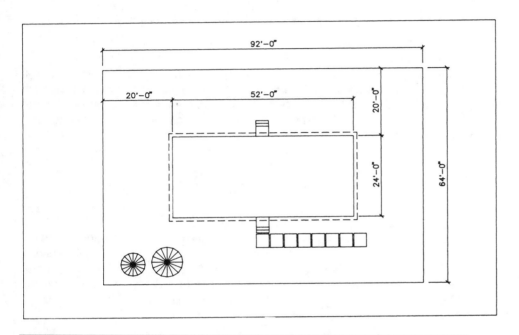

Figure 18.2
Plan view of the dwelling

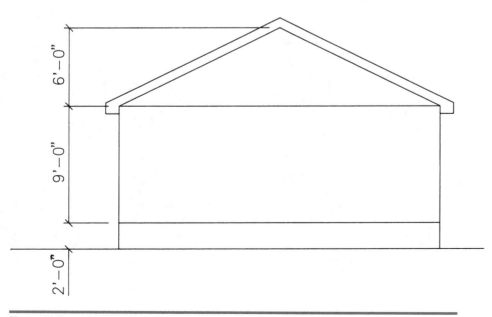

Figure 18.3
Side elevation view of the dwelling

Creation of the Lot

Draw Ground line/Lot area on layer LOT using the 3DFACE command so that it will appear as a surface. Refer to Figure 18.2. Begin at the lower left corner, 0,0,0.

Creation of the Foundation

What goes on below the ground line is not of concern in this project, so the foundation will start at the ground line and will extend 2′ above ground. Refer to Figures 18.2 and 18.3. While still displaying the plan view, proceed.

```
      SETTINGS
  Elevation = 0′
  Thickness = 2′
```

Using lines, draw the perimeter of the outside edge of the foundation. Remember to switch to the various view layers for the foundation: FR-FOUND, RI-FOUND, RE-FOUND, LE-FOUND.

Use the VPOINT command to see what you have created. It should look like Figure 18.4.

```
Command: VPOINT
Rotate/<View point>(current>: 1,−1,1
Return to the plan view.
Command: PLAN
<current UCS>/Ucs/World: W
```

Creation of the First-Floor Walls

The commands in this step are similar to those used to create the foundation, but now set the elevation as well as the thickness. The first floor will start on top of the foundation and will extend another 9′ into the air. Refer to Figures 18.2 and 18.3.

```
      SETTINGS
  Elevation = 2′
  Thickness = 9′
```

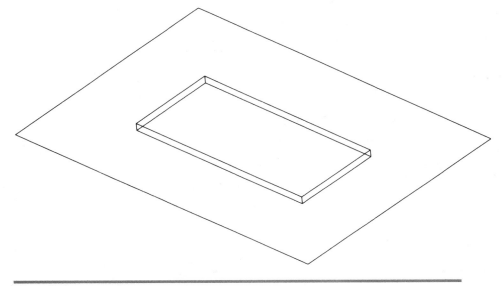

Figure 18.4
Isometric view of the foundation

Again using lines, draw the perimeter of the first floor, switching to the proper layers as each side is drawn. Use the VPOINT command to see what you have created.

Creation of Working Planes

Now that we have some 3D extruded geometry, it will be very easy to create some working planes aligned to that geometry. Create four working planes, one for each viewing side. Refer to Figure 18.5.

The following commands will create the first working plane—one for the front elevation. Remember to snap to key points when setting the UCS working planes.

```
Command: UCS
Origin/ZAxis/3point/.... /Save/Del/?/<World>: 3
Origin point <0,0,0>: refer to the front plane in
Figure 18.5 for P1
Point on positive portion of the X axis <default>:
refer to the front plane in Figure 18.5 for P2
Point on positive Y portion of the UCS X-Y plane
<default>: refer to the front plane in Figure 18.5
for P3
```

Use the UCS command to save the new working plane as FRONT. Switch to the plan view of the current UCS using the PLAN command, and save the view as FRONT using the VIEW command. Notice the UCS icon. It should be easy to tell which working plane is active by observing the position of the icon.

Now create the other three working planes (REAR, RIGHT, LEFT), as illustrated in Figure 18.5. Save them and their matching views (REAR, RIGHT, LEFT).

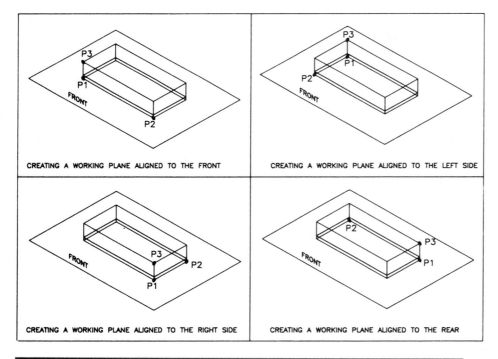

CREATING A WORKING PLANE ALIGNED TO THE FRONT

CREATING A WORKING PLANE ALIGNED TO THE LEFT SIDE

CREATING A WORKING PLANE ALIGNED TO THE RIGHT SIDE

CREATING A WORKING PLANE ALIGNED TO THE REAR

Figure 18.5
Creating the four working planes

Figure 18.6
Restoring the RIGHT working plane

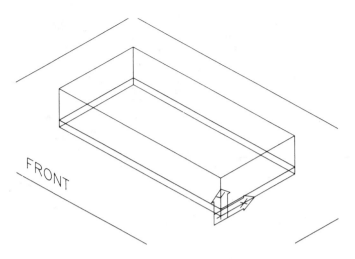

Creation of the Roof

The roof can be created very easily by extruding lines, similar to the way the walls were created. But the extrusion direction needs to be changed here. We'll do this by selecting a working plane that is perpendicular to the extrusion direction.

Begin this step by setting the elevation and the thickness:

```
SETTINGS
Elevation = 0'
Thickness = 1'
```

Now restore the UCS working plane RIGHT. Refer to Figure 18.6. Notice the UCS icon.

Freeze the FRont, REar, and LEft first-floor layers. By freezing these layers, we are ensuring that when we use the object snap modes, we will snap to the correct entities. When working in 3D space, it is possible to have entities (such as the right and left walls) completely overlap each other. If both left and right layers were on and you were looking at the right elevation, it would be impossible for you to tell to which side you might snap. So, to alleviate that difficulty, the layers containing the overlapping walls are frozen.

Restore the RIGHT view. Notice that the icon has moved off the 0,0,0 point. This is because the icon cannot display fully. Use ZOOM 0.8X to fix the problem by reducing the displayed image to 80% of its current size on the screen. The displayed view should now be the same as in Figure 18.7.

Figure 18.7
Displaying the right side parallel to the screen

337

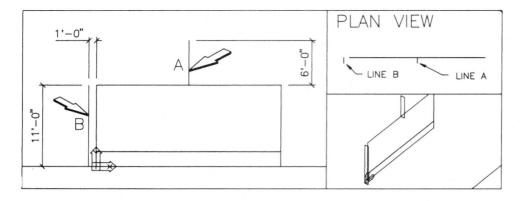

Figure 18.8
Adding temporary construction lines

Before the roof can be drawn, some temporary lines need to be created in order to set the height of the roof and the overhang. Switch to the RI-TMPOR layer and draw the lines A and B as shown in the first box of Figure 18.8. Use the midpoint object snap for the start of line A and give the length using relative coordinates. Then, use the ID command to reference the lower left of the right foundation wall and use relative coordinates to give the start and finish of line B. Line B should be 11′ long and should run along the 0Z axis.

Use the VPOINT command to display an isometric view with coordinates 1,−1,1. Because a thickness of 1′ was used, the displayed view should look like the second box of Figure 18.8.

Now, to draw the roof line, switch to layer FR-ROOF.

```
SETTINGS
Elevation = 0'
Thickness = −54'
```

The setting of 54′ represents the entire length of the roof, including the 1′ overhang on each end. The negative value causes the line to extrude back over the house.

Draw a line representing the roof by referring to Figure 18.9. Use end-point object snap to P1 for the start. For the end of the line, select filter .XY, endpoint snap to P2, and enter a value of 1′ for the *Z* coordinate. In other words, use the *X* and *Y* coordinates from P2, but enter in the *Z* distance of 1′ for the overhang. Line C represents the underside of the roof.

To draw the top of the roof, as shown in Figure 18.10, use the OFFSET command with a distance of 8″, and use the FILLET command with a radius of

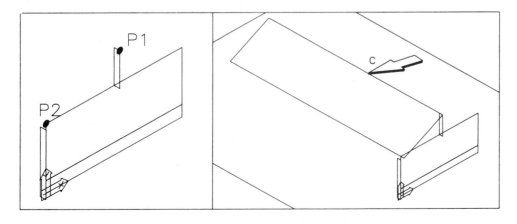

Figure 18.9
Adding one side of the roof

338

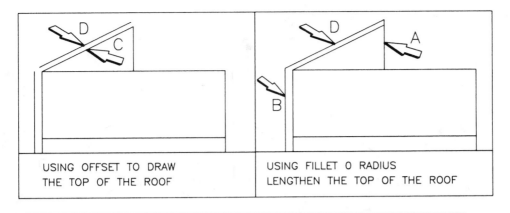

| USING OFFSET TO DRAW THE TOP OF THE ROOF | USING FILLET 0 RADIUS LENGTHEN THE TOP OF THE ROOF |

Figure 18.10
Creating the top of the roof

0 to extend line D to line B and bring it in line with line A. Then, erase line B and trim line A back to the lower roof, which is line C.

Now draw the fascia and soffits (lines E, F, and G), as shown in Figure 18.11. Lines E, F, and G have a thickness of –54′.

We will mirror the roof half later.

Stage 5: Initial Complex Surface Generation

So far, our house model has walls and a roof, but the fascia ends of the roof and the space between the peak of the roof and the right wall (gable end) are not enclosed. To enclose these spaces, we'll need to use the 3DFACE command. Do the gable end first, because it is the easier of the two.

SETTINGS
Freeze layer FR-ROOF. The roof should disappear.
Make sure that the RI-TMPOR layer is on and thawed.

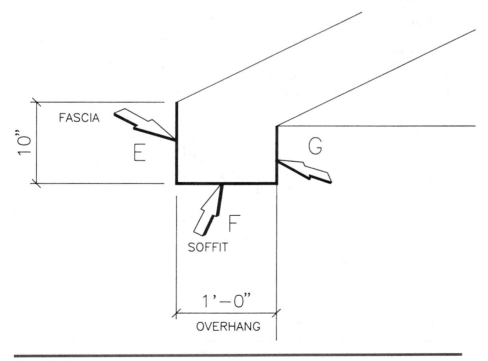

Figure 18.11
Adding in the fascia and soffits

Figure 18.12

Adding the gable end with the 3DFACE
command

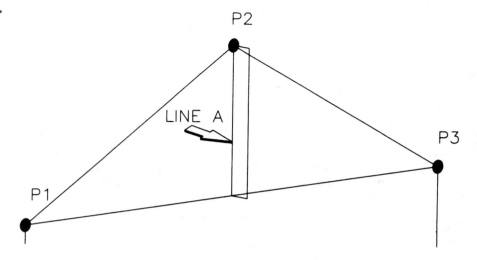

Switch to the RI-ROOF layer. The gable end surface is going to be placed on this layer.

```
Elevation = 0'
Thickness = 0'
```

Creation of Gable End Surface

Select the 3DFACE command. Referring to Figure 18.12, endpoint snap to points P1 and P3 on the top of the right wall and to P2 on the top of line A. Once you have input these three points, press the <Enter> key to complete the 3DFACE command, which places a surface in the peak area. (*Note:* The top of the temp line must be returned to a 6' length before adding the gable.)

Creation of Fascia End of the Roof

To create the fascia end of the roof, start with these settings:

> SETTINGS
>
> Thaw layer FR-ROOF.
>
> Switch to layer FR-ROOF. The fascia ends of the roof are going to be put on this layer.

Select the 3DFACE command. Referring to Figure 18.13, endpoint snap to points P1 and P2. Before endpoint snapping to point P3, select the Invisible

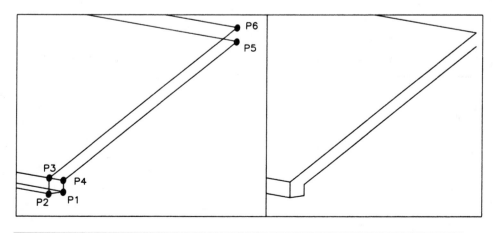

Figure 18.13

Adding the roof

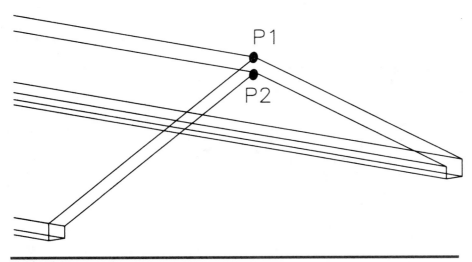

Figure 18.14
Mirroring one side of the roof to the other

edge option. Now snap to points P3 and P4. Do not exit from the 3DFACE command. Select the Invisible edge option again and endpoint snap to points P5 and P6. The 3DFACE command will refer to them as points 3 and 4. Now press <Enter> to exit from the 3DFACE command. Half of the roof should now be complete. Try the HIDE command to see the effect.

Mirroring the Roof

Note: Settings do not need to be changed at this point.

Use the MIRROR command to select the roof components, including the 3D face on the roof fascia end. Exclude the temporary lines, the right wall, and the gable end 3D face. Use endpoint object snaps at points P1 and P2 as shown in Figure 18.14 for the mirror line and respond "no" to the Delete Old Objects prompt.

Modifying the Roof

Modify the roof, fascia, and soffits so that they are on their proper layers (that is, front roof slope on FR-ROOF layer, front fascia on FR-ROOF layer, roof peak on RI-ROOF layer, and so forth).

Mirroring the 3D Faces

The right end of the building has 3D faces on the ends of the roof and the peak space. It is time now to copy them to the left end of the building.

>SETTINGS
>Freeze layers FR-ROOF, RE-ROOF, RI-1FLOR.
>Thaw layers FR-1FLOR, RE-1FLOR.
>Make sure that layers RE-ROOF and LE-ROOF are thawed.
>Switch to layer RI-TMPOR.
>Restore the UCS working plane FRONT.

Using the midpoints on the front wall as shown in Figure 18.15, mirror all the 3D faces on the right wall to the left wall. Modify the mirrored entities so that they are on their proper layers.

Thaw all layers except the temporary layers. The display should look like Figure 18.16.

Save the model as DWELL.

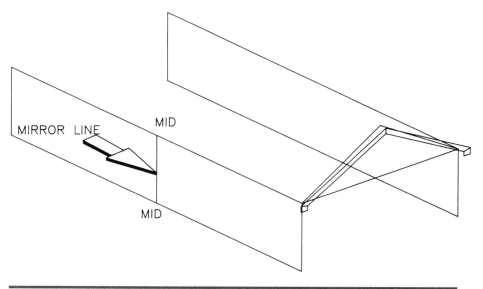

Figure 18.15
Mirroring one roof end to the other

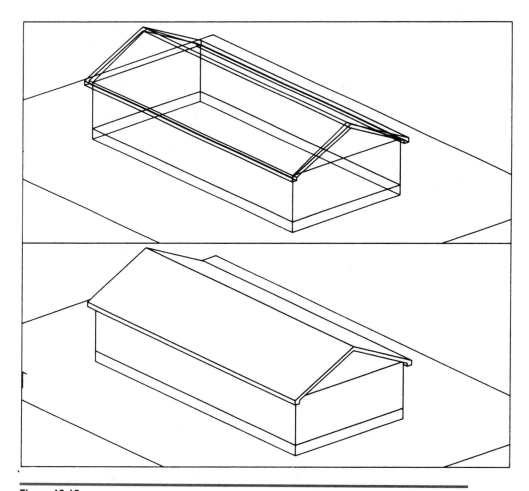

Figure 18.16
The model in wireframe with hidden lines removed

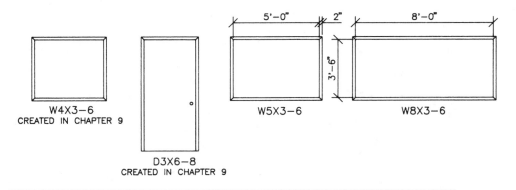

Figure 18.17
Window and door 3D symbols

The model should now have a surface over every area. Using the VPOINT command, move around the model—end to end, above, and below—and use the HIDE command at each view to see the effect (which should be similar to Figure 18.16). You have just created a semicomplex, fully surfaced 3D model. You have every right to feel proud. But there's more to do! Exit from the model, and let's continue.

Stage 6: Symbol Generation

In this stage, we'll create individual 3D symbols as shown in Figure 18.17. This stage could have been performed earlier because, once created, 3D symbols are independent and can be used at any time.

We'll create a 3D symbol of a concrete step here. If you read Chapter 13 in sequence and performed Lab 13.A, you have already created 3D symbols for a 4' × 3'6″ window (W4X3-6) and a 3' × 6'8″ door (D3X6-8). To complete this project, two more window symbols need to be created: one sized 5' × 3'6″ (W5X3-6) and the other sized 8' × 3'6″ (W8X3-6). Refer to Figure 18.17 and follow the procedures laid out in Lab 13.A. Once you have mastered those procedures, you can create any number of window and door symbols.

As was stated in Chapter 13, when 3D symbols are inserted into a model they orient themselves to the current UCS based on the WCS of the drawing on which they were initially created. In other words, the *X, Y,* and *Z* WCS coordinates of the original 3D symbol drawing align to the current UCS of the model into which they are to be inserted. Refer to Figure 18.18.

Figure 18.18
Aligning the UCS for insertion

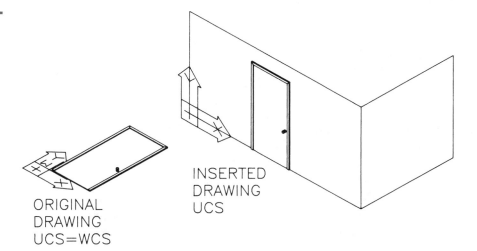

Figure 18.19
The layout of the steps

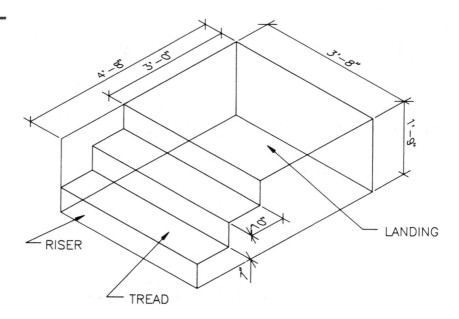

Start a new drawing called STEPS. This will be the original drawing for the 3D symbol of the concrete steps. Refer to Figure 18.19.

```
    SETTINGS
Units = Architectural
Limits = 0',0' to 5',6'
Grid = 6"
Snap Incr. = 2"
Thickness = 0'
Elevation = 0'
UCS = WCS
UCSICON = on and set to ORIGIN
Layers = 0 (all construction will take place on layer 0)
```

Creation of the Orientation Cube

Creating a box to surround the model that is about to be created is an excellent way to keep track of the orientation of the model and a quick way to create working planes. Refer to Figure 18.20.

Figure 18.20
Orientation cube and working plane

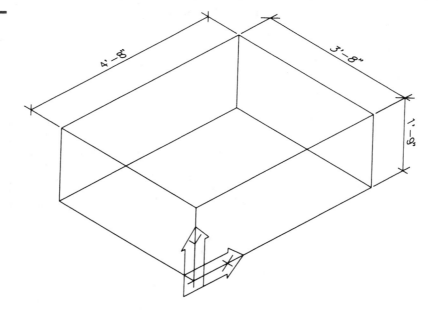

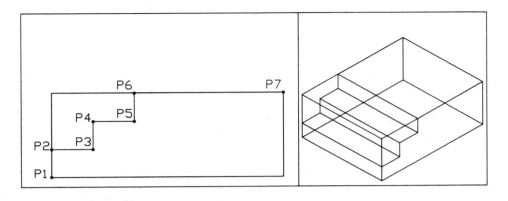

Figure 18.21
Adding the steps and viewing them from an isometric viewpoint

```
       SETTINGS
  Thickness = 1'9"
  Elevation = 0'
```

Draw a rectangle the same size as the concrete steps—with a width of 3'8" and a depth of 4'8". Use VPOINT (coordinates 1,–1,1) to view the model. Save the view as ISO.

Use the UCS 3POINT command to create a working plane on the right side of the box. Refer to Figure 18.20. Save the UCS as SIDE.

Creation of the Steps

Set only one setting for this step:

```
  Thickness = –3'8"
```

Use the PLAN command to set the view to the current UCS. Draw the outline of the landing and the treads and risers as shown in Figure 18.21. Refer to Figure 18.19 for the sizes. Then, use the VIEW/Restore command to redisplay the view ISO.

Creation of the Side Steps

First delete the top, front, and two side lines on the orientation box. Leave the back line for the back surface of the step. Use the 3DFACE command to place two surfaces—A and B—on the side of the step. Refer to Figure 18.22. Use endpoint snap to snap to points A1 through A6. (*Note:* You must use the Invisible edge option just before picking points A3 and A6.) Exit the 3DFACE command, and then reenter it to add surface B. Refer to Figure 18.22 for the points. Remember to use the Invisible edge option before picking point B4.

Repeat the 3DFACE command to create the other side of the steps, or use the COPY command to copy the surfaces just created.

Setting the Insertion Point

To insert the 3D symbol properly, you must set the insertion or base point before saving the drawing. Using the VPOINT command, display the rear of the steps. Use the BASE command to set the base point to the midpoint of the bottom of the rear line. Refer to Figure 18.23. Set UCS = WCS. Save the model as STEP.

Use the VPOINT command to move about the model and use the HIDE command to observe each view. The views should be similar to those depicted in Figure 18.23. Exit from this model.

Repeat the steps in stage 6 until you have created all the required 3D symbols.

Figure 18.22
Adding sides to the steps

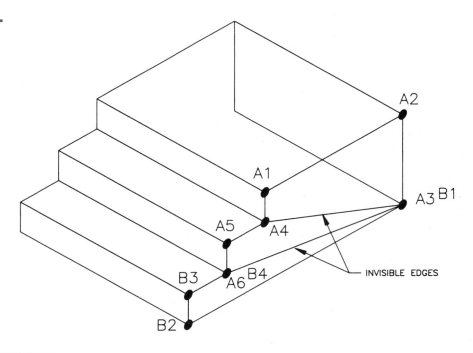

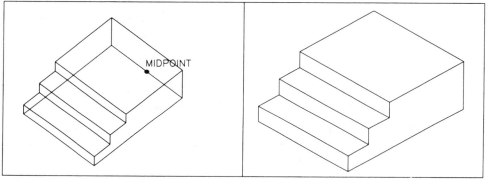

Figure 18.23
Setting the base and using hidden line removal

Stage 7: Insertion of Symbols

The following procedure details the insertion of the windows, door, and steps on the front of the dwelling. Repeat this procedure to generate the rest of the dwelling sides.

Open the master model for this project, DWELL, and enter the following settings:

```
SETTINGS
Freeze all layers except FR-FOUND, FR-1FLOR, FR-TMPOR, FR-
WINDO, FR-DOOR.

Thickness = 0'
Elevation = 0'
Current Layer = FR-TMPOR
UCS = set to FRONT working plane
Display = plan view of current UCS (FRONT)
Fill = off
```

Referring to Figure 18.24, draw the temporary lines used to determine the insertion points for the windows, door, and steps.

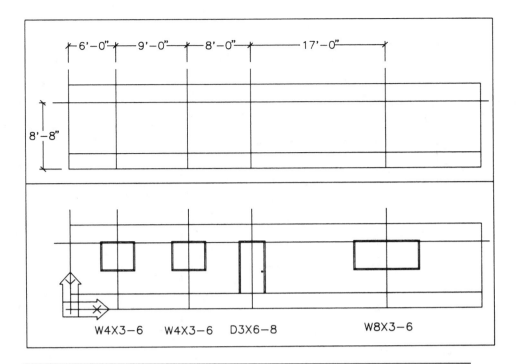

Figure 18.24
Temporary lines for insertion points and the inserted symbols

Window Insertion

Use this one new setting:

```
Current Layer = FR-WINDO
```

Use the INSERT command to place the windows on the wall. The block names are W4X3-6 and W8X3-6. Use insertion object snap for accurate placement. Refer to Figure 18.24.

Door Insertion

The setting is

```
Current Layer = FR-DOOR
```

Use the INSERT command again to place the door, D3X6-8. Refer to Figure 18.24.

Step Insertion

We need to change the working plane at this point or the concrete steps will not have the proper orientation to the model. Try to insert the steps without changing the UCS. Observe the results, and then undo the insertion. Refer to Figure 18.25.

```
    SETTINGS
Current Layer = FR-FEATU
UCS = WCS
Display = restore view ISO
```

Use the INSERT command to place the STEP 3D symbol at the proper location. Use the endpoint object snap. Refer to Figure 18.25.

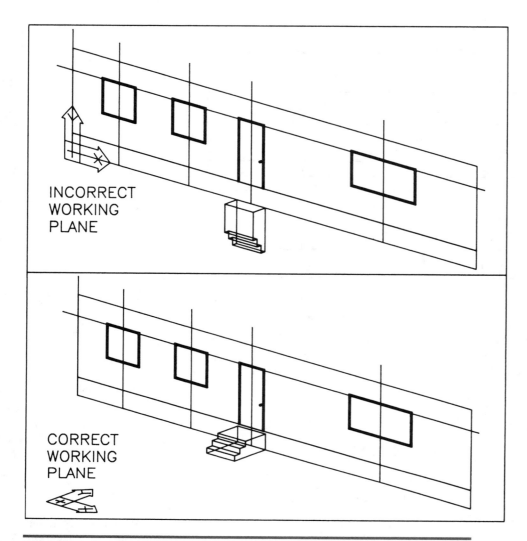

Figure 18.25
Using the incorrect working plane and using the correct working plane

At this point, the front elevation of the model is complete. It has windows, a door, and a set of steps. Using Figure 18.26 as your guide, complete the rest of the elevations. Remember to set the working plane to the side where you'll be inserting a symbol to ensure proper orientation of the 3D symbol. When you are done, save the model as DWELL.

Stage 8: Complex Surface Generation

If you use the HIDE command on the model at this point, the various features will be hidden but you will not be able to see through the windows. This is because we used the thickness property when creating the walls, so there is a complete surface over each window. What we have to do now is replace the walls created by lines with walls created by complex surfaces that allow openings where the windows appear. We will do this with the 3DFACE command, one of the most useful 3D commands.

Creation of the Front Wall

The front wall will be replaced by several 3DFACE surfaces.

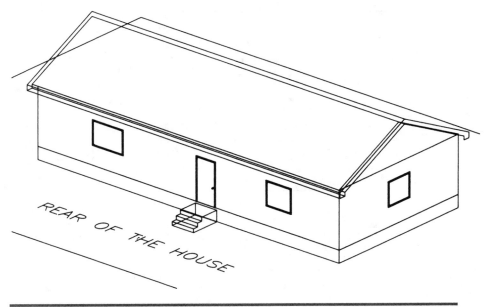

Figure 18.26
View of the rear left of the dwelling

Creation of a Temporary Frame around Windows

Erase the current front wall and replace it using lines, drawing the perimeter of the front wall on the FR-1FLOR layer.

Now erase the temporary lines on layer FR-TMPOR and, using the LINE command, trace around the windows. The new lines will be on layer FR-TMPOR. Be sure to use increment snap only; do not use object snap. This framing will be used to create the snap points for the 3DFACE command.

Creation of the Invisible Surfaces

Use these settings:

Freeze all layers except FR-1FLOR and FR-TMPOR.

Current Layer = FR-1FLOR

If you desire, you may want to experiment with regions instead of using 3D faces. Refer to Section 7.6 of Chapter 7 and the chapters on solid modeling (Chapters 9 through 12). If you use regions, you will need to create a region from the perimeter lines that represent the wall and regions from the lines that represent the window openings. You would then subtract the window regions from the wall using the SUBTRACT command. If you would rather use 3D faces, continue with the procedure on the creation of 3D faces.

Refer to Figure 18.27 for the 10 endpoints that will be used to generate four surfaces around the windows. (We could add points to go around the door as well, but in this project we are going to ignore the door opening.) Use the 3DFACE command to add the four surfaces. Remember that you must select

349

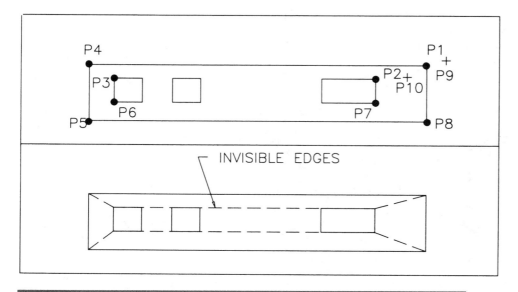

Figure 18.27
Using the 3DFACE command to create a wall with openings

the Invisible edge option of the 3DFACE command before you pick each point, including the very first point. Using invisible edges gives the illusion of one large surface, even though the model is made up of many smaller surfaces.

Now that there is a surface enclosing the windows, we need to place surfaces between the windows. These will be constructed using two separate surfaces—A and B. Refer to Figure 18.28 for the endpoints, and again use the Invisible edge option before picking every point. Exit the 3DFACE command after entering the first four points, and then reenter the 3DFACE command to enter the second four points. The two surfaces, A and B, are now placed between the windows.

Once you have replaced the solid wall with the surfaces that have openings for the windows, place a three-dimensional object inside the house in front of a window on the front wall. Use the HIDE command, and observe

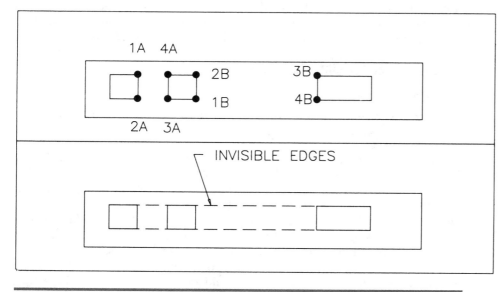

Figure 18.28
Completion of the wall

the results. You should be able to see the object through the window opening. Imagine how interesting the results would be if actual furniture were placed in the house!

Repeat the procedure outlined in stage 8 for the other three sides. *Note:* You can use many combinations of points to create openings in the walls. The procedure given here offers only one combination. It is up to you to determine whether another combination would be best for your particular circumstances.

Save the model as DWELL.

Stage 9: Exterior Features

This is the stage where we'll be adding features (such as railings, outside lamps, and walkways) to enhance the model. A variety of 3D commands can be used to generate these features. Some should be created as separate symbols to be inserted, while others can be created on the model itself. For example, as Figure 18.29 illustrates, railings and walkways can be created on the model very easily by using the 3D OBJECTS command and selecting the Box option. However, lamps and other similar features, which can be created by selecting the Sphere or Pyramid option of the 3D OBJECTS command, should be created as separate drawings to be used over and over again. (Recall that the lamppost and coach light were created in Chapter 13, Assignment 4.) For features you need to add to the model before proceeding to stage 10, refer to Figures 18.29, 18.30, and 18.31.

When you are done, save the drawing as DWELL.

Stage 10: Presentation Display

The construction of the model is now complete and it is time to consider how to display the model for presentation purposes. Chapter 15 discusses the display and presentation of models in detail. What follows here is specific to this particular dwelling model.

Figure 18.29
Front handrails and walkway

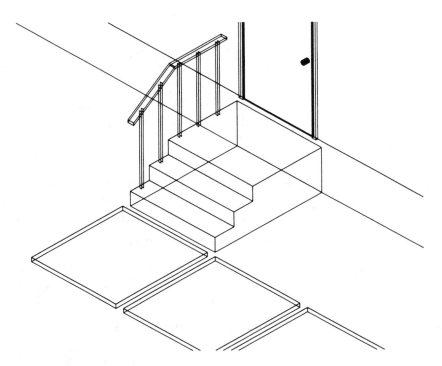

Figure 18.30
Front coach lamps, lamppost, and trees

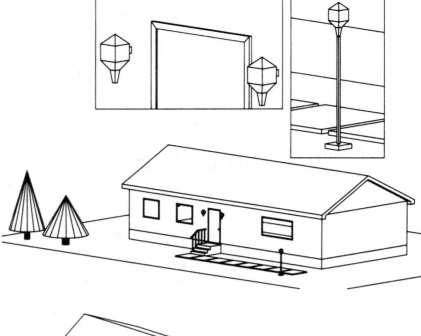

Figure 18.31
Rear coach lamp and steps

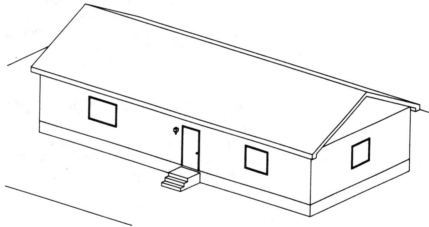

First we establish the options for displaying a perspective of the house, showing the front right side from above, as in Figure 18.32.

SETTINGS

Freeze all layers except the front and right-side layers, which are as follows: FR-FOUND, FR-1FLOR, FR-ROOF, FR-WINDO, FR-DOOR, FR-FEATU, RI-FOUND, RI-1FLOR, RI-ROOF, RI-WINDO, RI-DOOR, RI-FEATU.

`Display = Isometric view (ISO)`

Creation of the Preview Selection Set

Activate the DVIEW command and select the front wall, side wall, roof sections, and the front door as the Preview Selection Set.

Using the Camera Option

Now activate the Camera option. Move the cursor up and down and left and right until you achieve the desired elevation and horizontal view. Refer to Figure 18.33 for a sample view. Then press the pick button.

Setting the Camera Distance

Using the Distance option, place the camera at the desired distance away from the model. A suggested distance is 80′.

Figure 18.32
Perspective view of the model

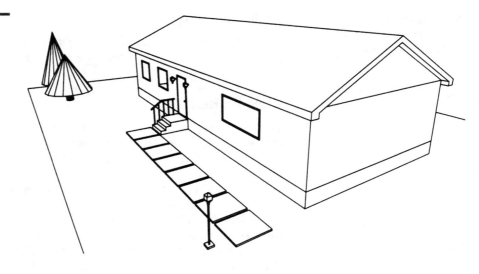

Figure 18.33
View displayed with one possible
location of the camera

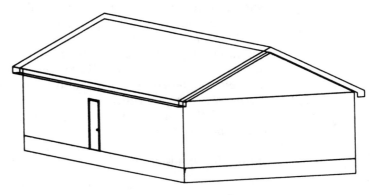

Using the Zoom Option to Get a Better Picture

Select the Zoom option to change the lens length. Move the cursor along the
slider bar or enter the length at the command line. A suggested length
is 25 mm.

Applying the Preview to the Entire Model

Select the Exit option once you have created the desired view using the
DVIEW options. Refer to Figure 18.34. (*Note:* All the roof layers should be
thawed at this point.)

Figure 18.34
Applying the DVIEW settings to the
entire model

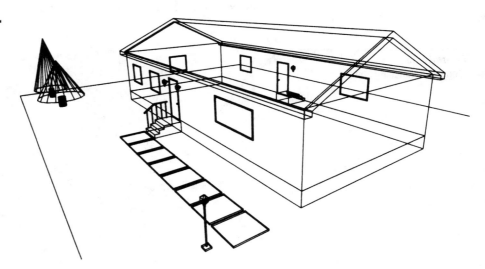

Saving the Perspective Settings

Select the VIEW command and save the current view as PERSP1. After you have done this, you can restore the perspective settings at any time using the VIEW command.

Using the HIDE Command

First, save the model as DWELL. The HIDE command can take a long time to complete, and something could affect the power supply during the procedure. To avoid an unfortunate accident, always save your model before attempting a long HIDE command.

Notice that only the layers that can be seen from this view have been left thawed. This will greatly save on the time it takes to hide the model.

Select the HIDE command and await the outcome. (This may be a good time to complete other homework or perhaps read a good book.) The display should be similar to Figure 18.1. When the HIDE command is finished, immediately make a slide of the display to avoid having to redo the HIDE command when you want to display the model again. You can redisplay the slide much faster than you can rehide the model. Call the slide DWELL1.

To enhance the hidden line removed view, use the BHATCH command to add various types of hatches to the model's surfaces. Remember that you need to set the UCS to each surface before performing the hatch. Once the model is hatched, use the HIDE command to see the results. Refer to Figure 18.35 for a view of the model with some hatching applied to the surfaces. This will not have any effect on the rendered view but does enhance the model if you plan only to plot the model on paper.

Rendering the Model

The project's final procedure is rendering the model in a way that creates a realistic image. This procedure should be thought of as your finishing touch, or what you can do to create truly impressive results. The rendering method you choose will be based on the software and hardware you possess.

Rendering can be accomplished in one of three ways, depending on the available software. The lowest level of realism can be accomplished using the SHADE features built into AutoCAD. If you have a graphics card that can display 256 colors or more, you can produce a moderately realistic image that is sufficient for most purposes.

The next level of realism can be accomplished using the RENDER features built into AutoCAD release 12 and later releases. The main benefit of using the RENDER command instead of the SHADE command is that it allows you to place lights to create different effects.

Figure 18.35
Model with hatching applied

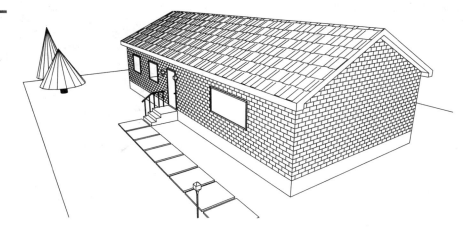

The highest level of realism can be achieved using programs such as Auto-Vision. Such rendering packages allow more flexibility in creating the final image and have some special capabilities, such as casting shadows.

With each increasing level of realism, the number of steps required to create the image also increases. To learn more about rendering models, refer to Chapter 17.

Here are sample settings to create a rendering of our house model using the RENDER utility. The three lamps will appear as if they are turned on because we are rendering the house at night. The lights are placed for viewing the model at PERSP1. See Figure 18.36 for a laser plot of the rendered model.

Rendering Preferences: Use default settings, and set the Rendering options to Smooth Shading.

Lights:

NAME	TYPE	INTENSITY	LIGHT LOCATION	TARGET LOCATION
street	distant	0.5	14′, −14′, 30′	69′, 43′, 0′
accent	point	23	105′, 42′, 5′	
lamp1	point	54	94′10″, 18′10″, 5′	
lamp2	point	54	63′11″, 29′1″, 8′	
lamp3	point	54	69′1″, 29′1″, 8′	
ambient		0.6		

Point Light Fall-off = inverse linear

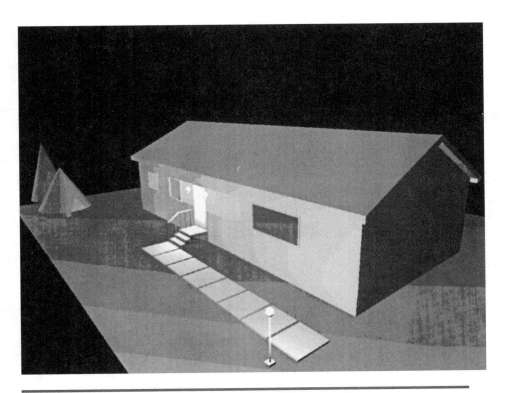

Figure 18.36
Rendered view of the house model

CHAPTER 19

Architectural Project: Commercial Building

Overview

You will find this chapter to be very similar to Chapter 18 in both methodology and content, but the project you will be doing here is a much broader one. In this chapter, you will apply your newly learned commands and techniques to a commercial project that is more complex and that will require you to make more decisions about how to apply your knowledge. To prepare you for the demands of this project, you should complete the Chapter 18 project first.

This chapter's project is not intended to teach you how to design a building or to construct a city; instead, it will provide you with hands-on practice in constructing a model and placing it into a three-dimensional setting. Because this project demands a basic level of expertise in all the techniques and procedures of 3D manipulation, it will serve as your stepping stone to even more complex creations.

Concepts Explored

- Continued exploration of the AutoCAD features
- Creation of a complex 3D model of a commercial building and a city environment
- Generation of 3D symbols to be inserted into the model
- Production of ideally located perspective views
- Creation of shaded and rendered images.

19.1 Introduction

The architectural project in this chapter involves the creation of an exterior model of a commercial building and its subsequent placement in a city environment, as illustrated in Figure 19.1. The building in question will be referred to as a convention center, with one section of the structure used for conventions and the other used as an exhibition hall. Once you have constructed the building, you will develop a simplified city environment in which to place it. The parameters of both the building and its city have already been determined so that you can apply 3D construction techniques.

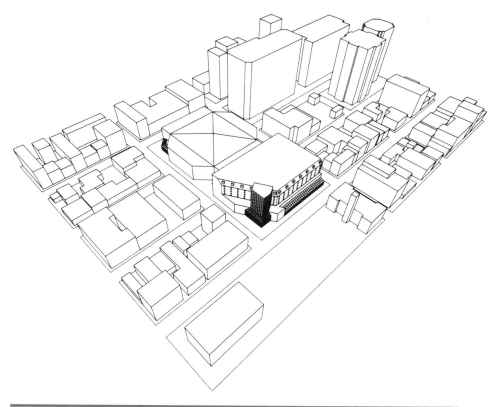

Figure 19.1
Perspective display of the commercial building in a city environment

When this model is finished, you should be able to view the city from any angle. This should generate some impressive perspective views of the commercial building in its environment and illustrate how powerful such a presentation can be.

19.2 Project Stages

Before we create it, we must organize the model. The importance of this first step was discussed in Chapter 18. As you should recall, we begin by determining the stages of development of the model. Some stages are common to all models; some stages are unique. The order in which the stages are performed depends on the particular model type.

Here are the stages in this project. Note that, after initial model division and layer designation, the stages will be done in two parts.

PROJECT STAGES
1. Division of the architectural model (into walls, features)
2. Layer designations (for elevations)

SECTION A: COMMERCIAL BUILDING CONSTRUCTION
3. Building settings (for units, base)
4. Building layout (as plan extrusion, wireframe)
5. Surface generation (for walls, roof)
6. 3D symbol creation (windows, parametric cube)
7. Insertion of symbols

SECTION B: CITY CONSTRUCTION AND BUILDING PLACEMENT
8. City settings (for units, limits)

9. City blocks layout (using parametric cube)
10. Creation of buildings (using parametric cube)
11. Placement of the commercial building
12. Presentation display (creating a perspective view, rendering)

19.3 Initial Stages

Stage 1: Division of the Model

Because the model you are about to create is more complex, it needs to be broken down into more manageable sections. A breakdown of the two sections is listed next.

SECTION A: COMMERCIAL BUILDING CONSTRUCTION
- Roof areas
- Walls
- Windows
- Glass features (solariums)
- External features (steps)
- Temporary construction entities.

SECTION B: CITY CONSTRUCTION
- Ground
- City blocks
- City block structures
- Surfaces of city block structures

Other divisions would be created if you chose to add extra elements.

The master model should be named at this point as well. In this project, the commercial building will be called CONV (CONVention center), and the city will be called CITY.

Stage 2: Layer Designations

As Chapter 18 noted, layer designation must take place in the early stages of development to facilitate the construction and later display of the final model. Most of the layers will be named now, but they will not all be created at this point. Some layers will not be created until they are actually needed during construction.

Because we will want to use the HIDE command to view our complex model with hidden features removed and because AutoCAD will ignore entities on a frozen layer during hidden line removal, thereby abbreviating the time that process takes, the model in this project is divided into individual city blocks (do not mistake these for AutoCAD blocks). Each block has its own designation. These designations allow you to freeze any number of city blocks, at any time, either for better viewing of the convention center or to speed up the processing time of the computer. Referring ahead to Figure 19.27, note that each block has a designated letter. Any construction taking place within that block will be on the layer for that block.

Recall that only the first 8 characters of a layer name are visible on the status line, even though the layer name can have as many as 31 characters. Because of this and for the sake of convenience, the names for the layers of this model have 8 or fewer characters. These names are self-explanatory. For example, A-WALLS would be the name of the layer containing the walls of the building on city block A.

Listed next are the layers you should create when starting the model. For section A (the commercial building construction), create the following layers.

(*Note:* The layer names use F for the prefix because the commercial building occupies city block F.)

LAYER COLOR	LAYER NAME	LAYER DESCRIPTION
1	F-ROOF	Commercial building roofs
2	F-WALLS	Commercial building walls
3	F-WIN1	Commercial building windows (separate symbol)
4	F-WIN2	Commercial building windows (parametric cube)
5	F-GLASS	Commercial building glass structures
6	F-FEATU	Commercial building external features (steps)
7	F-WIRES	Commercial building wireframe construction
12	F-TMPOR	Temporary construction

For section B (the city construction), create these layers. (*Note:* Replace the * with the appropriate city block designation.)

LAYER COLOR	LAYER NAME	LAYER DESCRIPTION
4	*-CBLOCK	City block base (parametric cube)
5	*-STRUCT	City block buildings (parametric cube)
6	*-STSURF	City block surfaces as required (3D faces)

Give each section type its own color to make it easier to distinguish what is on each layer. The color you choose for each section type is not important at this point.

Remember: It is customary to use continuous linetype for all construction of 3D models.

19.4 Section A: Commercial Building Construction
Stage 3: Initial Settings

Start a new model called CONV. Create the layers listed in stage 2, and assign the appropriate colors. Enter the following settings before beginning the model:

```
    SETTINGS
 Units = Architectural
 Limits = 0',0' to 360',660'
 Grid = 10'
 Snap Incr. = 10'
 Initial Elevation Thickness = 0'
 Initial Thickness = 0'
 UCS = WCS
 UCSICON = on and set to ORIGIN
```

Remember to ZOOM All, so that the display shows the set limits. In addition, if there are any other settings you would like to enter, now is the time to do so.

Note: To facilitate construction, start, intermediate, and end points will be given where required. They will be identified as P1, P2, and so forth. Simply enter each 3D point in sequence until the last point in the series has been entered. When exact coordinate numeric values are given, their locations will not be shown on the related figures.

Stage 4: Building Layout

Review the plan and elevation views of the building shown in Figure 19.2. At this stage, most of the building will be constructed with extrusion and wire-

Figure 19.2
Plan and elevation views of the building

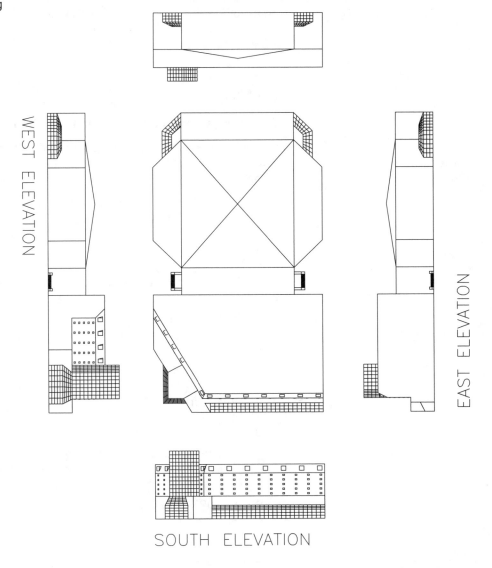

frame procedures. The missing surfaces will be added in stage 5. Some advanced surface commands, such as EDGESURF, will be used to construct the many-paned, glassed-in areas.

Let's begin construction. First, we'll tackle the walls that represent the major structure of the convention section of the building. REMEMBER TO SAVE YOUR DRAWING PERIODICALLY.

Creation of Major Structure of Convention Section

Create an orientation cube as a frame of reference. Use these settings:

```
    SETTINGS
Layer = F-TMPOR
Elevation = 0'
Thickness = 120'
UCS = WCS
Viewports = Split the screen into two viewports, one
above the other. The lower viewport should contain
the plan view. The top viewport should contain an
axonometric view (VPOINT = 2,-4,1).
```

Figure 19.3
Orientation cube

Using the LINE command, draw the perimeter representing the orientation cube, as shown in Figure 19.3. The orientation cube is 360′ in the *X* direction, 260′ in the *Y* direction, and 120′ in the *Z* direction. The lower left corner must start at 0,0,0. (*Note:* When entering 3D coordinates, *Z* values may be left off as long as the elevation is set to the desired height.)

```
P1 = 0',0',0'            P2 = 360',0',0
P3 = 360',260',0'        P4 = 0,260',0'
CLOSE.
```

Creation of Rooftop of Convention Section

We now construct the top of the roof, including the sloped edge of the roof, out of wireframe. We'll surface it in stage 5. The vertical wall that meets the sloped edge is constructed from a line with thickness. Refer to Figure 19.4.

```
SETTINGS
Layer = F-WIRES
Elevation = 120'
Thickness = 0'
UCS = WCS
```

Using the LINE command, draw the perimeter representing the sloped edge of the roof. Refer to Figure 19.4A.

```
P1 = 360',40',120'
P2 = 108'8",40',120'
P3 = 0',230'2",120'
```

```
SETTINGS
Layer = F-WALLS
Elevation = 50'
Thickness = 50'
UCS = WCS
```

Using the LINE command, draw the perimeter representing the vertical wall that meets the sloped edge of the roof. Refer to Figure 19.4B.

```
P1 = 360',30',50'
P2 = 102'10",30',50'
P3 = 0',210',50'
```

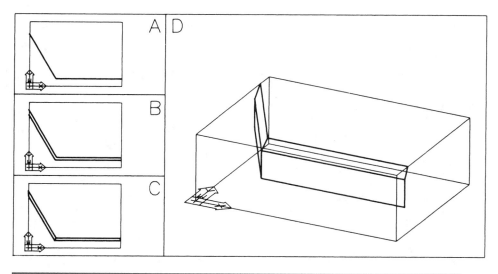

Figure 19.4
Wireframe representing the roof area

SETTINGS
```
Layer = F-WIRES
Elevation = 0'
Thickness = 0'
UCS = WCS
```

Using the LINE command and endpoint object snap, add the sloped lines connecting the roof to the walls. Refer to Figure 19.4C.

Creation of Extension Walls of Convention Section

The extension walls that run around the west and south wall are constructed now. The inner lines are wireframe, but the outer lines are extruded lines, because they represent a completely vertical wall.

SETTINGS
```
Layer = F-WIRES
Elevation = 50'
Thickness = 0'
UCS = WCS
```

Using the LINE command, draw the walls representing the inner perimeter of the extension. Refer to Figure 19.5A.

```
P1 = 360',30',50'
P2 = 102'10",30',50'
P3 = 0',210',50'
```

SETTINGS
```
Layer = F-WALLS
Elevation = 0'
Thickness = 50'
UCS = WCS
```

Using the LINE command, draw the walls representing the outer perimeter of the extension. Refer to Figure 19.5B. For line 1, use the following points:

```
P1 = 360',20',0'
P2 = 108'7",20',0'
```

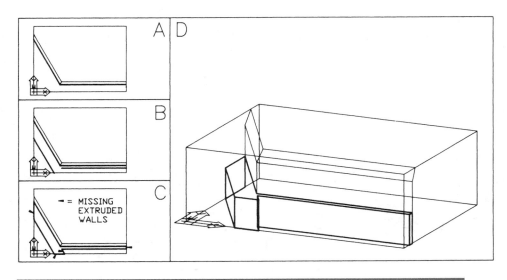

Figure 19.5
Creation of the extension walls

For line 2, use these points:

```
P1 = 80',0',0'
P2 = 0',140',0'
```

Using the LINE command, create the missing walls, as shown in parts C and D in Figure 19.5. Remember that these are extruded lines.

Creation of South Glass Solarium in Convention Section

The south glass solarium at the front of the building will first be constructed out of wireframe and then covered with meshes using the EDGESURF command.

```
SETTINGS
Layer = F-WIRES
Elevation = 0'
Thickness = 0'
UCS = WCS
```

Using the LINE command, construct the line representing the top of the solarium. Refer to Figure 19.6A.

```
P1 = 360',20',30'
P2 = 120',20',30'
```

Using the LINE command again, construct the line representing the bottom and top of the vertical wall of the solarium. Refer to Figure 19.6B. Use the following points for line 1:

```
P1 = 360',0',0'
P2 = 120',0',0'
```

For line 2, use these points:

```
P1 = 360',0',20'
P2 = 120',0',20'
```

Now add the missing lines as shown in Figure 19.6C. Use the LINE command and endpoint object snap.

```
SETTINGS
Layer = F-TMPOR
Freeze layer F-GLASS
```

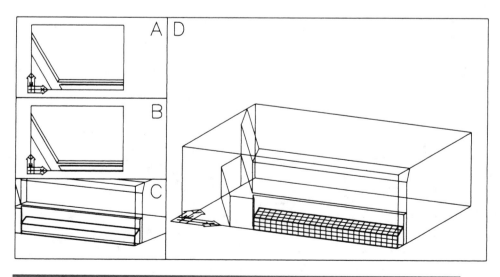

Figure 19.6
South solarium wireframe and mesh

```
SURFTAB1 = 26 (horizontal panes of glass)
SURFTAB2 = 3 (vertical panes of glass)
```

With the EDGESURF command, select groups of four lines to create a mesh. Refer to Figure 19.6D. Select horizontal lines first so that SURFTAB1 will control the number of horizontal panes. After you have created the first mesh, use CHPROP to move it to the F-GLASS layer. This allows you to select the wireframe to create a new mesh without being obstructed by the previously created mesh. Now create the second mesh and move it to the F-GLASS layer.

Creation of West Glass Solarium in Convention Section

The west glass solarium at the angled side of the building will be constructed in a manner similar to the construction of the south solarium.

```
    SETTINGS
Layer = F-WIRES
Elevation = 0'
Thickness = 0'
UCS = WCS
```

Using the LINE command, construct the line representing the top of the solarium. Refer to Figure 19.7A.

```
P1 = 62'10",30',50'
P2 = 30',30',50'
P3 = 30',87'6",50'
```

Using the LINE command again, construct the line representing the bottom and top of the vertical wall of the solarium. Refer to Figure 19.7B. For line 1, use these points:

```
P1 = 68'7",20',0'
P2 = 20',20',0'
P3 = 20',105',0'
```

For line 2, use these points:

```
P1 = 68'7",20',30'
P2 = 20',20',30'
P3 = 20',105',30'
```

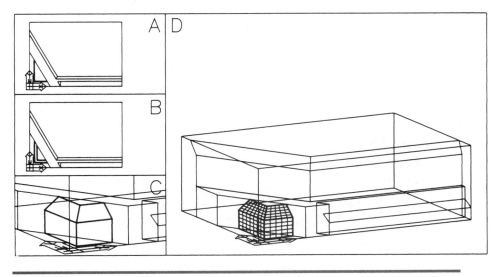

Figure 19.7
West solarium wireframe and mesh

Add the missing lines as shown in Figure 19.7C. Use the LINE command and endpoint object snap.

SETTINGS
Layer = F-TMPOR
SURFTAB1 = 5 (horizontal panes of glass)
SURFTAB2 = 5 (vertical panes of glass)
Freeze layer F-GLASS.

Using the EDGESURF command, select groups of four lines to create a mesh on the north face of the sloped surface. Select horizontal lines first so that SURFTAB1 will control the number of horizontal panes. After you have created the first mesh, use CHPROP to move it to the F-GLASS layer. Repeat this process for the north vertical face.

SURFTAB1 = 7 (horizontal panes of glass)
SURFTAB2 = 5 (vertical panes of glass)

Using the EDGESURF command again, select groups of four lines to create a mesh on the west face of the sloped surface. Select horizontal lines first so that SURFTAB1 will control the number of horizontal panes. Once you have created it, move the first mesh to the F-GLASS layer. Repeat this process for the west vertical face.

Thaw layer F-GLASS, observe the mesh, and then freeze the layer again.

Creation of Tower in Convention Section

The glass tower will sit half on the west solarium and half on the extension. It will be constructed out of wireframe and then covered with a mesh using the EDGESURF command.

SETTINGS
Layer = F-WIRES
Elevation = 50'
Thickness = 0'
UCS = WCS

Using the LINE command, construct the lines shown in Figure 19.8A.

P1 = 93',47'3",50'   P2 = 62'10",30',50'
P3 = 30',30',50'   P4 = 30',87'6",50'

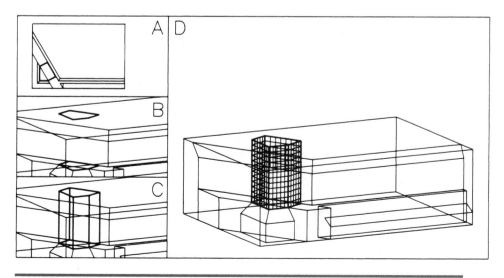

Figure 19.8
Glass tower construction

P5 = 60'2",104'9",50'

Using the LINE command again, construct the lines shown in part B of Figure 19.8, or copy the lines from part A to an elevation of 150'.

P1 = 93',47'3",150'   P2 = 62'10",30',150'
P3 = 30',30',150'   P4 = 30',87'6",150'
P5 = 60'2",104'9",150'

Using endpoint object snap, add the vertical lines as shown in Figure 19.8C.

    SETTINGS
Layer = F-TMPOR
Freeze layer F-GLASS.
SURFTAB1 = 5 (horizontal panes of glass)
SURFTAB2 = 12 (vertical panes of glass)

Note: Use SURFTAB1 = 7 for the west and east tower faces.

Using the EDGESURF command, select groups of four lines to create a mesh on one side of the tower. Select horizontal lines first so that SURFTAB1 will control the number of horizontal panes. Use CHPROP to move the newly created first mesh to the F-GLASS layer. Repeat this process for the other four sides.

Thaw layer F-GLASS, observe the mesh, and then freeze the layer again.

Save the model as CONV.

Creation of Extruded Walls of Exhibition Center

The walls of the exhibition portion of the building are vertical, so they will be created with lines that have thickness.

    SETTINGS
Layer = F-WALLS
Elevation = 0'
Thickness = 100'
UCS = WCS

Using the LINE command, draw the perimeter representing the walls as shown in Figure 19.9. For clarity, the convention center portion of the building is not shown in Figures 19.9, 19.10, and 19.11.

Figure 19.9
Extruded lines to create walls of the exhibition center

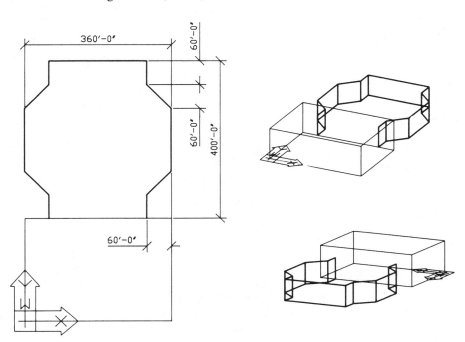

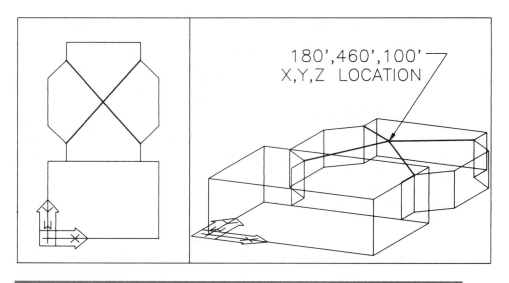

Figure 19.10
Wireframe of exhibition center roof

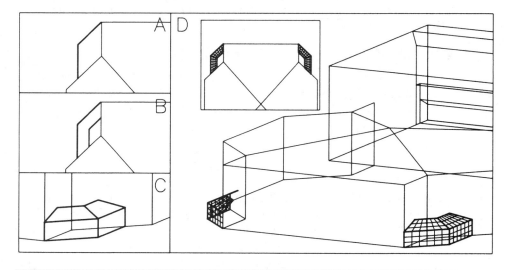

Figure 19.11
West and east solarium wireframe and mesh

Creation of Sloped Roof Structure of Exhibition Center

The sloped roof of the exhibition center will be constructed out of wireframe initially and then, in stage 5, it will be covered with surfaces.

```
    SETTINGS
Layer = F-WIRES
Elevation = 0'
Thickness = 0'
UCS = WCS
```

Using the LINE command, draw the four wires that represent the sloped structure of the roof as shown in Figure 19.10. The peak of the roof is numerically represented by the coordinates 180',460',100'. Use endpoint object snap to snap to the corners of the extruded walls, and then enter the coordinates for the peak. Be sure to work in the axonometric viewport so that the correct elevation is used as the endpoints.

Creation of West and East Glass Solariums in Exhibition Center

The exhibition center's solariums will be constructed in a fashion similar to the way the west solarium of the convention center was constructed. A wireframe model will be constructed first, and then it will be covered with a mesh.

```
     SETTINGS
Layer = F-WIRES
Elevation = 0'
Thickness = 0'
UCS = WCS
```

Using the LINE command, construct the top and bottom lines shown in Figure 19.11A. For the first line, use these points:

```
P1 = 20',560',0'
P2 = 20',620',0'
P3 = 60',660',0'
```

Use these points for the other line:

```
P1 = 20',560',20'
P2 = 20',620',20'
P3 = 60',660',20'
```

Using the LINE command again, construct the lines shown in Figure 19.11B.

```
P1 = 40',580',30'
P2 = 40',611'9",30'
P3 = 60',631'9",30'
```

Using endpoint object snap, add the missing sloped and vertical lines as shown in Figure 19.11C.

```
     SETTINGS
Layer = F-TMPOR
Freeze layer F-GLASS
SURFTAB1 = 6 (horizontal panes of glass)
SURFTAB2 = 3 (vertical panes of glass)
```

Using the EDGESURF command, select groups of four lines to create a mesh on one of the sloped surfaces. Select horizontal lines first so that SURFTAB1 will control the number of horizontal panes. When you have created the first mesh, use CHPROP to move it to the F-GLASS layer. Repeat this procedure for the other sloped surface. Thaw layer F-GLASS.

(Use the MIRROR command to mirror the west solarium to the east side.)

Observe the mesh, and then freeze the F-GLASS layer again.

Save the model as CONV.

Stage 5: Surface Generation

Now we need to add surfaces on the various portions of the building. We'll use the 3DFACE command to do this. Remember that 3D faces can be created with any three-dimensional coordinates and will not be forced to align to the current working plane. Thus, to add these surfaces, all we need to do is snap to the previously constructed wireframes. Follow these steps:

1. Using the 3DFACE command, add the missing surfaces by referring to Figures 19.12 and 19.13. Use object snap endpoint and intersection for most node points for the 3D faces.

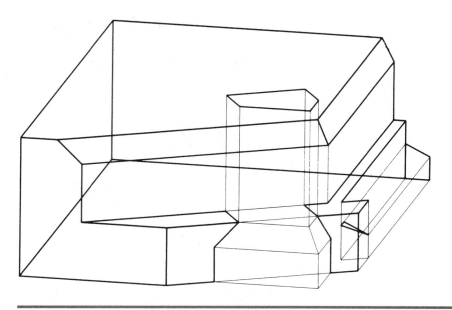

Figure 19.12
Surfaces to be added to the convention center

Figure 19.13
Surfaces to be added to the exhibition
center

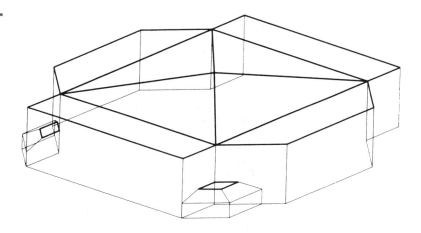

```
        SETTINGS
 Layer = F-ROOF
 Elevation = 0'
 Thickness = 0'
 UCS = WCS
```

Remember to use the Invisible edge option of the 3DFACE command
whenever necessary, so that no obstructing diagonal lines cross complex
surfaces. (Refer to Section 7.3 of Chapter 7 if you need a refresher.)

2. Freeze the F-TMPOR layer and thaw the F-GLASS layer.
3. Save the model as CONV.
4. Using the VPOINT and HIDE commands, move around the model and
   observe the results. The model should look similar to Figure 19.14.

Stage 6: 3D Symbol Generation

At this point, we create and add the various 3D features that are needed for the
building. We'll create two kinds of windows and a set of steps. If you desire, you

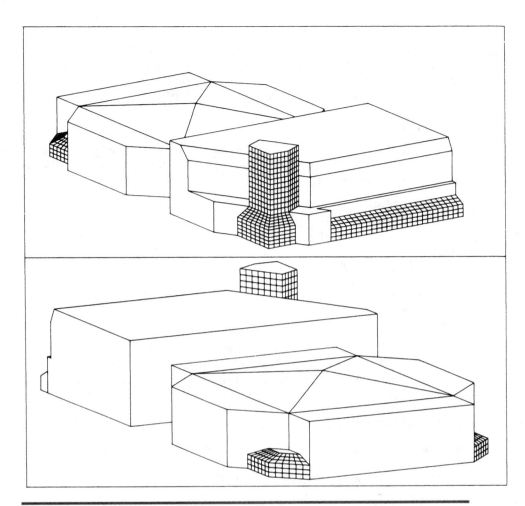

Figure 19.14
Model by the end of stage 5

can create more symbols and add them to the model for further enhancement. However, constructing the symbols specified here will give you sufficient practice in the necessary techniques. Once you become familiar with these procedures, there will be few limits to what you will be able to accomplish.

Creation of Parametric Cube

A parametric cube will serve several functions in the construction of the building and the city. Its first function will be to form windows that will line the convention center. Later, it will be used to create the city block lots and the city's other buildings. (This portion of our project should serve as a convincing illustration of the usefulness of parametric symbol design.)

Start a new model called FCUBE (parametric Foot CUBE) with the following settings:

```
    SETTINGS
Units = Architectural
Limits = −1',−1' to 1',1'
Grid = 1'
Snap Incr. = 1'
Elevation = 0'
Thickness = 0'
Current Layer = 0
```

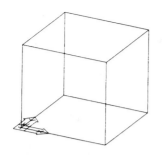

Figure 19.15
FCUBE model

UCS = WCS

We are going to use a 3D surface object for this symbol. Use the AI_BOX command to create a surface model that is a 1-foot cube (1′ × 1′ × 1′), as shown in Figure 19.15. The lower left corner should be at 0,0,0, and set the BASE point to 0,0,0. Then, save the model as FCUBE.

Creation of Sloped Window

A sloped window symbol will be placed along the sloped roof edge of the convention center. To construct it, start a new model called SWIN (Sloped WINdow) with the following settings:

```
  SETTINGS
Units = Architectural
Limits = −1′,−1′ to 12′,12′
Grid = 1′
Snap Incr. = 2″
Elevation = 0′
Thickness = 0′
Current Layer = 0
UCS = WCS
```

Using the LINE command, draw a wireframe of the illustration shown in Figure 19.16. (*Note:* The angle 63 degrees and the length 11′2″ are approximate.)

Using the 3DFACE command, add surfaces to the sides and the top of the wireframe. Set the BASE point to 0,0,0. Then, save the model as SWIN.

Creation of Exhibition Steps

The concrete steps to the exhibition center are constructed with lines that have thickness and 3D faces. See Figure 19.17.

Start a new drawing called STEP2 with these settings:

```
  SETTINGS
Units = Architectural
Limits = 0′,0′ to 35′,30′
Grid = 5′
Snap Incr. = 6″
```

Figure 19.16
SWIN model

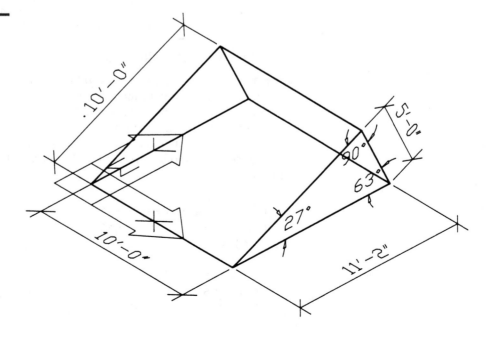

Figure 19.17
Concrete step model

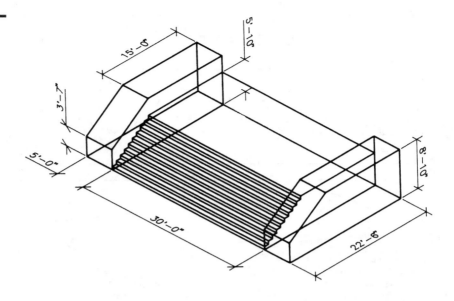

```
Thickness = 5'10"
Elevation = 0'
UCS = WCS
UCSICON = on and set to ORIGIN
Layers = 0 (all construction will take place on layer 0)
```

Draw a rectangle the same size as the concrete steps—with a width of 30' and a depth of 22'6", as shown in Figure 19.18. Next, display an axonometric view of the cube.

SETTING
```
Thickness = −30'
```

Create a working plane on the right side of the cube, as shown in Figure 19.19. Use the PLAN command to set the view to the current UCS. Draw the outline of the landing and the treads and risers, as shown in Figure 19.19.

SETTING
```
Thickness = 5'
```

Figure 19.18
Orientation cube and the working plane

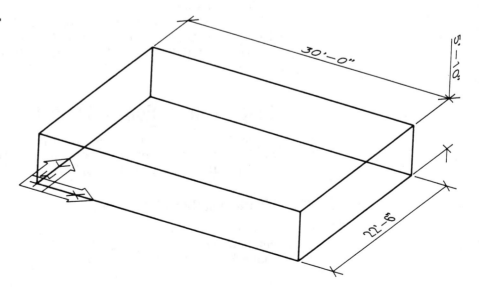

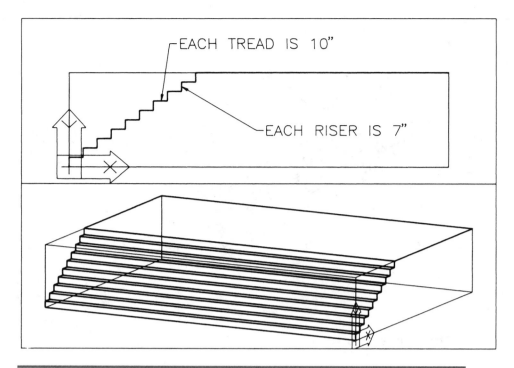

Figure 19.19
Adding the steps and viewing from an isometric viewpoint

Use the LINE command, and draw the sides of the steps, as shown in Figure 19.20.

Set the elevation to –30′ and the thickness to –5′ and draw in the other side of the steps, or use the COPY or MIRROR command and duplicate the first side.

```
    SETTING
Thickness = 0′
```

Delete the top, front, and two side lines of the orientation box. Leave the back line for the back surface of the step. Using the 3DFACE command, place two surfaces on the step sides. Refer to Figure 19.21. Use endpoint object snap to snap to points 1 through 5. *Note:* Remember to use the Invisible edge option just before picking point P3.

Use the COPY command to copy the 3D faces to the other three sides. Then, set the BASE point to 35′,22′6″,0′, as shown in Figure 19.21.

Use the HIDE command, and observe the results. The screen should look similar to Figure 19.21. Save the model as STEP2.

Stage 7: Insertion of Symbols

In this stage, we'll add the two window types and the concrete steps to the building. If you constructed other symbols during the last stage, add them now as well.

Open the building model CONV.

Insertion of Sloped Window

The first symbol to be inserted is the sloped window. To have the proper orientation upon insertion, align the working plane to the sloped surface of the roof edge.

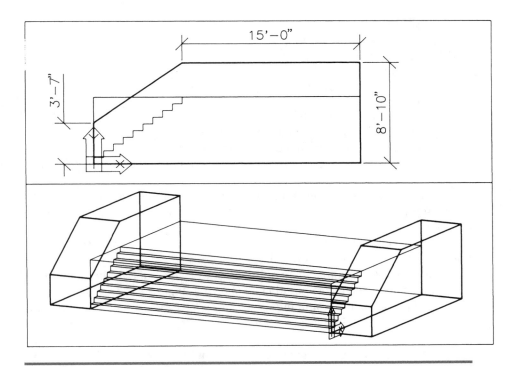

Figure 19.20
Sides of the steps

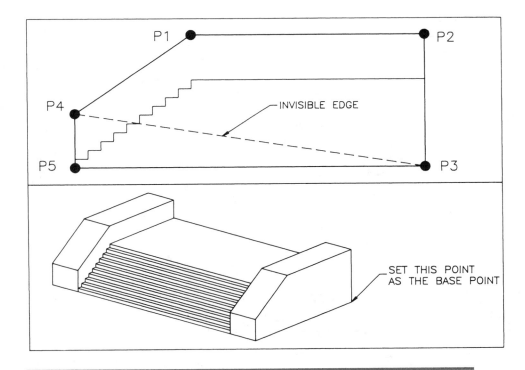

Figure 19.21
Adding surfaces to the sides

SETTINGS
```
Layer = F-WIN1
Elevation = 0'
Thickness = 0'
Freeze F-GLASS layer.
```

Using the UCS command, align the UCS working plane to the sloped roof edge of the west side of the building, as shown in Figure 19.22.

Using the INSERT command, place the SWIN 3D symbol at the coordinates 1'6",6'2",0'. Leave the scale of the 3D symbol at 1 and the rotation at 0.

Using the ARRAY command, copy the window along the wall. The number of rows is 1, and the number of columns is 4. The distance between the columns is 35'.

Insert another sloped window on the right side of the tower, as shown in Figure 19.22. Place it at the coordinates 191'6",6'2",0'.

Using the UCS command, align the UCS working plane to the sloped roof edge of the south side of the building, as shown in Figure 19.23.

Using the INSERT command, place the SWIN 3D symbol at the coordinates 10'10",6'2",0'. Leave the scale of the 3D symbol at 1 and the rotation at 0.

Using the ARRAY command, copy the window along the wall. The number of rows is 1, and the number of columns is 7. The distance between the columns is 38'6".

Insertion of Second Window Type

The windows along the vertical walls of the convention center are created using the second window type. This window type is formed using the parametric cube FCUBE. Refer to Figure 19.24.

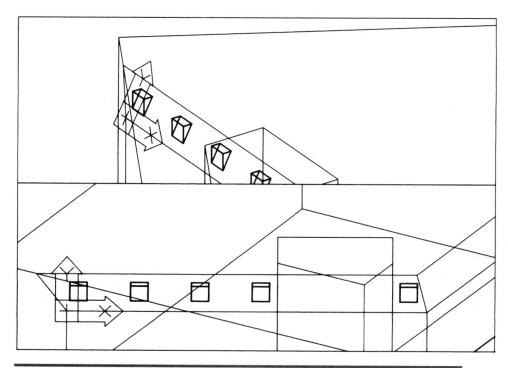

Figure 19.22
Sloped windows on the west side of the building

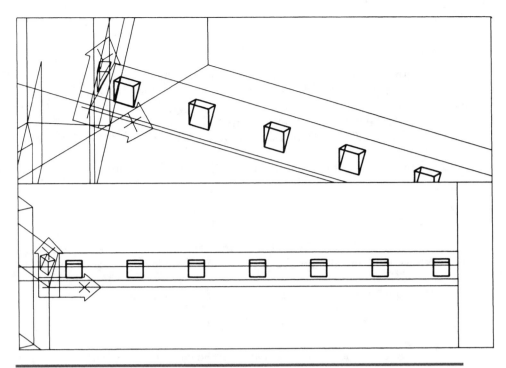

Figure 19.23
Sloped window on the south side of the building

Using the UCS command, align the UCS working plane to the west side of the building, as shown in Figure 19.24.

SETTING
Current Layer = F-WIN2

Using the INSERT command, place the FCUBE 3D symbol at the coordinates 10',4',0'.

Use the XYZ option to allow scaling of the cube in all three axes:

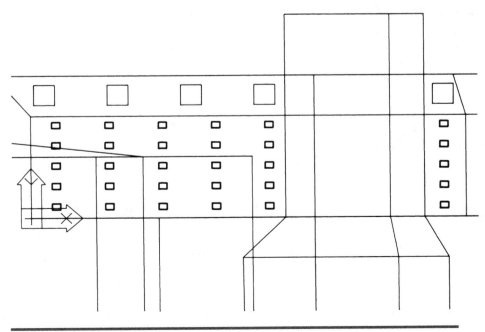

Figure 19.24
Parametric windows along the west side of the building

$X = 4$
$Y = 3$
$Z = 0.3$

This will create a window 4' wide, 3' high, and 3.6" thick.

Using the ARRAY command, copy the window along the wall. The number of rows is 5, and the number of columns is 5. The distance between the rows is 10', and the distance between the columns is 25'5".

Using the INSERT command, place the FCUBE 3D symbol at the right of the tower at the coordinates 195',4',0'.

Use the XYZ option to allow scaling of the cube in all three axes:

$X = 4$
$Y = 3$
$Z = 0.3$

Using the ARRAY command, copy the window along the wall. The number of rows is 5, and the number of columns is 1. The distance between the rows is 10'.

Using the UCS command, align the UCS working plane to the south side of the building, as shown in Figure 19.25.

Using the INSERT command, place the FCUBE 3D symbol at the coordinates 10',4',0'.

Use the XYZ option to allow scaling of the cube in all three axes:

$X = 4$
$Y = 3$
$Z = 0.3$

Using the ARRAY command, copy the window along the wall. The number of rows is 5, and the number of columns is 10. The distance between the rows is 10', and the distance between the columns is 26'4".

Insertion of Concrete Steps

A set of steps will be placed on each side of the exhibition center where it joins the convention center. The working plane will be set to match the WCS. Refer to Figure 19.26.

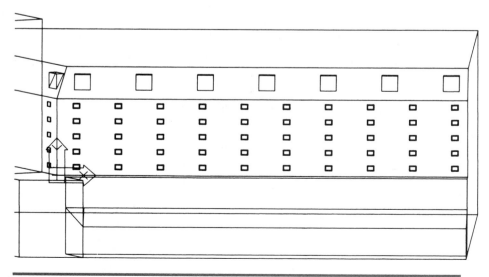

Figure 19.25
Parametric windows along the south side of the building

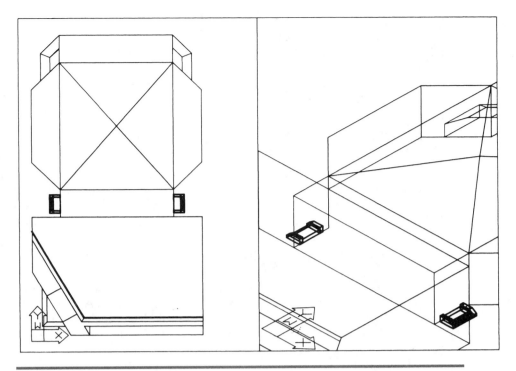

Figure 19.26
Placement of concrete steps

```
SETTINGS
Layer = F-FEATU
Elevation = 0'
Thickness = 0'
UCS = WCS
Freeze layers F-WIN1 and F-WIN2.
```

Using the INSERT command, first place the STEP2 3D symbol at the coordinates 60',270',0', at a scale of 1 and a rotation of 270 degrees. Then place the symbol at the coordinates 300',310',0' at a scale of 1 and a rotation of 90 degrees.

Save the model as CONV.

19.5 Section B: City Construction and Building Placement
Stage 8: City Settings

The following steps need to be completed before the modeling of the city blocks can begin.

Start a new model called CITY. Create the following layers and assign the appropriate colors:

LAYER COLOR	LAYER NAME	LAYER DESCRIPTION
3	GROUND	Ground surface (3D face)
4	*-CBLOCK	City block base (parametric cube)
5	*-STRUCT	City block buildings (parametric cube)
6	*-STSURF	City block surfaces as required (3D faces)

Replace the * with the appropriate city block designations A through P.

SETTINGS
```
Units = Architectural
Limits = -10',-10' to 1760',1210'
Grid = 10
Snap Incr. = 10'
Initial Elevation = 0'
Initial Thickness = 0'
UCS = WCS
UCSICON = on and set to ORIGIN
```

Remember to ZOOM All, so that the display shows the set limits.

Are there other settings you would like to set? If so, now is the time to set them, before entering stage 9. REMEMBER TO SAVE YOUR DRAWING PERIODICALLY.

Stage 9: City Blocks Layout

Figure 19.27 shows the plan views of the city blocks. These city blocks will be constructed out of the parametric cube FCUBE. The city blocks A, B, C, D, E, H, I, J, K, L, M, O, P are 400' × 200'. Blocks F, G, and N are made of modules sized 400' × 200' separated by street widths of 50'. Each block will have a thickness of 6".

SETTING
```
Layer = A-CBLOCK
```

Using the INSERT command, place the FCUBE at the coordinates 0',1000',0'.

Using the XYZ option, set the following scales. (You may use a 2D solid if desired.)

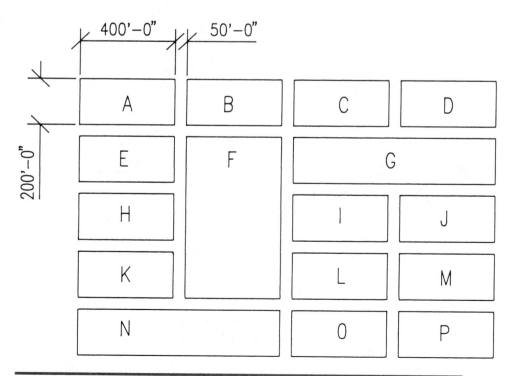

Figure 19.27
Plan views of the city blocks

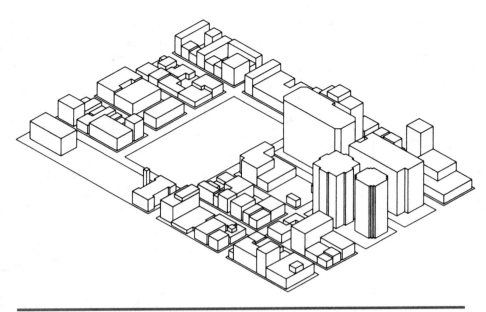

Figure 19.28
Isometric view of the city blocks

$$X = 400$$
$$Y = 200$$
$$Z = -0.5$$

Leave the rotation at 0.

The first city block has now been constructed at location A. Construct the remaining city blocks using the parametric 3D symbol FCUBE, as shown in Figure 19.27. All blocks are multiples of $400' \times 200'$ with $50'$ street spacing. Remember to change the layer before the formation of each city block so that each block is on its own layer.

When you are done, save the model as CITY.

Stage 10: Creation of Simple Buildings

Here we create simple buildings to represent the city setting into which the commercial building will be inserted, as shown in Figure 19.28. Most of the buildings will be constructed out of the FCUBE model. Those buildings with nonrectangular shapes will be constructed out of lines with thickness and then covered with 3D faces.

Look at Figure 19.29 now. Notice the enclosed numbers that are placed within each building area or near the area and directed to it. These numbers represent the roof elevation of each building (for example, "90" means that the roof is at an elevation of $90'$). If there is a plus sign before the number, it means that this building structure is on top of another and is so many feet higher. (For example, $+30$ represents that the roof elevation is $30'$ above the elevation of the roof it is sitting on.)

The smallest division in the X or Y direction is $10'$. The scale of the plan is $1'' = 200'$. The X and Y size of the buildings may be scaled directly from the plan. The scale bar on the drawing can be used to transfer the sizes as well.

```
        SETTINGS
Layer = *-STRUCT
Elevation = 0'
Thickness = 0'
UCS = WCS
```

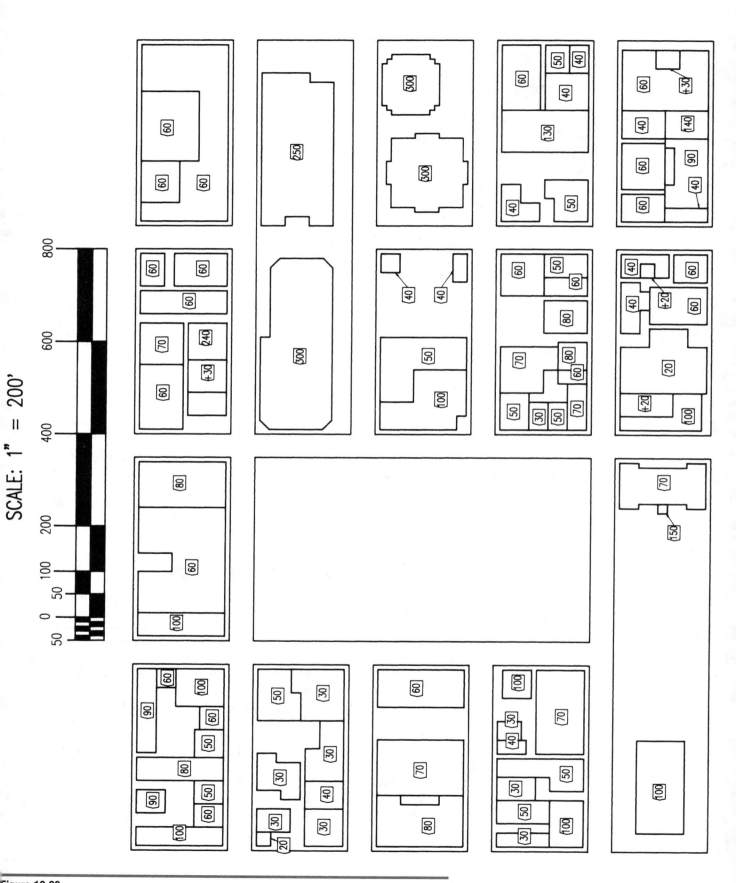

Figure 19.29
Plan view of the city buildings

Refer to both Figures 19.28 and Figure 19.29 as you create the buildings. Remember to change the layers as necessary. Layer *-STRUCT is for the FCUBE buildings and for the lines with thickness. Layer *-STSURF is for the 3D faces that are required to roof the nonrectangular buildings. Keep most of the elevations at 0'. However, to construct a building structure that is on top of another structure (indicated by a positive roof elevation number), set the elevation to the roof elevation of the bottom structure.

After you have created the simple buildings, save the model as CITY.

Stage 11: Placement of Commercial Building

Now it is time to insert the commercial building into the city setting.

```
    SETTINGS
Layer = F-STRUCT
Elevation = 0'
Thickness = 0'
UCS = WCS
```

Using the INSERT command, place the CONV model at the coordinates 470',270',0'. Keep the scale to 1, and then rotate the building as necessary. Refer to Figure 19.30 for the placement.

Save the model as CITY.

Stage 12: Presentation Display

The construction of the overall model is now complete, and we are ready to consider how to display the model for presentation purposes. Chapter 15 discusses presentation and display in detail; here, only the specifics for this commercial building model are given.

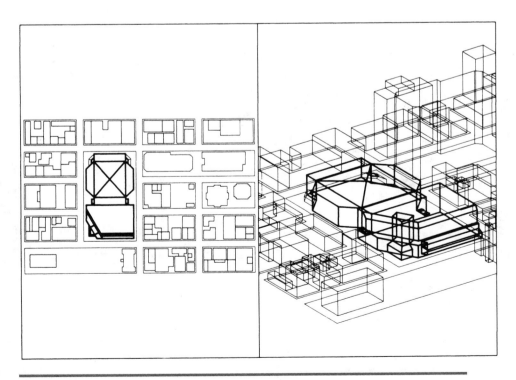

Figure 19.30
Commercial building placement

A project of this magnitude would be viewed in numerous ways. In fact, if you have access to AutoFlix (an animation program that is included with AutoShade) or Autodesk's Animator, you might consider creating an animated flyby of the city and the commercial building as an added challenge. However, we'll create only four perspective views for this project:

PERSP1: from above and to the southwest of the commercial building, looking at the commercial building

PERSP2: closer to the ground and closer to the southwest corner of the building, with emphasis on the glass tower and solarium

PERSP3: from the top of a building to the northwest of the exhibition center, looking toward the glass solarium on the northwest face of the exhibition center

PERSP4: from directly above the city, looking down

Creation of Preview Selection Set

When selecting objects for the Preview Selection Set, select only the commercial building, not the whole city. This will make it easier to modify the DVIEW settings to achieve the desired view. You may have to adjust the settings depending on your graphics.

Complete steps 1 through 5 to create and save the four perspective views:

1. The following settings will achieve the perspective view PERSP1 shown in Figure 19.31. Use the Points option of the DVIEW command to place the camera and the target points, and set the Distance and Zoom values.

```
Points-Target = 699'9",1007'4",−161'5"
Camera = −74'8",241'5",1078'
```

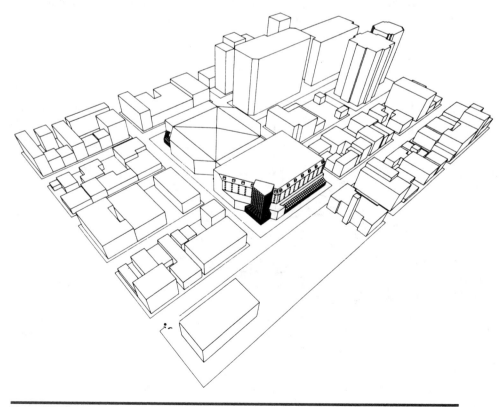

Figure 19.31
Perspective view PERSP1

Figure 19.32
Perspective view PERSP2

```
Distance = 1650'
Zoom = 22
```

Exit the DVIEW command to apply the settings to the entire model.
Using the VIEW command, save the perspective view as PERSP1.
2. The following settings will achieve the perspective view PERSP2 shown in Figure 19.32. Use the Points option to place the camera and the target points, and set the Distance and Zoom values.

```
Points-Target = 762'10",979'9",152'5"
Camera = 447'8",563'6",14'8"
Distance = 540'
Zoom = 25
```

Exit the DVIEW command to apply the settings to the entire model.
Using the VIEW command, save the perspective view as PERSP2.
3. The following settings will achieve the perspective view PERSP3 shown in Figure 19.33. Use the Points option to place the camera and the target points, and set the Distance and Zoom values.

```
Points-Target = 560',1331'9",30'
Camera = 440',1460',100'
Distance = 189'1"
Zoom = 20
```

Exit the DVIEW command to apply the settings to the entire model.
Using the VIEW command, save the perspective view as PERSP3.
4. The following settings will achieve the perspective view PERSP4 as shown in Figure 19.34. Use the Points option to place the camera and the target points, and set the Distance and Zoom values.

```
Points-Target = 925',1083'9",78'8"
Camera = 925',1083'9",1078'8"
Distance = 1000'
Zoom = 15
```

Exit the DVIEW command to apply the settings to the entire model.

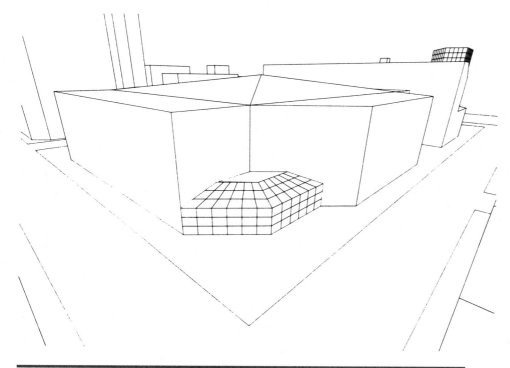

Figure 19.33
Perspective view PERSP3

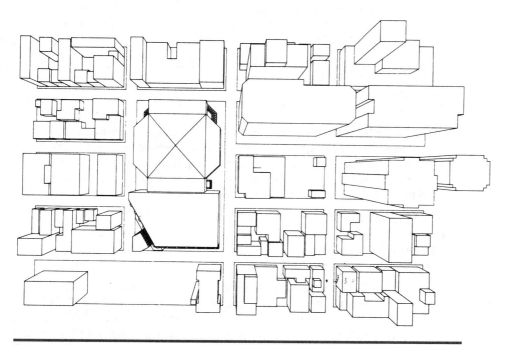

Figure 19.34
Perspective view PERSP4

Using the VIEW command, save the perspective view as PERSP4.

5. Save the model as CITY.

Using the HIDE Command

Select the HIDE command, and await the outcome. (This may be a good time to complete other homework, do a needlework project, or mow the neighbor's yard for extra cash!) When the HIDE command is finished, immediately make a slide of the display to avoid having to redo the HIDE command to display the model again. Call the slide PERSP4.

Using the VIEW command, restore the other three perspectives. Select the HIDE command after each view is restored and, when the command is finished, make a slide.

Rendering the Model

Note: For a discussion on rendering models, see the final section in Chapter 18.

Here are sample settings to create a rendering of the city in the daytime using the RENDER utility. There will be only one light, and that will represent the sun. Refer to Figure 19.35 for a laser plot of the rendered model.

> *Rendering Preferences:* Use default settings. There is no need for Smooth Shading.
>
> *Lights:*

NAME	TYPE	INTENSITY	LIGHT LOCATION	TARGET LOCATION
sun	distant	1.0	$-150', 1050', 1000'$	$815', 1073', 0'$
ambient		1.0		

Figure 19.35
Rendered view of the city model

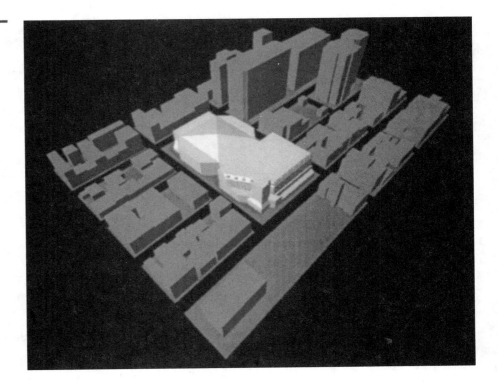

CHAPTER 20

Mechanical Project: Surface Modeling

Overview

In this chapter, you will create a surface model of a common mechanical object—a split pillow block. The project will illustrate techniques for creating holes in surfaces, forming unusual shapes, and adding curved and slotted surfaces. You will practice more complex techniques, rather than the extrusion methods required by the linear nature of the previous architectural projects.

Approaches to this type of model are varied, including the use of 3D meshes and solid modeling, which is perhaps the most desirable and popular method (see Chapter 12 for the solid modeling of a split pillow block). Here, we use surfaces to create a mechanical model. Also, to ensure that the final presentation view is not too cluttered with surface lines, we use 3D faces.

Concepts Explored

- Continued reinforcement of AutoCAD features
- Creation of a complex 3D model of a mechanical object
- Generation of 3D symbols
- Use of 3D symbols to construct the final model
- Creation of paper space layouts of multiple views
- Final production of shaded and rendered images.

20.1 Introduction

The project in this chapter will create a split pillow block model, illustrated in Figure 20.1, by generating individual parts and then assembling them into the final product. The parts are composed of curved, holed, and slotted surfaces, representing the complex aspects of mechanical design. When this model is finished, you should be able to manipulate it completely within 3D space, view it from any location, explode the parts for better viewing, and reassemble them. As with the other projects in this text, the goal here is not to train you in the design of a particular mechanical component; rather, it is to facilitate your understanding and application of the methods of 3D creation. To that end, this project is similar to Lab 12.B using solid modeling.

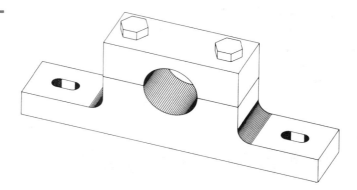

Figure 20.1
Axonometric display of assembled mechanical project

20.2 Project Stages

A project involving the creation of a mechanical assembly should be an organized one. Even though this project does not have numerous parts, organizing the fabrication will simplify the modeling and reinforce the techniques you will need to apply to more complex models in the future. This project lends itself to obvious divisions: (1) the manufacture of the individual components, (2) their assembly, and (3) their disassembly. Within those divisions, the fabrication can be organized by the common creation techniques. Normally, the order of fabrication in a mechanical design is unique for every project. In this project, however, you will be able to apply some of the underlying commonalities to subsequent mechanical projects.

PROJECT STAGES
1. Division of mechanical model (into parts)
2. Layer designations (for surfaces, symbols)
3. Upper yoke fabrication
4. Lower yoke fabrication
5. Connection bolt fabrication
6. Assembly of the components
7. Presentation display (in multiple views)
8. Disassembly of the model
9. Rendering the model

Stage 1: Division of the Mechanical Model

Creating a complex model is more easily accomplished if it can be done in sections. By identifying separate entities within the model, the creation task is simplified and the model is easier to manipulate after creation. The sections into which this model are divided are given in the following list:

- Creation of orientation cubes
- Creation of wireframe superstructure
- Addition of predefined surface models (holes and slots)
- Creation of surfaces to cover the combined symbols and superstructure.

Stage 2: Layer Designations

As noted before, it is very important that layer designation take place early in the development stages. Being able to make entities visible or invisible will facilitate the construction and later display of the final model. Most of the layers will be named now, but some layers will not be created until 3D creation actually takes place.

In this model, assembly is broken down into the following parts:

Part 1: Upper YOKE (UYOKE model)
Part 2: Lower YOKE (LYOKE model)
Part 3: Connecting bolt (BOLT model)

Because only the first 8 characters of the layer name (which can have as many as 31 characters) are visible on the status line, the names for the layers of this model will have only 8 characters. For example, P1-WIRE would represent the wireframe for part 1.

The layers to be created at the start of each model (UYOKE and LYOKE) are listed here:

LAYER COLOR	LAYER NAME	LAYER DESCRIPTION
**	P*-SYM	3D symbol model of individual part
1	P*-WIRE	Wireframe for individual part
2	P*-SURF	Surfaces for individual part
3	P*-HOLE	3D symbol of a hole
4	P*-ARCX	Arc extrusion to represent sides of holes
5	P*-TEMP	Layer used for temporary construction

Notes: The double asterisks (**) identify a layer with multiple colors. Remember that the single asterisk (*) will be replaced by the appropriate part number.

Two layers will automatically be created when the HOLE symbol blocks are inserted into the model. These layers are HOLESURF and MARKER, and they contain the surfaces and the marker locations of the hole.

For construction purposes, give each section type its own color. The separate colors will make it easier to distinguish what is on each layer. The color you choose for each section type is not important at this point.

Again, recall that it is customary to use continuous linetype for all construction.

Stage 3: Upper Yoke Fabrication

Initial Settings

Refer to Figure 20.2 for an illustration of the finished upper yoke model. Start a new model called UYOKE. Create the layers listed previously, and assign the appropriate colors. The following settings need to be entered before modeling can begin:

```
    SETTINGS
Units = Fractional
Limits = -1,-1, to 6,2
Grid = 1/8
Snap Incr. = 1/8
Initial Elevation = 0
Initial Thickness = 0
Pdmode = 2
Pdsize = 1/8
Splframe = 1
UCS = WCS
UCSICON = on and set to ORIGIN
```

Remember to ZOOM All, so that the display shows the set limits. If you would like to set any other settings, do so now, before creating the orientation cube.

To facilitate construction, start, intermediate, and end points will be given as required. They will be identified as P1, P2, and so on. Simply enter each 3D point in sequence until all points in the series have been entered.

Figure 20.2
Completed upper yoke model

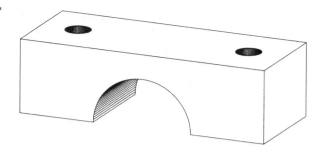

Creation of the Orientation Cube

An orientation cube (shown in Figure 20.3) will be created to define the 3D boundaries of the model.

```
    SETTINGS
  Layer = P1-TEMP
  Elevation = 0
  Thickness = 3/4
  UCS = WCS
  Viewports = single viewport displaying isometric view
  (1,-1,1)
```

Using the LINE command, draw the perimeter representing the orientation cube as shown in Figure 20.3. The orientation cube is 2-1/2″ in the X direction, 1″ in the Y direction, and 3/4″ in the Z direction. The lower left corner must start at 0,0,0.

```
P1 = 0,0,0              P2 = 2-1/2,0,0
P3 = 2-1/2,1,0          P4 = 0,1,0
CLOSE.
```

Insertion of Hole 3D Symbols on the Upper Yoke

Now insert the symbols for the hole models (HOLE2 and HOLE4) created in Lab 7.A in Chapter 7. These two symbols represent the holes through which the connecting bolts will pass. One hole symbol will be placed on the front of the cube to represent half the hole that goes through the front of the assembly. The other will be used as two smaller "whole" holes, placed on the top of the cube. Define a working plane for each surface to allow proper alignment when the symbols are inserted.

Once you have placed the hole symbols, you will create arcs with thicknesses to represent the sides of the holes. Refer to Figure 20.4.

```
    SETTINGS
  Layer = P1-HOLE
```

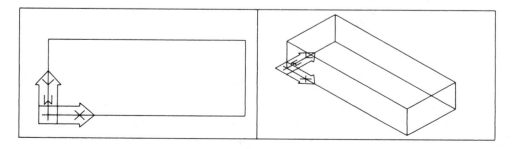

Figure 20.3
Orientation cube

392

Figure 20.4

The half hole and the arc on the front face

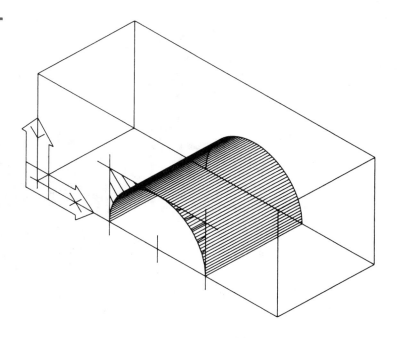

```
Elevation = 0
Thickness = 0
UCS = front plane of the cube as shown in Figure 20.4
```

Using the INSERT command, place the 3D symbol HOLE2 at the coordinates 1-1/4,0,0.

```
Scale = 1
Rotation = 0
```

Half a hole with a radius of 1/2″ should now be present. Copy this half hole to the rear surface of the cube.

```
        SETTINGS
Layer = P1-ARCX
Elevation = 0
Thickness = −1
```

Because the hole sides have no inside surfaces, you can use an extruded arc to create the inside surface of the half hole. Using the ARC command, create an arc to represent the inside of the half hole.

```
        SETTINGS
Layer = P1-HOLE
Elevation = 0
Thickness = 0
UCS = top plane of the cube as shown in Figure 20.5
```

Using the INSERT command, place the 3D symbol HOLE1 at the two coordinates 3/8,1/2,0 and 2-1/8,1/2,0

```
Scale = 0.25
Rotation = 0
```

The two inserted holes are 1/4″ in diameter.

```
        SETTINGS
Layer = P1-ARCX
Elevation = 0
Thickness = −3/4
```

Figure 20.5
Insertion of holes on the top face

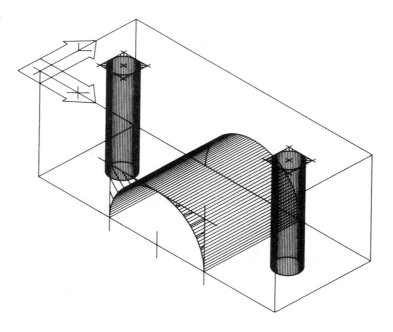

Using the ARC command, create two arcs for each hole to represent the sides of the holes. We use two arcs instead of a circle because a circle has a surface covering its area.

Creation of Surfaces on the Upper Yoke

Because the holes pass through the upper yoke, we need to create surfaces that surround the holes and yet leave them open. (If you need a refresher course in this technique, refer to Chapter 7, Lab 7.B.)

Special note: There is an AutoLISP program that can make 3DFACE edges visible and invisible after surfaces have been created. The program is called EDGE.LSP. Whenever you are going to use the 3DFACE command, load the EDGE program first so that if you forget to make an edge invisible, you can go back and correct it using the EDGE program.

```
    SETTINGS
  Layer = P1-SURF
  Elevation = 0
  Thickness = 0
  UCS = WCS
```

Also, thaw layer MARKER to show the snap points of the hole.

Using the 3DFACE command, draw the surfaces shown in Figure 20.6. Working in the isometric viewport, follow points P1 to P8 using object snaps. Make all the edges, except the outer perimeter, invisible. Remember to use the Invisible edge option before selecting the start of each of the edges.

Using the 3DFACE command again, draw the surfaces shown in Figure 20.7. Follow the points P1 to P8 using object snaps while working in the isometric viewport. Make all the edges, except the outer perimeter, invisible. Remember to use the Invisible edge option before selecting the start of each of the edges. Repeat this procedure for the inner surface marked PA to PD.

Finishing the Upper Yoke

The bottom and side surfaces of the yoke will be completed now. Create a new working plane for the bottom. Referring to Figure 20.8, copy the holes from the top or reinsert the hole symbol. After placing the holes, use the 3DFACE command to add new surfaces to the bottom and sides.

Figure 20.6
Adding surfaces on the front face

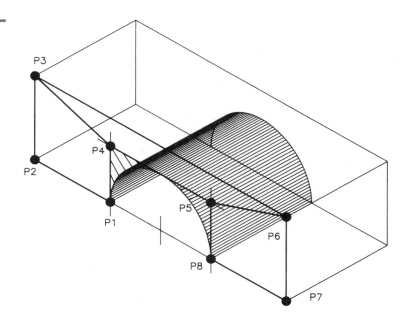

Figure 20.7
Adding surfaces on the top face

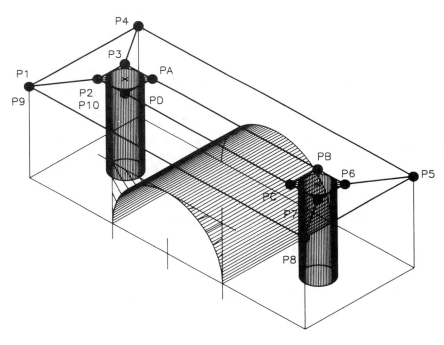

Figure 20.8
Completing the bottom face

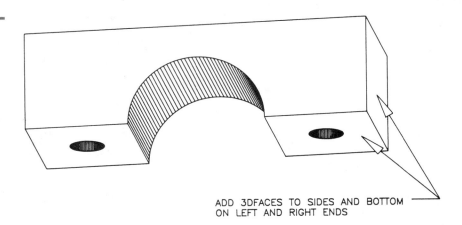

ADD 3DFACES TO SIDES AND BOTTOM
ON LEFT AND RIGHT ENDS

Because the bottom holes and surfaces will be needed for the lower yoke, make a copy of them and save them as a new file. Call the file BHOLES (Bolt HOLES). In this way, they can simply be inserted into the lower yoke model and will not have to be created again.

Freeze the P1-TEMP layer so that the orientation cube disappears. Then, save the current model as UYOKE (Upper YOKE). Finally, using the VPOINT and HIDE commands, move around the model and observe the results. The model should look similar to Figure 20.2.

Stage 4: Lower Yoke Fabrication

Initial Settings

Refer to Figure 20.9 for the finished model of the lower yoke. Call this model LYOKE. Create the layers listed in stage 2 and assign the appropriate colors. Enter the following settings before beginning construction:

```
SETTINGS
Units = Fractional
Limits = −1,−1, to 6,2
Grid = 1/8
Snap Incr. = 1/8
Initial Elevation = 0
Initial Thickness = 0
Pdmode = 2
Pdsize = 1/8
Splframe = 1
UCS = WCS
UCSICON = on and set to ORIGIN
```

Remember to ZOOM All, so that the display shows the set limits. If you would like to enter any other settings, now is the time to do so.

Start, intermediate, and end points (identified as P1, P2, and so forth) will be given as required. Enter each 3D point in sequence.

Creation of the Orientation Cube

Two orientation cubes will be created to define the 3D boundaries of the model.

```
SETTINGS
Layer = P2-TEMP
```

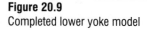

Figure 20.9
Completed lower yoke model

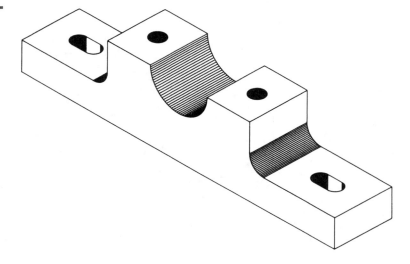

Figure 20.10
The two orientation cubes

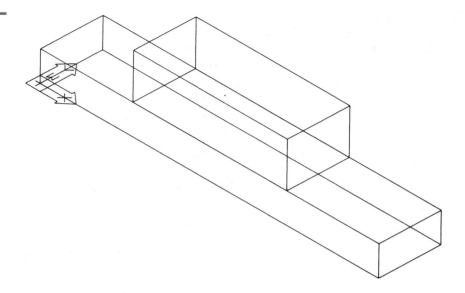

```
Elevation = 0
Thickness = 1/2
UCS = WCS
Viewports = single viewport displaying isometric view
(VPOINT 1,−1,1)
```

Using the LINE command, draw the perimeter representing the first orientation cube, as shown in Figure 20.10. The orientation cube is 5-1/2″ in the *X* direction, 1″ in the *Y* direction, and 1/2″ in the *Z* direction. The lower left corner must start at 0,0,0.

```
P1 = 0,0,0            P2 = 5-1/2,0,0
P3 = 5-1/2,1,0        P4 = 0,1,0
CLOSE.
```

```
      SETTINGS
Layer = P2-TEMP
Elevation = 0
Thickness = 3/4
UCS = WCS
Viewports = single viewport displaying isometric view
(VPOINT 1,−1,1)
```

Using the LINE command again, draw the perimeter representing the second orientation cube, as shown in Figure 20.10. The orientation cube is 2-1/2″ in the *X* direction, 1″ in the *Y* direction, and 3/4″ in the *Z* direction.

```
P1 = 1-1/2,0,1/2      P2 = 4,0,1/2
P3 = 4,1,1/2          P4 = 1-1/2,1,1/2
CLOSE.
```

Insertion of Hole 3D Symbols on the Lower Yoke

Now is the time to insert the symbols for the hole models (HOLE2 and HOLE4) created in Lab 7.A in Chapter 7. One hole symbol (HOLE2) will be placed on the front of the cube, representing half the hole that goes through the front of the assembly. On the same working plane, two fillets will be created to make use of the HOLE4 symbols.

On the top of the cube, two smaller "whole" holes will be placed, serving as the holes through which the connecting bolts will pass. The symbol model BHOLES (created during the construction of the upper yoke) will be used for these holes. We will also construct two slots in the base of the lower yoke. A working plane must be defined for each surface to allow proper alignment when the symbols are inserted. Refer to Figure 20.11.

```
       SETTINGS
Layer = P2-HOLE
Elevation = 0
Thickness = 0
UCS = front plane of the cube, as shown in Figure
20.11
```

Using the INSERT command, place the 3D symbol HOLE2 at the coordinates 2-3/4,1-1/4,0.

```
Scale = 1
Rotation = 180
```

Half a hole with a diameter of 1″ (radius of 1/2″) should now be present.

Using the INSERT command again, place the 3D symbol HOLE4 at the coordinates 4-1/4,3/4,0.

```
Scale = 0.5
Rotation = 90
```

Using the INSERT command one more time, place the 3D symbol HOLE4 at the coordinates 1-1/4,3/4,0.

```
Scale = 0.5
Rotation = 180
```

Two fillets with a diameter of 1/2″ (radius of 1/4″) should now be present.

```
       SETTINGS
Layer = P2-ARCX
Elevation = 0
Thickness =  −1
```

Using the ARC command, create arcs for the half hole and the fillets to represent the sides of the holes. Then, copy the hole symbols to the rear of the part.

```
       SETTINGS
Layer = P2-HOLE
Elevation = 0
Thickness = 0
UCS = top of the cube, as shown in Figure 20.12
```

Figure 20.11
Aligning the UCS and inserting the holes

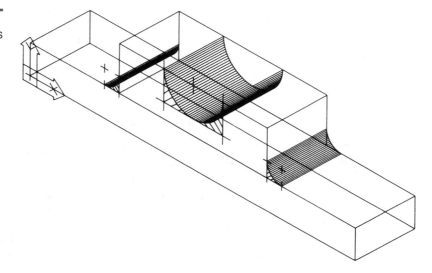

Figure 20.12
Aligning the UCS and adding the hole
symbols

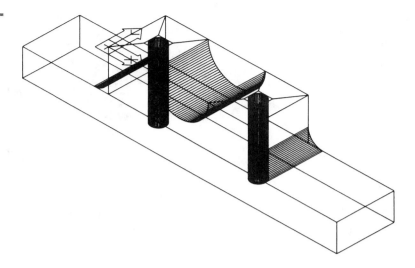

Using the INSERT command, place the 3D symbol BHOLES at the coordinates 0,0,0.

```
Scale = 1
Rotation = 0
```

The two bolt holes should now be on the top of the yoke.

```
        SETTINGS
Layer = P2-ARCX
Elevation = 0
Thickness = -1-1/4
```

Using the ARC command, create two sets of arcs to represent the sides of the holes.

```
        SETTINGS
Layer = P2-HOLE
Elevation = 0
Thickness = 0
UCS = top of the base plate, as shown in Figure 20.13
```

Using the INSERT command, first place the 3D symbol HOLE2 at the coordinates 1/2,1/2,0.

```
Scale = 1/4
Rotation = 90
```

Second, place the 3D symbol HOLE2 at the coordinates 3/4,1/2,0.

```
Scale = 1/4
Rotation = -90
```

Third, place the 3D symbol HOLE2 at the coordinates 4-3/4,1/2,0.

```
Scale = 1/4
Rotation = 90
```

Fourth, place the 3D symbol HOLE2 at the coordinates 5,1/2,0.

```
Scale = 1/4
Rotation = -90
        SETTINGS
Layer = P2-ARCX
Elevation = 0
Thickness = -1/2
```

Use the ARC command to create an arc for the half hole of each slot to represent the sides of the slots. Then, create the straight sides of the slots using the LINE command.

Figure 20.13
Aligning the UCS and adding the slots

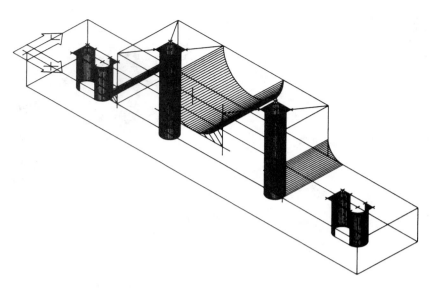

Creation of Surfaces on the Lower Yoke

Because the holes and slots pass through the lower yoke, surfaces need to be created that surround the holes and yet leave them open. (Check Chapter 7, Lab 7.B, for a refresher on this procedure.)

```
     SETTINGS
Layer = P2-SURF
Elevation = 0
Thickness = 0
UCS = WCS
Thaw layer MARKER (to show snap points of holes).
```

Using the 3DFACE command, draw the surfaces shown in Figures 20.14 and 20.15. Use the Invisible edge option as required. Copy the completed surface to the rear of the model and to the other side.

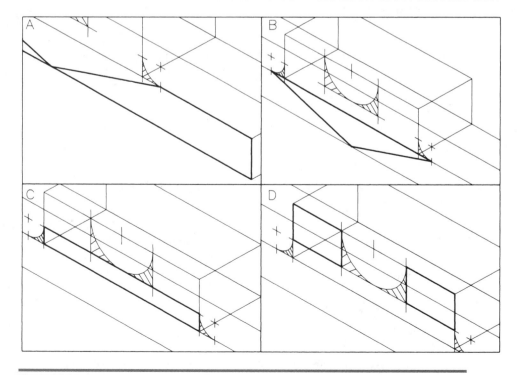

Figure 20.14
Adding surfaces around the holes

Figure 20.15
Adding surfaces around the slot

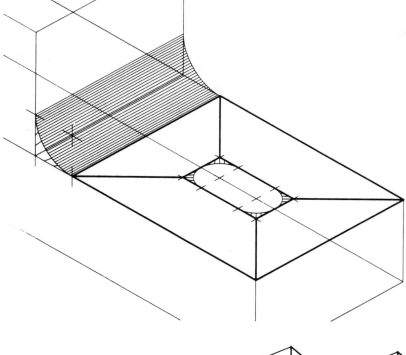

Figure 20.16
Finishing the lower yoke model

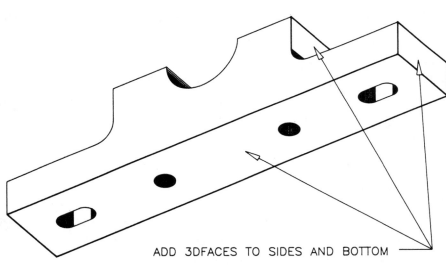

ADD 3DFACES TO SIDES AND BOTTOM

Finishing the Lower Yoke

To complete the bottom and side surfaces of the yoke, first create a new work-ing plane for the bottom. Referring to Figure 20.16, copy the hole symbols from the top, or reinsert the hole symbol. After you have placed the holes, use the 3DFACE command to add new surfaces to the bottom and sides. Then, save the current model as LYOKE (Lower YOKE).

Using the VPOINT and HIDE commands, move around the model and observe the results. The model should look similar to Figure 20.9.

Stage 5: Connection Bolt Fabrication

A three-dimensional model of a 1/4″ bolt is needed now. This bolt symbol will be used to connect the upper yoke to the lower yoke in the assembly. The model BOLT, created in Chapter 7, Assignment 1, will be used as this bolt sym-bol. (If you have not created the bolt at this point, turn back to the assignment and do so.) The bolt is illustrated in Figure 20.17.

Figure 20.17
Bolt model

401

Stage 6: Assembly of the Components

At this point in the project, all the required parts have been fabricated and are ready for assembly. Before we can insert the parts, a separate assembly file must be created. Call it SPB (Split Pillow Block).

Create the following layers and assign the appropriate colors. Then, enter the settings listed.

LAYER COLOR	LAYER NAME	LAYER DESCRIPTION
5	P1-SYM	3D symbol model of part 1
6	P2-SYM	3D symbol model of part 1
7	P3-SYM	3D symbol model of part 1

```
      SETTINGS
  Units = Fractional
  Limits = -1,-1, to 6,2
  Grid = 1/8
  Snap Incr. = 1/8
  Initial Elevation Thickness = 0
  Initial Thickness = 0
  Pdmode = 2
  Pdsize = 1/8
  Splframe = 0
  UCS = WCS
  UCSICON = on and set to ORIGIN
  Initial Layer = P2-SYM
```

Remember to ZOOM All, so that the display shows the set limits.

Inserting the Parts

Using the INSERT command, first insert part 2, LYOKE (Lower YOKE), at the coordinates 0,0,0. Refer to Figure 20.18A.

```
  Scale = 1
  Rotation = 0
      SETTINGS
  Layer = P1-SYM
  UCS = WCS
```

Second, insert part 1, UYOKE (Upper YOKE), at the coordinates 1-1/2,0, 1-1/4. Refer to Figure 20.18B.

```
  Scale = 1
  Rotation = 0
      SETTINGS
  Layer = P3-SYM
  UCS = WCS
```

Third, insert part 3, BOLT (connecting BOLT), at two sets of coordinates: 1-7/8,1/2,2 and 3-5/8,1/2,2. Refer to Figure 20.18C.

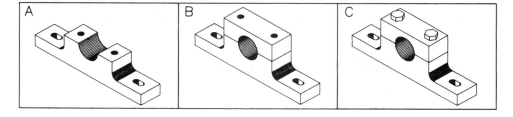

Figure 20.18
Assembly of parts

```
Scale = 1
Rotation = 0
Freeze the MARKER and P*-TEMP layers.
```

Save the model as SPB. You have now created an assembled model of a split pillow block. It can be viewed from any location.

Stage 7: Presentation Display

To present the model of the split pillow block, four paper space viewports will be created, each with its own scaled view of the model. If you have used paper space before now, turn off the layers containing the previously created viewports and create new ones as follows:

1. Using the TILEMODE command, switch to paper space by giving it the value of 0.
2. Create a layer called VPORTS, and make it active. Using the MVIEW command, split the screen into four equal viewports.
3. Using the MSPACE command, switch to model space and proceed to display the top, front, right-side, and isometric views of the model, as shown in Figure 20.19. By utilizing the XP option under the ZOOM command, the contents of each viewport will be the same size. Set the XP value to 1.
4. Using the PSPACE command, switch to paper space.
5. Using the MVIEW command, set each viewport to "Hideplot" so that, when plotted, each viewport will display a hidden line removed plot.
6. Freeze the layer called VPORTS so that the border of the viewport is not visible and will not plot.
7. Save the model as SPB.
8. If a plotter is available, plot the paper space layout.

Stage 8: Disassembly of the Model

Depending on the usage, it is sometimes desirable to have an exploded view of an assembly. Here is how you would accomplish that:

1. Open the model SPB.

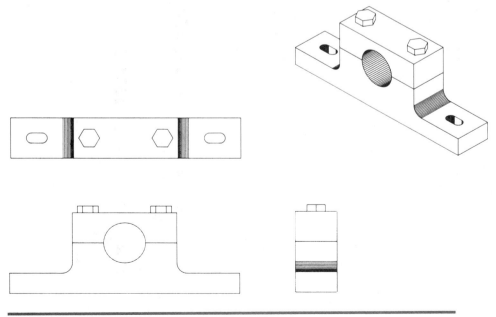

Figure 20.19
Four-view display of the model

SETTINGS
UCS = WCS
TILEMODE = 1

2. Using the MOVE command, select the upper yoke and the connecting bolt parts. Use a displacement of 0,0,1-1/4, and press <Enter> for the second point.
3. Using the MOVE command, select the connecting bolt part. Use a displacement of 0,0,2-1/4, and press <Enter> for the second point.
4. Using the VPOINT command and the XP option of the ZOOM command, display the new views at a proper scale. Refer to Figure 20.20.
5. Save the model as SPB2. You now have an exploded view of the split pillow block assembly.
6. If a plotter is available, plot the paper space layout. If a plotter is unavailable, switch to model space, and use the HIDE command in each viewport.

Stage 9: Rendering the Model

For general information about the rendering of models, refer to the final section in Chapter 18.

The sample settings listed here will create a rendering of the exploded split pillow block model using the RENDER utility. The settings place three lights so that their intensity can be increased or decreased to highlight any desired side. A laser plot of the rendered model is shown in Figure 20.21.

Rendering Preferences: Use default settings, and set the Rendering options to "no" for Smooth Shading and Apply Materials.

NAME	TYPE	INTENSITY	LIGHT LOCATION	TARGET LOCATION
front	distant	0.15	2¾, −2¾, 1¼	2¾, 0, 1¼
side	distant	0.5	8, ½, 1	5½, ½, 1
top	distant	0.3	2¾, ½, 6	2¾, ½, 2
ambient		0.6		

Figure 20.20
Exploded view of the split pillow block

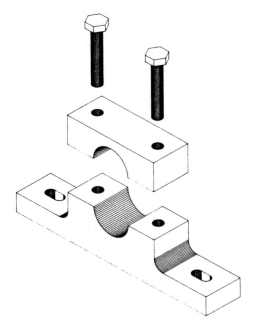

Figure 20.21
Rendered view of the exploded
assembly

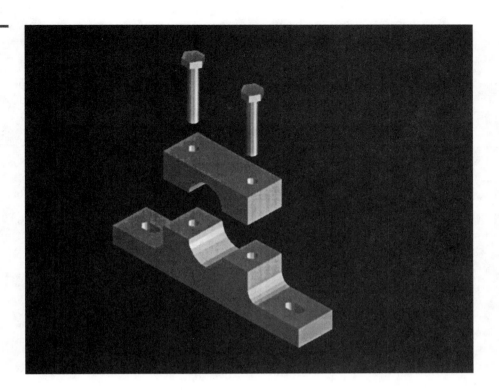

CHAPTER **21**

Mechanical Project: Solid Modeling

Overview

This chapter provides instruction on the creation of a cellular flip-phone using solid modeling techniques. The project will reinforce skills gained in the previous chapters on solid modeling and will demonstrate that using solid modeling can be easier than surface modeling, especially when adding holes to a model. This project uses filleting extensively, illustrating the ease with which it is possible in solid modeling.

Concepts Explored

- Extrusion of polylines to create a solid
- Filleting of edges of solid models and filleting behavior
- Creation of complex composite solids
- Generation of shaded and rendered images
- Possibilities of StereoLithography.

21.1 Introduction

The mechanical project in this chapter requires you to use solid modeling to create the body of a cellular flip-phone. Refer to Figure 21.1 for two views of the final model. If desired you could complete the project by creating all the pieces and assembling them into a complete flip-phone. The use of solid modeling to create this model also lends itself to the possibility of creating a physical prototype model using StereoLithography. By means of a laser, it is possible to create a tangible prototype of a 3D CAD model quickly. The process breaks down a CAD model into a series of "slices" of model data that is used to control a laser to form a prototype, slice by slice. One process, called Stereo-Lithography Apparatus (SLA), uses a laser to harden a liquid polymer. Refer to Figure 21.27 at the end of this chapter for a demonstration of SLA. Auto-CAD has the ability to create an ASCII text file of a solid model that can be used by SLA. The command to create the file is STLOUT.

Figure 21.1
Two views of flip-phone solid model

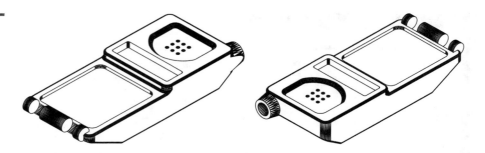

21.2 Project Stages

This project is broken into several stages to facilitate creation.

PROJECT STAGES

1. Division of the solid model into component sections
2. Layer designations
3. Creation of the extruded body
4. Rounding of vertical edges
5. Addition of hinge section
6. Rounding of horizontal body edges
7. Creation and subtraction of ear section
8. Creation and subtraction of display section
9. Creation and subtraction of control section
10. Addition of antenna section
11. Rendering the model
12. StereoLithography

Stage 1: Division of the Solid Model

Creation of any complex solid model is easily accomplished if it can be done in logical sections. Figure 21.2 shows the profile views of the model. There are various distinct component sections into which the model can be broken, as listed here:

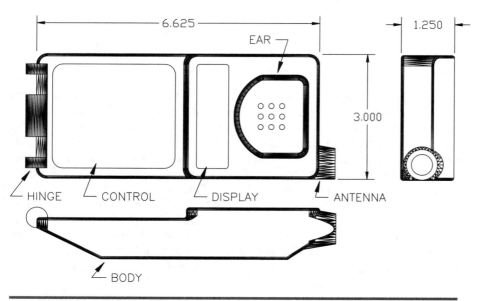

Figure 21.2
Profile views of the model

- The main body that will be used as the base
- The hinge section
- The ear section
- The display section
- The control section
- The antenna section.

Stage 2: Layer Designations

Using layers to differentiate between the various sections and components of a solid model will facilitate creation and display of the model. Layers can be frozen and thawed at will, making it easier to work on different parts of the model without other components obstructing views. The layers for this model are based on the component sections. Note that when one solid is added to another solid, it takes on the properties of the parent solid, including its color. So, don't be surprised if you add one solid to another and its color changes.

LAYER COLOR	LAYER NAME	LAYER DESCRIPTION
1	BODY	Main body of the phone
2	HINGE	Hinge solid before addition to the body
3	EAR	Ear solid before subtraction from the body
4	DISPLAY	Display solid before subtraction from the body
5	CONTROL	Control solid before subtraction from the body
6	ANTENNA	Antenna solid before addition to the body
7	OCUBE	Rectangular box to contain the model

Stage 3: Creation of the Extruded Body

Initial Settings

Start a new model called PHONE. Create the layers listed previously, and assign the appropriate colors. Proceed with the following settings:

```
     SETTINGS
Units = Decimal
Limits = —1,—1 to 4,7
Grid = 0.125
Snap Incr. = 0.125
Initial Elevation = 0
Initial Thickness = 0
UCS = WCS
UCSICON = ON and set to ORIGIN
```

Remember to ZOOM All, so that the display shows the set limits. If you would like to choose any other settings, do so now, before the creation of the orientation cube.

Creation of the Orientation Cube

An orientation cube (profile shown in Figure 21.3) will be created to define the three-dimensional boundaries of the body.

```
     SETTINGS
Layer = OCUBE
Elevation = 0
Thickness = 1.25
```

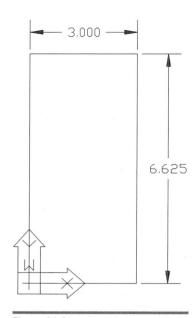

Figure 21.3
OCUBE profile

Using the LINE command, draw the perimeter representing the orientation cube as shown in Figure 21.3. The lower left corner must start at 0,0,0.

Creation of Body Profile

You are now going to create the profile of the body along the side of the orientation cube.

```
SETTINGS
Layer = BODY
Elevation = 0
Thickness = 0
UCS = set to the side of the body (Figure 21.4)
```

You may want to divide your screen into several viewports similar to the ones shown in Figure 21.4. Use the PLINE command to create the closed profile, as shown in Figure 21.4.

Extrusion of the Profile

Use the solid command EXTRUDE to create the extruded body, as shown in Figure 21.5. The thickness will be –3 inches and there will be no taper angle.

Stage 4: Rounding of Vertical Edges

Now that the body has been extruded, it is time to round (fillet) the vertical edges of the body. Because of the calculations involved when filleting a solid model, it should be broken down into small areas wherever possible.

Use the FILLET command and round the edges as shown in Figure 21.6. The radius is 0.25.

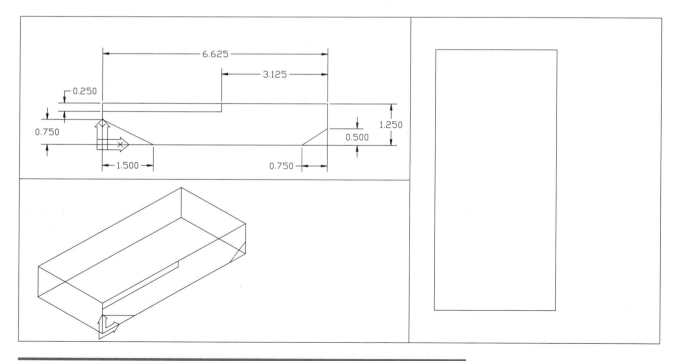

Figure 21.4
Profile of body

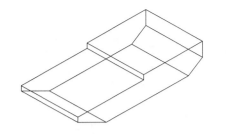

Figure 21.5
Extruded body

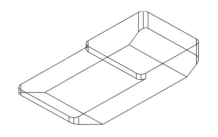

Figure 21.6
Rounding the vertical edges

Stage 5: Addition of Hinge Section

The hinge section must be broken down into two parts. The first part will be added to the body and the second part will need to be removed from the body.

```
    SETTINGS
  Layer = HINGE
  Freeze the OCUBE layer
  Elevation = 0
  Thickness = 0
  UCS = set to the side of the body (Figure 21.7)
```

Using the CYLINDER command, create the solid cylinder as shown in Figure 21.7. Note that the start of the cylinder is –0.250 inches in the Z direction from the face of the body.

Using the UNION command, add the hinge cylinder to the body.

Now create the two solid cylinders that will be subtracted from the body. Refer to Figure 21.8 for their size and placement. Use the SUBTRACT command to subtract them from the body. The results should look like Figure 21.9. The HIDE command was used to help show what was subtracted.

Stage 6: Rounding of Horizontal Body Edges

At this stage extensive filleting to round the edges of the body will take place. Most of the body will be rounded except for the hinge area and the area where the sloped edges meet the back. The filleting is broken into different steps to help clarify and simplify the process. Figures 21.10 through 21.13 illustrate each filleting step.

Figure 21.7
Solid cylinder creation

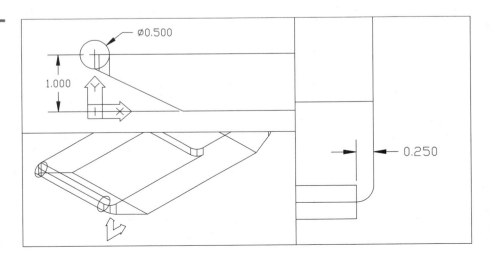

Figure 21.8
Subtracting the two cylinders from the body

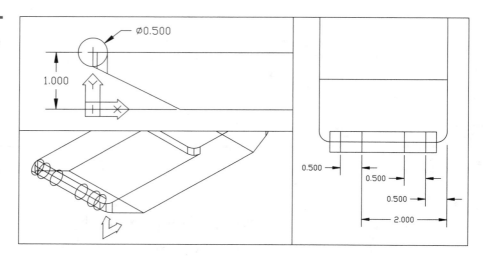

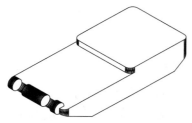

Figure 21.9
Results of subtracting cylinder from the body

Step 1	Figure 21.10 shows the filleting of the inner edge and curve.
Step 2	Figure 21.11 shows the filleting of the upper edge and curve. Remember to fillet both sides.
Step 3	Figure 21.12 shows the filleting of the top face edges. Remember to fillet all four edges at one time.
Step 4	Figure 21.13 shows the filleting of the bottom edges. All the bottom edges are filleted except for the curve that meets the hinge area and the two edges that are created where the slope meets the bottom.

Stage 7: Creation and Subtraction of Ear Section

You are going to create the ear section as a separate composite solid that includes the speaker holes. This composite solid will be subtracted from the body.

```
    SETTINGS
Layer = EAR
Thaw the OCUBE layer
Freeze the BODY layer
Elevation = 0
Thickness = 0
UCS = set to the top of the OCUBE
```

You can use lines and arcs or polylines to create the ear profile. No matter what method you initially use, you must turn the geometry into one closed

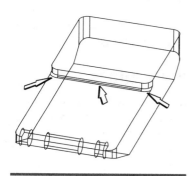

Figure 21.10
Fillet on inner edge and curve

Figure 21.11
Fillet on upper edge and curve

Figure 21.12
Fillet on top face edges

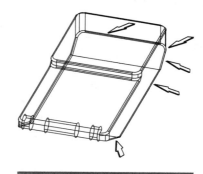

Figure 21.13
Fillet on bottom edges

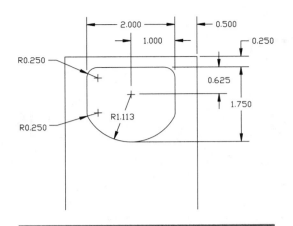

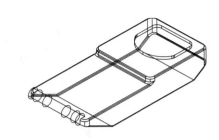

Figure 21.14
Creating the ear profile

Figure 21.15
Extruding the ear profile

polyline. If you use lines and arcs, use the PEDIT command to turn them into one closed polyline. Proceed to create the profile and refer to Figure 21.14.

Freeze the OCUBE layer and thaw the BODY layer.

Using the EXTRUDE command, turn the profile into a solid. Use –0.125 for the extrusion thickness and 0 for the taper angle. Refer to Figure 21.15 for the results.

Using the FILLET command, fillet the lower edge of the ear profile with a radius of 0.125. Refer to Figure 21.16.

Create the nine speaker holes using the CYLINDER command. The holes are 0.125 inches in diameter and 0.25 inches deep from the base of the ear solid. Each hole is 0.25 inches apart. Refer to Figure 21.17 for the center location of the pattern.

Once the holes are created, add them to the ear solid with the UNION command.

Using the SUBTRACT command, subtract the volume of the composite ear solid from the body. Use the HIDE command to observe the results.

Stage 8: Creation and Subtraction of Display Section

Create the rectangular box solid that represents the display area of the phone. This is where the digital readout of numbers dialed would be displayed.

```
    SETTINGS
Layer = DISPLAY
Elevation = 0
```

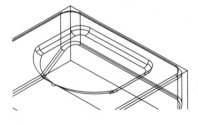

Figure 21.16
Fillet on lower edge of ear profile

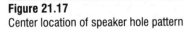

Figure 21.17
Center location of speaker hole pattern

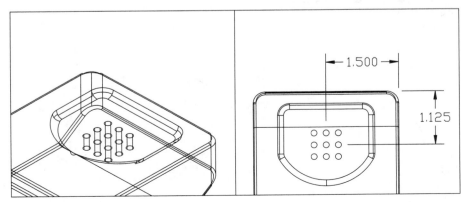

Figure 21.18
Creation of display solid

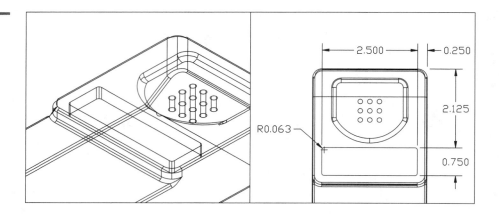

```
Thickness = 0
UCS = set to the top of the body
```

Refer to Figure 21.18 and create a closed polyline. Use the EXTRUDE command to create a solid with a depth of –0.25″.

Use the SUBTRACT command to take away the volume of the display solid from the body.

Stage 9: Creation and Subtraction of Control Section

Create the rectangular box solid that represents the control area of the phone. This is where the control buttons would be installed.

```
        SETTINGS
Layer = CONTROL
Elevation = 0
Thickness = 0
UCS = set to the top control area
```

Refer to Figure 21.19 and create a closed polyline. Use the EXTRUDE command to create a solid with a depth of –0.125″.

Use the SUBTRACT command to take away the volume of the control solid from the body.

Stage 10: Addition of Antenna Section

You are now going to create the antenna section of the phone. This area would house the antenna casing. You are going to use a circle to create a tapered truncated cone.

Figure 21.19
Creation of control solid

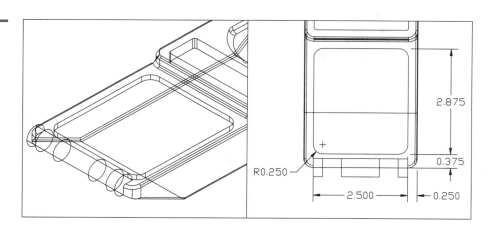

Figure 21.20
Creation of circle

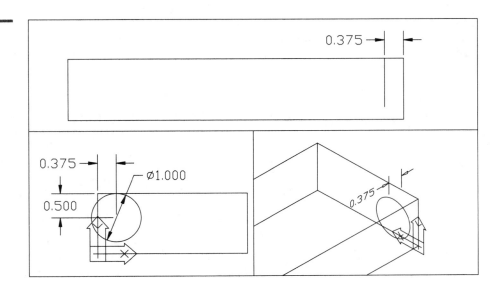

```
        SETTINGS
Layer = ANTENNA
Thaw the OCUBE layer
Freeze the BODY layer
Elevation = 0
Thickness = 0
UCS = set to the end of the OCUBE as shown in Figure
21.20
```

Use the CIRCLE command to draw the circle shown in Figure 21.20. Remember the center of the circle is –0.375″ from the end face.

Use the EXTRUDE command to turn the circle into a solid truncated cone. Use a thickness of 0.75 and a taper angle of 10 degrees. Refer to Figure 21.21 for the results of the extrusion. Notice how the edge of the antenna cone protrudes past the OCUBE and body. You are going to clip off this protrusion with the use of another solid.

Using the BOX command, create a solid as shown in Figure 21.22. Now, create a UCS working plane along the side of the OCUBE to help with the creation. Once the creation of the box is completed, use the SUBTRACT command to take its volume away from the cone volume. Refer to Figure 21.23 for the results.

Figure 21.21
Extrusion of circle

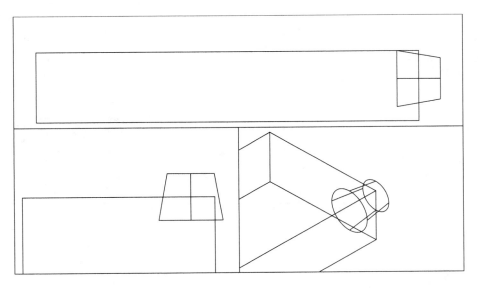

Figure 21.22
Creation of box solid

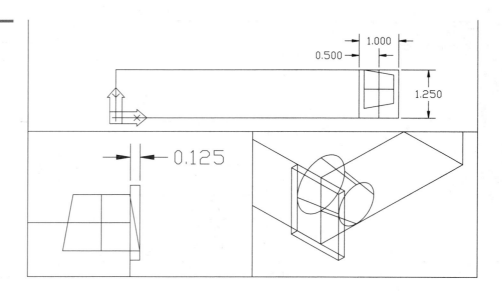

Figure 21.23
Subtracting box from cone

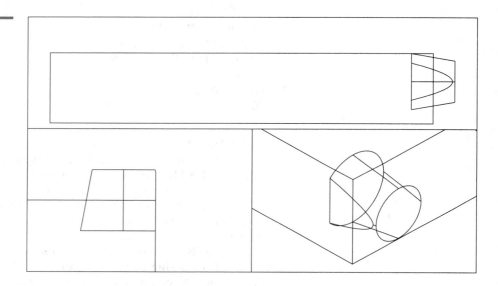

Using the UNION command, add the antenna solid to the body. Try the HIDE command to see the results. Refer to Figure 21.24, which shows the wireframe display and the hidden display.

Figure 21.24
Results of subtraction

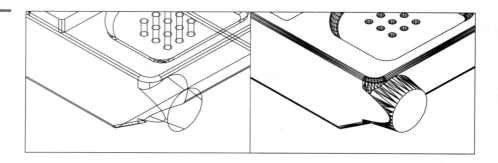

Figure 21.25
Subtracting a cylinder from the body

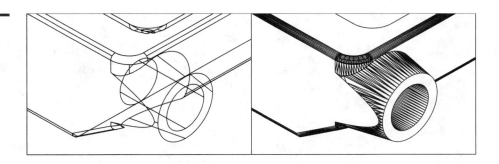

Figure 21.25
Subtracting a cylinder from the body

The antenna section requires a hole in it. Use the CYLINDER command to create a solid cylinder that is 0.5 inches in diameter and 0.625 inches deep. Place it in the center of the antenna section. Subtract the cylinder from the body. Refer to Figure 21.25 for the results.

Stage 11: Rendering the Model

For general information about rendering models, refer to the final section in Chapter 18.

The sample settings here will create a rendering of the phone solid model using the RENDER utility. The settings place two lights so the top and side surfaces may be highlighted. A laser plot of the rendered model is shown in Figure 21.26.

Lights:

NAME	TYPE	INTENSITY	LIGHT LOCATION	TARGET LOCATION
side	distant	1.00	5, 6.5, 2	2, 4, 1
top	point (inverse square)	1.24	1.5, 5.5, 3	
ambient		0.3		

Stage 12: StereoLithography

I wouldn't expect you to have access to a StereoLithography Apparatus (SLA), but if you refer to Figure 21.27 you can see the possible results of exporting your model using the STLOUT command.

Figure 21.26
Rendered view of flip-phone model

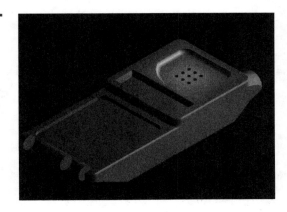

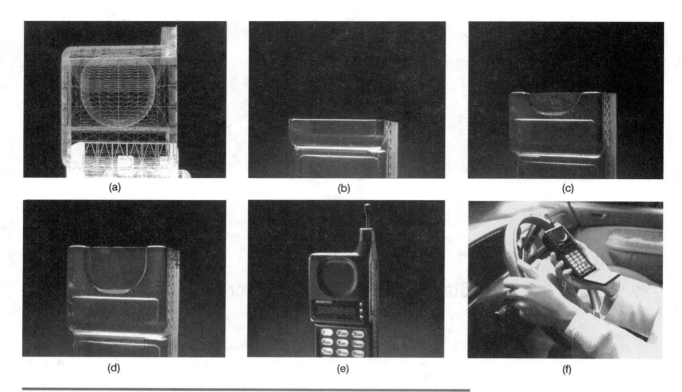

(a)　　　　　　　　　　(b)　　　　　　　　　　(c)

(d)　　　　　　　　　　(e)　　　　　　　　　　(f)

Figure 21.27
Physical model created from computer model using SLA
Source: Courtesy of 3D Systems, Inc., Valencia, California.

CHAPTER 22

Structural Project

Overview

In this project, you will model the structural members of a building. You will create and apply parametric (scalable) symbols and then compile the model with frames and supports represented by these symbols. (*A special note:* Third-party software that produces symbols similar to the ones you'll be creating in this project is available. By completing this project, however, you will learn how the symbols are produced and be able to create your own in future projects. Then, should you not have access to third-party software, all is not lost!)

Concepts Explored

- Continued use of AutoCAD features
- Creation of a complex three-dimensional model of the structural members of a commercial building
- Generation of 3D parametric symbols
- Use of 3D parametric symbols to create the model
- Discussion of 3D custom symbols and their creation for this project
- Production of ideally located perspective views
- Generation of shaded and rendered images.

22.1 Introduction

Although this project generates the structural framing for a warehouse, it does not create all the structural members that would be required for this type of building. It does, however, construct the most common members, which will illustrate the skills needed to create other structural members. Once this project is finished, you may want to construct other members to complete or enhance the model.

Like the other projects, this one is concerned with the application of three-dimensional modeling techniques, not with actual structural design. This project uses the structural discipline as a working environment to demonstrate the tools of three-dimensional modeling. In generating various 3D parametric models to compile the structure, the project demonstrates the usefulness of such symbols. And the presentation display stage will again enable you to create views from any location and display them. For a sample view of the completed project, see Figure 22.1.

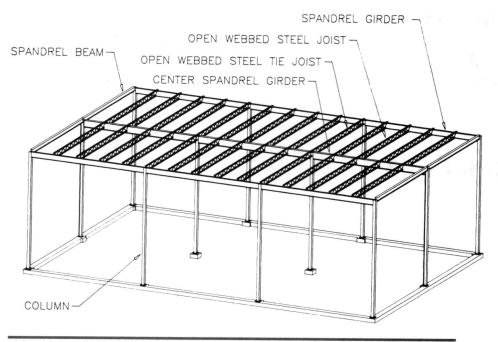

SPANDREL GIRDER

OPEN WEBBED STEEL JOIST

SPANDREL BEAM

OPEN WEBBED STEEL TIE JOIST

CENTER SPANDREL GIRDER

COLUMN

Figure 22.1
Axonometric view of the completed structural project

22.2 Project Stages

Dividing a project into stages allows for an organized progression. And when similarities in project stages can be identified and exploited, a project can be completed more efficiently.

This project is broken into stages that apply not only to the erection of the structural form but also to the creation of each member.

PROJECT STAGES
1. Division of structural form (into members)
2. Layer designations (for surfaces, symbols)
3. Parametric symbol creation (for beams, columns)
4. Custom symbol creation (for joists)
5. Foundation construction
6. Structural member erection
7. Presentation display.

Stage 1: Division of Structural Form

As with our previous models, this model is divided into separate stages of creation to facilitate generation. The obvious areas to be sectioned are the individual members and the foundation. Thus, this model is divided into the following sections:

- Creation of the column parametric symbol (scalable)
- Creation of the spandrel girder parametric symbol (scalable)
- Creation of the spandrel beam parametric symbol (scalable)
- Creation of the center spandrel beam parametric symbol (scalable)
- Creation of the column pad and grout symbols (custom)
- Creation of the open webbed steel joist symbol (custom)
- Creation of the open webbed steel tie joist symbol (custom)
- Creation of orientation cubes
- Creation of the bayline grid

- Creation of the foundation
- Creation of the covering surfaces.

If you plan to expand on the project model, this would be the ideal time to add further divisions. However, because you may be unfamiliar with the procedures this type of project requires and, consequently, unsure of what additions you might like to make, it would certainly be acceptable to return to this planning stage at the end of the project to make any needed adjustments.

Stage 2: Layer Designations

To enable us to make entities visible and invisible (one of the most powerful features of CAD) and to facilitate construction and the later display of the final model, we will name layers now. If you plan to make additions to the model, add their associated layers to our list if you can.

Even though the name of a layer can have as many as 31 characters, we will use only the first 8 characters in our layer names because only these characters will be visible on the status line. For example, 1-OWSJ would represent the open webbed steel joists for the ceiling of floor 1.

The layers to be created are listed next. Note that each layer in the main model is preceded by a number, representing the floor. Although there is only one floor in this project, there could be multiple floors in other projects. This stage, then, lays the procedural groundwork for future complex projects.

The main model (STRUCT) layers are listed here:

LAYER COLOR	LAYER NAME	LAYER DESCRIPTION
1	1-FNDEX	Foundation extrusions
1	1-FNDSUR	Foundation surfaces
2	1-COLUMN	Columns
3	1-SPGIRD	Spandrel girders
4	1-SPBEAM	Spandrel beams
5	1-CGIRD	Center girders
6	1-COLBAS	Column base plates and grout
7	1-OWSJ	Open webbed steel joists
8	1-OWSTJ	Open webbed steel tie joists
1	BGRID	Bayline grid

On the layer for parametric symbols (scalable), the parametric symbols will have all their entities on layer 0.

The layers for the column base plates and group symbols (custom) are as follows:

LAYER COLOR	LAYER NAME	LAYER DESCRIPTION
3	BPLATE	Column support base plate
4	GROUT	Pad to foundation grout

The layers for the open webbed steel joist symbols (custom) will contain the symbols for both the open webbed steel joist and the open webbed steel tie joist.

LAYER COLOR	LAYER NAME	LAYER DESCRIPTION
1	ANGLE	Angle member extrusions
1	ANGSURF	Angle member surfaces
2	ROD	Connecting rod
3	TEMPOR	Temporary construction
7	OCUBE	Orientation cube

Give each section type its own color to make it easier to distinguish what is on each layer.

Remember that it is customary to use continuous linetype for all 3D construction.

Stage 3: Parametric Symbols Creation

Repeat the steps in this stage to create the parametric symbols for the four structural members. The processes for creating the symbols are basically identical, except for the location of the BASE points. These locations vary for each parametric symbol.

The four parametric symbols are named and described next. Each of the symbols is a 2ES parametric symbol, which is explained in Chapter 14.

SYMBOL NAME	DESCRIPTION
W8X24	Column
W14X26	Spandrel girder
W10X21	Spandrel beam
W18X55	Center spandrel girder

Initial Settings

Enter the following settings before modeling. For each symbol, create a new model, and call the model by the symbol name (W8X24, W14X26, W10X21, or W18X55). All creation will take place on layer 0, with color 7 (white).

```
    SETTINGS
Units = architectural
Limits = −1,−1 to 8,19
Grid = 1/2"
Snap Incr. = 1/2"
Initial Elevation = 0
Initial Thickness = 1"
UCS = WCS
UCSICON = on and set to ORIGIN
```

Enter any other settings at this point. Remember to ZOOM All, so that the display shows the set limits.

Symbol Extension

Using the LINE command, draw the perimeter of the symbol as shown in Figure 22.2. Each symbol will have a 1" thickness along the Z axis.

Surface Creation

Using the 3DFACE command, place a surface on both ends of the extruded form.

Base Location

Using the BASE command, place the base point indicated for the model being created at this time.

FILE	BASE (INCHES)
W8X24	3-1/4,4,0
W14X26	2-1/2,14,0
W10X21	2-7/8,10,0
W18X55	3-3/4,18,0

Save each model using its symbol name. Make sure you have repeated the steps in stage 3 for all four 2ES parametric symbols.

Stage 4: Custom Symbol Creation

The three custom symbols to be created for this project are the BASE plate (BASE), Open Webbed Steel Joist (OWSJ), and the Open Webbed Steel Tie

Figure 22.2
2ES parametric symbols

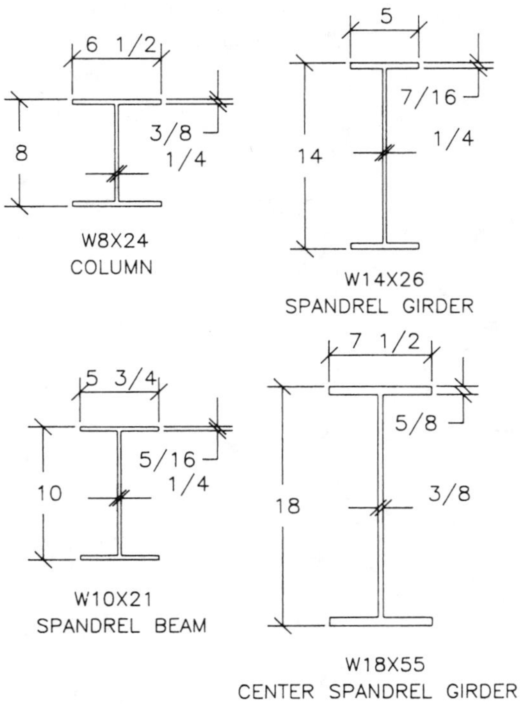
6 1/2
3/8
1/4
8
W8X24
COLUMN
5
7/16
1/4
14
W14X26
SPANDREL GIRDER
5 3/4
5/16
1/4
10
W10X21
SPANDREL BEAM
7 1/2
5/8
3/8
18
W18X55
CENTER SPANDREL GIRDER

Joist (OWSTJ). The requirements for these symbols are likely to change from project to project, so their creation processes will be unique.

Creation of Base Plate and Grout Symbol

The first custom symbol to be created will be the base plate and grout. The grout will eventually sit on the foundation, the plate will sit on the grout, and the columns will sit on the plate. Complete the numbered steps to create this symbol.

1. Start a new model called BASE and make the following layers:

LAYER COLOR	LAYER NAME	LAYER DESCRIPTION
3	BPLATE	Column support base plate
4	GROUT	Pad to foundation grout

SETTINGS

```
Units = architectural
Limits = -1",-1" to 14",14"
Grid = 1/2"
Snap Incr. = 1/2"
Initial Elevation Thickness = 0
Initial Thickness = 0
UCS = WCS
UCSICON = on and set to ORIGIN
```

Remember to ZOOM All, so that the display shows the set limits.

2. While on layer GROUT, use the LINE command to draw the perimeter of the grout in the plan view, as shown in Figure 22.3. Start the lower left corner at –6-1/8,–6-1/8, 0.
3. Using the ELEV command, set the elevation to 1-1/4″ and the thickness to 3/4″. Switch to layer BPLATE.
4. Using the LINE command, draw the perimeter of the base plate, as shown in Figure 22.3.
5. Using the 3DFACE command, add surfaces to the top of the plate.

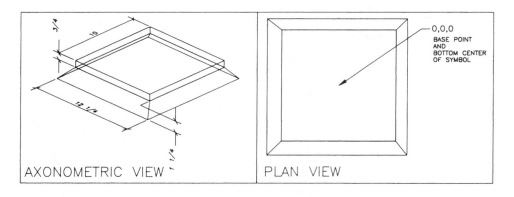

Figure 22.3
Finished symbol BASE

6. Return to layer GROUT and create the four sloped sides of the grout using the 3DFACE command.
7. Using the BASE command, set the base point to 0,0,0.
8. Save the model as BASE.

Creation of Open Webbed Steel Joist Symbol

Refer to Figures 22.4 and 22.5 for axonometric and orthographic views, respectively, of the custom symbol for the open webbed steel joist (OWSJ). Note that the connecting rods for this symbol will be rectangular instead of round.

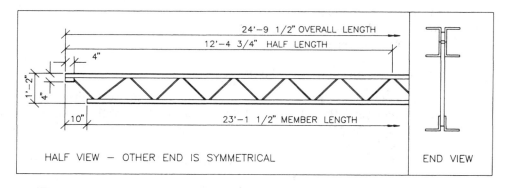

Figure 22.4
Axonometric view of finished symbol OWSJ

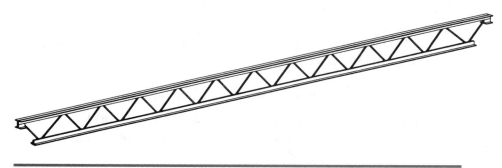

Figure 22.5
Orthographic views of symbol OWSJ

An orientation cube, a connecting rod, and several angle components must be created in order to model this symbol. Complete the numbered steps to create the symbol OWSJ.

1. Start a new model called OWSJ. Make the layers and enter the settings listed next.

LAYER COLOR	LAYER NAME	LAYER DESCRIPTION
1	ANGLE	Angle member extrusions
1	ANGSURF	Angle member surfaces
2	ROD	Connecting rod
3	TEMPOR	Temporary construction
7	OCUBE	Orientation cube

```
     SETTINGS
Units = architectural
Limits = −10",−10" to 30',5'
Grid = 1"
Snap Incr. = 1/4"
Initial Elevation Thickness = 0
Initial Thickness = 0
UCS = WCS
UCSICON = on and set to ORIGIN
```

Remember to ZOOM All, so that the display shows the set limits.

2. This step will create an orientation cube to define the 3D boundaries of the model.

```
     SETTINGS
Layer = OCUBE
Elevation = 0
Thickness = 1'2"
UCS = WCS
```

Using the LINE command, draw the perimeter representing the orientation cube as shown in part A of Figure 22.6. The orientation cube is 24'9-1/2" in the X direction, 4-1/2" in the Y direction, and 1'2" in the Z direction. The lower left corner must start at 0,0,0.

```
P1 = 0,0,0                          P2 = 24'9-1/2",0',0'
P3 = 24'9-1/2",4-1/2",0'            P4 = 0',4-1/2",0'
CLOSE
```

Figure 22.6
Orientation cube and the new working plane

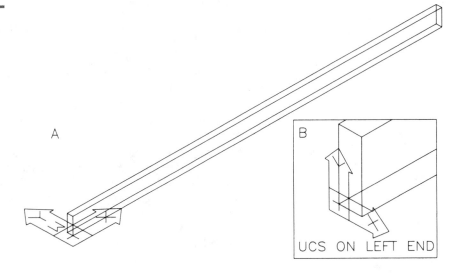

425

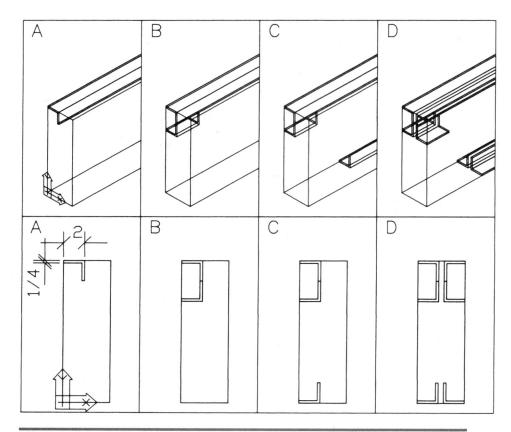

Figure 22.7
End views of angle components

Change the working plane to the end of the orientation cube, as shown in part B of Figure 22.6.

3. This step will create three components made of angle iron. These will be mirrored twice to create all the required angle components. All three components have the same dimensions for the X and Y axes. Only the dimensions for the Z axis change.

```
SETTINGS
Layer = ANGLE
Elevation = 0
Thickness = -24'9-1/2"
```

Using the LINE command, draw the first angle component as shown in part A of Figure 22.7.

Change the thickness to –4″.

Using the LINE command, draw the second angle component as shown in part B of Figure 22.7.

Change the elevation to –10″ and the thickness to –23′1-1/2″.

Using the LINE command, draw the third component as shown in Figure 22.7.

Change both the elevation and the thickness back to 0.

Set the current layer to ANGSURF. Using the 3DFACE command, add a surface to all the exposed ends of the angle components.

Using the MIRROR command, mirror the three components as shown in part D of Figure 22.7.

Set the working plane to WCS. Mirror the left end components to the right end, as shown in Figure 22.8.

Save the model as OWSJ.

USE MID POINT —
FOR MIRROR LINE

Figure 22.8
Angle components

4. This step will create the square connecting rod. The rod will be created at an angle of 45 degrees, except for the first two bends on each end. Refer to Figure 22.9, line A and line C.

SETTINGS
```
Layer = TEMPOR
Elevation = —2-1/2″
Thickness = 0
UCS = front plane, as shown in part A of Figure 22.9
```

Using the LINE command, draw line A, as shown in Figure 22.9. The coordinates for P1 are 3″, 1′, –2-1/2″, and the coordinates for P2 are 1′2″, 1″, –2-1/2″.

Using the LINE command again, draw the number of lines indicated as B from the center of the OCUBE at an angle of 45 degrees. Use relative coordinates @ 1′5″<225 and @ 1′5″<135 for each alternate line.

The last line, indicated as C, should be drawn by snapping onto the end of line A.

SETTINGS
```
Layer = ROD
Elevation = —2-1/2″
Thickness = 1/2″
Freeze all layers except the TEMPOR layer.
```

Using the PLINE command, draw the connecting rod (1/2″ square) by endpoint object snapping to the ends of each of the temporary lines, as shown in Figure 22.10. The polyline should have a width of 1/2″.

Freeze layers TEMPOR and OCUBE and turn on the other layers.

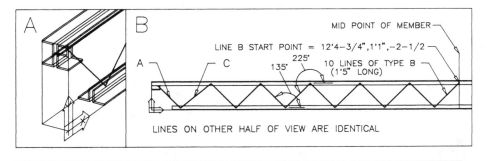

Figure 22.9
Creation of temporary lines

Figure 22.10
Connecting rod created by polyline

Figure 22.11
Open webbed steel tie joist symbol

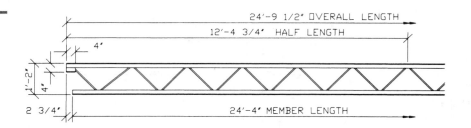

Set the UCS to the WCS, and set the BASE command to –1-1/4″, 2-1/4″, 10″.

Save the model as OWSJ. Do not exit the drawing. This model will be used to create the symbol for the open webbed steel tie joist as well.

If you wish, use the VPOINT and HIDE commands to move around and observe the newly created model. The model should look like Figure 22.4.

Creation of Open Webbed Steel Tie Joist Symbol

To modify the open webbed steel joist symbol to use as the symbol for the open webbed steel tie joist, the two lower angle components need to be moved and then lengthened. Figure 22.11 shows the modifications. Complete the numbered steps to alter the symbol.

1. Set the UCS working plane to the left end of the OCUBE, as shown in part A of Figure 22.12.
2. Using the MOVE command, move the lower components a distance of 7-1/4″ positively along the *Z* axis. This is illustrated in part B of Figure 22.12.
3. Using the CHPROP command, change the thickness of the angle components' extrusions to –24′4″.

    Remember to replace/move the surfaces on either end of the angle extrusions.
4. Set the UCS to the WCS, and set the BASE command to –1-1/4″, 2-1/4″, 10″.
5. Save the model as OWSTJ (notice the location of the *T* in the file name).

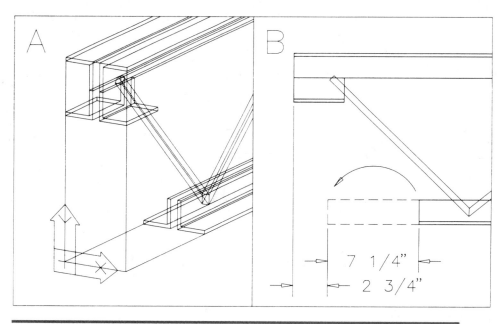

Figure 22.12
Increasing the length of the lower member

Stage 5: Foundation Construction

Now that all the symbols have been created, it is time to construct the foundation. It will be constructed out of lines with thickness and topped with surfaces using the 3DFACE command. The base plate and grout symbol will be added at this point as well.

Start a new model called STRUCT (STRUCTural model). Make the following layers and enter the settings listed below.

LAYER COLOR	LAYER NAME	LAYER DESCRIPTION
1	1-FNDEX	Foundation extrusions
1	1-FNDSUR	Foundation surfaces
2	1-COLUMN	Columns
3	1-SPGIRD	Spandrel girders
4	1-SPBEAM	Spandrel beams
5	1-CGIRD	Center girders
6	1-COLBAS	Column base plates and grout
7	1-OWSJ	Open webbed steel joists
8	1-OWSTJ	Open webbed steel tie joists
1	BGRID	Bayline grid

```
    SETTINGS
  Units = architectural
  Limits = -5',-5' to 80',55'
  Grid = 5'
  Snap Incr. = 5'
  Initial Elevation Thickness = 0
  Initial Thickness = 0
  UCS = WCS
  UCSICON = on and set to ORIGIN
```

Remember to ZOOM All, so that the display shows the set limits.

Creation of Bayline Grid

The baylines that form the building grid will now be laid out. They are 55' long and spaced at 25' intervals. They will be drawn at an initial elevation of 10" and later moved to an elevation of 1'. We will snap to these grid lines when placing symbols.

```
    SETTINGS
  Layer = BGRID
  Elevation = 10"
  Thickness = 0
  UCS = WCS
```

Using the LINE command, draw the grid as shown in Figure 22.13.

Creation of Extruded Foundation

The extruded foundation is 10" high and is topped with surfaces. The outer edge of the wall is 10" from the grid, and the inner edge is 5". The projections around the wall extend 5" into the interior of the building. The two foundation pads that are in the middle of the building are 20" square. Refer to Figure 22.14.

```
    SETTINGS
  Layer = 1-FNDEX
  Elevation = 0
  Thickness = 10"
```

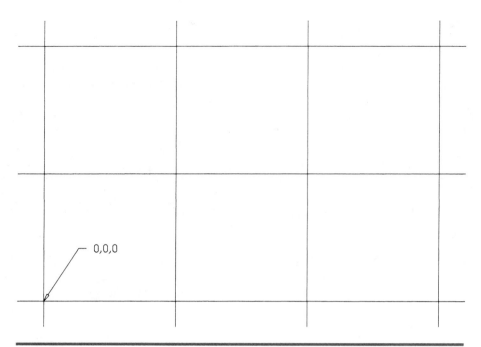

Figure 22.13
Bayline grid

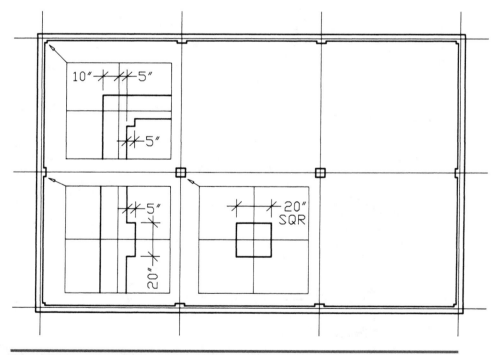

Figure 22.14
Extruded foundation

Using the LINE command, draw the extruded foundation, as shown in Figure 22.14.

```
SETTINGS
Layer = 1-FNDSUR
Elevation = 10"
Thickness = 0
```

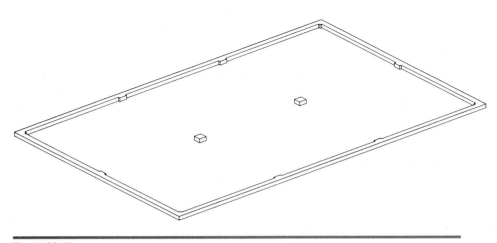

Figure 22.15
Foundation surface

Using the 3DFACE command, create surfaces over the extruded foundation lines. Remember to use invisible edges where needed. Refer to Figure 22.15.

The symbol BASE will now be inserted.

```
      SETTINGS
Layer = 1-COLBAS
Elevation = 10"
Thickness = 0
UCS = WCS
Snap Incr. = 25',25'
```

Using the INSERT command, place the BASE symbol at the intersection of each grid line, as shown in Figure 22.16. After you have placed one symbol, you can use the COPY command with the multiple option to place the others.

Save the model as STRUCT.

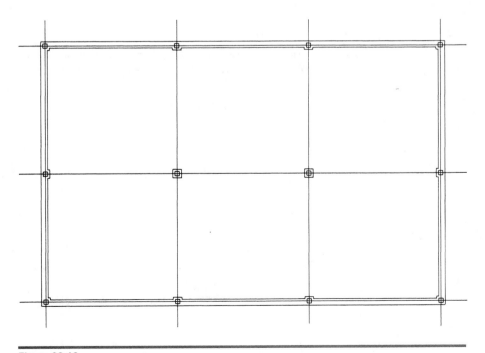

Figure 22.16
BASE symbol placement

Stage 6: Structural Member Erection

Placement of Column Symbol

The column parametric symbol will be placed on top of the base plates at the intersection of the grid. Because the column symbol is a 2ES parametric symbol, we will need to give a length upon insertion. The length of the column is 300″ (25′).

```
    SETTINGS
Layer = 1-COLUMN
Elevation = 1′
Thickness = 0
UCS = WCS
Snap Incr. = 25′,25′
```

Using the MOVE command, move the grid lines to an elevation of 1′. Using the INSERT command, place the W8X24 (column) symbol at the intersection of each grid line, as shown in Figure 22.17. After placing one symbol, use the COPY command with the Multiple option to place the others. The orientation of a column depends on its location. Refer to Figure 22.17 to observe the orientation of each column. *Note:* When placing the block, do not use object snap; instead, use increment snap.

```
Command: INSERT
Block Name (or?): W8X24
Insertion point: place the column symbol at the
intersection of one of the grid lines; use increment
snap so that the proper elevation is maintained
X scale factor <1>/Corner/XYZ: XYZ
X scale factor <1>/Corner/XYZ: 1
Y scale factor <default=X>: 1
Z scale factor <default=X>: 300 (inches) = (25′)
Rotation angle <0>: 0
```

Save the model as STRUCT.

Placement of Spandrel Girder Symbol

The spandrel girder parametric symbol will be placed between each outer column and will run along the *X* axis of the WCS. Because it is a 2ES parametric

Figure 22.17
Placement of column symbol

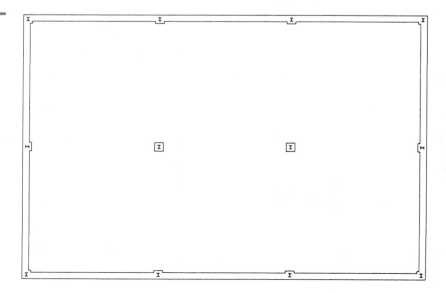

symbol, we will need to give a length upon insertion. The length of the girder is 299.75" (24'11-3/4").

```
    SETTINGS
Layer = 1-SPGIRD
Elevation = 0
Thickness = 0
UCS = WCS
Snap Incr. = 1/8",1/8"
```

The location and orientation of the UCS working plane is crucial to the placement of the remaining parametric symbols. The UCS commands for each placement are listed in detail. When you have completed them, refer to the associated figures to check that location and orientation are correct.

Using the UCS command, rotate the UCS working plane to align with the upper left beam when looking at a plan view. The command is as follows:

```
Command: UCS
Origin/ZAxis/ . . . /X/Y/Z/Prev/ . . . <World>: W
Command: UCS
Origin/ZAxis/ . . . /X/Y/Z/Prev/ . . . <World>: Z
Rotation about Z axis <0>: 90
Command: UCS
Origin/ZAxis/ . . . /X/Y/Z/Prev/ . . . <World>: X
Rotation about X axis <0>: 90
Command: UCS
Origin/ZAxis/ . . . /X/Y/Z/Prev/ . . . <World>: O
Origin point: using object snap endpoint, snap to the
point indicated in part A in Figure 22.18
```

Using the INSERT command, place the W14X26 (spandrel girder) symbol at the center of the inside face of the column, as shown in part B in Figure 22.18. Once you have placed a symbol, use the COPY command with the multiple option to place the others. Refer to Figure 22.19 for the correct placement of the symbols. Make sure the UCS is equal to the WCS before using the COPY command.

```
Command: INSERT
Block Name (or?): W14X26
```

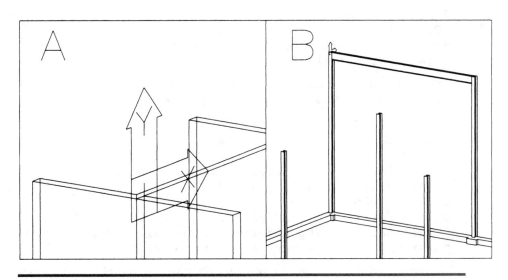

Figure 22.18
Placement of spandrel girder symbol

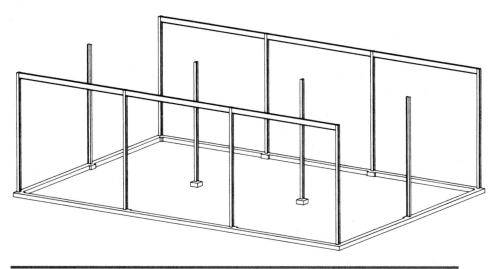

Figure 22.19
Copying of spandrel girder symbol

```
Insertion point: 3-3/8",0,0
X scale factor <1>/Corner/XYZ: XYZ
X scale factor <1>/Corner/XYZ: 1
Y scale factor <default=X>: 1
Z scale factor <default=X>: 299.75 = (24' 11-3/4")
Rotation angle <0>: 0
```

Save the model as STRUCT.

Placement of Spandrel Beam Symbol

The spandrel beam parametric symbol will be placed between each outer column and will run along the *Y* axis of the WCS. Because it is a 2ES parametric symbol, we will need to give a length upon insertion. The length of the beam is 295.875″ (24′7⅞″).

```
SETTINGS
Layer = 1-SPBEAM
Elevation = 0"
Thickness = 0
UCS = WCS
Snap Incr. = 1/8",1/8"
Freeze layer 1-SPGIRD.
```

Using the UCS command, rotate the UCS working plane to align with the upper left beam when looking at a plan view. The command is as follows:

```
Command: UCS
Origin/ZAxis/ ... /X/Y/Z/Prev/ ... <World>: W
Command: UCS
Origin/ZAxis/ ... /X/Y/Z/Prev/ ... <World>: X
Rotation about X axis <0>: 90
Command: UCS
Origin/ZAxis/ ... /X/Y/Z/Prev/ ... <World>: 0
Origin point: using object snap endpoint, snap to the
point indicated in part A in Figure 22.20
```

Using the INSERT command, place the W10X21 (spandrel beam) symbol at the center of the face of the column, as shown in part B of Figure 22.20.

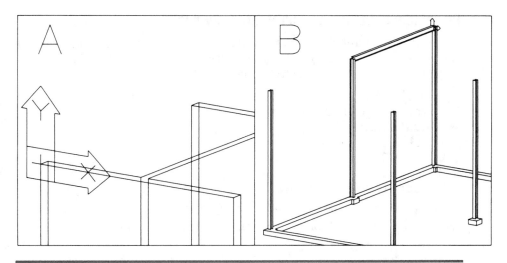

Figure 22.20
Placement of spandrel beam symbol

Once you have placed a symbol, use the COPY command with the Multiple option to place the others. Refer to Figure 22.21 for the correct placement of the symbols. Make sure the UCS is equal to the WCS before using the COPY command.

```
Command: INSERT
Block Name (or?): W10X21
Insertion point: 3-1/4",4",0"
X scale factor <1>/Corner/XYZ: XYZ
X scale factor <1>/Corner/XYZ: 1
Y scale factor <default=X>: 1
Z scale factor <default=X>: 295.875 (24'7-7/8")
Rotation angle <O>: 0
```

The spandrel beams are 4″ above the columns so that their tops will align with the tops of the joists when they are inserted later.

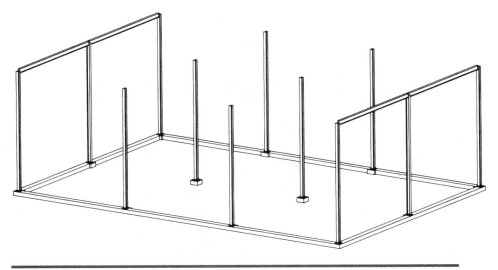

Figure 22.21
Copying of spandrel beam symbol

Placement of Central Spandrel Girder Symbol

The central spandrel girder symbol will be placed between each center column and will run along the *Y* axis of the WCS. The two outer central girders are 24′ 7-7/8″ long, and the center central girder is 24′11-3/4″ long.

```
SETTINGS
Layer = 1-CGIRD
Elevation = 0"
Thickness = 0
UCS = WCS
Snap Incr. = 1/8",1/8"
Freeze layer 1-SPBEAM.
```

Using the UCS command, rotate the UCS working plane to align with the center left beam when looking at a plan view. The command is as follows:

```
Command: UCS
Origin/ZAxis/ . . . /X/Y/Z/Prev/ . . . <World>: W
Command: UCS
Origin/ZAxis/ . . . /X/Y/Z/Prev/ . . . <World>: Z
Rotation about Z axis <0>: 90
Command: UCS
Origin/ZAxis/ . . . /X/Y/Z/Prev/ . . . <World>: X
Rotation about X axis <0>: 90
Command: UCS
Origin/ZAxis/ . . . /X/Y/Z/Prev/ . . . <World>: O
Origin point: using object snap endpoint, snap to the
point indicated in part A in Figure 22.22
```

Using the INSERT command, place the W18X55 (center spandrel girder) symbol at the center of the face of the column as shown in part B in Figure 22.22. Once you have placed the first symbol, use the COPY command with the Multiple option to place another at the other end, as shown in Figure 22.23. *Remember:* The UCS must equal the WCS when using the COPY command.

```
Command: INSERT
Block Name (or?): W18X55
Insertion point: 3-1/4",0,0"
X scale factor <1>/Corner/XYZ: XYZ
X scale factor <1>/Corner/XYZ: 1
```

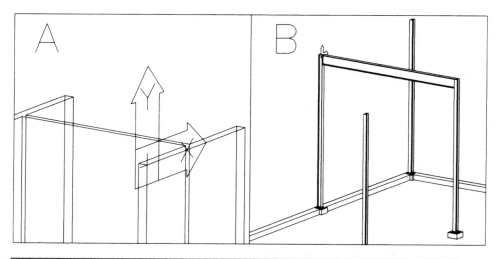

Figure 22.22
Placement of outer central spandrel girder symbol

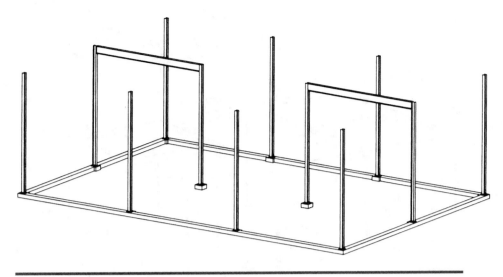

Figure 22.23
Copying of outer central spandrel girder symbol

```
Y scale factor <default=X>: 1
Z scale factor <default=X>: 295.875 = (24'7-7/8")
Rotation angle <O>: 0
```

The center girder is a different length, so it will need to be inserted at a new length and with a new origin for the UCS. The procedure is as follows:

```
Command: UCS
Origin/ZAxis/ . . . /X/Y/Z/Prev/ . . . <World>: O
Origin point: using object snap endpoint, snap to the
point indicated in part A in Figure 22.24
Command: INSERT
Block Name (or?): W18X55
Insertion point: 3-5/8",0",0"
X scale factor <1>/Corner/XYZ: XYZ
X scale factor <1>/Corner/XYZ: 1
Y scale factor <default=X>: 1
Z scale factor <default=X>: 299.75 = (24'11-3/4")
Rotation angle <O>: 0
```

Save the model as STRUCT.

Figure 22.24
Placement of center central spandrel girder symbol

Figure 22.25
Placement of OWSTJ symbols

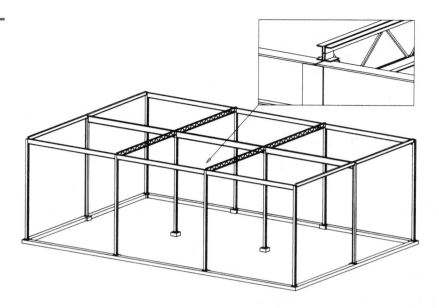

Placement of Open Webbed Steel Tie Joist Symbol

The open webbed steel tie joist symbol is custom designed for this project. This means that it will be inserted at a constant scale for all axes. It will be placed on the top of the inner four columns, as shown in Figure 22.25.

```
     SETTINGS
  Layer = 1-OWSTJ
  Elevation = 0"
  Thickness = 0
  UCS = WCS
  Snap Incr. = 1/8",1/8"
  Freeze layer 1-CGIRD
```

Use the INSERT command to place four OWSTJ symbols at the following coordinates. Each will have an overall scale of 1 and a rotation of 90 degrees, as shown in Figure 22.25.

```
P1 = 25',0',26'          P2 = 25',25',26'
P3 = 50',0',26'          P4 = 50',25',26'
```

Placement of Open Webbed Steel Joist Symbol

The open webbed steel joist symbol is custom designed for this project. This means that it will be inserted at a constant scale for all axes. It will be placed on the top of the girders, as shown in Figure 22.26.

Figure 22.26
Placement of OWSJ symbols

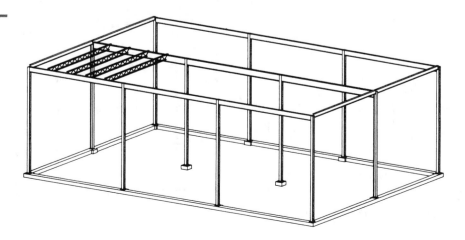

Figure 22.27
Copying of OWSJ symbols

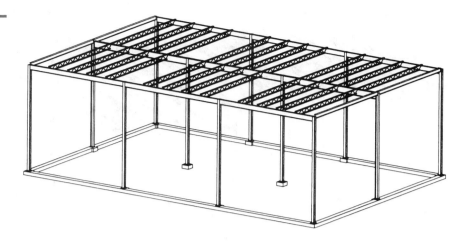

```
      SETTINGS
 Layer = 1-OWSJ
 Elevation = 0"
 Thickness = 0
 UCS = WCS
 Snap Incr. = 1/8",1/8"
 Freeze layer 1-OWSTJ.
 Thaw layers 1-CGIRD and 1-SPGIRD.
```

Use the INSERT command to place four OWSJ symbols. Insert them at the coordinates listed below. Each will have an overall scale of 1 and a rotation of 90 degrees, as shown in Figure 22.26.

```
P1 = 5',0',26'            P2 = 10',0',26'
P3 = 15',0',26'           P4 = 20',0',26'
```

Use the COPY command with the Multiple option to copy the six sets of four OWSJ symbols, as shown in Figure 22.27.

Thaw the 1-SPBEAM and 1-OWSTJ layers, and save the model as STRUCT.

The model construction is finished now. You have created a model of the *initial* framework for the structural portion of a building, not a model of the complete structural framing. However, the techniques learned during this model construction should enable you to complete any type of structural project.

Stage 7: Presentation Display

With construction complete, the display of the model for presentation purposes must be considered. Refer to Figure 22.28 for an axonometric view of the structural framework model. This type of viewing is necessary for construction purposes, but it is not as useful for presentation. For example, the viewer will have difficulty imagining the size of the building. Now look at Figure 22.29, which shows the perspective view. Here, the magnitude and realism of the structure are more effectively demonstrated.

We will create two perspective views of this project. The two views are described next. You may create other perspective views according to your needs (refer to Chapter 15 for a discussion of presentation and display).

PERSP1:   from a height of 12'8", to the right of the structure, and looking over the entire building

PERSP2:   from a height of 6', to the right of the structure, and looking upward, toward the open webbed steel joists

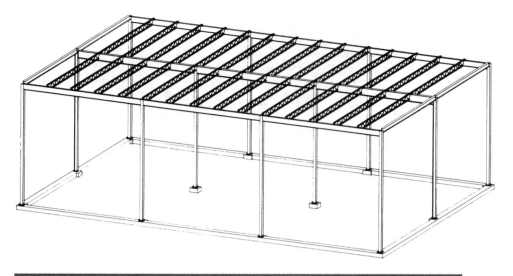

Figure 22.28
Axonometric view of the model

Figure 22.29
Perspective view of the model
(PERSP1)

Creating the Preview Selection Set

When selecting objects for the Preview Selection Set, select only the columns, not the whole model. This will make manipulating in the DVIEW environment easier and quicker.

Completion of the following steps will achieve the perspective view PERSP1, as shown in Figure 22.29.

1. Use the POINTS option to place the camera and the target points. Enter these settings:

```
Points-Target = 36'2",27'6",12'8"
Camera = 96'5",-17'2",12'8"
Distance = 75'
Zoom = 20
```

2. Exit the DVIEW command to apply the settings to the entire model.

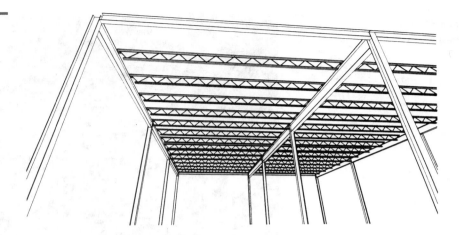

Figure 22.30
Perspective view of the model (PERSP2)

3. Use the VIEW command to save the perspective view as PERSP1.

Completing the following steps will achieve the perspective view PERSP2, as shown in Figure 22.30.

1. Use the POINTS option to place the camera and the target points. Enter these settings:

```
Target = 66'9",12'5",25'
Camera = 91',10',6'
Distance = 28'8"
Zoom = 20
```

2. Exit the DVIEW command to apply the settings to the entire model.
3. Use the VIEW command to save the perspective view as PERSP2.

Save the model as STRUCT.

Using the HIDE Command

Select the HIDE command and await the outcome. With a model of this magnitude, you are going to be waiting for a while.

Once the HIDE command is finished, immediately make a slide of the display to avoid having to redo the HIDE command next time you want to show the model. You can redisplay a slide much faster than you can redo a HIDE command. Call the slide PERSP2.

Using the VIEW command, restore the other perspective. Select the HIDE command and, when it is done, make a slide called PERSP1.

Rendering the Model

If you need to review the discussion on rendering, turn back to the final section in Chapter 18.

The following sample settings will create a rendering of the structure in the daytime using the RENDER utility. Only one light, representing the sun, will be used. A laser plot of the rendered model displaying PERSP1 is shown in Figure 22.31.

Rendering Preferences: Use default settings. Smooth Shading is not needed.

Lights:

NAME	TYPE	INTENSITY	LIGHT LOCATION	TARGET LOCATION
sun	distant	1.00	110', 0', 50'	37'6", 27'3", 10"
ambient		0.7		

Figure 22.31
Rendered view of the structural model

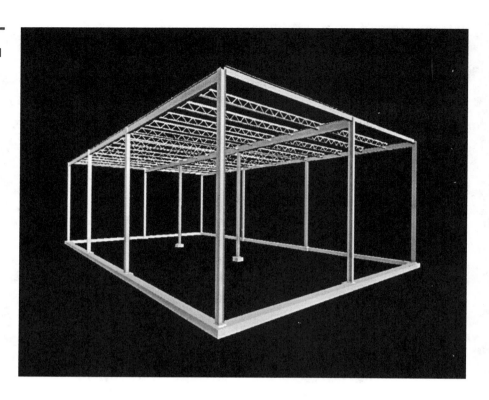

CHAPTER 23

Civil Project

Overview

In this project, you will use polygon mesh techniques to create a terrain model. You will record varied topographical data as a text file and then learn how to use that text file to make the program create imagery automatically.

Concepts Explored

- Further application of AutoCAD features
- Generation of a complex three-dimensional terrain model
- Creation of a script/data file of topographical coordinates
- Generation of a polygon mesh terrain
- Exploration of polyline contours
- Creation of an elevation view of the contour lines.

23.1 Introduction

The project in this chapter involves the creation of the terrain model shown in Figure 23.1. Although the data for this terrain model is supplied for you, you

Figure 23.1
Final terrain model

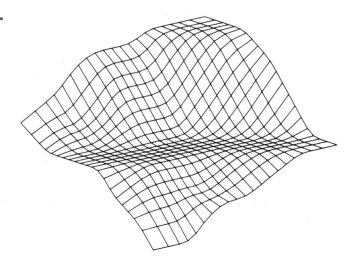

will acquire the skills you'll need to select a topographical map, determine the elevation coordinates, and create your own unique terrain model because the steps given here can be applied to any map.

The coordinate values given in this project are simple, so as not to complicate the steps and risk you losing sight of the procedure. The theoretical topographical map measures 100 units by 100 units and shows contour lines at elevation intervals of 10 units (refer to Figure 23.2). You will convert this map into coordinated data in a text file that can be read into AutoCAD to create the terrain model automatically. You also will use the data to create automatic profile lines that cut cross-sections through the terrain so that, when the models are finished and you are viewing the terrain, you will be able to selectively view cross-section profiles.

As a point of interest, note that modern survey equipment can automatically store survey points similar to those used in this project. The data can then be transferred to the computer and used to create a topographical map.

23.2 Project Stages

Like any project, this one should be performed in an organized manner that will allow efficient execution and easy repetition of the modeling process. To that end, this project is separated into stages that apply to the initial generation of a terrain model from topographical data and the subsequent generation of cross-section profiles.

PROJECT STAGES
1. Division of the terrain model
2. Layer designation
3. Development of the topographical data
4. Creation of the mesh script/data file
5. Creation of the polygon mesh terrain model
6. Creation of the profile script/data file
7. Creation of the profile model
8. Display of selected profiles

Stage 1: Division of the Terrain Model

Any map could be selected for this project as long as it had distinct contour lines that indicate the various elevations. Refer to the contour map shown in Figure 23.2. The map's contour lines indicate that the highest elevation is at the top right corner, where there is a small plateau with an elevation of 70′. The terrain slopes downward and toward the left of the map, ending at an elevation of 0′ at the bottom left corner of the map.

Stage 2: Layer Designations

This project will need only two layers. If other topographical features were added, or another map was substituted, then more layers would need to be named. Listed here are the layers to be created for this project:

LAYER COLOR	LAYER NAME	LAYER DESCRIPTION
1	CMESH	Contour MESH (representing the terrain)
2	PROFL	PROFile Lines (representing the cross-sectional profiles of the terrain)

Stage 3: Development of Topographical Data

To create a three-dimensional model of the terrain of any map, you need to generate a series of coordinates. The coordinates are the X, Y, and Z locations

Figure 23.2
Contour map

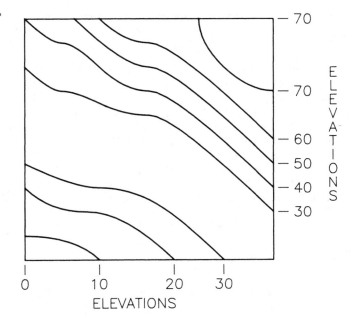

of various points on the map. These coordinates must be extracted in a grid-type pattern so that the data will be read into AutoCAD in the proper sequence.

Refer to Figures 23.2 and 23.3. The topographic contour lines in Figure 23.2 are converted to lines that correspond to the 10 by 10 unit division grid in Figure 23.3. The grid represents the format of the coordinate data to be placed into the data file. (*Note:* Any number of divisions could be used; however, the greater the number of divisions, the more accurate the model.)

The vertical lines of the grid represent each line of data as a cross section through the terrain. The lines travel from the left to the right, numbered 1 to 11. These lines also represent a location of 10′ along the X axis (that is, line 1 is 10′ along the X axis, line 2 is 20′ along the X axis, and so on).

The horizontal lines of the grid represent an individual field or coordinate of data along a line. There are 11 fields of data for each line, meaning that there are 11 X, Y, Z coordinate points for each of the 11 lines. The horizontal

Figure 23.3
Stylized contour lines overlaid on a grid

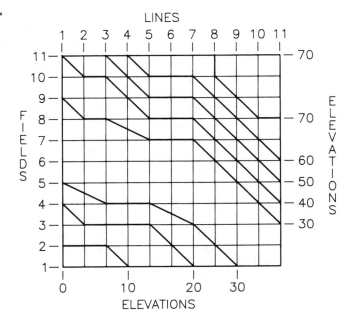

Lines	Field 1	Field 2	Field 3	Field 4	Field 5	Field 6	Field 7	Field 8	Field 9	Field 10	Field 11
1	10,10,0	10,20,10	10,30,15	10,40,20	10,50,30	10,60,30	10,70,30	10,80,30	10,90,30	10,100,35	10,110,40
2	20,10,0	20,20,10	20,30,20	20,40,25	20,50,30	20,60,30	20,70,30	20,80,30	20,90,35	20,100,40	20,110,45
3	30,10,0	30,20,10	30,30,20	30,40,30	30,50,30	30,60,30	30,70,30	30,80,30	30,90,35	30,100,40	30,110,50
4	40,10,10	40,20,15	40,30,20	40,40,30	40,50,30	40,60,30	40,70,30	40,80,35	40,90,40	40,100,50	40,110,60
5	50,10,15	50,20,15	50,30,20	50,40,30	50,50,30	50,60,30	50,70,30	50,80,40	50,90,50	50,100,60	50,110,65
6	60,10,15	60,20,20	60,30,25	60,40,30	60,50,30	60,60,30	60,70,30	60,80,40	60,90,50	60,100,60	60,110,65
7	70,10,20	70,20,25	70,30,30	70,40,30	70,50,30	70,60,30	70,70,30	70,80,40	70,90,50	70,100,60	70,110,65
8	80,10,25	80,20,30	80,30,30	80,40,30	80,50,30	80,60,30	80,70,40	80,80,50	80,90,60	80,100,70	80,110,70
9	90,10,30	90,20,30	90,30,30	90,40,30	90,50,30	90,60,40	90,70,50	90,80,60	90,90,70	90,100,70	90,110,70
10	100,10,30	100,20,30	100,30,30	100,40,30	100,50,40	100,60,50	100,70,60	100,80,70	100,90,70	100,100,70	100,110,70
11	110,10,30	110,20,30	110,30,30	110,40,40	110,50,50	110,60,60	110,70,65	110,80,70	110,90,70	110,100,70	110,110,70

Table 23.1
Coordinate data for each topographical point

lines also represent location along the Y axis in the same way the vertical lines represent location along the X axis.

The next step is to take the coordinate location of each field location and tabulate the X, Y, and Z values. Refer to Figure 23.3 again and specifically observe the location of line 1, field 1. The elevation is 0, the X location is 10, and the Y location is 10. This means the coordinate data for that location is 10,10,0. Now refer to line 1, field 2, which coincides with the contour line for the elevation of 10′. This means that the coordinate data for line 1, field 2, is 10,20,10. This procedure would be followed to identify each coordinate location on the map. For this project, all the data has already been extracted and tabulated in Table 23.1. If you have selected your own map, then you must create a similar table.

Stage 4: Creation of the Mesh Script/Data File

Once the data has been collected for each coordinate point, it needs to be placed into a file in a way that AutoCAD can read. This procedure creates a script file. A *script file* is a file containing a series of commands that AutoCAD can read and then perform.

The command that we are going to use in this project is the 3DMESH command. (This command is explained in Section 8.3 of Chapter 8.) Auto-CAD refers to the function of the 3DMESH command as the creation of topographically rectangular polygon meshes. To use this command, you define the size of a grid and then enter the X, Y, and Z locations for each point on the grid. This will place a surface mesh over the points. The script we are going to create will enter such data automatically.

A script file must have the suffix .SCR for AutoCAD to recognize it. Our file will be called MESH.SCR. The first line of the script will activate the 3DMESH command and define the size of the mesh. After that, each line will represent a line from Table 23.1. Refer now to Table 23.2; the data file MESH.SCR should appear identical to this table.

Any text editor can be used to create the script, as long as it can create straight ASCII text that contains no formatting, such as justification or page breaks. If a word-processing program such as WordPerfect is used, make sure that the data file is saved as DOS text.

In the script, there should be one (and only one) space placed between each field of data. Also, there should not be any extra blank lines at the bottom of the file or blank spaces at the end of each line. If an extra blank line or space is inserted, AutoCAD will then try to repeat the last command at that location in the script.

Table 23.2
Script file MESH.SCR

```
3DPOLY
10,10,0 10,20,10 10,30,15 10,40,20 10,50,30 10,60,30 10,70,30
10,80,30 10,90,30 10,100,35 10,110,40

20,10,0 20,20,10 20,30,20 20,40,25 20,50,30 20,60,30 20,70,30
20,80,30 20,90,35 20,100,40 20,110,45

30,10,0 30,20,10 30,30,20 30,40,30 30,50,30 30,60,30 30,70,30
30,80,30 30,90,35 30,100,40 30,110,50

40,10,10 40,20,15 40,30,20 40,40,30 40,50,30 40,60,30 40,70,30
40,80,35 40,90,40 40,100,50 40,110,60

50,10,15 50,20,15 50,30,20 50,40,30 50,50,30 50,60,30 50,70,30
50,80,40 50,90,50 50,100,60 50,110,65

60,10,15 60,20,20 60,30,25 60,40,30 60,50,30 60,60,30 60,70,30
60,80,40 60,90,50 60,100,60 60,110,65

70,10,20 70,20,25 70,30,30 70,40,30 70,50,30 70,60,30 70,70,30
70,80,40 70,90,50 70,100,60 70,110,65

80,10,25 80,20,30 80,30,30 80,40,30 80,50,30 80,60,30 80,70,40
80,80,50 80,90,60 80,100,70 80,110,70

90,10,30 90,20,30 90,30,30 90,40,30 90,50,30 90,60,40 90,70,50
90,80,60 90,90,70 90,100,70 90,110,70

100,10,30 100,20,30 100,30,30 100,40,30 100,50,40 100,60,50
100,70,60 100,80,70 100,90,70 100,100,70 100,110,70

110,10,30 110,20,30 110,30,30 110,40,40 110,50,50 110,60,60
110,70,65 110,80,70 110,90,70 110,100,70 110,110,70
```

Stage 5: Creation of the Polygon Mesh Terrain Model

After the script file has been created, all that is needed to create the three-dimensional terrain is running the script.

Initial Settings

Start a new file called TERR (TERRain model). Create the two layers listed in stage 2 and assign the appropriate colors. Then enter the settings.

```
    SETTINGS
Units = engineering
Limits = −10,−10 to 250,250
Grid = 10
Snap Incr. = 10
Initial Elevation Thickness = 0
Initial Thickness = 0
UCS = WCS
UCSICON = on and set to ORIGIN
VPOINT = −2,−3,1 (set to an axonometric view)
Current Layer = CMESH
```

Running the Script

Using the SCRIPT command, enter MESH as the script file name. Now you can sit back and watch AutoCAD do its thing. You will see AutoCAD read each line of data and place each point on the screen. Then it will place a mesh over the grid points forming the terrain. It's as simple as that. The resulting terrain model should look similar to Figure 23.4.

If some points on the grid look very much out of place, it is probably because some of the coordinate data is incorrect. In that case, use UNDO to remove the terrain model, save the file as TERR, and go back and correct the script file. Once you have corrected the script, reenter the TERR file, and run the script again.

Figure 23.4
Rough terrain model from raw data

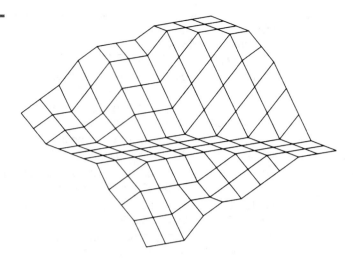

Smoothing the Terrain

The terrain created from the raw data has a rough, jagged appearance. You can modify the appearance of the terrain using the PEDIT command. PEDIT will modify both polylines and polygon meshes.

Select the PEDIT command and pick the mesh as the object to modify. Before you can smooth the mesh, you need to set some variables. Select the POLYVARS option from the sidebar menu. A dialog box should appear; select Quadratic as the curve type. Set the DENSITY to 20, the SPLINESEG to 8, and the SPLFRAME to 0. Now return to the PEDIT menu and select the SPLINE option. The resulting enhancement of the mesh should look similar to Figure 23.5.

Save the modified mesh as TERR. Use the VPOINT command to move about the terrain, observing it from any location. If your computer is capable of 256 colors or more, return to VPOINT −2,−3,1, and shade the terrain. The results should be interesting.

Stage 6: Creation of the Profile Script/Data File

You can use the same data entered to create the terrain mesh to create profile lines showing the cross section through the terrain. You do this by modifying the original data file so that it will automatically create 3D polylines instead of 3D polygon meshes. The modification is a simple procedure: Replace the 3DMESH line with the 3DPOLY command at the beginning of the file and add two blank

Figure 23.5
Enhanced terrain model

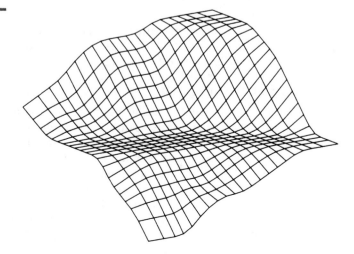

Table 23.3
Script file MESH2.SCR

3DPOLY
10,10,0 10,20,10 10,30,15 10,40,20 10,50,30 10,60,30 10,70,30
10,80,30 10,90,30 10,100,35 10,110,40

20,10,0 20,20,10 20,30,20 20,40,25 20,50,30 20,60,30 20,70,30
20,80,30 20,90,35 20,100,40 20,110,45

30,10,0 30,20,10 30,30,20 30,40,30 30,50,30 30,60,30 30,70,30
30,80,30 30,90,35 30,100,40 30,110,50

40,10,10 40,20,15 40,30,20 40,40,30 40,50,30 40,60,30 40,70,30
40,80,35 40,90,40 40,100,50 40,110,60

50,10,15 50,20,15 50,30,20 50,40,30 50,50,30 50,60,30 50,70,30
50,80,40 50,90,50 50,100,60 50,110,65

60,10,15 60,20,20 60,30,25 60,40,30 60,50,30 60,60,30 60,70,30
60,80,40 60,90,50 60,100,60 60,110,65

70,10,20 70,20,25 70,30,30 70,40,30 70,50,30 70,60,30 70,70,30
70,80,40 70,90,50 70,100,60 70,110,65

80,10,25 80,20,30 80,30,30 80,40,30 80,50,30 80,60,30 80,70,40
80,80,50 80,90,60 80,100,70 80,110,70

90,10,30 90,20,30 90,30,30 90,40,30 90,50,30 90,60,40 90,70,50
90,80,60 90,90,70 90,100,70 90,110,70

100,10,30 100,20,30 100,30,30 100,40,30 100,50,40 100,60,50
100,70,60 100,80,70 100,90,70 100,100,70 100,110,70

110,10,30 110,20,30 110,30,30 110,40,40 110,50,50 110,60,60
110,70,65 110,80,70 110,90,70 110,100,70 110,110,70

lines between each line of data. Refer to Table 23.3 to discover what the modified file should look like.

Copying the Original Data

Exit AutoCAD and copy the original script file MESH.SCR to a new file called MESH2.SCR.

Editing the Data

Use a text editor to modify the data so that it looks exactly like the data shown in Table 23.3. *Note:* This script needs one blank line at the end of the file to exit from the 3DPOLY command. The other rules regarding extra spaces and lines still apply.

Stage 7: Creation of the Profile Model

Create the terrain profiles in the same manner you created the terrain model.

1. Open the original model TERR.
2. Freeze the CMESH layer, and make the PROFL layer current.
3. Run the newly modified script MESH2. The resulting 3D polylines should look like Figure 23.6.

Smoothing the Profile Lines

As with the terrain model, the profile lines created from raw data are somewhat ragged and need to be smoothed. The technique to smooth them is identical to the technique you used earlier on the mesh.

1. Select the PEDIT command and pick one of the polylines.
2. Use the SPLINE option to smooth the line.

Figure 23.6
Rough profile lines from raw data

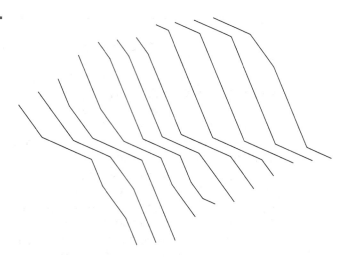

3. Repeat for the other 10 lines. The resulting figure should appear similar to Figure 23.7.
4. Save the modified mesh as TERR.

Stage 8: Display of Selected Profiles

The next step is to display a cross-sectional view of the profiles and then selectively display each profile in turn. To allow the display of a single profile while hiding the rest, place each profile on its own layer.

1. Create layers for each profile line—a total of 11.

COLOR	LAYER
1	PLINE1
2	PLINE2
3	PLINE3
4	PLINE4
5	PLINE5
6	PLINE6
7	PLINE7
8	PLINE8
9	PLINE9
10	PLINE10
11	PLINE11

2. Using the CHPROP command, move each profile line to its own layer.
3. Save the model as TERR.
4. Using the VPOINT command, set the coordinates to –1,0,0 and ZOOM Extents. This will give an elevation view of the profile lines that should be similar to Figure 23.8.
5. Freeze all layers except PLINE1. The cross-section profile of PLINE1 should now be easy to interpret.
6. Proceed to display each profile line in turn and observe the cross-section.

The project is finished: You have created a topographical polygon mesh of a selected terrain and then created and displayed a series of cross-section profiles on that terrain. You now have the skills to recreate any terrain of your choice. Practice the procedures by translating a small portion of any contour map into a 3D topographic model. For a real challenge, try to translate a portion of a contour map of the Rocky Mountains or the Appalachians.

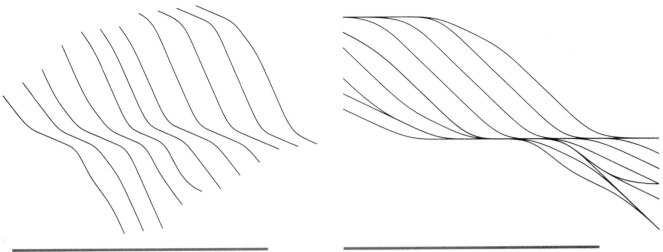

Figure 23.7
Enhanced profile lines

Figure 23.8
Elevation view of profile lines

Rendering

To create a rendering, redisplay the terrain mesh only, set the Rendering Preferences to Smooth Shading, and then render the model. No lights are needed to give a representative view. Refer to Figure 23.9 for a laser plot of the rendered view. (If necessary, return to Chapter 17 for a review of the rendering process.)

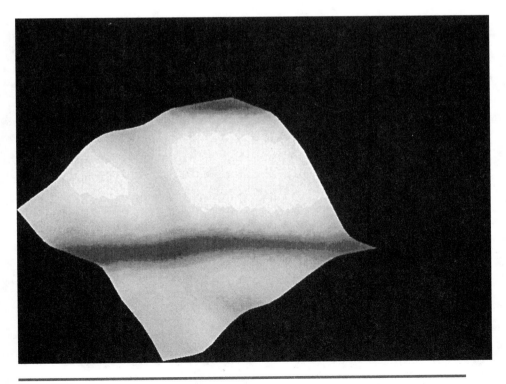

Figure 23.9
Rendered view of the terrain model

PART

Application Programs

This final section, encompassing Chapters 24, 25, and 26, explores three add-on programs that, although not provided with AutoCAD software, act as a complement to it. In the same way that specialized menus and libraries make AutoCAD more valuable to specific users, add-ons like these can add capabilities that neither program could achieve on its own.

Designer, 3D Studio R4, and 3D Studio MAX, the three application programs explored here, point the way to the future for AutoCAD, and, in showing the extraordinary abilities of the programs, it seems fitting that we saved them, like a rich dessert, for last.

CHAPTER 24

AutoCAD Designer

24.1 Introduction

AutoCAD Designer is a parametric, feature-based, solid modeling utility the operates through the AutoCAD Development System (ADS). It is separate from AutoCAD so it must be purchased independently and added on. Its purpose is to automate the production of mechanical designs and drawings by integrating a feature-based parametric solid modeler into the standard Auto-CAD package. You will find that many of the solid modeling options that were part of the Advanced Modeling Extension (AME) are now part of the Designer utility.

Feature-based parametric modeling refers to applying geometric features to a model, such as holes or slots, through dimensional constraints in much the same way as you would normally draw using AutoCAD. However, the difference lies in the fact that with parametric design, you can change a dimensional value on the model and the model is automatically modified to suit the change. Refer to Figure 24.1.

The Designer utility allows you to create a solid modeled part by applying dimensional constraints (or controls) to the model that you can change at any time. This is very useful in prototype design. This is referred to as the part mode. Secondarily, but equally important, Designer also has a drawing mode. In this mode you lay out the part views and apply drawing dimensions. Part mode and drawing mode are integrated, meaning you can make changes in either mode and the changes are reflected in the other mode.

The purpose of this chapter is to give you some insight into the Designer utility and how it can be used within AutoCAD.

Figure 24.1
Parametric changes to a model

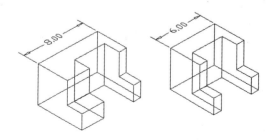

The Parametric Design Process

You have already had some exposure to parametrics in Chapter 14, 3D Parametric Design, in which you made use of parametric blocks. As mentioned in Chapter 14, parametrics is the application of a set of parameters or variables to a model to control its shape and size. Refer to Figure 24.2, which shows the dimensions of a model. Some dimensions control the shape of the object, some control the location of features such as holes or cutouts, and others control the size of the features. By having the ability to change those parameters of the model, you can change the design at any time. And that is exactly what the Designer utility does—it gives you control over those parameters. Designer often refers to the parameters controlling the model as constraints. Some common constraints that apply to a model are whether the surfaces are horizontal or parallel.

The Part

The solid model you create with Designer is referred to as the *part.* The part is the highest level modeling entity. There can be more than one part in the entire layout (referred to as an assembly), but there is only one part active at one time. The part is composed of various parametric features created in a variety of ways, from sketching the desired profile and extruding, revolving, or sweeping it into a three-dimensional shape to applying standard industry forms such as holes (Drilled, C'Bore, C'Sink) and fillets. The creation of the part takes place in model space.

The Drawing

Once you have created a part, you can then create the drawing associated with the part. You switch from the part mode to the drawing mode using the ADMODE command. The drawing mode allows you to lay out the various two-dimensional views of the model. The drawing and its views are associated with the part. This means that when you change the part, the drawing changes as well. The reverse is true also: Change the drawing annotation or dimensions and the part will change. The creation of the drawing takes place in paper space.

Features

Features, the parametric objects used to create the part, come in two types: geometric and work.

Figure 24.2
Parameters that control the model

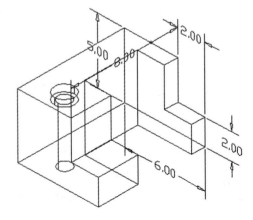

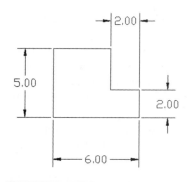

Figure 24.3
Base feature profiles

Geometric Features

Geometric features are used to create the shape of the part and the integral components such as holes. The shape is created through the use of sketched features, whereas the integral components use form features that are completely defined mechanical forms such as drilled or counterbored holes.

Sketched Feature Creation

Most of the solid modeling with Designer is done through "sketched" features. The following is a simplified procedure to create features through sketches:

1. Create a sketch plane.
2. Draw a rough sketch of the desired shape using standard AutoCAD commands to create lines, arcs, circles, or non-spline-fit polylines.
3. Turn your rough sketch into a Designer sketch using ADPROFILE or ADPATH commands.
4. Use Designer commands such as ADADDCON to apply specific geometric or dimensional model related constraints.
5. Turn the active sketch into a solid feature using Designer commands such as ADEXTRUDE, ADREVOLVE, or ADSWEEP.
6. Edit a feature using the ADEDITFEAT command.

Base Feature

To apply parametric controls to the model, you must start with something. This something is referred to as the *base* feature because it provides the base on which the other features are built. The base feature can be as simple as a rectangle or as complex as the Brooklyn Bridge. However, you will find that if you start with a simple rectangle and build on it, you will have more parametric control of your model. If there is a possibility that the beginning profile may change shape if the design changes, stick with a rectangle; if it won't, draw the complex profile as the base feature to save time.

To decide on a base feature, you must review your basic design and break it down into various stages or components—similar to the projects in Chapters 18 through 23. Identify the most controlling feature of the design. It is usually some profile shape that can be extruded, revolved, or swept (refer to Figure 24.3). Use this as the starting point for the base feature.

Geometric Constraints

When you are sketching a profile to create a base feature or another feature further on in the model, you need not be overly concerned with the accuracy of the initially sketched geometry. Lines do not have to be perfectly horizontal or vertical; endpoints do not have to touch perfectly. The reason for this is that Designer has several commands to correct your rough sketch. The ADPROFILE or ADPATH commands are used to apply geometric constraints to the sketch and turn your rough sketch into a sketch Designer can use. The ADPROFILE command creates an active sketch profile by solving closed 2D geometry. The ADPATH command is similar to the ADPROFILE command except that the sketch may be open and it creates an active sketch path. The resulting active sketch can be used to create the solids from extrusion, revolutions, and sweeps. Refer to Figure 24.4.

Some of the constraints that are used in ADPROFILE and ADPATH are horizontal, vertical, perpendicular, parallel, and so on. How they are applied is set by the following variables:

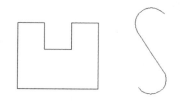

Figure 24.4
Active sketch closed and open

ADSKMODE	Controls whether Designer assumes the sketch to be precise or rough. If ADSKMODE is 1, the constraint rules are applied to your rough sketch. If ADSKMODE is 0, Designer assumes the sketch is precise. It does not make alterations or corrections to the sketch.
ADSKANGTOL	Controls the angular tolerance within which Designer applies constraint rules. It defaults to 4 degrees. If a line is slightly off the horizontal or vertical by less than 4 degrees, Designer straightens it to the axis. You can set the constraint angle.
ADRULEMODE	Controls whether Designer automatically applies constraints. If ADRULEMODE is 1, all constraints are applied. If it is set to 0, only endpoints are joined.
PICKBOX	The standard PICKBOX variable controls how Designer checks entities that touch. If there is a gap between entities and that gap is smaller than the pickbox, then the entities are considered to be touching.

Parametric Constraints

When the active sketch is created, certain parametric constraints are applied to the profile to control its shape. Different constraints are applied based on the shape and how the profile was initially drawn. As you work on the model you will find that more parametric constraints are required depending on your design and you will use constraints to tie your new sketches to an existing part. The ADADDCON command is used to add specific constraints to your model.

Sketching Rules

When you use the ADPROFILE or ADPATH commands to create the Designer sketch, your rough sketch is analyzed and changed to meet a set of rules. The following explains the rules that are applied:

- Lines sketched nearly horizontal are horizontal.
- Lines sketched nearly vertical are vertical.
- Two arcs or an arc/circle and a line sketched nearly tangent are tangent.
- Two arcs or circles whose centers are sketched nearly coincident are concentric.
- Two lines sketched nearly overlaying the same line as each other are collinear.
- Lines sketched nearly parallel are parallel.
- Lines sketched nearly perpendicular are perpendicular. The lines must be attached for perpendicularity to be inferred automatically.
- Any arcs and circles sketched with nearly the same radius have the same radius. One of the arcs or circles must include a radius dimension before the rule is applied.
- Objects are attached using endpoints.
- Objects are attached using the endpoint of one object and the near point of the other object.

Form Features

Form features are predefined mechanical features that do not require sketching such as chamfers, fillets, and holes. Figure 24.5 is an illustration of the Designer Hole dialog box. This type of feature does require a sketch plane to be created; the command automatically creates a plane when you identify a work plane, planar, face, or work point on the active part.

Figure 24.5
Designer Hole dialog box

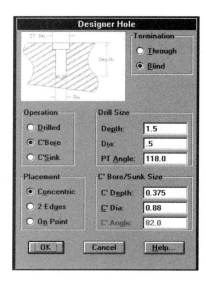

Sketch Planes

Sketch planes are used to create sketches by providing a flat two-dimensional plane on which to draw. Sketch planes are very similar to the UCS except that the UCS uses three axes, *X, Y,* and *Z,* whereas a sketch plane has only two, *X* and *Y.* The sketch plane uses the UCS to form the bases of the plane formation. The *X* and *Y* of the UCS coincides with the *X* and *Y* of the sketch plane.

The command used to set a sketch plane is ASSKPLN. Its options let you set the plane to the World XY, YZ, ZX, or the current UCS or a previously created work plane or planar face. The most common method is to select a face on a part, which causes the sketch plane to align itself to the plane. It is useful to have the UCS icon turned on so that you can see the orientation of the sketch plane. Only one sketch plane can be active at one time.

Work Features

Work features are used to place geometric features on the active part. There are three types of work features: work planes, work axes, and work points. They are created on the ADP_WORK layer. Do not tamper directly with objects on this layer; doing so could ruin your model.

Work Planes

Work planes are considered construction planes. Not only can they be used as planes on which sketch planes can be created, but they are also used to create parametric planes in relation to the model. When this occurs, you can modify the plane, such as rotate it about an axis, and the geometry associated (constrained) with the plane will move as well. Refer to Figure 24.6 for the Designer Work Plane dialog box.

Figure 24.6
Designer Work Plane dialog box

Parametric work planes are parametrically constrained to the active part. You specify the relationship, such as on the edge or parallel to a location on the active part.

Nonparametric work planes are fixed to the UCS or WCS.

Work Axes

Work axes are used as construction lines that run along the centerlines of analytical curved surfaces including cylindrical, conical, or toroidal surfaces or holes. They use the centerline linetype.

Work axes are useful to place a work plane or locate a sketched feature along a curved surface.

Work Points

Work points are used in the location of holes. They appear as three mutually perpendicular lines that originate at a point.

24.4 Dimensioning a Feature

To control the sketch feature that was created with ADPROFILE or ADPATH, you must dimension the sketch using parametric dimensioning. The easiest way is to use the ADPARDIM command that applies parametric dimensions to features that you specify. You could also use standard AutoCAD commands but you would then have to use ADPROFILE or ADPATH again to connect the dimensions with the feature.

To use ADPARDIM, pick two entities, or a single entity. If you pick two entities, Designer assumes you are entering a location or linear size dimension. If you pick at the endpoints, a linear dimension is created, if you pick at the middle an angular dimension is created, and if you pick a single entity, Designer assumes you are creating a radial, diametral, or length dimension. When you have determined the type of dimension and you pick in empty space, Designer assumes you are identifying where to place the dimension value. Refer to Figure 24.7. Each parametric dimension is given an identification such as d1 or d2. The parametric dimension can be in different forms—a numeric value (6.25) or a formula (d2 = d1 * 2).

Editing a Parametric Dimension

To edit the parametric dimensions of a feature, use the ADEDITFEAT command. Once you have selected the feature to edit, the constraining dimensions are displayed. You need only select the one to change and enter the new value.

Figure 24.7
Parametric dimensioning

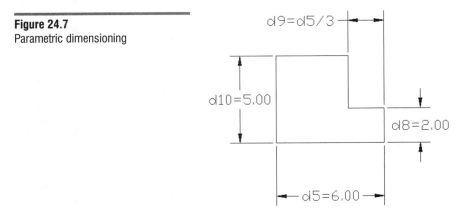

However, the part does not reflect the change until it is updated using the ADUPDATE command. The application of this command is required whenever you edit a feature on a part.

24.5 Drawing Creation

A drawing is a collection of views of the part. Dimensions and annotations are added to the appropriate views. The dimensions and annotations are associated with the part as well. In this way modifications to the part or the dimensions are reflected in each other.

Drawing Views

There are seven different types of views you can create using the ADVIEW command. A dialog box is used to identify the view type and its relation to the part or parts. Refer to Figure 24.8. The first type is the base view on which the others are built. The following list describes the various view types:

Base Views	A general view of a drawing without predefined orientation. This is the first view that you create by selecting a work plane or planar face on the part.
Parent Views	Any view that is used to control the other views. A base view is considered a parent view. When you make changes to the parent view, the other views associated with it change.
Orthographic Views	Standard mechanical orthographic views such as top, right side, or front. These are created from a base view. Where you place the orthographic view in relation to the base view determines the view type. Designer automatically generates the appropriate view.
Auxiliary Views	True size views of selected planes on the part. You pick an edge on a view. This view becomes the parent view for the auxiliary view. The auxiliary view is created on either side of the selected edge, perpendicular to the edge.

Figure 24.8
Designer Drawing View dialog box

Detail Views	Enlarged view of the part. These are used to clarify small details on the part by enlarging only a selected portion of a parent view. You cannot cut a cross section while creating a detail view.
Isometric Views	A standard isometric view of the part where the part view is rotated evenly on all three axes.
Cross-section Views	A view created as if you cut through the part revealing the interior. You can create two types of sections, full and half, with or without hatching. The sectioning plane is identified by either work planes or a point on the parent view.

Projection Orientation

There are two types of projection used to create views: first angle and third angle. Third-angle projection is the common projection method in North America, whereas first-angle projection is common in Europe. The variable ADPROJTYPE controls the type of projection used for orthographic and cross-sectional views. A value of 1 results in a third-angle projection and a value of 0 results in a first-angle projection.

Editing Views

You can edit the various view once they have been created and placed. Orthographic and auxiliary views are always tied to their parent views. The base, detail, and isometric views can be moved to any location on the drawing. You can use the ADEDITVIEW command to change the scale, text label, and hidden line properties of the views. You can also change the area enlarged in a detail view.

Dimensioning

When you create your views, you will find that the parametric dimensions created on the part in part mode now appear in the drawing mode. You may need to use the ADFRZDIM command to freeze parametric dimensions that appear in the drawing, but are unnecessary for the drawing. The freezing of parametric dimensions will not affect their function. The ADTHAWDIM command will redisplay the frozen dimensions if you desire.

The ADMOVEDIM command allows you to move the dimensions to more desirable locations.

To add more dimensions in drawing mode, you need to use the ADREFDIM command. This adds dimensions that are not parametric but only reference in origin. In this way you won't be duplicating parametric dimensions which would alter the part's parametric nature. The reference dimensions define the part but do not control the geometry.

The ADMODDIM command allows you to change dimension values on a drawing or the active sketch on a part. If you change parametric values you need to update the part using the ADUPDATE command.

Refer to Figure 24.9 for dimensioned views highlighting the various dimension types.

Annotations

To add annotations, such as notes, part balloons, or tolerance symbols, to the drawing, use standard AutoCAD commands, such as CIRCLE and DTEXT. If you want the annotation to attach itself to a particular view so that it moves if the view moves, use the ADANNOTE command. The ADANNOTE command will also create a leader from the part to the annotation if desired.

Figure 24.9
Drawing dimension types

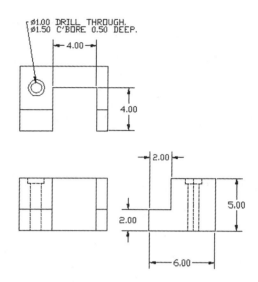

Hole Notes

The ADHOLENOTE command will extract the hole feature information of a selected arc or circle and place it in a note on the desired view along with a leader line.

24.6 Designer Command and Variable Listing

Here is a listing of the various Designer commands and variables. Most of the variables can be accessed through the Designer Settings dialog box through the ADSETTINGS command.

COMMANDS	DESCRIPTION
ADACTPART	Selects the part to be active when there is more than one part.
ADADDCON	Adds parametric constraints to paths or profiles for features.
ADANNOTE	Adds or modifies annotations on a drawing.
ADASFCONV	Creates AutoSURF surface model from a Designer part.
ADAXISDSP	Displays the work axis of a part.
ADCHAMFER	Creates a chamfer on a part.
ADDELCON	Changes relationships between sketched entities.
ADDELFEAT	Deletes features from a part.
ADDELREF	Deletes dimensions from drawing views.
ADDELVIEW	Deletes a specified view.
ADDIMATT	Modifies the appearance, precision, and tolerance of a view's dimensions.
ADDIMDSP	Changes dimensioning display mode.
ADEDITFEAT	Displays/modifies the dimensions of a part.
ADEDITVIEW	Modifies scale, text, and hidden line display of a view.
ADEXTRUDE	Creates an extruded solid feature from a sketch.
ADFILLET	Creates a fillet on a part's edge.
ADFIXPT	Fixes an immovable point in XYZ space on a sketch.
ADFRZDIM	Guides a dimension on a drawing.
ADHOLE	Creates a hole in a part.
ADHOLENOTE	Creates a note (diameter depth and angle) on a hole.
ADISOLINES	Controls the wireframe display of a part (controls variables ADISOCYL and ADISONURB).

ADLIST	Provides information on parts, features, and views.
ADMAKEBASE	Makes a part nonactive and compresses its information.
ADMASSPROP	Lists the mass properties of a part.
ADMESH	Displays wireframe surfaces as mesh surfaces.
ADMODDIM	Allows modification of dimension values of a part.
ADMODE	Selects part or drawing mode.
ADMOVEDIM	Moves dimensions while maintaining association to drawing geometry.
ADMOVELDR	Moves the leader arrowhead.
ADMOVEVIEW	Moves a drawing view.
ADNEWPART	Creates a new solid part definition while in part mode.
ADPARM	Creates/deletes/lists/exports global parameters.
ADPARDIM	Allows interactive dimensioning of a sketch.
ADPARTIN	Reads an outside part into a current file.
ADPARTOUT	Saves selected part in a separate file.
ADPARTVIEW	Changes view orientation in the part mode.
ADPATH	Creates an open path sketch used for Sweep features.
ADPLNDSP	Displays/hides work planes of a part.
ADPROFILE	Creates a closed profile sketch for creating solids.
ADPTDSP	Displays/hides work points on a part.
ADREFDIM	Creates a reference dimension on a view.
ADREVOLVE	Creates a revolved solid feature on a profile.
ADSATIN	Reads a .SAT file (ACIS) into AutoCAD designer.
ADSATOUT	Writes a designer file into .SAT format.
ADSETTINGS	Allows AutoCAD designer variables to be set.
ADSHOWACT	Highlights the active part, sketch, or plane.
ADSHOWCON	Displays the constraint symbols on a sketch.
ADSKPLN	Sets the sketch plane and *XY* axes.
ADSWEEP	Creates a solid feature by sweeping a profile along a specified path.
ADTHAWDIM	Displays dimensions frozen with ADFRZDIM.
ADUPDATE	Updates and regenerates an active part.
ADVER	Displays the release number of AutoCAD designer.
ADVIEW	Creates a variety of drawing types from a designer solid model.
ADWORKAXIS	Creates a work axis at the center of cylindrical, conical, and toroidal surfaces.
ADWORKPLN	Creates the construction plane of a part.
ADWORKPT	Creates work points for hole location.

VARIABLES	VALUE	DESCRIPTION
ADBORDER	1 or 0	Controls the display of view borders.
ADCONDSPSZ	1 to 19	Controls the height of display constraints on the sketch.
ADHIDLTYPE	Linetype	Controls the linetype of hidden lines.
ADISOCYL	0 to 100	Controls the number of isolines on a cylinder/sphere.
ADISONURB	0 to 100	Controls the number of isolines in NURBS surfaces.
ADPARFILE	File name	Names the file for sharing parameters between .DWG files.
ADPROJTYPE	1 or 0	Controls the unfolding of orthographic and ancillary vies.
ADREUSEDIM	1 or 0	Toggles display of parametric dimensions.
ADRULEMODE	1 or 0	Controls the application of automatic constraints.

ADSECLTYPE	Linetype	Sets linetype for section lines in a cross section.
ADSKANGTOL	0.001 to 10.0	Controls constraint tolerance angle.
ADSKMODE	1 or 0	Controls interpretation of a sketch as precise or rough.
ADSKSTYLE	Linetype	Lists linetypes used for sketch boundaries.

CHAPTER 25

3D Studio (R4)

25.1 Introduction

3D Studio is a complete three-dimensional modeling, rendering, and animation program produced by Autodesk. It is separate from AutoCAD, but is able to make use of 3D AutoCAD models. With 3D Studio, you can create a variety of 3D models, as you can in AutoCAD, for instance by drawing a 2D profile and extruding it into three dimensions and applying materials to surfaces or objects using AutoVision's image bitmaps and mapping coordinates. However, in the area of animation, 3D Studio is more impressive than AutoVision/AutoCAD in its creation of animated stills (see Figure 25.1).

In architectural design, walk-throughs or flybys can be created for preliminary designs. The animated presentation can show the client what the structure will look like, inside and out, as if the client were walking through or around the building.

Similarly, in mechanical design, mechanical movement can be shown—gears rotate and robotic arms swing into motion. This application allows the designer or client to see how a particular piece of equipment will operate in an easily studied environment.

In the area of graphic design, the artist can create impressive and dynamic presentations of ideas and concepts—from flying corporate logos to a quick mock-up of a video advertisement without the production overhead.

Even computer game designers make use of 3D Studio to create creatures and the virtual environments they inhabit.

In fact, this explanation barely touches on the areas in which 3D Studio is being utilized. The program is currently being used by ballet and theater producers to orient their actors on stage without wasting valuable time and money; it is helping criminologists decide the course of events that culminated in a murder, thereby helping to solve the case; athletics coaches use the program to teach the ideal plays visually, before they hit the field; air traffic controllers use it to try to decide what went wrong upon approach, and how to avoid the problem in future; even historical researchers use it as they continue to ask what went on behind the grassy knoll. In much the same way as flight simulators were originally used to train pilots, 3D Studio is found where it makes more sense—in terms of time, money, and safety—for the program to go before the actual people go or before the real money is spent.

This chapter provides an overview of 3D Studio and the basics of the program.

25.2 3D Studio Concepts

3D Studio creates an animation by assembling rendered still frames into a movie, as shown in Figure 25.1. To accomplish this, 3D Studio is broken down into logical environments that are used at various stages to create the geometry, cover it with materials, prepare the scene, and produce the animation. In this way, you can switch to any of the different environments at any time, to work on your project. The environments interact with each other. You can begin simply, by creating a few objects, giving them some material coverings, and animating them. Once this is working the way you want, you can switch back to other environments and continue to add and modify your project until you have completed your complex model and animation. The environment modules are referred to as programs in 3D studio.

3D Studio Programs

The following is a list of the different environment modules within 3D Studio. Once 3D Studio is loaded, you can switch between the modules by using the pull-down menu or the function keys.

2D Shaper	(F1)	Used to create 2D profiles or shapes.
3D Lofter	(F2)	Used to take the 2D shapes and project them in various ways to create 3D objects.
3D Editor	(F3)	Used to assemble the scene and place objects at various locations. You will apply materials to objects and add lights and cameras. Even simple primitive objects can be created.
Keyframer	(F4)	Used to create the animation. This is where the action takes place. You decide how long the animation will be in frames, where objects will move to, if the lights or camera moves, and more.
Materials Editor	(F5)	Used to analyze materials from the material libraries or create your own to be used in the 3D Editor.

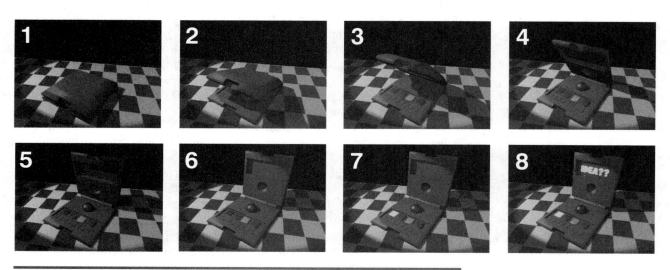

Figure 25.1
Still frames to create animation

Saving and Loading Files

Each program has its own form of saving and loading files. In this way you can save individual pieces to be used in other projects. 2D Shaper shapes are saved or loaded as files with the extension .SHP; 3D Lofter lofts are saved or loaded as files with the extension .LFT; and 3D Editor scenes (whether one object or many) are saved or loaded as files with the extension .3DS. The Keyframer has no individual save but its information is saved when you save in the 3D Editor. A file with the extension .3DS contains the 3D model and the animation information. Materials are not saved but are manipulated using GET or PUT. You can "get" them from a library or the 3D Editor scene and "put" them into a scene or a library. The material libraries can be saved or loaded.

It is also possible to save all the information currently stored in the various programs into one file. This is referred to as a project. When you save a project, a file is created with the extension .PRJ. If you open a project, the information is loaded into the various programs—2D Shaper, 3D Lofter, 3D Editor, Keyframer, and Materials Editor. This is useful when working on a current project for which you wish to retain all the pieces.

25.3 The 3D Studio Interaction

To use 3D Studio you must be able to navigate the program, become familiar with the screen and menus, and learn the different functions performed by the mouse buttons.

Screen

There are different screens for each program environment but most have a similar layout. Refer to Figure 25.2.

Figure 25.2
The 3D Editor program screen

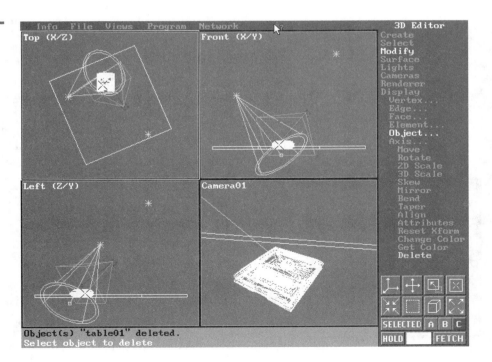

Status Line and Pull-Down Menus

Along the top edge of the screen are the status line and pull-down menus. When you are working with various commands, information about the commands is displayed here, such as coordinate information. When you bring your cursor into this area, the pull-down menu bar appears. You can select from any one of the menus by picking on them with your pointing device. You should look though each menu and become familiar with its contents.

One item to note for AutoCAD users is the coordinate axis. In AutoCAD the WCS has the X and Y axes for the top or plan view. The Z axis is usually the projecting axis. In 3D Studio the X and Z axes form the top or plan view, while the Y axis is the projecting axis. This is the default setting, although it is possible to change this using the 3DS.SET configuration file.

Command Columns

Along the right side of the screen lies the command column. This menu changes with the program module currently in use. The menu hierarchy is divided into branches.

The leftmost column at the top of the menu column is the main branch. As you select an item of this menu, menu branches form below, allowing access to more command options. There are as many as four levels of branches.

Colors are used to emphasize your menu selection. As you scroll though a menu, the items are highlighted in light blue to show you where you are. When you pick an item, it turns yellow or white. A white item indicates that it is an intermediate item and that there are further options below. A yellow item indicates that there are no further options. Note that it may flash yellow and turn blue again if an action took place when picking the menu item.

Some menu items are toggles, meaning they may be on or off, such as the Modify/Axis/Show menu item in the 2D Shaper module. An asterisk is placed next to the toggle item if it has been turned on.

As you move through menu branches, you will notice that they are bookmarked. What this means is that when you leave a main menu branch and go to another totally different branch, 3D Studio places a bookmark where you were before. If you go back to the previous menu, it displays your exit point.

Prompt Line

Information will appear at the bottom of the screen when you are using a command to give you further information about the command. This is referred to as the prompt line. Current information will appear white, whereas previous command information or a sentence describing results will appear in black. The command line looks familiar to AutoCAD users; however, you cannot enter commands there as you can with the command line in AutoCAD.

Icon Panel

In the lower right corner of the screen you will see a series of icons in an area called the icon panel. These icon buttons control the views in the drawing area and activate various modes. Pick on an icon button to use it as indicated in Figure 25.3.

The SELECTED icon and the A, B, and C that follow are used when you want to perform an action on a group of objects instead of only one object. You create a group of selected items using the Select column menu item and the objects will turn red to denote that they are in a group. To use the selected items, activate the desired command, and when you are asked to select items, pick on the SELECTED icon to turn it red and then pick anywhere in the

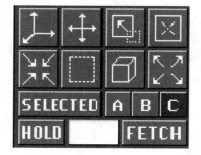

Figure 25.3
Icon panel

desired viewport. The objects that were red are then acted upon. You can work with three different groups at any time—A, B, or C group.

The HOLD and FETCH icons are a form of undo for 3D Studio. Before you perform a command whose results you are unsure of, pick on the HOLD icon. It stores the current state of the program module. You then perform the command. If the results are not what you want, simply pick on the FETCH icon to return to your initial state.

Some icons are global for all program modules, whereas others are specific to specific modules. The following view control icons are global to most of the modules.

Axis Tripod Icon (U):   Used to adjust the 3D viewpoint in a user viewport with an *XYZ* tripod axis. If the axis is white, the positive axis points towards you. If it is black, the positive axis points away from you.

Pan Icon (P):   Used to move the image in the active viewport.

Full Screen Toggle Icon (W):   Toggles between displaying multiple viewports and a single viewport.

Local Axis Icon (X):   Used to activate the axis of the object being manipulated. Used in 2D Shaper and 3D Editor to manipulate an object about its own axis. When it is off, operations are based on a global axis.

Switch Viewports Icon (X):   Used in the 3D Lofter to switch views between the large viewport and the smaller ones.

Zoom In Icon (Shift + Z):   Magnifies the active view by 50 percent.

Window Zoom Icon (Alt + Z):   Used to magnify a specified area of the active view.

Zoom Extent Icon (Ctrl + Z):   Magnifies or reduces the displayed active view so that the objects in the view fill the view.

Zoom Out Icon (Z):   Reduces the display in the active view by 50 percent. The opposite of Zoom In.

Using the Input Device

You can use a mouse or a digitizer with 3D Studio. The left button on the mouse is your pick button, used for selecting most commands and objects on the screen. The right button has special features depending on where you are in the program. For instance, if you use the Pick button to select the Zoom Extent icon, the current viewport redraws to display the extent of your objects. If you use the right button to select the icon, all viewports redraw to display their extents.

The cursor icon can change appearance depending on what action is being performed. Refer to Figure 25.4 for an illustration of the different cursor icon types. The tab key can be used to toggle through various cursor icon types. For instance, if the unidirectional cursor is displayed, each time you press the <Tab> key, the direction will cycle through up, down, left, and right.

The help cursor icon will appear when you hold down the <Alt> key and move the cursor over the pull-down menus or the command columns. Picking on an item at this point will display some help information.

Figure 25.4
Cursor icons

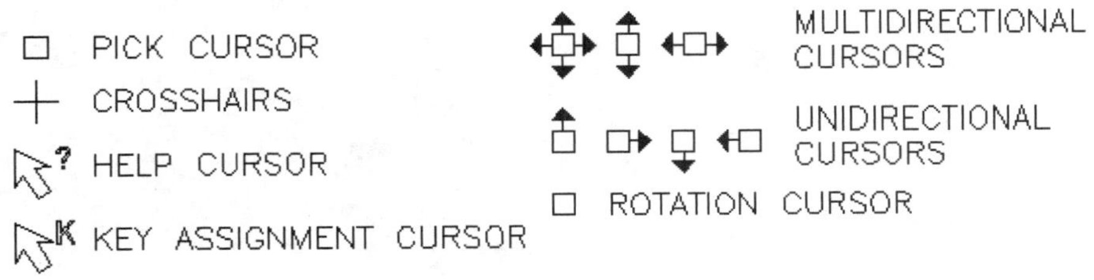

□ PICK CURSOR

+ CROSSHAIRS

? HELP CURSOR

K KEY ASSIGNMENT CURSOR

MULTIDIRECTIONAL CURSORS

UNIDIRECTIONAL CURSORS

□ ROTATION CURSOR

Viewports

Depending on which program you are in, you can have single or multiple viewports displayed on the screen. Each one will give you different viewpoints of the model. Each viewport type has a name associated with it:

L	left
R	right
F	front
K	back
B	bottom
T	top
C	camera
U	user

To activate a viewport you pick within the viewport border. To change a viewpoint inside a viewport, enter the letter associated with the view on the keyboard. You can also use the Views/Viewports pull-down menu item.

25.4 2D Shaper

The 2D Shaper is used to create and edit two-dimensional spline polygons. Refer to Figure 25.5. These polygon profiles are used in the following ways:

- Creates 3D mesh objects in the 3D Lofter.
- Replaces the current path for a new path in the 3D Lofter.
- Creates flat, 2D mesh objects in the 3D Editor.
- Creates complex paths for objects, lights, and cameras in the Keyframer.

Use the Create menu item from the command column to create shapes. If you have created more than one shape in the shaper, you must identify which one(s) will be used in the other modules using the Shape Assign command. The assigned polygons will appear yellow. When used in another model, all the assigned shapes will be treated as one complex shape.

Figure 25.5
The 2D Shaper screen

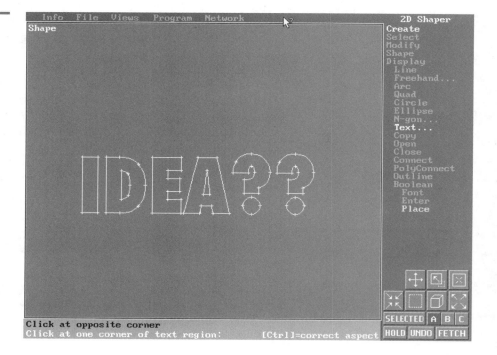

To make use of a 2D shape you enter the appropriate program model. For instance, the 3D Lofter is used to take the 2D shape and loft it into a 3D meshed object. First, bring the shape into the lofter with the Shapes/Get/Shaper command. Then, turn it into a 3D object using the Objects/Make command or make the shape into a path in the 3D Lofter by using the Path/Get/Shaper command.

The 3D Editor is used to turn the shape into a 2D meshed object using the Create/Object/Get Shape command.

At a later stage, the Keyframer uses the shape to define paths used to direct the motion of objects, lights, and cameras. This is done using the Paths/Get/Shaper command in the Keyframer module.

25.5 3D Lofter

The 3D Lofter assembles one or more 2D Shaper shapes and uses them to create a three-dimensional meshed object. Refer to Figure 25.6 for an illustration of the 3D Lofter screen. The term lofter comes from ancient times when wooden ships were built. The builders assembled a series of wooden cross sections of the shape, held together with "lofts." The process of hoisting the cross sections into the lofts became known as lofting. This is exactly what you do in 3D Lofter.

Place one or more shapes and use the 3D Lofter commands to turn those 2D shapes into complex 3D meshes. A path is used to determine the direction in which the lofting will take place. You can create and modify a path in the 3D Lofter or bring in a shape from the 2D Shaper to be used as a lofting path.

Once you have assembled the shapes and defined the path, use the Objects/Make command to create a meshed object to be sent to the 3D Editor when the lofting is performed.

25.6 3D Editor

The 3D Editor module provides the spot where you assemble your objects and place lights and cameras to create a scene. It is the main controlling program. You take shapes from the 2D Shaper, mesh objects from the 3D Lofter, and

Figure 25.6
The 3D Lofter screen

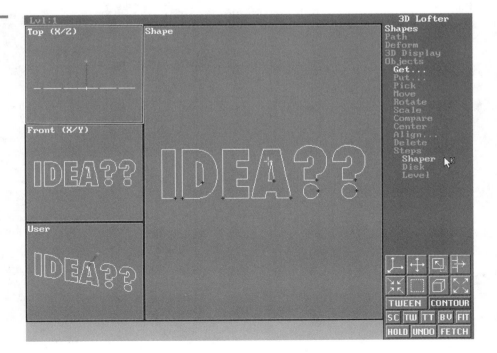

apply materials from the Materials Editor. You, as the director, decide where the various objects should go, where the lights should be placed and how and where the camera should be set. Figure 25.7 shows a view of the 3D Editor screen.

The following paragraphs explain the items listed in the main column menu and provide a description of their purpose.

Create

The Create menu is used to create primitive objects such as boxes or spheres. Remember that any objects that are created require a name. You should assign appropriate names to objects so that you can manipulate them by name, such as Chair or Tire. You can add or delete vertices on already created objects. Vertices are used to create faces (flat surfaces). 2D Shaper profiles can be imported. You can edit and copy vertices, faces, and objects.

Select

The Select menu is used to group objects into selection sets so that you can manipulate several items at once. This temporary group is stored under one of three letter groups: A, B, or C.

To select and use the group:

1. Pick the desired letter (A, B, C) from the icon panel.
2. Use the Select menu options to pick the various objects to be added to the group.
3. Check that the appropriate letter is highlighted in the icon panel.
4. Select the desired command such as Modify/Object/Move.
5. Highlight the SELECTED button in the icon panel. You can use the space bar to turn this button on or off.
6. Pick in an active viewport (camera, or spotlight viewports do not work).
7. The selected group will be acted on.
8. Turn off the SELECTED button when finished.

Figure 25.7
The 3D Editor screen

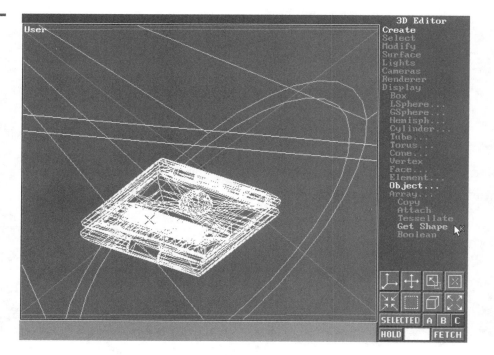

If you want to modify a single object, a quick way of selecting it is to use the CTRL + N key sequence. This brings up a list of named objects from which you can select.

Modify

The Modify menu is used to edit objects, elements, faces, edges, or vertices. You can move, rotate, scale, or make other changes to those entities and you can alter the attributes of an object, including its name.

The Modify menu can also be used to display, hide, or move the location of the global axis. This axis is used as the focal point for modifications such as rotate or scale.

Surface

The Surface menu is used to control the appearance of surfaces for rendering. Such tasks as assigning materials from the Materials Editor (or Materials Library) to objects, adjusting the smoothing groups for different shading types (Gouraud, Phong, or metal), and assigning mapping coordinates to objects are all performed from this menu.

Lights

The Lights menu is used to pick different light types and place them in the scene. You can also reposition existing lights and change their properties.

The different light types are:

Ambient   Used for the overall brightness of a scene. It brightens or darkens all surfaces uniformly.

Omni   Used for placing light sources that radiate light in all directions. They do not cast shadows.

Spot   Used for placing light sources that have direction to their light (beam of light). Spotlights cast shadows.

The Alt + L key sequence will display or hide lights in a scene.

Cameras

The Cameras menu is used to create cameras, place them, and locate their target points. When you create a camera, you can adjust such items as lens size, field of view, and roll (twist). In addition, you can modify the location or settings of any existing camera.

The Alt + C key sequence will display or hide cameras in a scene.

Render

The Render menu is used to perform rendering on the current 3D Studio scene. You can render all, or a portion, of the current viewport.

When rendering, you control the appearance of the rendered file with the Render Still Image dialog. Items in the dialog box include render type (from simple, Flat, to complex, Metal) and output (such as Display or Disk).

Display

The Display menu is used to change the display of graphic components by hiding and unhiding selected faces, elements, and objects.

The Keyframer is used to animate the scene that you assembled in the 3D Editor. Basically, you create a series of still frames with each of the scenes progressively transformed. Figure 25.8 shows the Keyframer screen.

Key Frames

To make life simpler for you, there are frames that you can use as key frames. For instance, suppose you have an object in a certain position in frame 1 and you want the object to slide across the scene and come to rest in frame 10. Instead of moving the object in each frame from 2 to 10, you go to frame 10 and move the object to its new position. Frame 10 becomes a key frame. The Keyframe module knows that you want to object to move from its position in frame 1 to its new position in frame 10. It visually creates the movements in the frames from 2 to 9 automatically. However, you may not make any changes in frame 1, or these changes will also be reflected in the 3D Editor.

Tracks

The movements or transformations that take place through an animation are recorded as keys on tracks. Every object, including cameras and lights, has tracks. When you add a key frame or make a change to an existing key, it is recorded on the objects track. You use tracks to make changes to keys.

Hierarchical Linking

When you have objects whose movements affect other objects, you must link them in some way. Think of a human arm—you have a hand, a lower arm, and an upper arm. When the upper arm swings up at the shoulder, the lower arm and hand obviously move with it. They are physically linked. This is the same within the Keyframer; you decide which objects are linked. This is referred to as hierarchical linking.

Figure 25.8
The Keyframer screen

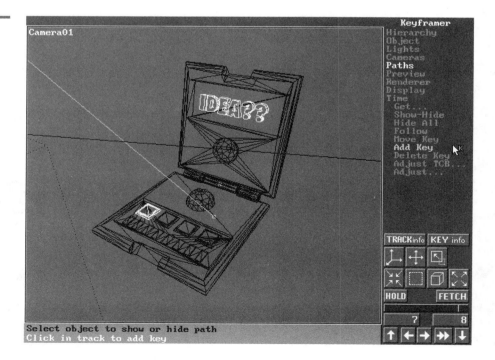

Rendering

Once you have made the transformations to your animation, it is time to render it. Each frame is rendered and automatically assembled into a single movie file with the extension .FLC (or .FLI for 320 × 200 resolution). This can take quite a while depending on the complexity of the scene, render type, and the resolution of the created images (320 × 200 versus 640 × 480). The flic can be played back in 3D Studio or outside the program using another animation display program such as ANIPLAY.EXE.

25.8 Materials Editor

The Materials Editor allows you to create and edit surface materials. Every object has surface material properties. The default material is shiny white plastic and is assigned to newly created objects by default. With the Materials Editor, you can create your own materials or modify already created materials from a materials library. Refer to Figure 25.9 for the Materials Editor screen.

Sample Windows

The sample windows let you view sample renderings of materials you have loaded or created. You can display them on a sphere or a cube as set in the Control Panel. There are seven windows, each of which can display its own material. However, depending on your computer's display (8-bit versus 16-bit), only the active window may display color. The rest of the windows turn black and white.

Shading Mode Buttons and Special Attributes

The shading mode buttons determine the shading mode of the current material. The lowest mode is flat and the highest is metallic. You decide what mode to use on a material. The special attribute buttons control whether the material will render as wireframe and/or two sided. Two sided is used when you want a material to be displayed on both sides of a surface.

Figure 25.9
The Materials Editor screen

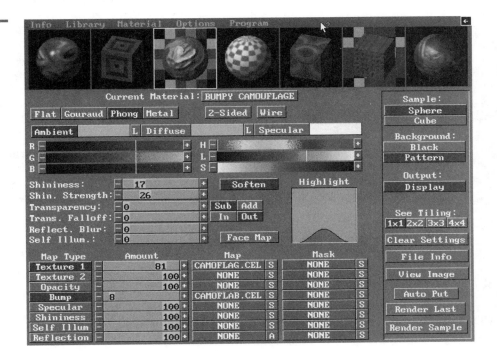

Material Color Controls

The material color buttons control the color of all nonmapped materials:

Ambient | Controls the color of the portion of an object not in direct light.
Diffuse | Controls the color of the lighted portion of the object.
Specular | Controls the color of the highlight on a shiny object.

Material Property Controls

The material property controls are used to adjust the various properties of the surface material:

Shininess | Controls the size of the specular highlight.
Shin. Strength | Controls the brightness of the highlight.
Transparency | Controls how transparent an object is.
Sub and Add | Control whether the color of a transparent material is subtracted or added to the background color, respectively.
Trans. Falloff | Controls the size of an object's transparent area.
Out and In | Control the effect of transparency fall-off.
Reflect. Blur | Controls the sharpness of reflection bitmaps.
Self Illum. | Controls how much of the diffuse color is displayed on an object.
Soften | Used only for Phong shading and to soften specular highlights.
Face Map | Controls whether a map is applied to every face of an object or the surface.
Highlight | Displays the intensity and area of the highlight with the use of a graph.

Mapping Assignment

This area controls how bitmap images are applied to surfaces. Note that the use of bitmaps requires a lot of memory depending on their use. Each bitmap used in a material has to be loaded into memory when it is used in a scene.

With Texture 1 and Texture 2 maps, the image is painted onto the surface. Opacity causes white pixels of the map to be opaque and black pixels to be transparent. Bump creates an embossed effect, or bumpiness. Specular shows up only in areas of specular highlight and affects the color. Shininess shows up only in areas of specular highlight and affects the intensity. Self-illumination is used to apply a map that appears to glow from within. Reflection creates the effect of a reflected image.

Control Panel

The Control Panel controls the manner in which the images are displayed.

CHAPTER 26

3D Studio MAX

26.1 Introduction

3D Studio MAX is a complete three-dimensional modeling, rendering, and animation program that runs within the Windows NT or Windows 95 environment. Whatever your field or intended field, 3D Studio MAX has a place—from creating photorealistic static presentations of a mechanical part to dynamic flybys of a new architectural complex.

It has the ability to import 3DS files that AutoCAD can export. In this way you can make use of models already created in AutoCAD. This chapter gives you an overview of the program and its many features.

26.2 The Scene

All your creation and manipulation takes place in a scene in which you form objects and place them in the desired layout. The material properties added in the scene make them look more realistic, lights create shadow and highlights, and the correct camera placement provides the most effective viewpoint. Once a scene is complete you can render a single, static frame to get a photo-realistic picture or take the objects contained in your scene and animate them. The starting point, however, is the objects you create.

Object-oriented Design

Because object behavior is governed by the object's assigned properties, it is the objects and their properties that, in effect, control what may happen within a scene. These properties vary depending on the object type, which in turn depends on the plug-in (external programs) software available. Some plug-ins accompany 3D Studio MAX; others can be purchased from third-part developers.

The following list contains the basic object types that can be created within 3D Studio MAX:

Standard Primitives   Parametric objects for creating standard-shaped primitive objects such as boxes or spheres. Parametric design is the process of supplying varying data, such as length, width, and height, to create different forms. Primitives are building blocks that can be used as the basis for final complex objects such as table legs, room floors, and planetary bodies.

Shapes	2D or 3D spline curves. These curves can be open or closed. When closed they define outlines used to loft (sweep) a complex 3D form or to create flat, meshed objects. When open, they can define paths that are used for loft direction or for animated motion paths that objects follow.
Lofts	Compound objects created by sweeping (pushing) profile objects along a path. The profile can be any shape, closed or open. The path, another shape, may be straight, curved, or extremely convoluted, such as a helix. The resulting object can be simple or complex, defined by the profile and path combined.
Patch Grids	A surface object referred to as a Bezier surface patch. Think of it as a paper shape. It has no thickness, but you can rotate and bend it at any angle; by welding the surfaces together, you can create a 3-dimensional object.
Meshes	Collection of vertices connected by triangular faces to form an object.
Morphs	Compound objects used to cause an object to change shape over time. Usually two objects are used, with the first object changing into the second object over time. Note that the two objects must contain the same number of vertices for successful morphing.
Booleans	Compound objects created by the action of Boolean operations such as union (adding together) and subtraction (taking one from the other) of two objects.
Particles	Objects that emit 2D and 3D particles to simulate rain or other similar effects.
Lights	Three types of lights, Omni, Spot, and Directional, used to light a scene, cast shadows, project images, and create other effects.
Cameras	Behave like real-life cameras, allowing you to set the camera lens and field of vision. These are used to view movement or move themselves.
Helpers	Objects that are used to define 3D points, measure distances and angles, and create working grid planes.
Space Warps	Special objects that are used to influence other objects that come within a space warp's boundary. A space warp can deform or move objects that move over them.

26.3 Working Planes and Viewing

Working with 3D Studio MAX's world involves understanding how objects relate to one another and how they are positioned. There are two spatial coordinate systems within 3D Studio MAX. These two systems are called Object Space and World Space.

Object Space

Object space is a coordinate system based on the object itself. Each object created has its own vertices, placement modifiers, mapping coordinates, and materials, and these are located in reference to the object's object space.

Refer to Figure 26.1 showing an object's pivot point axes and bounding box. The pivot point, defined in object space, governs the object's movement and modification. The bounding box is a rectangular box that defines the dimensional extent or limit of the object.

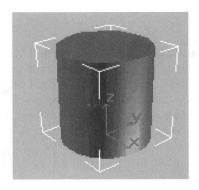

Figure 26.1
An object showing pivot point and bounding box.

World Space

World space is 3D Studio MAX's universal 3-dimensional coordinate system used to keep track of all objects in a scene. The Home Grid, discussed next, is based on world space and is used as the initial ground working plane. Refer to Figure 26.2, which indicates that the world axis sits in the center of the Home Grid. Every object is positioned in world space. Consequently, world space is fixed and cannot be moved or rotated.

Home Grid

The Home Grid is three coordinate planes (working planes) aligned to the world space coordinates. Refer to Figure 26.3, showing the intersection of the three planes. Each plane is a combination of two of the three axes, creating *XY*, *XZ*, and *YZ* planes. They intersect at the 0,0,0 point in world space. This means that the *XY* plane sits on the 0*Z* axis, the *XZ* plane sits on the 0*Y* axis, and the *YZ* plane sits on the 0*X* axis. When you create, the object is positioned on one of the planes. You are also able to create your own construction planes with Grid Objects.

Grid Objects

Grid objects are helper objects; their sole purpose is to create construction planes in any scene location. You can position them anywhere in world space and are not forced to match the fixed Home Grid. Refer to Figure 26.4 for a representation of a grid object.

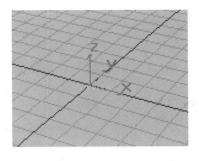

Figure 26.2
World space axis icon

Viewports

Viewports behave as the windows to a scene and control the planes upon which you construct. The standard orthographic viewports that align with the Home Grid, such as Front, Top, and Right Side, are the default method of creation. When you activate such a viewport, you are drawing on one of these three views.

Perspective, user, camera, light, and grid object viewports are available, in addition to the standard viewports. A grid object viewport can be used for creation, whereas the others are used mainly to get a clearer view of the 3D scene.

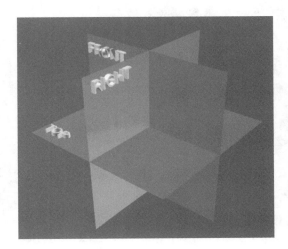

Figure 26.3
Intersection of three working planes

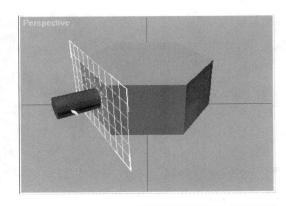

Figure 26.4
Grid helper object used as construction plane

26.4 | Modeling and Editing

When first you create an object, it is called a master object and is controlled by an initial set of creation parameters. Take a box, for instance. Initially the box is defined by its length, width, height, the number of segments along each of those shape descriptors, and the original position and orientation of its pivot point. The object is also assigned surface properties. Once an object has been created, you can edit it by transforming it (by moving or rotating, for example) or modify it (by changing the length or surface properties, for example).

Creation Parameters

Creation parameters are the initial values used to describe the shape, size, and position of an object. Refer to Figure 26.5, showing the creation dialog and the creation parameters. They can be altered during the creation process but only until you generate another object. Remember to give a unique name to every object you create.

Pivot Point

The pivot point defines the object's local coordinate system (object space) and the object's location in world space. It is also used as the center of rotation and scaling. Refer to Figure 26.6, showing the tripod axis of the pivot point. It is possible to modify the orientation of this pivot point using the hierarchy command panel. This is discussed later.

Bounding Box

The *bounding box* defines the dimensional extents or limit of the object. It appears as the corners of a rectangular box when the object is displayed in a shaded mode or as a complete box when the object is displayed in box mode. Refer to Figure 26.6. Notice the rectangular shape that represents the bounding box.

Figure 26.5
Creation dialog showing creation parameters.

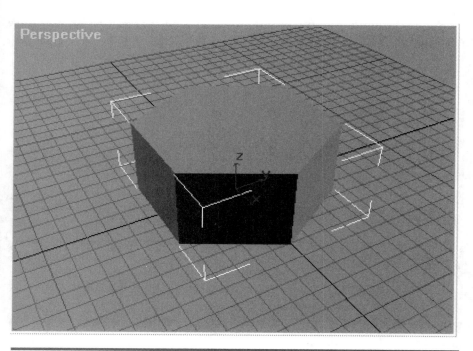

Figure 26.6
Shaded display showing bounding box and pivot point

Surface Properties

Every geometric object you create has a set of surface properties. These are called face normals, smoothing groups, and mapping coordinates.

A *face normal* is a vector that defines the direction in which a face is pointing. Remember that a face has two sides. The face normal decides which side of a face is visible. During the usual creation of objects, the face normals usually face outward and do not need modification. Refer to Figure 26.7, showing the vectors pointing outward on an object. However, imported objects from other programs may have their normals reversed. You can modify the entire object's face normals or adjust individual ones.

Smoothing groups affect pairs of faces joined at an edge. When an object is rendered, sometimes you want to see an edge and sometimes you want the edge to be smoothly blended. Each face is assigned a smoothing group. If two adjacent faces have the same smoothing group, they will be blended. If they do not share the same smoothing group, the edge between them will be defined. During the creation of objects you can turn smoothing on or off; once an object is created you can modify the object's smoothing groups. Refer again to Figure 26.5, which shows the creation panel. Near the bottom of the panel is a box to check for automatic smoothing.

Mapping coordinates are used to tell 3D Studio MAX how to apply mapped materials to an object. If an object is going to have mapped materials applied, it needs mapping coordinates. When an object is initially created, it can have mapping coordinates automatically applied to it. You can also modify a previously created object so that it has mapping coordinates or adjust existing ones. Refer again to Figure 26.5. At the bottom of the creation panel there is a box for the automatic application of mapping coordinates.

Note: If an object has mapping coordinates, it takes longer to render. As a rule of thumb, don't use mapping coordinates if an object is not going to have bitmap image material applied to it.

Selecting Objects

Whenever you want to make a change to an object, whether you're deleting, moving, or modifying it, you need to be able to select it. There are several ways to go about this.

Figure 26.7
Face normals pointing outward

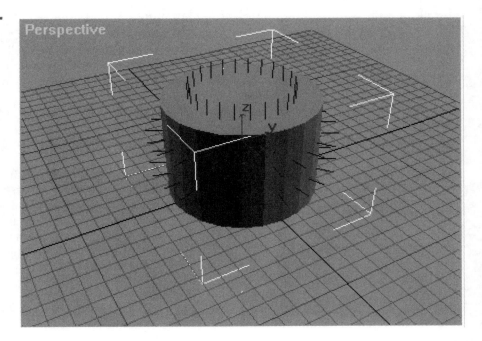

To select an object or objects, activate the Select Object icon on the toolbar at the top of screen. Then, if you want to select a single object, move across an object and the cursor changes to a thick, stubby cross. This tells you that you can pick that object to select it. If you pick an object that hasn't yet been selected, it will turn white, letting you know you have selected it. If you pick open space, any selected objects will be unselected.

To select several objects at once, activate the Select Object Icon, pick and hold in open space, drag the cursor, forming a window around the objects to be selected, and release the button. All the objects will be added to the selection set.

If you want to select objects one after another or add to ones already picked, hold down the CTRL key while picking objects. They will be added to the selection set.

If you want to remove one or more objects from a selection set, hold down the ALT key as you pick previously selected objects. They will be removed from the selection set.

Once you have picked your objects, you can lock your selection using the lock icon on the status bar at the bottom of the screen. When this is active, no more objects can be selected or unselected. If you turn the lock icon off, you can select and unselect objects as normal.

Object Modifiers

Once you select an object or objects, you can then open the Modify command panel, as shown in Figure 26.8. At the top of the modifier panel is the name of the object, which you can change. There will be no name if you have selected more than one object. Below this is the list of modifiers. Here you can pick a particular modifier and use it to make changes to the object. When you make a modifier change, it goes in the modifier stack, which is shown as a pull-down list in the middle of the panel. To review the different modifiers you have used on an object, select the modifier from the stack. Before you make any modifier changes, the only item in the modifier stack is the original object itself. This modifier is used to modify creation parameters such as length and width.

Object Transforms

Transforms affect position, rotation, and scale changes and are activated with the transform tool icon buttons on the toolbar. The transform tools have the added feature of a built-in select option. To use them you do not have to have previously picked the object. You can pick on the tool and then pick on the object to transform.

Object Clones

There are several ways to make clones with 3D Studio MAX: Shift-Clone, Array, Mirror, and Snapshot. Clones are like copies, but there are some differences.

The Shift-Clone method of making clones involves holding down the Shift key while performing a Transform. For instance, if you wanted to make a clone of an object and move it to a new location, you would activate the Move tool, hold down on the Shift key, and pick the object. As you move the cursor away, a clone of the object will travel with it.

Figure 26.8
Modify panel

The Array method creates repeated clones and allows you to control all three transforms, position, rotation, and scale. Refer to Figure 26.9 for an illustration of the original object, the Array dialog, and the final arrayed clones.

The Mirror method creates a clone that mirrors the original object. The Mirror command has the added ability to transform the original into the mirror image instead of cloning it. Refer to Figure 26.10 for the Mirror dialog.

The Snapshot method clones an animated object over time.

Copies versus Instances or References

When you make a clone of an object, you select from three choices for the type of clone: copy, instance, and reference.

A copy is a new, independent, master object that has all the characteristics of the original but is not tied to the original in any way.

An instance is bound to the original object's creation parameters and object modifiers. This means if you change the creation length of the original, the instance clone will change to match it. The instance is separate from the original with regard to transforms, space warps, and object properties such as materials. This means that you can move the instance or change its materials separately from the original. Remember that if you make a change to the creation parameters or modifiers of any instance clone, you will make the change to all the instance clones of the original object.

A reference is the same as an instance, except that a reference can have its own object modifiers as well as being controlled by the original object's modifiers.

Undo: Edit, View

To undo a change to a scene, either use the Undo icon button or the Edit/Undo pull-down menu item. This will work for most changes in 3D Studio MAX. For extra insurance make sure you use the Edit/Hold pull-down menu items discussed earlier.

There is also an Undo for reversing the changes made to a viewport. This command can be found under the View pull-down menu.

For both the Edit/Undo and View/Undo, there are Redos. Redo undoes the effect of the Undo.

26.5 Cameras and Lights

This section introduces camera and light objects. Cameras are used to display a view that can be altered as you would alter a camera lens. Lights are used to give light to a scene and enhance the visibility and realism. There are different camera and light types for different effects.

Cameras

Cameras are objects that can simulate still-image or motion picture viewing. 3D Studio MAX's cameras have features that mimic real-life cameras. The first is the lens size, which controls the focal length and the field of view (FOV). You can select from stock (preset) lens sizes or create your own custom size. Small lens sizes give a wide-angle FOV, whereas large lens sizes give

Figure 26.9
Original object, the Array dialog, and
the final arrayed clones

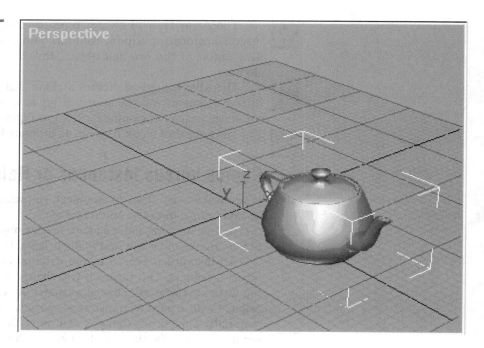

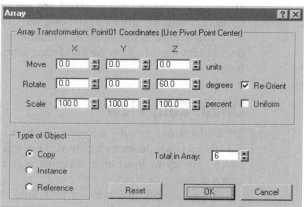

Figure 26.10
Mirror dialog

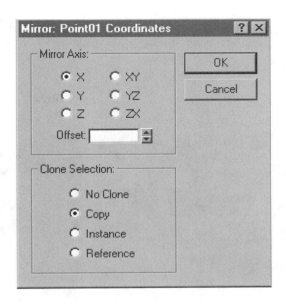

you a small, magnified (zoomed-in) FOV. Refer to Figure 26.11, which shows two different views of the same objects using different lens sizes.

There are two types of cameras you can place in your scene: target and free. Target cameras are usually used for fixed camera placement with a target that moves. Free cameras are used when the camera itself will be animated.

Because cameras are objects, you will find the camera button in the Creation command panel. When you pick it, you will be presented with the camera options, allowing you to pick either target or free. Once you pick the type, you will be presented with the camera type's creation parameters, as shown in Figure 26.12. Don't forget to give your camera a name to help you keep track of it. You can transform and modify cameras as well.

When you have placed a camera, you can activate one of the viewports and display a camera view by pressing C on the keyboard. If you have more than one camera, you can pick from a list.

Lights

If you render a scene in which you have not placed any lights, 3D Studio MAX uses its own default lighting. This way you can render even before you have mastered lighting. As soon as you place a light, default lighting is turned off, and the scene relies on your expertise. You may be shocked the first time a well-lit scene suddenly changes drastically when you add your first light. However, the key to a realistic scene lies in its lighting. Many of these techniques are discussed in Chapter 10. Here you will get just a taste.

3D Studio MAX has different light types to light a scene in virtually any way you wish: ambient, omni, and directional light and target and free spotlights.

Ambient light in 3D Studio simulates background light or light that reflects from objects. It can be used to increase or decrease the overall lighting of a scene. The Ambient light value can be adjusted by selecting the Rendering/Environment pull-down menu item. Normally it is set to black, providing the greatest contrast available to the scene.

Omni light radiates light equally in all directions, like a lightbulb. However, omni lights cannot cast shadows. Omni lights are useful in lighting a scene in which there is no necessary direction for the light source. Refer to Figure 26.13.

Because it casts parallel light rays, directional light is used to simulate the sun. It can cast shadows and project bitmap images. When you place a directional light, you direct its beam by using the rotate transform. Refer to Figure 26.13

Figure 26.11
Two views with different lens sizes

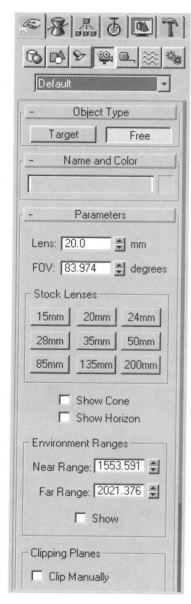

Figure 26.12
Camera creation parameters

Spotlights cast a focused beam of light similar to a flashlight, theater spot, or automobile headlight. There are two types: target and free. Their placement and directional behavior are similar to target and free cameras. Like directional light, they can cast shadows and project bitmap images. Refer to Figure 26.13.

26.6 Rendering and Materials

Rendering and materials work hand in hand because the choice of materials controls the generation of a realistically rendered scene. This section introduces the concept of materials and how to apply them. Once you have assigned materials to an object, it's time to render.

Figure 26.13
Directional and omni lights and spotlights

Materials

Materials are the properties of an object. According to which properties are assigned, objects can reflect or absorb light and can have pictures on their surfaces.

The selection, creation, and application of materials happens in the Material Editor dialog. To access this dialog, pick the Material Editor icon button near the right end of the tool bar. Refer to Figure 26.14 for an illustration of the Material Editor dialog. When you first open this dialog, it shows six standard materials that bear six different colors and have no bitmaps associated with them. To assign one of these materials to an object in your scene, pick one of the six sample display boxes, identify the object to which you wish to apply the material, and then pick the Assign Material to Selection button.

There are many premade materials available, stored in the material library. To access the library, pick the Get Material button. This displays the Material/Map Browser dialog, as shown in Figure 26.15. If you pick the Material Library box in the Browse From area of the dialog, you will have access to all the materials that are contained in the currently opened material library. Figure 26.15 shows some of the material listings in the default material library, 3DSMAX.MAT. You can scroll through the various materials and then double-click on the one you want. It will be placed in the sample display box that was currently active, replacing whatever material was previously displayed. You can then assign that material to a selected object or objects. You must remember that

Figure 26.14
Material Editor dialog

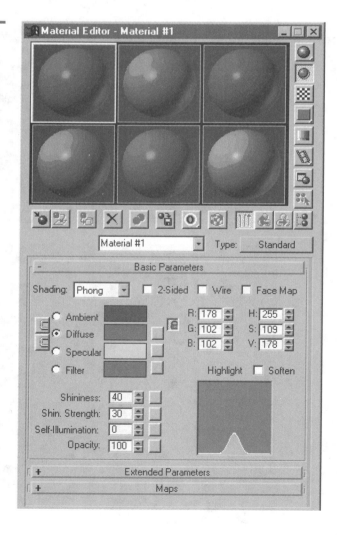

Figure 26.15
Material/Map Browser dialog

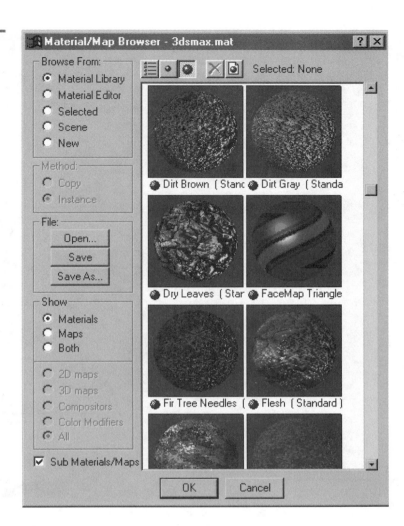

you need to assign a mapping coordinate property to an object if it is going to have a material that makes use of bitmaps. Note that you assign mapping coordinates during creation, as mentioned in Section 26.4 under Surface Properties.

Rendering

Although you can render at any time, your scene will be more realistic once you have added lights and assigned materials to your objects. To render, pick either the Render Scene or Quick Render icon buttons at the right end of the tool bar.

The Render Scene button will bring up the Render Scene dialog, as shown in Figure 26.16. Here you can control different options that will affect the final rendering. Review the figure, noting such areas as Time Output and Output Size.

Time Output is used to control whether a single frame, part of an animation, or the entire animation is rendered. Output size controls the size, in pixels, of the rendered image. Once you have chosen your settings, pick the Render button at the bottom of the dialog. A separate window will open, and the rendering will take place in this window. Refer to Figure 26.17.

The Quick Render button will perform a rendering using previously set options in the Render Scene dialog. This button is useful when you want to render a scene without changing any settings.

Near the end of the tool bar, just after the Render Scene and Quick render buttons, is the Render Type pull-down list. Use this list to select the areas of the scene you wish to render: View, Selected, Region, and Blowup.

Figure 26.16
Render Scene dialog

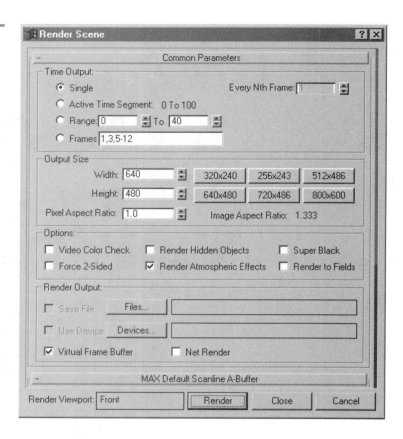

Figure 26.17
Rendered window

26.7 Animation

Animation is the act of imparting motion or activity. Almost any object in your scene can be animated, as long as that object is altered in some way, such as by movement or shape, over a period of time. Within 3D Studio MAX, these changes occur over frames. Each frame can contain a different change to a scene. When the frames are played one after another, animation occurs. A frame can be a frame of the scene or a unit of time.

Key Frames

To make the animation process even easier, there are special frames you can use as key frames. For instance, an object sits in a certain position in frame 1 and you want the object to slide across the scene, coming to rest in another position in frame 8. Instead of moving the object in each frame from 2 to 8, you go to frame 8 and move the object to its new position. Frame 8 is a key frame. 3D Studio MAX knows that you want the object to move from its position in frame 1 to its new position in frame 8. It then creates the movements in the frames from 2 to 7 automatically. Refer to Figure 26.18 for a rendering of frames 1 to 8. This animation shows an electronic panel opening and the word "IDEA??" appearing on its screen. Frame 1 shows the instrument closed, frame 6 shows the panel fully open, panel 7 shows the leftmost button lit up, and panel 8 shows the word "IDEA??" appearing on the panel's display screen.

Tracks

The movements or transformations that take place through an animation are recorded as keys on tracks. Every object, including cameras and lights, has tracks. When you add a key frame or make some changes to an existing key, it is recorded on the object's track. The track represents the length of the animation in frames. You use tracks to make changes to keys. Refer to Figure 26.19 for the Track View dialog. Notice the list on the left of the dialog. It is called the *hierarchy list* and contains all the objects in the scene. Each object can be broken down into the various properties associated with it. Along the right is the window that contains the tracks associated with each object property. The tracks provide a visual indicator showing when a particular property is acted upon during the animation, and the oval dots indicate the frame in which an action occurs. The track view dialog is modeless, which means it can stay visible while you work on your scene. To display the dialog, pick the Track View button on the right along the tool bar.

Animate button

To make a change that will be animated, use the large Animate button at the bottom of the screen. When it is on (red), any transform or change to an animatable parameter will create a key. The basic procedure for animating is as follows:

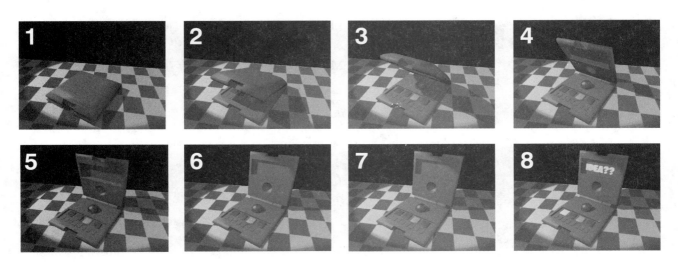

Figure 26.18
Rendered frames

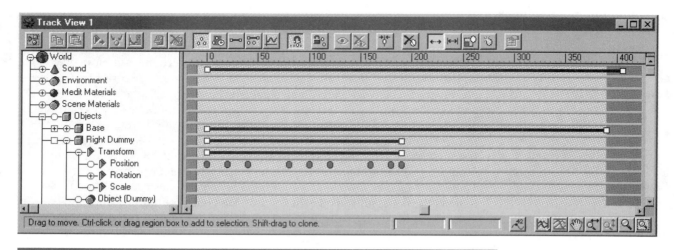

Figure 26.19
Track View dialog

1. Select the desired frame/time using the time slider at the bottom of the screen. Do not use frame 0. Frame 0 is used to contain the original parameters of the objects in your scene.
2. Turn on (red) the Animate button.
3. Select the object or objects and perform the change and a key will be created or modified.

Animation Tools

The following describes some of the animation tools available to you.

Animation Tools

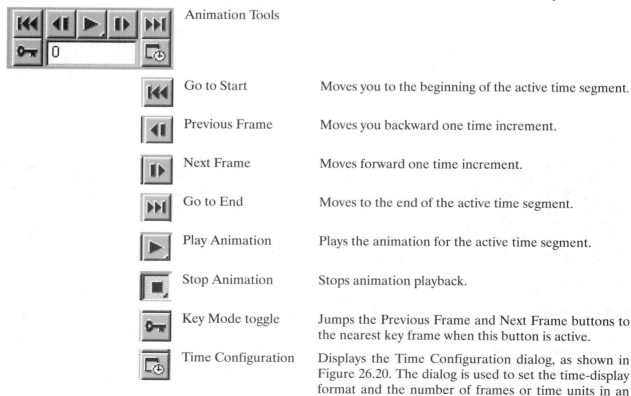

	Go to Start	Moves you to the beginning of the active time segment.
	Previous Frame	Moves you backward one time increment.
	Next Frame	Moves forward one time increment.
	Go to End	Moves to the end of the active time segment.
	Play Animation	Plays the animation for the active time segment.
	Stop Animation	Stops animation playback.
	Key Mode toggle	Jumps the Previous Frame and Next Frame buttons to the nearest key frame when this button is active.
	Time Configuration	Displays the Time Configuration dialog, as shown in Figure 26.20. The dialog is used to set the time-display format and the number of frames or time units in an animation.

Figure 26.20
Time Configuration dialog

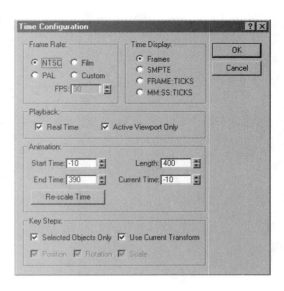

Hierarchical Linking

When you have objects whose movement affects other objects, you must link them in some way. Think of a human arm: you have a hand, a lower arm, and an upper arm. When you move that arm, the upper arm swings up at the shoulder, and the lower arm and hand obviously move with it. They are physically linked together. This principle remains true in 3D Studio MAX; you decide which objects are linked together and under what parameters. This is referred to as *hierarchical linking*.

Index

Thickness property, *continued*
   effect on object snap, 87
   explanation, 87
   modification of, 87
Tilemode, 287–289
TILEMODE command, 287
Toolbars
   modify, 185
   rendering, 306
   solids, 174
   surfaces, 153
   UCS, 70
   view, 47
Topologically rectangular meshes, 149
TORUS command, 172
Trimetric, 37
True 3D, 6, 99
   concept behind, 99
   definition, 6

UCS command, 65–66
UCSICON command, 68
UCS icon options, 68
User Coordinate System (UCS), 64–69
   description, 64
   icon, 68
   options, 65–66

Vanishing point, 264
Video Walk-throughs, 22
Vpoint, 35–42
   compass input, 39–40
   coordinate input, 36–37

lab, Vpoint exploration, 48–52
lab, Vpoint options, 52–55
options, 42
orientation control, 42–43
plan, 42–43
preset input, 40–41
rotation input, 38
VPOINT command, 33, 35, 46
Vport, 43–44
   control, 43–44
   lab, Vport exploration, 55–58
   options, 44
VPORTS command, 33, 43

WEDGE command, 172
What if situations, 3
Wireframe, 99–104
   definition, 6, 99
   examples, 24–25, 28
   role of nodes, 99
   uses, 99
Working drawings, 292
Working planes, 11–12
   alignment to, 64
   definition, 11
   elevated, 69–70
   model insertion, 215–218
   purpose, 63–64
   warning, 68–69
World Coordinate System (WCS), 64

Xrefs, 218–222

4408